01089001

821.4 MIL
MILTON
79/2522

79/2522

D1179473

DISCARD
B.C.H.E. – LIBRARY

00124482

THE POETICAL WORKS
OF
JOHN MILTON

Bring the rathe primrose that unwedded dies
colouring the pale cheeke of unim̄joyd Love
and that sad floure that strove
to write his owne woes on the vermeil graine
next adde Narcissus y[t] still weeps in baine
the woodbine and y[e] pansie freakt wth jet
the glowing violet
the cowslip wan that hangs his pensive head
and every bud that sorrows liverie weares
let Daffadillies fill thire cups wth teares
bid Amaranthus all his beautie shed
to strew the Laureat herse ⌐y⌐

Bring the rathe primrose that forsaken dies
the tufted crowtoe and pale Gessamie
the white pinks, and y[e] pansie freakt wth jet
the glowing violet the well-ati'd woodbine
the musk̄ rose and the garish columbine
wth cowslips wan that hang the pensive head ✗   peares
and every flower that sad escutcheon bearis imbroidrie
2[tha]t daffadillies fill thire cups wth teares
1^bid Amaranthus all his beauties shed
to strew ⌐y⌐

                    what could the muse her selfe that Orpheus bore
        ✗   the muse her selfe for her inchanting son.
        for her inchanting son
        whome universal nature did lament
        when by the rout that made the hideous roare
✗   his divine visage downe the streame was sent
goarie   downe the swift Hebrus to y[e] Lesbian shoare.

THE POETICAL WORKS
OF
JOHN MILTON

Volume II

PARADISE REGAIN'D, SAMSON AGONISTES
POEMS UPON SEVERAL OCCASIONS, BOTH
ENGLISH AND LATIN

EDITED BY

HELEN DARBISHIRE

OXFORD
AT THE CLARENDON PRESS

Oxford University Press, Ely House, London, W.1

GLASGOW NEW YORK TORONTO MELBOURNE WELLINGTON
CAPE TOWN IBADAN NAIROBI DAR ES SALAAM LUSAKA ADDIS ABABA
DELHI BOMBAY CALCUTTA MADRAS KARACHI LAHORE DACCA
KUALA LUMPUR SINGAPORE HONG KONG TOKYO

ISBN 0 19 811820 1

First published 1955

NEWTON PARK
COLLEGE
BATH
DISCARD
LIBRARY

CLASS
NO. 821. 4 MIL

ACC.
NO. 79/2522

*Printed in Great Britain
at the University Press, Oxford
by Vivian Ridler
Printer to the University
1966, 1973*

PREFACE

FOLLOWING Milton's first editors, I place *Paradise Regain'd* and *Samson Agonistes* next in order after *Paradise Lost*; after these, the other poems which Milton selected for publication in his lifetime, that is in the editions of 1645 and 1673: I include here four Sonnets, Numbers XVI, XVII, XVIII, XXII, prepared by him for publication in 1673, but finally for politic reasons held back (*v.* Commentary p. 324), and two copies of early Latin verses preserved, on a separate leaf, in his common-place-book (B.M. Add. MS. 41063). I arrange these poems of the editions of 1645 and 1673 in the order adopted in 1673, but with three changes: first, according to Milton's injunction in the Errata of 1673, I place 'At a Vacation Exercise' after 'On the Death of a fair Infant', and on my own judgement I place 'On the new forcers of Conscience' at the end of the Sonnets, followed by 'The Fifth Ode of Horace. Lib. i'. Milton's arrangement in the different groups is in part, but not rigidly, chronological.

I have revised the text of *Paradise Regain'd* and *Samson Agonistes* on the principles that I laid down in my Introduction to *Paradise Lost*, Vol. I. For the spelling of particular words the reader is also referred to the Word-List at the end of that volume.

I have dealt with the text of the minor poems in a different way— inevitably as I believe, and as I have tried to show in my Introduction to the present volume. As in Volume I, I have preferred not to overload the pages of Milton's verse with textual apparatus; I place underneath the text only those variants which are significant for difference of meaning: in my textual commentary at the end of the volume I note other variants which may have interest for the student; I have drawn freely upon the manuscripts for significant readings. It has been no part of my plan to offer a complete collation: for this readers will turn to the Columbia University edition of *The Works of John Milton* and to vols. i and iv of Mr. H. F. Fletcher's most useful facsimile edition of *John Milton's Complete Poetical Works*, where all the texts published in Milton's lifetime together with his manuscripts are reproduced in clear and reliable form. My object has been to present a text as near as may be to that which Milton himself seems to have intended to offer his readers. My procedure may perhaps be dubbed bold, but it is not rash: I have attended carefully to an accumulation of detailed evidence.

I am grateful to the Librarian of Trinity College, Cambridge, for allowing me to spend several days with the valuable Trinity College manuscript, Milton's holograph; this has enabled me, especially with *Lycidas* and *Comus*,[1] to trace, more closely than has hitherto been attempted, Milton's hand at work in the process of shaping his poem.

Professor H. W. Garrod has most kindly undertaken the critical editing of the Latin Poems, a task which no editor has seriously undertaken before. Mr. John Purves has with equal kindness made himself responsible for the Italian Poems. I am sensible of the great debt which this volume owes to the contribution of these two scholars.

For my notes on Milton's renderings of the Psalms and for the spelling of Biblical names I have had the help and advice of Dr. Chaim Rabin, Cowley Lecturer in Post-Biblical Hebrew at Oxford, to whom I am glad to express my thanks. I am also grateful to Dr. Onions for help and confirmation in some of my notes on Milton's spellings.

Dr. R. W. Chapman has from time to time over the years sent me notes and queries on the subject of Milton's text; he has also allowed me to see the late George Gordon's lecture notes on the Trinity College manuscript. From the suggestions of both these acute and sensitive scholars I have benefited, I hope, by closer insight into significant minutiae which might have eluded my duller eyes.

Miss Margaret Crum has kindly drawn my attention to what appears to be an early version of Milton's poem *On Time* in a manuscript collection of the early seventeenth century in the Bodleian Library.

H. D.

---

[1] I adopt for convenience the generally accepted title of *Comus*, though Milton never gave it any heading but *A Mask*—*v*. Introduction to *Comus*, p. 336 *infra*.

CONTENTS

Contents

INTRODUCTION

Paradise Regain'd and *Samson Agonistes*

THE right way, as I conceive it, of dealing with the text of *Paradise Regain'd* and of *Samson Agonistes*, published together in 1671, only four years after *Paradise Lost*, is determined by my procedure with *Paradise Lost* in Vol. I of this edition, where I have tried to carry out Milton's considered rules of spelling and punctuation as closely as seemed reasonable.[1] For the volume of 1671 he had a new printer, John Starkey, who has not attended to these rules as faithfully as Samuel Simmons, the exemplary printer of *Paradise Lost*. But there is enough evidence that Milton intended carrying out his system in *Paradise Regain'd* and *Samson Agonistes* to convince his editor that these texts also must be brought under the poet's mandate. Typical forms appear, though not consistently, in both poems: *anough, highth, perfet, persue, rowl* or *roul*; the pronouns— *thir*[2] normally, with *their* for emphasis, *we, me,* and the rest, with *wee, mee* for emphasis. The printer partly respects, partly neglects Milton's useful distinction between the participle ending in *t* and the preterite in *d*: thus on the first page of *Paradise Regain'd* he prints *flock'd* (preterite) and *Unmarkt* (participle), but often ignores the distinction, as in l. 297 where he prints *mark'd* for participle where it should be *markt*. Again he sometimes follows Milton in his spelling of sonant *n* as in *soft'n* (*Paradise Regain'd*, ii. 163), *happ'ns* (i. 334), but slips back into *spoken* (ii. 90). I have revised these spellings along with others that transgress Milton's considered principles, so as to bring the text into line with his clear intentions. Further, where the printer of the 1671 volume has idiosyncrasies of his own, or is adopting idiosyncrasies of Milton's amanuensis, I follow Milton. The printer spells in some places *uttr'ed, entred, wandred,* whereas Milton spelt *utterd, enterd, wanderd*— spellings which also come through in *Paradise Regain'd* and *Samson Agonistes* (*vide* note to *Paradise Regain'd*, i. 320). An item in the Errata of the volume of 1671, *demurring* for *demuring* (*Paradise Regain'd*, i. 373), proclaims Milton's persistent desire to make spelling indicate pronunciation.

It must always be remembered that with Milton spelling and

---

[1] *v.* Vol. I, Introduction and Word-List.

[2] *Their*, unemphatic, has been corrected to *thir* as the sheets went through the press: *v.* notes to *Paradise Regain'd*, iv. 424 and *Samson Agonistes*, 1183.

punctuation are not harmless idiosyncrasies: he used them deliberately as aids to carry over to his reader the sense, sound, and movement of his lines as he wished them to be read.

The punctuation of the first edition of *Paradise Regain'd* and *Samson Agonistes* is throughout easy-going. Commas are used lavishly—often where Milton would have used colon or semi-colon. I have revised the punctuation of those texts in accordance with his principles and practice.[1] (With Milton principle and practice are one.)

No second edition of these poems appeared in Milton's lifetime, and no manuscript copies have survived. The edition of 1680, Ed. 2, is carelessly printed, shows no close revision, and neglects the carefully listed Errata of Ed. 1: *vide* notes *infra* to *Paradise Regain'd*, i. 62, 226, 373, 400, 417; ii. 128, 313, 341, 371; iii. 324; iv. 102; and to *Samson Agonistes*, 126, 157, 222, 354, 656, 660, 1248, 1313, 1325, 1552. These necessary corrections with a few others are listed by Peck in his *New Memoirs of Milton*, 1740, but most of them had to wait till 1747 to be incorporated in the text in Tonson's edition of that year, and till 1752 to be picked out for annotation by Newton.[2] Truly the text of *Paradise Regain'd* and *Samson Agonistes* had a bad start in the posthumous second edition. Editors before Newton from time to time made useful corrections, notably those of the volumes published in 1705, 1713, 1720 (Tickell), 1725 (Fenton), 1747.[3]

Poems published in 1645 and 1673, &c.

The right way of dealing with the text of the poems published in these volumes is more open to question.

In 1645 Milton published his first volume of poetry with the title

Poems of Mr. John Milton, both English & Latin, Compos'd at several times. Printed by his true Copies.

In 1673 he put out a second edition including a few more poems, under the title

Poems, &c. upon Several Occasions. By Mr. John Milton: Both English and Latin, &c. Composed at several times.

---

[1] *v.* Vol. I, Introduction, xx–xxiii.
[2] *v.* Textual Commentary *infra*.
[3] I have given a list in my Appendix, p. 375, of the more important later editions.

These volumes, comprising what he modestly thought of as occasional poems, 'Poems upon Several Occasions', had clearly for him a secondary importance compared with the two Epics and the classical Tragedy. It is significant that he is particular in assigning dates to many of the poems, especially to the Juvenilia.

The volume of 1645 contained *A Mask* (*Comus*) and *Lycidas*, both already published separately, so that for these two poems we have the choice of three texts. A glance at the first printed texts of *A Mask* (*Comus*), 1637, and *Lycidas*, 1638, will be enough to convince a critical reader that in all the minutiae of spelling and punctuation they represent Milton himself very imperfectly: the printer has done pretty much as he liked, according to the current conventions of the printing-house. A close scrutiny of the volume of 1645 reveals a careful printer who followed Milton's copy with what he would have thought reasonable faithfulness, but took his own line freely in what were to him accepted conventions or variations. Thus he gives the typical Miltonic spellings, *hunderd, forren, agen, anough, vers, wildernes, oft'n, rott'nness, furder,* but he has not adopted Milton's unusual spelling of *their*—*thir* for the normal form, *their* for emphasis (a solitary example of *thir* slips through in *The Passion*, l. 53)—nor does he distinguish the unemphatic and emphatic forms of the other pronouns, with the alternative spellings *me, mee; we, wee; ye, yee*: again he does not distinguish consistently, as I think Milton himself did not at this time distinguish, the past participle in *t* from the preterite in *d*.[1]

A similar scrutiny applied to the text of 1673 will show that Milton, now blind, made his printer carry out one important piece of revision (in Stanza XV of the Nativity *Hymn*) and two characteristic corrections in *At a Solemn Musick*: in line 6 *content* to *concent* (the musical term of precise definition) and in line 23 *perfect* to *perfet*—Milton's chosen spelling to indicate the pronunciation (the same correction is made in the *Hymn*, l. 166),[2] but that apart from this he has left the printer to his own devices, with the result that ignorant miscorrections appear (thus in *Comus*, l. 474, *sensuality* is printed in 1673, where Milton has written in the Trinity MS. *sensualtie*, and 1645 reads *sensualty*, the form he needs metrically);[3] and that on every page characteristic Miltonic spellings are ironed out: thus *onely, vers, els, wildernes, Goddes,* familiar forms in

---

[1] *v.* Introduction, Vol. I, pp. xv and xxxi.

[2] It is noteworthy that the only corrections in the text of 1673 which are clearly Milton's own are in the Nativity *Hymn* and in *At a Solemn Musick.*

[3] Other readings in *Comus* telling the same tale are: line 547 *meditate upon* 1673: *meditate* MSS., 1637, 1645; line 556 *stream* 1673: *steame* MSS., 1637, 1645.

1645, are replaced by the more conventional *only, verse, else, wilderness, Goddess* in 1673.

There can be no doubt that the volume of 1645 represents what Milton wrote far better than that of 1673, and that the earlier printed texts of *Comus* and *Lycidas* will be useful only in supplying a few interesting variants.

There is no case, as I see it, for imposing upon the *Poems* of 1645 and 1673 Milton's mature system of spelling and punctuation. By 1645 he was indeed moving towards his own system, which he was to work out fully by the time he wrote *Paradise Lost*, and which at that later time he made every effort to get his printer to adopt. But in the volume of 1645, although, as we have seen, a few of his characteristic spellings come through, he seems to have made no attempt to enforce his system (still not fully thought out) upon his printer; and when he came to republish the *Poems* in 1673 he did not overhaul the spelling according to his system then matured.

In his punctuation he is not, as in *Paradise Lost*, attempting to carry through a careful system of his own: he has offered the printer a 'copy' punctuated in the main, we must believe, according to his own principles, but he has accepted some of the contemporary conventions of the printing-press.[1] In the Trinity College manuscript he punctuates very little.[2]

I have thought it best to base my text upon the edition of 1645 (Ed. 1), applying not a drastic but a light revision—in two ways: I adopt a few readings from other versions found in Milton's manuscripts or printed copies (Ed. 2 revises to some extent the punctuation), and I carry through a few of the particular spellings such as *perfet, anow, anough*,[3] which Milton quite certainly intended at that time. The text of Poems added in 1673 must inevitably follow that edition, similarly modified.[4]

The general appearance of my text is thus of a different character from that of my text of *Paradise Lost*, *Paradise Regain'd*, and *Samson Agonistes*. The stamp of the early seventeenth century is upon it, and not the stamp of Milton's post-restoration period. This, I think, is as it should be.

[1] I have attempted to indicate some of these principles and conventions in my Commentary—*v.* notes *infra* on Nativity Hymn, ll. 3, 15, 36, 240 and Comus, l. 275, and *Song on May Morning*, ll. 6–8. The whole field of seventeenth-century punctuation awaits an enlightened and pertinacious investigator.

[2] *v. Lycidas*, 21, note *infra*.

[3] *v.* notes to H. 166, *Lyc.* 114.

[4] For the text of Sonnets added from the Trinity MS., *v.* notes, pp. 324–5.

The Manuscripts

We have no manuscripts of *Paradise Regain'd* or *Samson Agonistes*. Of several of the 'occasional' poems drafts survive in Milton's own holograph manuscript, now in the library of Trinity College, Cambridge, known to scholars from the eighteenth century onwards as the Trinity College manuscript.[1] This manuscript Milton used and preserved as a working copy in which he entered drafts of his poems as he wrote them, further correcting and revising the drafts in preparation for the press. Interesting versions of *Comus*, *Lycidas*, *At a Solemn Musick*, and most of the Sonnets are found in this manuscript. I have drawn on these both in illustration and sometimes in modification of his printed text.

Apart from this we have for *Comus* a fair copy, by an amanuensis, of the acting version of *A Mask*, preserved in the Bridgwater Library; and secondly versions of separate poems in some of the manuscript Collections of Poems dating from the first half of the seventeenth century: these include *An Epitaph on the Marchioness of Winchester*, *On Time*, and the two poems *On the University Carrier*.[2] Of the Latin poems we have a copy (not holograph) in the Bodleian Library of Milton's *Ode to John Rouse*, and in the British Museum an exercise in his own early hand which he never published (B.M. Add. MS. 41063.)[3]

H. D.

The Italian Poems

Milton's Italian poems offer few textual problems. No manuscript authority exists for any of these poems, and the only contemporary texts are those of 1645 and 1673. Of these 1645 is undoubtedly the superior. 1673 has six positive errors: *sui* for *suoi* (Son. II, 6), *fian* for *sian* (Son. V, 2), *e trovar* for *a trovar* (Son. V, 12), *indubbio* for *in dubbio* (Son. VI, 2), omission of *e* (Son. VI, 8), and in punctuation *arco.* for *arco,* (Son. II, 7). Also in Son. II, 3, *Bene* for *Ben* involves a hiatus which

---

[1] The first reference to it which I know is in Jonathan Richardson's *Commentary on Paradise Lost*, 1734. Thomas Birch in his preface to *A Complete Collection of the Historical Political and Miscellaneous Works of John Milton*, 1738, gave a list of substantially faithful readings from the manuscript, and was followed in this by Bishop Newton in his edition of the *Poems* 1752, Thomas Warton in his *Occasional Poems of John Milton* 1785, and Todd in various editions beginning with his *Comus* 1798, and ending with his final edition of the *Poetical Works*, 1826. Newton, Warton, and Todd all add details from their own examination of the manuscript.

[2] *v*. pp. 308, 311, 313–14 *infra*.

[3] *v*. pp. xix, 288, 370–1 *infra*.

Milton, with his knowledge of Italian poetry, would hardly have allowed. On the other hand *occhi*, for *occhi* (Son. V, 1) is an improvement, although here one would expect also the addition of a comma after *mia*.

In general Italian punctuation, as found in the printed texts of the sixteenth and seventeenth centuries, especially from such presses as those of Aldus, the Giunti, and Giolito de' Ferrari, did not differ greatly from modern English practice, although it is apt to be erratic in the work of inferior printers. There is a wider use of the colon, which may take the place sometimes of the full stop, sometimes of the semicolon. A frequent use of the comma, unfamiliar in modern texts, is its insertion after the first of two adjectives or nouns linked by a conjunction, or between two verbs similarly joined, as for example in Tasso, *Rime* (Aldus, 1583, p. 120):

> Vecchio, & alato Dio, nato col Sole,
>
> . . . .
>
> Che distruggi le cose, e rinovelle,
> Mentre per torte vie vole, e rivole:

So in Milton, Son. II, 9:

> Quando tu vaga parli, o lieta canti

Son. V, 9:

> Parte rinchiusa, e turbida si cela

Son. VI, 9:

> Tanto del forse, e d'invidia sicuro.

The structure of the regular Petrarchan sonnet, with its elaborate symmetry and parallelism, called for a similar regularity in punctuation. Since there is usually a clear division between each of the quatrains and tercets, these being to a large extent self-contained, this is generally indicated by a full stop or its nearest equivalents, colon, semicolon, or mark of interrogation. Pauses within the line, if they occur, are generally brief and indicated only with a comma; if longer, by a colon or semicolon; while the octave almost invariably ends with a full stop or a colon, although even in Petrarch there are exceptions to this. In the sixteenth century, however, there was a certain loosening of the structure, when writers began to seek for a less artificial and more organic form, by permitting the sense to overflow from one unit of the poem to another and by a more varied use of the pauses within the line, while seeking to preserve the essential unity of the Sonnet. Hence a greater variety in punctuation, although the regular divisions are still frequently retained. This is true even of the sonnets of Della Casa, the

chief of these reformers, to whom Milton's debt is now generally
admitted. But if we assume that Milton supervised the punctuation
of his Italian poems in the text of 1645, it would seem that he favoured
an unusually light system of pointing. It is more likely, however, that
the punctuation was due in the first instance to a somewhat careless
printer, and that the poet gave less attention to this than he after-
wards showed in his English poems. It has seemed right, therefore,
in this edition to bring the punctuation as far as possible into line with
contemporary Italian practice (of *c.* 1550–1650).

Accentuation is much scantier in 1673 than in 1645, another proof
of the carelessness with which the later text was prepared. Indeed the
comparative fullness with which 1645 is accented suggests that it
was Milton's desire to provide some guide to pronunciation, for not
only are the usual verbal accents inserted (*è, dirò, farò, può—puo*,
however, in Son. V, 2), but *natía, soléa, ridéa* are similarly marked.
Several monosyllables such as *a, o, fra, qui,* &c., which are no longer
accented, frequently carry an accent in sixteenth- and seventeenth-
century texts, but here Milton's printers anticipated modern practice
by their omission, in which they have been naturally followed in the
present edition. *Perche,* on the other hand, with similar compounds in
che, and pronominal *se,* are unaccented in the same texts, and so too in
Milton.

Spelling, both in 1645 and 1673, is much as it was in contemporary
Italian practice. The redundant or vestigial *h* (*honora, herbosa, herbetta,
ad hor ad hor, hebbi, huom, honesti*) remained common until well after Mil-
ton's time. *Rheno,* however (Son. II, 2), calls for further remark. This
was taken apparently by readers in the eighteenth century to refer to
the Rhine—an error perpetuated in Cowper's translation of the sonnet.
In the Aldine edition of Tasso's *Rime* (1583) the spellings *Reno* and
Rheno both occur,[1] with reference apparently to the stream in Emilia to
which Milton alludes. The poet, or his printer, probably adopted the

---

[1] Cf. Tasso, *Delle Rime et Prose. Parte Prima.* (Vinetia, M.D. LXXXI, Presso Aldo), p. 19:
> Poiche'n vostro terren vil Tasso alberga
> Dal Ren translato, ond' empia man lo svelse,

and (ib., p. 141):
> Quella spada, Signor, che con tant' arte
> Girate, il tempo misurando, e i passi,
> Che'l gran vostro avversario in dubbio stassi
> De la vittoria, e del favor di Marte,
> Di tronche membra, e d'arme incise, e sparte
> Empir l'onde del Rheno, e i duri sassi
> Mollir potria col sangue, e novi passi
> Aprir ne l'Alpi in vie più alpestra parte:

form *Rheno* from the example of Lat. *Rhenus* (which, like modern Italian *Reno*, applied either to the German river or to the tributary of the Po). *Trueva* (Son. II, 12) is an archaic survival, although found as late as the sixteenth century (e.g. in Ariosto); but *giamai* (Son. II, 6) for mod. *giammai*, and *gratta* (Son. II, 13) for *grazia* are the usual spellings in the seventeenth century, and *inanti* for *innanzi* is also found at least until the end of the sixteenth century, and has the authority of Florio.

Of the emendations suggested at various times in these poems only two have met with general acceptance: *mostrasi* for *mostra si* (Son. II, 5) and *scossomi* for *scosso mi* (Son. V, 10), the latter suggested by Masson. Both are obvious and do not involve interference with Milton's text. On the other hand, attempts to improve his grammar and syntax by words not found in the original, as for example Gabriele Rossetti's suggestion of *cui* for *qual* (= *il quale*) in Son. II, 4, are inadmissible. In line 7 of the same sonnet an Italian critic, F. Olivero, has suggested the omission of the initial *E*, but this, though it would ease the syntax, is to mistake Milton's meaning (*v.* Textual Commentary, *infra*, p. 318). There remain two suggested emendations in the Columbia University edition which require a closer examination.[1] In line 13 of Son. III the editors would read *foss' il mio cuor lento e duro 'l seno* for *e 'l duro seno* of the text. This would be a natural improvement if the clause were followed by an independent sentence. But since the *cuor lento* and the *duro seno* are in apposition to the *buon terreno* of line 14, no change is called for. Again in line 8 of Son. VI the substitution of *f è* for *se* is not convincing. *S'arma di se* seems more in keeping with the proud and confident note of this, the most individual and personal of the Italian sonnets, than the more conventional *S'arma di f è*, as when Marino speaks in one of his sonnets of

> tanti
> Più di fè, che di ferro armati heroi.

And cf. Tasso:

> Solo di se, nè d'altra lode adorno
>
> (*Rime*, 1583, p. 60).

In fixing the text of the Italian poems for this edition, it has been the editor's aim to depart as little as possible from that of 1645, or, as was stated in the General Introduction, to provide 'a text as near as possible to that which Milton himself desired to offer his readers'. Emendation

---

[1] Both had appeared already in the notes to the Clarendon Press type-facsimile of Ed. 1 (1924).

has been confined, therefore, to matters of punctuation and accentuation, and the principle followed has been merely to bring the text in some small necessary points into conformity with the best Italian practice. This has involved only slight interference with the original, and the general conservatism of Milton's text suggests that in punctuation as in spelling he had mainly earlier models in view.

In several respects the text of Francini's Ode (pp. 232–4) is more modern than that of Milton's poems. The redundant *h* has disappeared from *onora*, although it is retained in *huom*, *Chorde*, and the combination of article and preposition is the general rule. In the present text it has been made regular throughout, and punctuation and accents have been added in the few cases where this was necessary. A suggested emendation made by the translator of this poem in the Columbia University edition, viz. *mortal* for *moral* in line 66, seems very plausible, and has been tentatively introduced in brackets.

JOHN PURVES

Poemata

In the volume of 1645, *Poems of Mr. John Milton, both English & Latin*, &c., the English Poems were followed by a collection of Latin Poems with a separate title-page (see p. 229). In the Ode to John Rouse (see p. 284) Milton speaks of the volume as *gemellus liber*, two books in one. The two books are, in fact, except for the title-page to the English Poems, as disjunct as could be. Their pages are separately numbered (as they are also in 1673) and, more important, the Latin Poems have a separate series of signatures, starting with A, clearly showing that the two portions of the book were, from the printer's point of view, separate. (In 1673 the series of signatures is continuous throughout the volume, signature L giving the last six pages of the English Poems and the first ten pages of the *Poemata*.) It seems likely that the Latin book of 1645 sometimes—perhaps more often than not—crossed to the Continent without its twin English brother. In a letter to Carlo Dati of 21 April 1647 Milton says that it is no good sending his English Poems to Florence, but that he will send the Latin ones—'Poematum quae pars Latina est'. More than one copy of the Latin Poems separate from the English ones survives.[1] In general, the Continental scholars, when they speak of the Latin book, say nothing of any English Poems

---

[1] One in the library of the University of Illinois, one in the Bodleian Library (8° T. 14. Art. B.S.).

accompanying it. The Latin verses were criticized for the false quantities in which they abound. Salmasius noted three metrical atrocities: *Eleg.* v, 30, *quotannĭs; In Quint. Nov.* 143, *sĕmifractaque;* ibid. 165, *păruere* (see *Responsio ad Milt.*, Dijon, P. Chavance, 1600, p. 6). Milton's enemies enjoyed these blunders. Scholars friendly to him noted them regretfully (as Heinsius, in Burmann's *Sylloge,* iii. 669). But beyond correcting his two worst false quantities Milton did nothing. In his 1673 edition *quotannis* is replaced by *perennis, semifractaque* by *præruptaque.* But *paruere* is left standing, with at least a dozen other false quantities (*Eleg.* vii. 37, *Cȳdŏniusque; In obit. Præsul. Eliens.* 29, *temerĕ; Mansus* 93, *egō; Epit. Damon* 1, *Hȳlan;* ibid. 86, *bĭs; Ad Sals.* 3, *sentĭs;* ibid. 33 *emĭrabitur;* ibid. 22 and *In Salmas. Hund.* 8, *mēlos; Psalm.* 114, 6, εἰλῠμένη; *Phil. ad Reg.* 4, ὀδύρη (fut. indic.), *In Effig. Sculpt.* 4 δυσμίμημα).

This list of metrical irregularities, common to the editions of 1645 and 1673, takes no account of 27 examples of a vowel kept short before an initial *sc., sp., st.* in the word following; nor of 19 scazons, out of a total of 41, in which Milton allows himself the licence of a spondee in the fifth foot.

The 1645 *Poemata* was full of faults. The 1673 edition—in which the poems are still spoken of, oddly, as *nunc primum edita*—does little to remedy these. It gets rid of two of the false quantities of which Salmasius complained. And it corrects two bad misprints on p. 10 of 1645—*vastitate* for *venustate,* and *terrararum* for *terrarum.* In line 92 of *In Quint. Nov.* it has *artus?,* correctly, for the *artus* of 1645. In *In Quint. Nov.* 125 its *casumque* is to be preferred to *casuque;* and in six places it improves on the punctuation of 1645: p. 4 *Epigramma Salsilli* 3–4, *undas,* (1645 has no comma); *Eleg.* ii. 12, *tuo,* (for *tuo*); *Nat. non pati* 38, *raptat* 1673, *raptat,* 1645; *Ad Patrem* 13, *ista,* (for *ista*); ibid. 35, *orbes,* 1673 (for *orbes*); *Ad Salsillum* 5, *lectum,* (for *lectum*). But the number of new misprints which 1673 introduces is considerable. For convenience, these may be tabled here, so that I may not cumber my apparatus criticus with them:

Eleg. iii. 27, *potetas* (for *potestas*); *Eleg.* iv. 123, *miseri* (for *miseris*); *Eleg.* vi, prefatory note 4, *amisis* (for *amicis*); *Eleg.* vi. 13, *queretis* (for *quereris*); ibid. 22, *modis,* (for *modis?*); *Eleg.* vii. 50, *erat,* (for *erat.*); ibid. 59, *misi* (for *misi,*); p. 254, *In Eandem* 8, *Deos,* (for *Deos.*); p. 254, *In Eandem* 4, *corona* (for *cornua*); p. 255, *Ad Eandem* 8, *desipulisset* (for *desipuiiset*); *In obitum Procancell.* 40, *Fausibus* (for *Faucibus*); *In Quint. Nov.* 43, *tantamina possunt.* (for *tentamina possunt,*); ibid. 84, *salaces.* (for *salaces*); ibid. 108, *pontum* (for *Pontum*); ibid. 146, *fauces* (for *fauces,*); ibid. 148, *timor* (for *Timor*); *In obit. Præsul. Eliens.* 2, *lumina;* (for *lumina*); *De Idea Plat.* 23, *iis* (for *diis*); *Ad Patrem* 8, *possunt* (for *possint*); ibid. 58, *Munete* (for *Munere*); *Mansus* 4, *galli* (for *Galli*); ibid. 27, *longinguam* (for *longinquam*); *Epit. Damon.* 8, *perrerans* (for *pererrans*).

Most of the errors common to 1645 and 1673 reappear in the edition of 1695; where, however, editorial conjecture has made a number of corrections: *Epigramma Salsilli* 4, *te, Milto, par* (for *te Milto par*); *Eleg.* v. 110, *Virgineos* (for *Virgineas*—but it is possible that Milton did not know the gender of *sinus*); *Eleg.* vii. 2, *fuit* (for *suit*); *Ad Eandem,* p. 255, 8, *desipuisset; In Quint. Nov.* 219, *omnem.* (for *omnem*); *In obit. Præsul. Eliens.* 30, *percita,* (for *percita.*); ibid. 67, *loci?* (for *loci*); *Ad Patrem* 14, *Clio,* (for *Clio*).

The text of the *Poemata* which this edition offers is the text of 1645; taking in, however, from 1673 the *Apologus de Rustico et Hero*, with which in that year Milton concluded the section of 'Elegies', and the verses *Ad Joannem Rousium*, written in 1646–7 and placed at the end of the 1673 volume. I have appended the two epigrams on *Salmasius* printed in the *Pro Populo Anglicano Defensio*, 1651, and the *Defensio Secunda*, 1654; the distich on More in the second *Defensio* (attributed by Milton to a writer *lepidi ingenii*, but probably his own composition); together with the two sets of verses preserved in the British Museum Add. MS. 41063, which is a photograph of the original manuscript (almost certainly in Milton's early hand), now lost. The manuscript was a single folio leaf, the recto of which contained a short prose essay, the verso two poems sharing the title *Carmina Elegiaca*. The leaf was preserved with the manuscript of Milton's commonplace-book. The photograph was given to the British Museum by Mr. C. H. Candy, who collated it for me as long ago as 1934. The collation has been checked for me by Miss Darbishire.

In my critical footnotes I have noted all deviations from the text of 1645 which affect the meaning. But I have admitted into the text a good many changes in punctuation which I have not thought it worth while to record in the footnotes, lest they should overload the page. A large proportion of them consists in the addition of commas before and after a noun or proper name in the vocative. About these vocative commas Milton had his own whims, in English as well as in Latin. With the Latin texts Newton and Warton have helped him against his will and whim, intruding commas infinitely helpful to the casual reader, but not enough of them, even so. For the benefit of readers more scrupulous, or more pedantic, than those of Newton and Warton, I have listed in a supplement to the apparatus criticus *all* changes of punctuation.

A good many of my critical notes reproduce notes contributed by me to the type-facsimile edition of the volume of 1645 published by the Clarendon Press in 1924, now out of print.

H. W. GARROD

PARADISE
REGAIN'D.

A
POEM.

In IV *BOOKS*.

To which is added

SAMSON AGONISTES

The Author
JOHN MILTON.

LONDON,

Printed by *J. M* for *John Starkey* at the
Mitre in *Fleetſtreet*, near *Temple-Bar*.
MDCLXXI.

PARADISE REGAIN'D

THE FIRST BOOK

I WHO ere while the happy Garden sung,
By one mans disobedience lost, now sing
Recoverd Paradise to all mankind,
By one mans firm obedience fully tri'd
Through all temptation, and the Tempter foild   5
In all his wiles, defeated and repulst,
And *Eden* rais'd in the wast Wilderness.
 Thou Spirit who ledst this glorious Eremite
Into the Desert, his Victorious Field
Against the Spiritual Foe, and broughtst him thence   10
By proof th' undoubted Son of God, inspire,
As thou art wont, my prompted Song else mute,
And bear through highth or depth of natures bounds
With prosperous wing full summd to tell of deeds
Above Heroic, though in secret done,   15
And unrecorded left through many an Age,
Worthy t' have not remaind so long unsung.
 Now had the great Proclaimer with a voice
More awful then the sound of Trumpet, cri'd
Repentance, and Heav'ns Kingdom nigh at hand   20
To all Baptiz'd: to his great Baptism flockd
With aw the Regions round, and with them came
From *Nazareth* the Son of *Joseph* deemd
To the flood *Jordan*, came as then obscure,
Unmarkt, unknown; but him the Baptist soon   25
Descri'd, divinely warnd, and witness bore
As to his worthier, and would have resign'd
To him his Heav'nly Office, nor was long
His witness unconfirmd: on him baptiz'd
Heav'n op'nd, and in likeness of a Dove   30
The Spirit descended, while the Fathers voice
From Heav'n pronounc'd him his beloved Son.
That heard the Adversary, who roving still
About the World, at that assembly fam'd

Would not be last, and with the voice divine   35
Nigh Thunder-strook, th' exalted man, to whom
Such high attest was giv'n, a while survey'd
With wonder, then with envy fraught and rage
Flies to his place, nor rests, but in mid air
To Councel summons all his mighty Peers,   40
Within thick Clouds and dark ten-fold involv'd,
A gloomy Consistory; and them amidst
With looks agast and sad he thus bespake.
   O ancient Powers of Air and this wide World,
For much more willingly I mention Air,   45
This our old Conquest, then remember Hell
Our hated habitation; well ye know
How many Ages, as the years of men,
This Universe we have possest, and rul'd
In manner at our will th' affairs of Earth,   50
Since *Adam* and his facil consort *Eve*
Lost Paradise deceiv'd by me, though since
With dread attending when that fatal wound
Shall be inflicted by the Seed of *Eve*
Upon my head: long the decrees of Heav'n   55
Delay, for longest time to him is short;
And now too soon for us the circling hours
This dreaded time have compast, wherein we
Must bide the stroak of that long threat'nd wound,
At least if so we can, and by the head   60
Brok'n be not intended all our power
To be infring'd, our freedom and our being
In this fair Empire won of Earth and Air;
For this ill news I bring, the Womans seed
Destind to this, is late of Woman born: 65
His birth to our just fear gave no small cause,
But his growth now to youths full flowr, displaying
All vertue, grace and wisdom to atchieve
Things highest, greatest, multiplies my fear.
Before him a great Prophet, to proclaim   70
His coming, is sent Harbinger, who all
Invites, and in the Consecrated stream
Pretends to wash off sin, and fit them so
Purifi'd to receive him pure, or rather

To do him honour as thir King; all come, 75
And he himself among them was baptiz'd,
Not thence to be more pure, but to receive
The testimony of Heaven, that who he is
Thenceforth the Nations may not doubt; I saw
The Prophet do him reverence; on him rising 80
Out of the water, Heav'n above the Clouds
Unfold her Crystal Dores; thence on his head
A perfet Dove descend, what e're it meant,
And out of Heav'n the Sovran voice I heard,
This is my Son belov'd, in him am pleas'd. 85
His Mother then is mortal, but his Sire,
Hee who obtains the Monarchy of Heav'n,
And what will he not do to advance his Son?
His first-begot we know, and sore have felt,
When his fierce thunder drove us to the deep; 90
Who this is we must learn, for man he seems
In all his lineaments, though in his face
The glimpses of his Fathers glory shine.
Ye see our danger on the utmost edge
Of hazard, which admits no long debate, 95
But must with something sudden be oppos'd,
Not force, but well coucht fraud, well woven snares,
Ere in the head of Nations he appear
Thir King, thir Leader, and Supream on Earth.
I, when no other durst, sole undertook 100
The dismal expedition to find out
And ruin *Adam*, and th' exploit performd
Successfully; a calmer voyage now
Will waft me; and the way found prosperous once
Induces best to hope of like success. 105
   He ended, and his words impression left
Of much amazement to th' infernal Crew,
Distracted and surpriz'd with deep dismay
At these sad tidings; but no time was then
For long indulgence to thir fears or grief: 110
Unanimous they all commit the care
And management of this main enterprize
To him thir great Dictator, whose attempt
At first against mankind so well had thriv'd

In *Adams* overthrow, and led thir march   115
From Hells deep-vaulted Den to dwell in light,
Regents and Potentates, and Kings, yea gods
Of many a pleasant Realm and Province wide.
So to the Coast of *Jordan* he directs
His easie steps, girded with snaky wiles,   120
Where he might likeliest find this new-declar'd,
This Man of men, attested Son of God,
Temptation and all guile on him to try;
So to subvert whom he suspected rais'd
To end his Raign on Earth so long enjoy'd: 125
But contrary unweeting he fulfilld
The purpos'd Counsel pre-ordaind and fixt
Of the most High, who in full frequence bright
Of Angels, thus to *Gabriel* smiling spake.
　　Gabriel this day by proof thou shalt behold,   130
Thou and all Angels conversant on Earth
With man or mens affairs, how I begin
To verifie that solemn message late,
On which I sent thee to the Virgin pure
In *Galilee*, that she should bear a Son   135
Great in Renown, and calld the Son of God;
Then toldst her doubting how these things could be
To her a Virgin, that on her should come
The Holy Ghost, and the power of the highest
Ore-shadow her: this man born and now up-grown,   140
To shew him worthy of his birth divine
And high prediction, henceforth I expose
To Satan; let him tempt and now assay
His utmost suttlety, because he boasts
And vaunts of his great cunning to the throng   145
Of his Apostasie; he might have learnt
Less over-weening, since he faild in *Job*,
Whose constant perseverance overcame
Whate're his cruel malice could invent.
He now shall know I can produce a man   150
Of femal Seed, far abler to resist
All his sollicitations, and at length
All his vast force, and drive him back to Hell,
Winning by Conquest what the first man lost

By fallacy surpriz'd. But first I mean   155
To exercise him in the Wilderness,
There he shall first lay down the rudiments
Of his great warfare, ere I send him forth
To conquer Sin and Death the two grand foes,
By Humiliation and strong Sufferance: 160
His weakness shall orecome Satanic strength
And all the World, and mass of sinful flesh;
That all the Angels and Ætherial Powers,
They now, and men hereafter may discern,
From what consummat vertue I have chose   165
This perfet Man, by merit calld my Son,
To earn Salvation for the Sons of men.
    So spake th' Eternal Father, and all Heaven
Admiring stood a space, then into Hymns
Burst forth, and in Celestial measures mov'd,   170
Circling the Throne and Singing, while the hand
Sung with the voice, and this the argument.
    Victory and Triumph to the Son of God
Now entring his great duel, not of arms,
But to vanquish by wisdom hellish wiles.   175
The Father knows the Son; therefore secure
Ventures his filial Vertue, though untri'd,
Against whate're may tempt, whate're seduce,
Allure, or terrifie, or undermine.
Be frustrate all ye stratagems of Hell,   180
And devilish machinations come to naught.
    So they in Heav'n thir Odes and Vigils tun'd:
Mean while the Son of God, who yet some days
Lodg'd in *Bethabara* where *John* baptiz'd,
Musing and much revolving in his brest,   185
How best the mighty work he might begin
Of Saviour to mankind, and which way first
Publish his God-like office now mature,
One day forth walkd alone, the Spirit leading,
And his deep thoughts, the better to converse   190
With solitude, till farr from track of men,
Thought following thought, and step by step led on,
He enterd now the bordering Desert wild,
And with dark shades and rocks environd round,

His holy Meditations thus persu'd.   195
  O what a multitude of thoughts at once
Awak'nd in me swarm, while I consider
What from within I feel my self, and hear
What from without comes oft'n to my ears,
Ill sorting with my present state compar'd.   200
When I was yet a child, no childish play
To me was pleasing, all my mind was set
Serious to learn and know, and thence to do
What might be publick good; my self I thought
Born to that end, born to promote all truth,   205
All righteous things: therefore above my years,
The Law of God I red, and found it sweet,
Made it my whole delight, and in it grew
To such perfection, that ere yet my age
Had measur'd twice six years, at our great Feast   210
I went into the Temple, there to hear
The Teachers of our Law, and to propose
What might improve my knowledge or thir own;
And was admir'd by all, yet this not all
To which my Spirit aspir'd, victorious deeds   215
Flam'd in my heart, heroic acts, one while
To rescue *Israel* from the *Roman* yoke,
Then to subdue and quell ore all the earth
Brute violence and proud Tyrannick pow'r,
Till truth were freed, and equity restor'd: 220
Yet held it more humane, more heav'nly first
By winning words to conquer willing hearts,
And make perswasion do the work of fear;
At least to try, and teach the erring Soul
Not wilfully mis-doing, but unware   225
Misled; the stubborn onely to subdue.
These growing thoughts my Mother soon perceiving
By words at times cast forth inly rejoyc'd,
And said to me apart, high are thy thoughts
O Son, but nourish them and let them soar   230
To what highth sacred vertue and true worth
Can raise them, though above example high;
By matchless Deeds express thy matchless Sire.

226 subdue] erratum Ed. 1 : destroy Edd. 1, 2

For know, thou art no Son of mortal man,
Though men esteem thee low of Parentage,   235
Thy Father is th' Eternal King, who rules
All Heav'n and Earth, Angels and Sons of men;
A messenger from God fore-told thy birth
Conceiv'd in me a Virgin, he fore-told
Thou shouldst be great and sit on *Davids* Throne,   240
And of thy Kingdom there should be no end.
At thy Nativity a glorious Quire
Of Angels in the fields of *Bethlehem* sung
To Shepherds watching at thir folds by night,
And told them the Messiah now was born,   245
Where they might see him, and to thee they came;
Directed to the Manger where thou laist,
For in the Inn was left no better room:
A Starr, not seen before in Heav'n appearing
Guided the Wise Men thither from the East,   250
To honour thee with Incense, Myrrh, and Gold,
By whose bright course led on they found the place,
Affirming it thy Starr new grav'n in Heaven,
By which they knew thee King of *Israel* born.
Just *Simeon* and Prophetic *Anna*, warnd   255
By Vision, found thee in the Temple, and spake,
Before the Altar and the vested Priest,
Like things of thee to all that present stood.
    This having heard, strait I again revolv'd
The Law and Prophets, searching what was writ   260
Concerning the Messiah, to our Scribes
Known partly, and soon found of whom they spake
I am; this chiefly, that my way must lie
Through many a hard assay eev'n to the death,
Ere I the promisd Kingdom can attain,   265
Or work Redemption for mankind, whose sins
Full weight must be transferrd upon my head.
Yet neither thus disheart'nd or dismay'd,
The time prefixt I waited, when behold
The Baptist, (of whose birth I oft had heard,   27
Not knew by sight) now come, who was to come
Before Messiah and his way prepare.

254 thee] Ed. 1 : the Ed. 2

I as all others to his Baptism came,
Which I believ'd was from above; but hee
Strait knew me, and with loudest voice proclaimd   275
Mee him (for it was shewn him so from Heaven)
Mee him whose Harbinger he was; and first
Refus'd on mee his Baptism to conferr,
As much his greater, and was hardly won;
But as I rose out of the laving stream,   280
Heav'n op'nd her eternal doors, from whence
The Spirit descended on me like a Dove,
And last the sum of all, my Father's voice,
Audibly heard from Heav'n, pronounc'd me his,
Mee his beloved Son, in whom alone   285
He was well pleas'd; by which I knew the time
Now full, that I no more should live obscure,
But op'nly begin, as best becomes
The Autority which I deriv'd from Heaven.
And now by some strong motion I am led   290
Into this Wilderness, to what intent
I learn not yet, perhaps I need not know;
For what concerns my knowledge God reveals.
   So spake our Morning Starr then in his rise,
And looking round on every side beheld   295
A pathless Desert, dusk with horrid shades;
The way he came not having markt, return
Was difficult, by human steps untrod;
And he still on was led, but with such thoughts
Accompanied of things past and to come   300
Lodg'd in his brest, as well might recommend
Such Solitude before choicest Society.
Full forty days he passd, whether on hill
Sometimes, anon in shady vale, each night
Under the covert of some ancient Oak,   305
Or Cedar, to defend him from the dew,
Or harbourd in one Cave, is not reveald;
Nor tasted human food, nor hunger felt
Till those days ended, hungerd then at last
Among wild Beasts: they at his sight grew mild,   310
Nor sleeping him nor waking harmd, his walk
The fiery Serpent fled, and noxious Worm,

The Lion and fierce Tiger glar'd aloof.
But now an aged man in Rural weeds,
Following, as seemd, the quest of some stray Ewe, 315
Or witherd sticks to gather; which might serve
Against a Winters day when winds blow keen,
To warm him wet returnd from field at Eve,
He saw approach, who first with curious eye
Perus'd him, then with words thus utterd spake. 320
   Sir, what ill chance hath brought thee to this place
So farr from path or road of men, who pass
In Troop or Caravan, for single none
Durst ever, who returnd, and dropd not here
His Carcass, pin'd with hunger and with droughth? 325
I ask the rather, and the more admire,
For that to me thou seem'st the man, whom late
Our new baptizing Prophet at the Ford
Of *Jordan* honourd so, and calld thee Son
Of God; I saw and heard, for wee sometimes 330
Who dwell this wild, constraind by want, come forth
To Town or Village nigh (nighest is farr)
Where aught we hear, and curious are to hear,
What happ'ns new; Fame also finds us out.
   To whom the Son of God. Who brought me hither 335
Will bring me hence, no other Guide I seek.
   By Miracle he may, reply'd the Swain,
What other way I see not, for we here
Live on tough roots and stubs, to thirst inur'd
More then the Camel, and to drink go farr, 340
Men to much misery and hardship born;
But if thou be the Son of God, Command
That out of these hard stones be made thee bread;
So shalt thou save thy self and us relieve
With Food, whereof we wretched seldom taste. 345
   He ended, and the Son of God reply'd.
Think'st thou such force in Bread? is it not writt'n
(For I discern thee other then thou seem'st)
Man lives not by Bread onely, but each Word
Proceeding from the mouth of God; who fed 350
Our Fathers here with Manna; in the Mount
Moses was forty days, nor eat nor drank,

And forty days *Elijah* without food
Wanderd this barren waste, the same I now:
Why dost thou then suggest to me distrust,   355
Knowing who I am, as I know who thou art?
   Whom thus answerd th' Arch-Fiend now undisguis'd.
'Tis true, I am that Spirit unfortunate,
Who leagu'd with millions more in rash revolt
Kept not my happy Station, but was driv'n   360
With them from bliss to the bottomless deep,
Yet to that hideous place not so confin'd
By rigour unconniving, but that oft
Leaving my dolorous Prison I enjoy
Large liberty to round this Globe of Earth,   365
Or range in th' Air, nor from the Heav'n of Heav'ns
Hath he excluded my resort sometimes.
I came among the Sons of God, when he
Gave up into my hands *Uzzean Job*
To prove him, and illustrat his high worth;   370
And when to all his Angels he propos'd
To draw the proud King *Ahab* into fraud
That he might fall in *Ramoth*, they demurring,
I undertook that office, and the tongues
Of all his flattering Prophets glibbd with lyes   375
To his destruction, as I had in charge.
For what he bids I do; though I have lost
Much lustre of my native brightness, lost
To be belov'd of God, I have not lost
To love, at least contemplat and admire   380
What I see excellent in good, or fair,
Or vertuous, I should so have lost all sense.
What can be then less in me then desire
To see thee and approach thee, whom I know
Declar'd the Son of God, to hear attent   385
Thy wisdom, and behold thy God-like deeds?
Men generally think me much a foe
To all mankind: why should I? they to me
Never did wrong or violence, by them
I lost not what I lost, rather by them   390
I gaind what I have gaind, and with them dwell
Copartner in these Regions of the World,

If not disposer; lend them oft my aid,
Oft my advice by presages and signs,
And answers, oracles, portents and dreams, 395
Whereby they may direct thir future life.
Envy they say excites me, thus to gain
Companions of my misery and wo.
At first it may be; but long since with wo
Nearer acquainted, now I feel by proof, 400
That fellowship in pain divides not smart,
Nor light'ns aught each mans peculiar load.
Small consolation then, were Man adjoind:
This wounds me most (what can it less) that Man,
Man fall'n shall be restor'd, I never more. 405
　　To whom our Saviour sternly thus reply'd.
Deservedly thou griev'st, compos'd of lyes
From the beginning, and in lies wilt end;
Who boast'st release from Hell, and leave to come
Into the Heav'n of Heavens; thou com'st indeed, 410
As a poor miserable captive thrall
Comes to the place where he before had sat
Among the Prime in Splendour, now depos'd,
Ejected, emptied, gaz'd, unpitied, shunnd,
A spectacle of ruin or of scorn 415
To all the Host of Heaven; the happy place
Imparts to thee no happiness, no joy,
Rather inflames thy torment, representing
Lost bliss, to thee no more communicable,
So never more in Hell then when in Heaven. 420
But thou art serviceable to Heav'ns King.
Wilt thou impute to obedience what thy fear
Extorts, or pleasure to do ill excites?
What but thy malice mov'd thee to misdeem
Of righteous *Job*, then cruelly to afflict him 425
With all inflictions, but his patience won?
The other service was thy chosen task,
To be a lyer in four hunderd mouths;
For lying is thy sustenance, thy food.
Yet thou pretend'st to truth; all Oracles 430
By thee are giv'n, and what confest more true
Among the Nations? that hath been thy craft,

By mixing somewhat true to vent more lyes.
But what have been thy answers, what but dark
Ambiguous and with double sense deluding,   435
Which they who askd have seldom understood,
And not well understood as good not known?
Who ever by consulting at thy shrine
Returnd the wiser, or the more instruct
To flye or follow what concernd him most,   440
And run not sooner to his fatal snare?
For God hath justly giv'n the Nations up
To thy Delusions; justly, since they fell
Idolatrous, but when his purpose is
Among them to declare his Providence   445
To thee not known, whence hast thou then thy truth,
But from him or his Angels President
In every Province, who themselves disdaining
To approach thy Temples, give thee in command
What to the smallest tittle thou shalt say   450
To thy Adorers; thou with trembling fear,
Or like a Fawning Parasite obey'st;
Then to thy self ascrib'st the truth fore-told.
But this thy glory shall be soon retrencht;
No more shalt thou by oracling abuse   455
The Gentiles; henceforth Oracles are ceast,
And thou no more with Pomp and Sacrifice
Shalt be enquir'd at *Delphos* or elsewhere,
At least in vain, for they shall find thee mute.
God hath now sent his living Oracle   460
Into the World, to teach his final will,
And sends his Spirit of Truth henceforth to dwell
In pious Hearts, an inward Oracle
To all truth requisite for men to know.
    So spake our Saviour; but the suttle Fiend,   465
Though inly stung with anger and disdain,
Dissembl'd, and this Answer smooth returnd.
    Sharply thou hast insisted on rebuke,
And urg'd me hard with doings, which not will
But misery hath wrested from me; where   470
Easily canst thou find one miserable,
And not inforc't oft-times to part from truth,

If it may stand him more in stead to lye,
Say and unsay, feign, flatter, or abjure?
But thou art plac't above me, thou art Lord;   475
From thee I can and must submiss endure
Check or reproof, and glad to scape so quit.
Hard are the ways of Truth, and rough to walk,
Smooth on the tongue discourst, pleasing to th' ear,
And tuneable as Silvan Pipe or Song;   480
What wonder then if I delight to hear
Her dictates from thy mouth? most men admire
Vertue, who follow not her lore: permit me
To hear thee when I come (since no man comes)
And talk at least, though I despair to attain.   485
Thy Father, who is holy, wise and pure,
Suffers the Hypocrit or Atheous Priest
To tread his Sacred Courts, and minister
About his Altar, handling holy things,
Praying or vowing, and voutsaf'd his voice   490
To *Balaam* Reprobate, a Prophet yet
Inspir'd; disdain not such access to me.

   To whom our Saviour with unalterd brow.
Thy coming hither, though I know thy scope,
I bid not or forbid; do as thou find'st   495
Permission from above; thou canst not more.

   He added not; and Satan bowing low
His gray dissimulation, disappeard
Into thin Air diffus'd: for now began
Night with her sullen wing to double-shade   500
The Desert, Fowls in thir clay nests were coucht;
And now wild Beasts came forth the woods to roam.

THE END OF THE FIRST BOOK

THE SECOND BOOK

MEAN while the new-baptiz'd, who yet remaind
At *Jordan* with the Baptist, and had seen
Him whom they heard so late expresly calld
Jesus Messiah Son of God declar'd,
And on that high Autority had believ'd,   5
And with him talkt, and with him lodg'd, I mean
Andrew and *Simon*, famous after known
With others though in Holy Writ not nam'd,
Now missing him thir joy so lately found,
So lately found, and so abruptly gone,   10
Began to doubt, and doubted many days,
And as the days increas'd, increas'd thir doubt:
Sometimes they thought he might be onely shewn,
And for a time caught up to God, as once
Moses was in the Mount, and missing long;   15
And the great *Thisbite* who on fiery wheels
Rode up to Heaven, yet once again to come.
Therefore as those young Prophets then with care
Sought lost *Elijah*, so in each place these
Nigh to *Bethabara*; in *Jerico*   20
The City of Palms, *Ænon*, and *Salem* Old,
Machærus and each Town or City walld
On this side the broad lake *Genezaret*,
Or in *Perea*, but returnd in vain.
Then on the bank of *Jordan*, by a Creek,   25
Where winds with Reeds, and Osiers whisp'ring play,
Plain Fishermen, no greater men them call,
Close in a Cottage low together got
Thir unexpected loss and plaints out breath'd.

  Alas, from what high hope to what relapse   30
Unlookt for are we fall'n; our eyes beheld
Messiah certainly now come, so long
Expected of our Fathers; we have heard
His words, his wisdom full of grace and truth:
Now, now, for sure, deliverance is at hand,   35
The Kingdom shall to *Israel* be restor'd:
Thus we rejoyc'd, but soon our joy is turnd

Into perplexity and new amaze:
For whither is he gone, what accident
Hath rapt him from us? will he now retire   40
After appearance, and again prolong
Our expectation? God of *Israel*,
Send thy Messiah forth, the time is come;
Behold the Kings of th' Earth how they oppress
Thy chosen, to what highth thir pow'r unjust   45
They have exalted, and behind them cast
All fear of thee; arise and vindicate
Thy Glory, free thy people from thir yoke:
But let us wait; thus farr he hath performd,
Sent his Anointed, and to us reveald him,   50
By his great Prophet, pointed at and shown,
In publick, and with him we have converst;
Let us be glad of this, and all our fears
Lay on his Providence; he will not fail
Nor will withdraw him now, nor will recall,   55
Mock us with his blest sight, then snatch him hence,
Soon we shall see our hope, our joy return.
    Thus they out of thir plaints new hope resume
To find whom at the first they found unsought:
But to his Mother *Mary*, when she saw   60
Others returnd from Baptism, not her Son,
Nor left at *Jordan*, tidings of him none;
Within her brest, though calm; her brest though pure,
Motherly cares and fears got head, and rais'd
Some troubl'd thoughts, which she in sighs thus clad.   65
    O what avails me now that honour high
To have conceiv'd of God, or that salute
Hale highly favour'd, among women blest;
While I to sorrows am no less advanc't,
And fears as eminent, above the lot   70
Of other women, by the birth I bore,
In such a season born when scarce a Shed
Could be obtain to shelter him or me
From the bleak air; a Stable was our warmth,
A Manger his, yet soon enforc't to flye   75
Thence into *Egypt*, till the Murd'rous King
Were dead, who sought his life, and missing filld

With Infant blood the streets of *Bethlehem*;
From *Egypt* home returnd, in *Nazareth*
Hath been our dwelling many years, his life   80
Privat, unactive, calm, contemplative,
Little suspicious to any King; but now
Full grown to Man, acknowledg'd, as I hear,
By *John* the Baptist, and in publick shown,
Son ownd from Heaven by his Father's voice;   85
I lookd for some great change; to Honour? no,
But trouble, as old *Simeon* plain fore-told,
That to the fall and rising he should be
Of many in *Israel*, and to a sign
Spok'n against, that through my very Soul   90
A sword shall pierce, this is my favour'd lot,
My Exaltation to Afflictions high;
Afflicted I may be, it seems, and blest;
I will not argue that, nor will repine.
But where delays he now? some great intent   95
Conceals him: when twelve years he scarce had seen,
I lost him, but so found, as well I saw
He could not lose himself; but went about
His Father's buisness; what he meant I mus'd,
Since understand; much more his absence now   100
Thus long to some great purpose he obscures.
But I to wait with patience am inur'd;
My heart hath been a store-house long of things
And sayings laid up, portending strange events.
       Thus *Mary* pondering oft, and oft to mind   105
Recalling what remarkably had past
Since first her Salutation heard, with thoughts
Meekly compos'd awaited the fulfilling:
The while her Son tracing the Desert wild,
Sole but with holiest Meditations fed,   110
Into himself descended, and at once
All his great work to come before him set;
How to begin, how to accomplish best
His end of being on Earth, and mission high:
For Satan with slye preface to return   115
Had left him vacant, and with speed was gon
Up to the middle Region of thick Air,

Where all his Potentates in Council sate;
There without sign of boast, or sign of joy,
Sollicitous and blank he thus began.   120
    Princes, Heav'ns ancient Sons, Æthereal Thrones,
Demonian Spirits now, from th' Element
Each of his reign allotted, rightlier calld,
Powers of Fire, Air, Water, and Earth beneath,
So may we hold our place and these mild seats   125
Without new trouble; such an Enemy
Is risen to invade us, who no less
Threat'ns then our expulsion down to Hell;
I, as I undertook, and with the vote
Consenting in full frequence was impowr'd,   130
Have found him, viewd him, tasted him, but find
Farr other labour to be undergon
Then when I dealt with *Adam* first of Men,
Though *Adam* by his Wives allurement fell,
However to this Man inferior farr,   135
If he be Man by Mothers side at least,
With more then human gifts from Heav'n adornd,
Perfections absolute, Graces divine,
And amplitude of mind to greatest Deeds.
Therefore I am returnd, lest confidence   140
Of my success with *Eve* in Paradise
Deceive ye to perswasion over-sure
Of like succeeding here; I summon all
Rather to be in readiness, with hand
Or counsel to assist; lest I who erst   145
Thought none my equal, now be over-matcht.
    So spake th' old Serpent doubting, and from all
With clamour was assur'd thir utmost aid
At his command; when from amidst them rose
Belial the dissolutest Spirit that fell,   150
The sensuallest, and after *Asmodai*
The fleshliest Incubus, and thus advis'd.
    Set women in his eye and in his walk,
Among daughters of men the fairest found;
Many are in each Region passing fair   155
As the noon Skie; more like to Goddesses
Then Mortal Creatures, graceful and discreet,

Expert in amorous Arts, enchanting tongues
Perswasive, Virgin majesty with mild
And sweet allayd, yet terrible to approach,   160
Skilld to retire, and in retiring draw
Hearts after them tangl'd in Amorous Nets.
Such object hath the power to soft'n and tame
Severest temper, smooth the rugged'st brow,
Enerve, and with voluptuous hope dissolve,   165
Draw out with credulous desire, and lead
At will the manliest, resolutest brest,
As the Magnetic hardest Iron draws.
Women, when nothing else, beguil'd the heart
Of wisest *Solomon*, and made him build,   170
And made him bow to the Gods of his Wives.
    To whom quick answer Satan thus returnd.
Belial, in much uneven scale thou weigh'st
All others by thy self; because of old
Thou thy self doat'st on womankind, admiring   175
Thir shape, thir colour, and attractive grace,
None are, thou think'st, but tak'n with such toys.
Before the Flood thou with thy lusty Crew,
False-titl'd Sons of God, roaming the Earth
Cast wanton eyes on the daughters of men,   180
And coupl'd with them, and begot a race.
Have we not seen, or by relation heard,
In Courts and Regal Chambers how thou lurk'st,
In Wood or Grove by mossie Fountain side,
In Valley or Green Meadow to way-lay   185
Some beauty rare, *Calisto*, *Clymene*,
Daphne, or *Semele*, *Antiopa*,
Or *Amymone*, *Syrinx*, many more
Too long, then lay'st thy scapes on names ador'd,
Apollo, *Neptune*, *Jupiter*, or *Pan*,   190
Satyr, or Fawn, or Silvan? But these haunts
Delight not all; among the Sons of Men,
How many have with a smile made small account
Of beauty and her lures, easily scornd
All her assaults, on worthier things intent?   195
Remember that *Pellean* Conquerour,
A youth, how all the Beauties of the East

He slightly viewd, and slightly over-passd;
How hee sirnam'd of *Africa* dismissd
In his prime youth the fair *Iberian* maid.   200
For *Solomon* he liv'd at ease, and full
Of honour, wealth, high fare, aimd not beyond
Higher design then to enjoy his State;
Thence to the bait of Women lay expos'd;
But hee whom we attempt is wiser far   205
Then *Solomon*, of more exalted mind,
Made and set wholly on th' accomplishment
Of greatest things; what woman will you find,
Though of this Age the wonder and the fame,
On whom his leisure will voutsafe an eye   210
Of fond desire? or should she confident,
As sitting Queen ador'd on Beauties Throne,
Descend with all her winning charms begirt
To enamour, as the Zone of *Venus* once
Wrought that effect on *Jove*, so Fables tell;   215
How would one look from his Majestick brow
Seated as on the top of Vertues hill,
Discount'nance her despis'd, and put to rout
All her array; her femal pride deject,
Or turn to reverent awe? for Beauty stands   220
In th' admiration onely of weak minds
Led captive; cease to admire, and all her Plumes
Fall flat and shrink into a trivial toy,
At every sudden slighting quite abasht:
Therefore with manlier objects we must try   225
His constancy, with such as have more shew
Of worth, of honour, glory, and popular praise;
Rocks whereon greatest men have oftest wreckt;
Of that which onely seems to satisfie
Lawful desires of Nature, not beyond;   230
And now I know he hungers where no food
Is to be found, in the wide Wilderness;
The rest commit to mee, I shall let pass
No advantage, and his strength as oft assay.
　　He ceas'd, and heard thir grant in loud acclaim;   235
Then forthwith to him takes a chosen band

232 wide] Ed. 1 : wild Ed. 2

Of Spirits likest to himself in guile
To be at hand, and at his beck appear,
If cause were to unfold some active Scene
Of various Persons each to know his part;   240
Then to the Desert takes with these his flight;
Where still from shade to shade the Son of God
After forty days fasting had remaind,
Now hungring first, and to himself thus said.

    Where will this end? four times ten days I have past   245
Wandring this woody maze, and human food
Nor tasted, nor had appetite; that Fast
To Vertue I impute not, or count part
Of what I suffer here; if Nature need not,
Or God support Nature without repast   250
Though needing, what praise is it to endure?
But now I feel I hunger, which declares,
Nature hath need of what she asks; yet God
Can satisfie that need some other way,
Though hunger still remain: so it remain   255
Without this bodies wasting, I content me,
And from the sting of Famin fear no harm,
Nor mind it, fed with better thoughts that feed
Mee hungring more to do my Fathers will.

    It was the hour of night, when thus the Son   260
Commun'd in silent walk, then laid him down
Under the hospitable covert nigh
Of Trees thick interwoven; there he slept,
And dreamd, as appetite is wont to dream,
Of meats and drinks, Natures refreshment sweet;   265
Him thought, he by the Brook of *Cherith* stood
And saw the Ravens with thir horny beaks
Food to *Elijah* bringing Ev'n and Morn,
Though ravenous, taught to abstain from what they brought:
He saw the Prophet also how he fled   270
Into the Desert, and how there he slept
Under a Juniper; then how awak't,
He found his Supper on the coals prepar'd,
And by the Angel was bid rise and eat,
And eat the second time after repose,   275
The strength whereof suffic'd him forty days;

Sometimes that with *Elijah* he partook,
Or as a guest with *Daniel* at his pulse.
Thus wore out night, and now the Harald Lark
Left his ground-nest, high towring to descry   280
The morns approach, and greet her with his Song:
As lightly from his grassy Couch up rose
Our Saviour, and found all was but a dream;
Fasting he went to sleep, and fasting wak'd.
Up to a hill anon his steps he reard,   285
From whose high top to ken the prospect round,
If Cottage were in view, Sheep-cote or Herd;
But Cottage, Herd or Sheep-cote none he saw,
Onely in a bottom saw a pleasant Grove,
With chaunt of tuneful Birds resounding loud;   290
Thither he bent his way, determind there
To rest at noon, and enterd soon the shade
High rooft and walks beneath, and alleys brown
That op'nd in the midst a woody Scene,
Natures own work it seemd (Nature taught Art)   295
And to a Superstitious eye the haunt
Of Wood-Gods and Wood-Nymphs; he viewd it round,
When suddenly a man before him stood,
Not rustic as before, but seemlier clad,
As one in City, or Court, or Palace bred,   300
And with fair speech these words to him addressd.
   With granted leave officious I return,
But much more wonder that the Son of God
In this wild solitude so long should bide
Of all things destitute, and well I know,   305
Not without hunger. Others of some note,
As story tells, have trod this Wilderness;
The Fugitive Bond-woman with her Son
Out cast *Nebaioth*, yet found he relief
By a providing Angel; all the race   310
Of *Israel* here had famisht, had not God
Raind from Heav'n Manna, and that Prophet bold
Native of *Thebez* wandring here was fed
Twice by a voice inviting him to eat.
Of thee these forty days none hath regard,   315

309 he] Edd. 1, 2: here 1705

Forty and more deserted here indeed.
    To whom thus Jesus; what conclud'st thou hence?
They all had need, I as thou seest have none.
    How hast thou hunger then? Satan reply'd,
Tell me if Food were now before thee set,   320
Wouldst thou not eat? Thereafter as I like
The giver, answerd Jesus. Why should that
Cause thy refusal, said the suttle Fiend,
Hast thou not right to all Created things,
Owe not all Creatures by just right to thee   325
Duty and Service, nor to stay till bid,
But tender all thir power? nor mention I
Meats by the Law unclean, or offerd first
To Idols, those young *Daniel* could refuse;
Nor profferd by an Enemy, though who   330
Would scruple that, with want opprest? behold
Nature asham'd, or better to express,
Troubl'd that thou shouldst hunger, hath purveyd
From all the Elements her choicest store
To treat thee as beseems, and as her Lord   335
With honour: onely deign to sit and eat.
    He spake no dream, for as his words had end,
Our Saviour lifting up his eyes beheld
In ample space under the broadest shade
A Table richly spred, in regal mode,   340
With dishes pil'd, and meats of noblest sort
And savour, Beasts of chase, or Fowl of game,
In pastry built, or from the spit, or boild,
Gris-amber-steamd; all Fish from Sea or Shore,
Freshet, or purling Brook, of shell or fin,   345
And exquisitest name, for which was draind
Pontus and *Lucrine* Bay, and *Afric* Coast.
Alas how simple, to these Cates compar'd,
Was that crude Apple that diverted *Eve*!
And at a stately side-board by the wine   350
That fragrant smell diffus'd, in order stood
Tall stripling youths rich clad, of fairer hew
Then *Ganymed* or *Hylas*; distant more
Under the Trees now trippd, now solemn stood
Nymphs of *Diana*'s train, and *Naiades*   355

With fruits and flowers from *Amalthea*'s horn,
And Ladies of th' *Hesperides*, that seemd
Fairer then feignd of old, or fabl'd since
Of Fairy Damsels met in Forest wide
By Knights of *Logres*, or of *Lyones*, 360
Lancelot or *Pelleas*, or *Pellenore*,
And all the while Harmonious Airs were heard
Of chiming strings, or charming pipes, and winds
Of gentlest gale *Arabian* odors fannd
From their soft wings, and *Flora*'s earliest smells. 365
Such was the Splendour, and the Tempter now
His invitation earnestly renewd.
　　What doubts the Son of God to sit and eat?
These are not Fruits forbidd'n, no interdict
Defends the touching of these viands pure; 370
Thir taste no knowledge works, at least of evil,
But life preserves, destroys life's enemy,
Hunger, with sweet restorative delight.
All these are Spirits of Air, and Woods, and Springs,
Thy gentle Ministers, who come to pay 375
Thee homage, and acknowledge thee thir Lord:
What doubt'st thou Son of God? sit down and eat.
　　To whom thus Jesus temperatly reply'd.
Said'st thou not that to all things I had right?
And who withholds my pow'r that right to use? 380
Shall I receive by gift what of my own,
When and where likes me best; I can command?
I can at will, doubt not, as soon as thou,
Command a Table in this Wilderness,
And call swift flights of Angels ministrant 385
Arrayd in Glory on my cup to attend:
Why shouldst thou then obtrude this diligence,
In vain, where no acceptance it can find,
And with my hunger what hast thou to do?
Thy pompous Delicacies I contemn, 390
And count thy specious gifts no gifts but guiles.
　　To whom thus answerd Satan malecontent.
That I have also power to give thou seest;
If of that pow'r I bring thee voluntary
What I might have bestowd on whom I pleas'd, 395

And rather opportunely in this place
Chose to impart to thy apparent need,
Why shouldst thou not accept it? but I see
What I can do or offer is suspect;
Of these things others quickly will dispose   400
Whose pains have earnd the far-fet spoil. With that
Both Table and Provision vanishd quite
With sound of Harpies wings, and Talons heard;
Onely th' importune Tempter still remaind,
And with these words his temptation persu'd.   405
   By hunger, that each other Creature tames,
Thou art not to be harmd, therefore not mov'd;
Thy temperance invincible besides,
For no allurement yeilds to appetite,
And all thy heart is set on high designs,   410
High actions; but wherewith to be atchiev'd?
Great acts require great means of enterprise,
Thou art unknown, unfriended, low of birth,
A Carpenter thy Father known, thy self
Bred up in poverty and streights at home;   415
Lost in a Desert here and hunger-bit:
Which way or from what hope dost thou aspire
To greatness? whence Autority deriv'st,
What Followers, what Retinue canst thou gain,
Or at thy heels the dizzy Multitude,   420
Longer then thou canst feed them on thy cost?
Money brings Honour, Friends, Conquest, and Realms;
What rais'd *Antipater* the *Edomite*,
And his Son *Herod* plac'd on *Judahs* Throne;
(Thy throne) but gold that got him puissant friends?   425
Therefore, if at great things thou wouldst arrive,
Get Riches first, get Wealth, and Treasure heap,
Not difficult, if thou heark'n to me,
Riches are mine, Fortune is in my hand;
They whom I favour thrive in wealth amain,   430
While Virtue, Valour, Wisdom sit in want.
   To whom thus Jesus patiently reply'd.
Yet Wealth without these three is impotent,
To gain dominion or to keep it gaind.
Witness those ancient Empires of the Earth,   435

In highth of all thir flowing wealth dissolv'd:
But men endu'd with these have oft attaind
In lowest poverty to highest deeds;
Gideon and *Jephtha*, and the Shepherd lad,
Whose off-spring on the Throne of *Judah* sat　　　　440
So many Ages, and shall yet regain
That seat, and reign in *Israel* without end.
Among the Heathen, (for throughout the World
To me is not unknown what hath been done
Worthy of Memorial) canst thou not remember　　　445
Quintius, Fabricius, Curius, Regulus?
For I esteem those names of men so poor
Who could do mighty things, and could contemn
Riches though offerd from the hand of Kings.
And what in mee seems wanting, but that I　　　　450
May also in this poverty as soon
Accomplish what they did, perhaps and more?
Extoll not Riches then, the toil of Fools,
The wise mans cumbrance if not snare, more apt
To slack'n Virtue, and abate her edge,　　　　455
Then prompt her to do aught may merit praise.
What if with like aversion I reject
Riches and Realms; yet not for that a Crown,
Gold'n in shew, is but a wreath of thorns,
Brings dangers, troubles, cares, and sleepless nights　460
To him who wears the Regal Diadem,
When on his shoulders each mans burden lies;
For therein stands the office of a King,
His Honour, Vertue, Merit and chief Praise,
That for the Publick all this weight he bears.　　465
Yet he who reigns within himself, and rules
Passions, Desires, and Fears, is more a King;
Which every wise and vertuous man attains:
And who attains not, ill aspires to rule
Cities of men, or head-strong Multitudes,　　　470
Subject himself to Anarchy within,
Or lawless passions in him which he serves.
But to guide Nations in the way of truth
By saving Doctrin, and from errour lead
To know, and knowing worship God aright,　　　475

Is yet more Kingly, this attracts the Soul,
Governs the inner man, the nobler part;
That other ore the body onely reigns,
And oft by force, which to a generous mind
So reigning can be no sincere delight.   480
Besides to give a Kingdom hath been thought
Greater and nobler done, and to lay down
Far more magnanimous, then to assume.
Riches are needless then, both for themselves,
And for thy reason why they should be sought,   485
To gain a Scepter, oftest better misst.

THE END OF THE SECOND BOOK

THE THIRD BOOK

So spake the Son of God, and Satan stood
A while as mute confounded what to say,
What to reply, confuted and convinc't
Of his weak arguing, and fallacious drift;
At length collecting all his Serpent wiles,   5
With soothing words renewd, him thus accosts.
    I see thou know'st what is of use to know,
What best to say canst say, to do canst do;
Thy actions to thy words accord, thy words
To thy large heart give utterance due, thy heart   10
Conteins of good, wise, just, the perfet shape.
Should Kings and Nations from thy mouth consult,
Thy Counsel would be as the Oracle
Urim and *Thummim*, those oraculous gems
On *Aarons* brest: or tongue of Seers old   15
Infallible; or wert thou sought to deeds
That might require th' array of warr, thy skill
Of conduct would be such, that all the World
Could not sustain thy Prowess, or subsist
In battel, though against thy few in arms.   20
These God-like Vertues wherefore dost thou hide?
Affecting privat life, or more obscure
In savage Wilderness, wherefore deprive
All Earth her wonder at thy acts, thy self
The fame and glory, glory the reward   25
That sole excites to high attempts the flame
Of most erected Spirits, most temperd pure
Ætherial, who all pleasures else despise,
All treasures and all gain esteem as dross,
And dignities and powers all but the highest?   30
Thy years are ripe, and over-ripe, the Son
Of *Macedonian Philip* had ere these
Won *Asia* and the Throne of *Cyrus* held
At his dispose, young *Scipio* had brought down
The *Carthaginian* pride, young *Pompey* quelld   35
The *Pontic* King and in triumph had rode.
Yet years, and to ripe years judgment mature,

Quench not the thirst of glory, but augment.
Great *Julius*, whom now all the World admires,
The more he grew in years, the more inflam'd   40
With glory, wept that he had liv'd so long
Inglorious: but thou yet art not too late.
    To whom our Saviour calmly thus reply'd.
Thou neither dost perswade me to seek wealth
For Empires sake, nor Empire to affect   45
For glories sake by all thy argument.
For what is glory but the blaze of fame,
The peoples praise, if always praise unmixt?
And what the people but a herd confus'd,
A miscellaneous rabble, who extoll   50
Things vulgar, and well weighd, scarce worth the praise;
They praise and they admire they know not what,
And know not whom, but as one leads the other;
And what delight to be by such extolld,
To live upon their tongues and be their talk,   55
Of whom to be disprais'd were no small praise?
His lot who dares be singularly good.
Th' intelligent among them and the wise
Are few, and glory scarce of few is rais'd.
This is true glory and renown, when God   60
Looking on th' Earth, with approbation marks
The just man, and divulges him through Heaven
To all his Angels, who with true applause
Recount his praises; thus he did to *Job*,
When to extend his fame through Heav'n and Earth,   65
As thou to thy reproach mayst well remember,
He askd thee, hast thou seen my servant *Job*?
Famous he was in Heaven, on Earth less known;
Where glory is false glory, attributed
To things not glorious, men not worthy of fame.   70
They err who count it glorious to subdue
By Conquest farr and wide, to over-run
Large Countries, and in field great Battels win,
Great Cities by assault: what do these Worthies,
But rob and spoil, burn, slaughter, and enslave   75
Peaceable Nations, neighbouring, or remote,
Made Captive, yet deserving freedom more

Then those thir Conquerours, who leave behind
Nothing but ruin wheresoe're they rove,
And all the flourishing works of peace destroy,   80
Then swell with pride, and must be titl'd Gods,
Great Benefactors of mankind, Deliverers,
Worship with Temple, Priest and Sacrifice;
One is the Son of *Jove*, of *Mars* the other,
Till Conquerour Death discover them scarce men,   85
Rowling in brutish vices, and deformd,
Violent or shameful death thir due reward.
But if there be in glory aught of good,
It may by means far different be attaind
Without ambition, warr, or violence;   90
By deeds of peace, by wisdom eminent,
By patience, temperance; I mention still
Him whom thy wrongs with Saintly patience born,
Made famous in a Land and times obscure;
Who names not now with honour patient *Job*?   95
Poor *Socrates* (who next more memorable?)
By what he taught and sufferd for so doing,
For truths sake suffering death unjust, lives now
Equal in fame to proudest Conquerours.
Yet if for fame and glory aught be done,   100
Aught sufferd; if young *African* for fame
His wasted Country freed from *Punic* rage,
The deed becomes unprais'd, the man at least,
And loses, though but verbal, his reward.
Shall I seek glory then, as vain men seek   105
Oft not deserv'd? I seek not mine, but his
Who sent me, and thereby witness whence I am.
   To whom the Tempter murmuring thus reply'd.
Think not so slight of glory; therein least,
Resembling thy great Father: hee seeks glory,   110
And for his glory all things made, all things
Orders and governs, nor content in Heaven
By all his Angels glorifi'd, requires
Glory from men, from all men good or bad,
Wise or unwise, no difference, no exemption;   115
Above all Sacrifice, or hallowd gift
Glory he requires, and glory he receives

Promiscuous from all Nations, Jew, or Greek,
Or Barbarous, nor exception hath declar'd;
From us his foes pronounc't glory he exacts.   120
    To whom our Saviour fervently reply'd.
And reason; since his Word all things produc'd,
Though chiefly not for glory as prime end,
But to shew forth his goodness, and impart
His good communicable to every soul   125
Freely; of whom what could he less expect
Then glory and benediction, that is thanks,
The slightest, easiest, readiest recompence
From them who could return him nothing else,
And not returning that, would likeliest render   130
Contempt instead, dishonour, obloquy?
Hard recompence, unsutable return
For so much good, so much beneficence.
But why should man seek glory? who of his own
Hath nothing, and to whom nothing belongs   135
But condemnation, ignominy, and shame?
Who for so many benefits receiv'd
Turnd recreant to God, ingrate and false,
And so of all true good himself despoild,
Yet, sacrilegious, to himself would take   140
That which to God alone of right belongs;
Yet so much bounty is in God, such grace,
That who advance his glory, not thir own,
Them he himself to glory will advance.
    So spake the Son of God; and here again   145
Satan had not to answer, but stood strook
With guilt of his own sin, for he himself
Insatiable of glory had lost all,
Yet of another Plea bethought him soon.
    Of glory as thou wilt, said he, so deem,   150
Worth or not worth the seeking, let it pass:
But to a Kingdom thou art born, ordaind
To sit upon thy Father *Davids* Throne;
By Mother's side thy Father, though thy right
Be now in powerful hands, that will not part   155
Easily from possession won with arms;
Judæa now and all the promisd land

Reduc't a Province under *Roman* yoke,
Obeys *Tiberius*; nor is always rul'd
With temperat sway; oft have they violated   160
The Temple, oft the Law with foul affronts,
Abominations rather, as did once
Antiochus: and think'st thou to regain
Thy right by sitting still or thus retiring?
So did not *Machabeus*: he indeed   165
Retir'd unto the Desert, but with arms;
And ore a mighty King so oft prevaild,
That by strong hand his Family obtaind,
Though Priests, the Crown, and *Davids* Throne usurpd,
With *Modin* and her Suburbs once content.   170
If Kingdom move thee not, let move thee Zeal,
And Duty; Zeal and Duty are not slow;
But on Occasions forelock watchful wait.
They themselves rather are occasion best,
Zeal of thy Fathers house, Duty to free   175
Thy Country from her Heathen servitude;
So shalt thou best fulfill, best verifie
The Prophets old, who sung thy endless raign,
The happier raign the sooner it begins:
Raign then; what canst thou better do the while?   180
   To whom our Saviour answer thus returnd.
All things are best fulfilld in thir due time,
And time there is for all things, Truth hath said:
If of my raign Prophetic Writ hath told
That it shall never end, so when begin   185
The Father in his purpose hath decreed,
He in whose hand all times and seasons roul.
What if he hath decreed that I shall first
Be try'd in humble state, and things adverse,
By tribulations, injuries, insults,   190
Contempts, and scorns, and snares, and violence,
Suffering, abstaining, quietly expecting
Without distrust or doubt, that he may know
What I can suffer, how obey? who best
Can suffer, best can do; best reign, who first   195
Well hath obeyd; just tryal ere I merit
My exaltation without change or end.

But what concerns it thee when I begin
My everlasting Kingdom, why art thou
Sollicitous, what moves thy inquisition?   200
Know'st thou not that my rising is thy fall,
And my promotion will be thy destruction?
    To whom the Tempter inly rackt reply'd.
Let that come when it comes; all hope is lost
Of my reception into grace; what worse?   205
For where no hope is left, is left no fear;
If there be worse, the expectation more
Of worse torments me then the feeling can.
I would be at the worst; worst is my Port,
My harbour and my ultimate repose,   210
The end I would attain, my final good.
My error was my error, and my crime
My crime; whatever for it self condemnd,
And will alike be punisht; whether thou
Raign or raign not; though to that gentle brow   215
Willingly I could flye, and hope thy raign,
From that placid aspect and meek regard,
Rather then aggravate my evil state,
Would stand between me and thy Fathers ire,
(Whose ire I dread more then the fire of Hell)   220
A shelter and a kind of shading cool
Interposition, as a summers cloud.
If I then to the worst that can be hast,
Why move thy feet so slow to what is best,
Happiest both to thy self and all the World,   225
That thou who worthiest art should'st be thir King?
Perhaps thou linger'st in deep thoughts detain
Of the enterprise so hazardous and high;
No wonder, for though in thee be united
What of perfection can in man be found,   230
Or human nature can receive, consider
Thy life hath yet been privat, most part spent
At home, scarce viewd the *Gallilean* Towns,
And once a year *Jerusalem*, few days
Short sojourn; and what thence could'st thou observe?   235
The World thou hast not seen, much less her glory,
Empires, and Monarchs, and thir radiant Courts,

Best school of best experience, quickest insight
In all things that to greatest actions lead.
The wisest, unexperienc't, will be ever   240
Timorous and loth, with novice modesty,
(As he who seeking Asses found a Kingdom)
Irresolute, unhardy, unadventrous:
But I will bring thee where thou soon shalt quit
Those rudiments, and see before thine eyes   245
The Monarchies of th' Earth, thir pomp and state,
Sufficient introduction to inform
Thee, of thy self so apt, in regal Arts,
And regal Mysteries; that thou may'st know
How best thir opposition to withstand.   250
      With that (such power was giv'n him then) he took
The Son of God up to a Mountain high.
It was a Mountain at whose verdant feet
A spacious plain out strecht in circuit wide
Lay pleasant; from his side two rivers flowd,   255
Th' one winding, th' other strait, and left between
Fair Champain with less rivers interveind,
Then meeting joind thir tribute to the Sea:
Fertil of corn the glebe, of oil and wine,
With herds the pastures throngd, with flocks the hills,   260
Huge Cities and high towr'd, that well might seem
The seats of mightiest Monarchs, and so large
The Prospect was, that here and there was room
For barren desert fountainless and dry.
To this high mountain top the Tempter brought   265
Our Saviour, and new train of words began.
      Well have we speeded, and ore hill and dale,
Forest and field, and flood, Temples and Towers
Cut shorter many a league; here thou behold'st
Assyria and her Empires ancient bounds,   270
Araxes and the *Caspian* lake, thence on
As farr as *Indus* East, *Euphrates* West,
And oft beyond; to South the *Persian* Bay,
And inaccessible th' *Arabian* drouth:
Here *Ninevee*, of length within her wall   275
Several days journey, built by *Ninus* old,
Of that first gold'n Monarchy the seat,

And seat of *Salmanassar*, whose success
Israel in long captivity still mourns;
There *Babylon* the wonder of all tongues,   280
As ancient, but rebuilt by him who twice
Judah and all thy Father *Davids* house
Led captive, and *Jerusalem* laid waste,
Till *Cyrus* set them free; *Persepolis*
His City there thou seest, and *Bactra* there;   285
Ecbatana her structure vast there shews,
And *Hecatompylos* her hunderd gates,
There *Susa* by *Choaspes*, amber stream,
The drink of none but Kings; of later fame
Built by *Emathian*, or by *Parthian* hands,   290
The great *Seleucia*, *Nisibis*, and there
Artaxata, *Teredon*, *Ctesiphon*,
Turning with easie eye thou may'st behold.
All these the *Parthian*, now some Ages past,
By great *Arsaces* led, who founded first   295
That Empire, under his dominion holds
From the luxurious Kings of *Antioch* won.
And just in time thou com'st to have a view
Of his great power; for now the *Parthian* King
In *Ctesiphon* hath gatherd all his Host   300
Against the *Scythian*, whose incursions wild
Have wasted *Sogdiana*; to her aid
He marches now in hast; see, though from farr,
His thousands, in what martial equipage
They issue forth, Steel Bows, and Shafts thir arms   305
Of equal dread in flight, or in persuit;
All Horsemen, in which fight they most excell;
See how in warlike muster they appear,
In Rhombs and wedges, and half-moons, and wings.

    He lookd and saw what numbers numberless   310
The City gates out powr'd, light armed Troops
In coats of Mail and military pride;
In Mail thir horses clad, yet fleet and strong,
Prauncing thir riders bore, the flower and choice
Of many Provinces from bound to bound;   315
From *Arachosia*, from *Candaor* East,
And *Margiana* to th' *Hyrcanian* cliffs

Of *Caucasus*, and dark *Iberian* dales,
From *Atropatia* and the neighbouring plains
Of *Adiabene*, *Media*, and the South 320
Of *Susiana* to *Balsara*'s hav'n.
He saw them in thir forms of battel rang'd,
How quick they wheeld, and flying behind them shot
Sharp sleet of arrowie showers against the face
Of thir persuers, and overcame by flight; 325
The field all iron cast a gleaming brown,
Nor wanted clouds of foot, nor on each horn,
Cuirassiers all in steel for standing fight;
Chariots or Elephants endorst with Towers
Of Archers, nor of labouring Pioners 330
A multitude with Spades and Axes armd
To lay hills plain, fell woods, or valleys fill,
Or where plain was raise hill, or over-lay
With bridges rivers proud, as with a yoke;
Mules after these, Camels and Dromedaries, 335
And Waggons fraught with Utensils of warr.
Such forces met not, nor so wide a camp,
When *Agrican* with all his Northern powers
Besieg'd *Albracca*, as Romances tell;
The City of *Gallaphrone*, from thence to win 340
The fairest of her Sex *Angelica*
His daughter, sought by many Prowest Knights,
Both *Paynim*, and the Peers of *Charlemane*.
Such and so numerous was thir Chivalrie;
At sight whereof the Fiend yet more presum'd, 345
And to our Saviour thus his words renewd.
   That thou may'st know I seek not to engage
Thy Vertue, and not every way secure
On no slight grounds thy safety; hear, and mark
To what end I have brought thee hither and shewn 350
All this fair sight; thy Kingdom though foretold
By Prophet or by Angel, unless thou
Endeavour, as thy Father *David* did,
Thou never shalt obtain; prediction still
In all things, and all men, supposes means; 355
Without means us'd, what it predicts revokes.
But say thou wert possest of *Davids* Throne

By free consent of all, none opposite,
Samaritan or *Jew*; how could'st thou hope
Long to enjoy it quiet and secure, 360
Between two such enclosing enemies
Roman and *Parthian*? therefore one of these
Thou must make sure thy own, the *Parthian* first
By my advice, as nearer and of late
Found able by invasion to annoy 365
Thy country, and captive lead away her Kings
Antigonus, and old *Hyrcanus* bound,
Maugre the *Roman*: it shall be my task
To render thee the *Parthian* at dispose;
Chuse which thou wilt by conquest or by league; 370
By him thou shalt regain, without him not,
That which alone can truly reinstall thee
In *Davids* royal seat, his true Successour,
Deliverance of thy brethren, those ten Tribes
Whose off-spring in his Territory yet serve 375
In *Habor*, and among the *Medes* disperst,
Ten Sons of *Jacob*, two of *Joseph* lost
Thus long from *Israel*, serving as of old
Thir Fathers in the land of *Egypt* serv'd,
This offer sets before thee to deliver. 380
These if from servitude thou shalt restore
To thir inheritance, then, nor till then,
Thou on the Throne of *David* in full glory,
From *Egypt* to *Euphrates* and beyond
Shalt raign, and *Rome* or *Cæsar* not need fear. 385
　　To whom our Saviour answerd thus unmov'd.
Much ostentation vain of fleshly arm,
And fragile arms, much instrument of warr
Long in preparing, soon to nothing brought,
Before mine eyes thou hast set; and in my ear 390
Vented much policy, and projects deep
Of enemies, of aids, battels and leagues,
Plausible to the World, to mee worth naught.
Means I must use thou say'st, prediction else
Will unpredict and fail me of the Throne: 395
My time I told thee, (and that time for thee
Were better fardest off) is not yet come;

When that comes think not thou to find me slack
On my part aught endeavouring, or to need
Thy politic maxims, or that cumbersome   400
Luggage of warr there shewn me, argument
Of human weakness rather then of strength.
My brethren, as thou call'st them; those Ten Tribes
I must deliver, if I mean to raign
Davids true heir, and his full Scepter sway   405
To just extent over all *Israels* Sons;
But whence to thee this zeal, where was it then
For *Israel*, or for *David*, or his Throne,
When thou stood'st up his Tempter to the pride
Of numbring *Israel*, which cost the lives   410
Of threescore and ten thousand *Israelites*
By three days Pestilence? such was thy zeal
To *Israel* then, the same that now to me.
As for those captive Tribes, themselves were they
Who wrought thir own captivity, fell off   415
From God to worship Calves, the Deities
Of *Egypt*, *Baal* next and *Ashtaroth*,
And all th' Idolatries of Heathen round,
Besides thir other worse then heathenish crimes;
Nor in the land of thir captivity   420
Humbl'd themselves, or penitent besought
The God of thir fore-fathers; but so dy'd
Impenitent, and left a race behind
Like to themselves, distinguishable scarce
From Gentils, but by Circumcision vain,   425
And God with Idols in thir worship joind.
Should I of these the liberty regard,
Who freed, as to thir ancient Patrimony,
Unhumbl'd, unrepentant, unreformd,
Headlong would follow; and to thir Gods perhaps   430
Of *Bethel* and of *Dan*? no, let them serve
Thir enemies, who serve Idols with God.
Yet hee at length, time to himself best known,
Remembring *Abraham* by some wond'rous call
May bring them back repentant and sincere,   435
And at thir passing cleave the *Assyrian* flood,
While to thir native land with joy they hast,

As the Red Sea and *Jordan* once he cleft,
When to the promisd land thir Fathers passd;
To his due time and providence I leave them.   440
   So spake *Israels* true King, and to the Fiend
Made answer meet, that made void all his wiles.
So fares it when with truth falshood contends.

THE END OF THE THIRD BOOK

THE FOURTH BOOK

PERPLEXT and troubl'd at his bad success
The Tempter stood, nor had what to reply,
Discoverd in his fraud, thrown from his hope,
So oft, and the perswasive Rhetoric
That sleekd his tongue, and won so much on *Eve*,   5
So little here, nay lost; but *Eve* was *Eve*,
This farr his over-match, who self deceiv'd
And rash, before-hand had no better weigh'd
The strength he was to cope with, or his own:
But as a man who had been matchless held   10
In cunning, over-reacht where least he thought,
To salve his credit, and for very spite
Still will be tempting him who foils him still,
And never cease, though to his shame the more;
Or as a swarm of flies in vintage time,   15
About the wine-press where sweet moust is powrd,
Beat off, returns as oft with humming sound;
Or surging waves against a solid rock,
Though all to shivers dasht, the assault renew,
Vain battry, and in froth or bubbles end;   20
So Satan, whom repulse upon repulse
Met ever; and to shameful silence brought,
Yet gives not ore though desperat of success,
And his vain importunity persues.
He brought our Saviour to the Western side   25
Of that high mountain, whence he might behold
Another plain, long but in bredth not wide;
Washt by the Southern Sea, and on the North
To equal length backt with a ridge of hills
That screend the fruits of th' earth and seats of men   30
From cold *Septentrion* blasts, thence in the midst
Divided by a river, of whose banks
On each side an Imperial City stood,
With Towers and Temples proudly elevate
On seven small Hills, with Palaces adornd,   35
Porches and Theatres, Baths, Aqueducts,
Statues and Trophees, and Triumphal Arcs,

Gardens and Groves presented to his eyes,
Above the highth of Mountains interpos'd.
By what strange Parallax or Optic skill   40
Of vision multipli'd through air, or glass
Of Telescope, were curious to enquire:
And now the Tempter thus his silence broke.
    The City which thou seest no other deem
Then great and glorious *Rome*, Queen of the Earth   45
So farr renownd, and with the spoils enricht
Of Nations; there the Capitol thou seest
Above the rest lifting his stately head
On the *Tarpeian* rock, her Cittadel
Impregnable, and there Mount *Palatine*   50
Th' Imperial Palace, compass huge, and high
The Structure, skill of noblest Architects,
With gilded battlements, conspicuous farr,
Turrets and Terrases, and glittering Spires.
Many a fair Edifice besides, more like   55
Houses of gods (so well I have dispos'd
My Aerie Microscope) thou may'st behold
Outside and inside both, pillars and roofs
Carv'd work, the hand of fam'd Artificers
In Cedar, Marble, Ivory or Gold.   60
Thence to the gates cast round thine eye, and see
What conflux issuing forth, or entring in,
Pretors, Proconsuls to thir Provinces
Hasting or on return, in robes of State;
Lictors and rods the ensigns of thir power,   65
Legions and Cohorts, turmes of horse and wings:
Or Embassies from Regions farr remote
In various habits on the *Appian* road,
Or on th' *Æmilian*, some from fardest South,
Syene, and where the shadow both way falls,   70
Meroe Nilotic Ile, and more to West,
The Realm of *Bocchus* to the Black-moor Sea;
From the *Asian* Kings and *Parthian* among these,
From *India* and the gold'n *Chersoness*,
And utmost *Indian* Ile *Taprobane*,   75
Dusk faces with white silk'n Turbants wreath'd:
From *Gallia*, *Gades*, and the *Brittish* West,

Germans and *Scythians*, and *Sarmatians* North
Beyond *Danubius* to the *Tauric* Pool.
All Nations now to *Rome* obedience pay,   80
To *Romes* great Emperour, whose wide domain
In ample Territory, wealth and power,
Civility of Manners, Arts, and Arms,
And long Renown thou justly may'st preferr
Before the *Parthian*; these two Thrones except,   85
The rest are barbarous, and scarce worth the sight,
Shar'd among petty Kings too farr remov'd;
These having shewn thee, I have shewn thee all
The Kingdoms of the World, and all thir glory.
This Emperour hath no Son, and now is old,   90
Old, and lascivious, and from *Rome* retir'd
To *Capreæ* an Iland small but strong
On the *Campanian* shore, with purpose there
His horrid lusts in privat to enjoy,
Committing to a wicked Favourite   95
All publick cares, and yet of him suspicious,
Hated of all, and hating; with what ease
Indu'd with Regal Vertues as thou art,
Appearing, and beginning noble deeds,
Might'st thou expell this monster from his Throne   100
Now made a stye, and in his place ascending
A victor people free from servil yoke?
And with my help thou may'st; to me the power
Is given, and by that right I give it thee.
Aim therefore at no less then all the World,   105
Aim at the highest, without the highest attaind
Will be for thee no sitting, or not long
On *Davids* Throne, be propheci'd what will.
     To whom the Son of God unmov'd reply'd.
Nor doth this grandeur and majestic show   110
Of luxury, though calld magnificence,
More then of arms before, allure mine eye,
Much less my mind; though thou should'st add to tell
Thir sumptuous gluttonies, and gorgeous feasts
On *Cittron* tables or *Atlantic* stone;   115
(For I have also heard, perhaps have red)
Thir wines of *Setia*, *Cales*, and *Falerne*,

Chios and *Creet*, and how they quaff in Gold,
Crystal and Myrrhine cups imbost with Gems
And studs of Pearl, to me should'st tell who thirst   120
And hunger still: then Embassies thou shew'st
From Nations farr and nigh; what honour that,
But tedious wast of time to sit and hear
So many hollow complements and lies,
Outlandish flatteries? then proceed'st to talk   125
Of the Emperour, how easily subdu'd,
How gloriously; I shall, thou say'st, expell
A brutish monster: what if I withall
Expell a Devil who first made him such?
Let his tormenter Conscience find him out,   130
For him I was not sent, nor yet to free
That people victor once, now vile and base,
Deservedly made vassal, who once just,
Frugal, and mild, and temperat, conquerd well,
But govern ill the Nations under yoke,   135
Peeling thir Provinces, exhausted all
By lust and rapine; first ambitious grown
Of triumph that insulting vanity;
Then cruel, by thir sports to blood enur'd
Of fighting beasts, and men to beasts expos'd,   140
Luxurious by thir wealth, and greedier still,
And from the daily Scene effeminate.
What wise and valiant man would seek to free
These thus degenerat, by themselves enslav'd,
Or could of inward slaves make outward free?   145
Know therefore when my season comes to sit
On *Davids* Throne, it shall be like a tree
Spreading and over-shadowing all the Earth,
Or as a stone that shall to pieces dash
All Monarchies besides throughout the World,   150
And of my Kingdom there shall be no end:
Means there shall be to this, but what the means,
Is not for thee to know, nor mee to tell.
    To whom the Tempter impudent repli'd.
I see all offers made by me how slight   155
Thou valu'st, because offerd, and reject'st:
Nothing will please the difficult and nice,

Or nothing more then still to contradict:
On th' other side know also thou, that I
On what I offer set as high esteem,   160
Nor what I part with mean to give for naught;
All these which in a moment thou behold'st,
The Kingdoms of the World to thee I give;
For giv'n to me, I give to whom I please,
No trifle; yet with this reserve, not else,   165
On this condition, if thou wilt fall down,
And worship me as thy superior Lord,
Easily done, and hold them all of me;
For what can less so great a gift deserve?
   Whom thus our Saviour answerd with disdain.   170
I never lik'd thy talk, thy offers less,
Now both abhorr, since thou hast dar'd to utter
Th' abominable terms, impious condition;
But I endure the time, till which expir'd,
Thou hast permission on me. It is writt'n   175
The first of all Commandments, Thou shalt worship
The Lord thy God, and onely him shalt serve;
And dar'st thou to the Son of God propound
To worship thee accurst, now more accurst
For this attempt bolder then that on *Eve*,   180
And more blaspheamous? which expect to rue.
The Kingdoms of the World to thee were giv'n,
Permitted rather, and by thee usurpt,
Other donation none thou canst produce:
If giv'n, by whom but by the King of Kings,   185
God over all supream? if giv'n to thee,
By thee how fairly is the Giver now
Repaid? But gratitude in thee is lost
Long since. Wert thou so void of fear or shame,
As offer them to mee the Son of God,   190
To mee my own, on such abhorred pact,
That I fall down and worship thee as God?
Get thee behind me; plain thou now appear'st
That Evil one, Satan for ever damnd.
   To whom the Fiend with fear abasht reply'd.   195
Be not so sore offended, Son of God;
Though Sons of God both Angels are and Men,

If I to try whether in higher sort
Then these thou bear'st that title, have propos'd
What both from Men and Angels I receive,   200
Tetrarchs of fire, air, flood, and on the earth
Nations besides from all the quarterd winds,
God of this World invok't and World beneath;
Who then thou art, whose coming is foretold
To mee so fatal, mee it most concerns.   205
The tryal hath indamag'd thee no way,
Rather more honour left and more esteem;
Mee naught advantag'd, missing what I aimd.
Therefore let pass, as they are transitory,
The Kingdoms of this World; I shall no more   210
Advise thee, gain them as thou canst, or not.
And thou thy self seem'st otherwise inclin'd
Then to a worldly Crown, addicted more
To contemplation and profound dispute,
As by that early action may be judg'd,   215
When slipping from thy Mothers eye thou went'st
Alone into the Temple; there wast found
Among the gravest Rabbi's disputant
On points and questions fitting *Moses* Chair,
Teaching not taught; the childhood shews the man,   220
As morning shews the day. Be famous then
By wisdom; as thy Empire must extend,
So let extend thy mind ore all the World,
In knowledge, all things in it comprehend,
All knowledge is not coucht in *Moses* Law,   225
The *Pentateuch* or what the Prophets wrote,
The Gentiles also know, and write, and teach
To admiration, led by Natures light;
And with the Gentiles much thou must converse,
Ruling them by perswasion as thou mean'st;   230
Without thir learning how wilt thou with them,
Or they with thee hold conversation meet?
How wilt thou reason with them, how refute
Thir Idolisms, Traditions, Paradoxes?
Error by his own arms is best evinc't.   235
Look once more ere we leave this specular Mount
Westward, much nearer by Southwest, behold

Where on the *Ægean* shore a City stands
Built nobly, pure the air, and light the soil,
Athens the eye of *Greece*, Mother of Arts   240
And Eloquence, native to famous wits
Or hospitable, in her sweet recess,
City or Suburban, studious walks and shades;
See there the Olive Grove of *Academe*,
Plato's retirement, where the *Attic* Bird   245
Trills her thick-warbl'd notes the summer long,
There flowrie hill *Hymettus* with the sound
Of Bees industrious murmur oft invites
To studious musing; there *Ilissus* rouls
His whispering stream; within the walls then view   250
The schools of ancient *Sages*; his who bred
Great *Alexander* to subdue the World,
Lyceum there, and painted *Stoa* next:
There thou shalt hear and learn the secret power
Of harmony in tones and numbers hit   255
By voice or hand, and various-measur'd verse,
Æolian charms and *Dorian Lyric* Odes,
And his who gave them breath, but higher sung,
Blind *Melesigenes* thence *Homer* calld,
Whose Poem *Phœbus* challeng'd for his own.   260
Thence what the lofty grave Tragœdians taught
In *Chorus* or *Iambic*, teachers best
Of moral prudence, with delight receiv'd
In brief sententious precepts, while they treat
Of fate, and chance, and change in human life;   265
High actions, and high passions best describing:
Thence to the famous Orators repair,
Those ancient, whose resistless eloquence
Wielded at will that fierce Democratie,
Shook th' Arsenal and fulmind over *Greece*,   270
To *Macedon*, and *Artaxerxes* Throne;
To sage Philosophy next lend thine ear,
From Heav'n descended to the low-rooft house
Of *Socrates*, see there his Tenement,
Whom well inspir'd the Oracle pronounc'd   275
Wisest of men; from whose mouth issu'd forth
Mellifluous streams that waterd all the schools

Of Academics old and new, with those
Sirnam'd *Peripatetics*, and the Sect
Epicurean, and the *Stoic* severe;   280
These here revolve, or, as thou lik'st, at home,
Till time mature thee to a Kingdoms waight;
These rules will render thee a King compleat
Within thy self, much more with Empire joind.
    To whom our Saviour sagely thus repli'd.   285
Think not but that I know these things, or think
I know them not; not therefore am I short
Of knowing what I ought: he who receives
Light from above, from the fountain of light,
No other doctrin needs, though granted true;   290
But these are false, or little else but dreams,
Conjectures, fancies, built on nothing firm.
The first and wisest of them all professd
To know this onely, that he nothing knew;
The next to fabling fell and smooth conceits;   295
A third sort doubted all things, though plain sense;
Others in vertue plac'd felicity,
But vertue joind with riches and long life;
In corporal pleasure hee, and careless ease;
The Stoic last in Philosophic pride,   300
By him calld vertue; and his vertuous man,
Wise, perfet in himself, and all possessing
Equal to God, oft shames not to preferr,
As fearing God nor man, contemning all
Wealth, pleasure, pain or torment, death and life, 305
Which when he lists, he leaves, or boasts he can,
For all his tedious talk is but vain boast,
Or suttle shifts conviction to evade.
Alas what can they teach, and not mislead;
Ignorant of themselves, of God much more,   310
And how the World began, and how man fell
Degraded by himself, on Grace depending?
Much of the Soul they talk, but all awrie,
And in themselves seek vertue, and to themselves
All glory arrogate, to God give none,   315
Rather accuse him under usual names,
Fortune and Fate, as one regardless quite

Of mortal things. Who therefore seeks in these
True wisdom, finds her not, or by delusion
Farr worse, her false resemblance onely meets,   320
An empty cloud. However many books
Wise men have said are wearisom; who reads
Incessantly, and to his reading brings not
A spirit and judgment equal or superior,
(And what he brings, what needs he elsewhere seek)   325
Uncertain and unsettl'd still remains,
Deep verst in books and shallow in himself,
Crude or intoxicate, collecting toys,
And trifles for choice matters, worth a spunge;
As Childern gathering pibles on the shore.   330
Or if I would delight my privat hours
With Music or with Poem, where so soon
As in our native Language can I find
That solace? All our Law and Story strew'd
With Hymns, our Psalms with artful terms inscrib'd,   335
Our Hebrew Songs and Harps in *Babylon*,
That pleas'd so well our Victors ear, declare
That rather *Greece* from us these Arts deriv'd;
Ill imitated, while they loudest sing
The vices of thir Deities, and thir own   340
In Fable, Hymn, or Song, so personating
Thir Gods ridiculous, and themselves past shame.
Remove thir swelling Epithetes thick laid
As varnish on a Harlots cheek, the rest,
Thin sown with aught of profit or delight,   345
Will farr be found unworthy to compare
With *Sions* songs, to all true tasts excelling,
Where God is prais'd aright, and Godlike men,
The Holiest of Holies, and his Saints;
Such are from God inspir'd, not such from thee;   350
Unless where moral vertue is exprest
By light of Nature not in all quite lost.
Thir Orators thou then extoll'st, as those
The top of Eloquence, Statists indeed,
And lovers of thir Country, as may seem;   355
But herein to our Prophets farr beneath,
As men divinely taught, and better teaching

The solid rules of Civil Goverment
In thir majestic unaffected stile
Then all the Oratory of *Greece* and *Rome*.   360
In them is plainest taught, and easiest learnt,
What makes a Nation happy, and keeps it so,
What ruins Kingdoms, and lays Cities flat;
These onely with our Law best form a King.
    So spake the Son of God; but Satan now   365
Quite at a loss, for all his darts were spent,
Thus to our Saviour with stern brow reply'd.
    Since neither wealth, nor honour, arms nor arts,
Kingdom nor Empire pleases thee, nor aught
By mee propos'd in life contemplative,   370
Or active, tended on by glory, or fame,
What dost thou in this World? the Wilderness
For thee is fittest place, I found thee there,
And thither will return thee, yet remember
What I foretell thee, soon thou shalt have cause   375
To wish thou never hadst rejected thus
Nicely or cautiously my offerd aid,
Which would have set thee in short time with ease
On *Davids* Throne; or Throne of all the World,
Now at full age, fulness of time, thy season,   380
When Prophesies of thee are best fulfilld.
Now contrary, if I read aught in Heaven,
Or Heav'n write aught of Fate, by what the Starrs
Voluminous, or single characters,
In thir conjunction met, give me to spell,   385
Sorrows, and labours, opposition, hate,
Attends thee, scorns, reproaches, injuries,
Violence and stripes, and lastly cruel death,
A Kingdom they portend thee, but what Kingdom,
Real or Allegoric I discern not,   390
Nor when, eternal sure, as without end,
Without beginning; for no date prefixt
Directs me in the Starry Rubric set.
    So saying he took (for still he knew his power
Not yet expir'd) and to the Wilderness   395
Brought back the Son of God, and left him there,
Feigning to disappear. Darkness now rose,

As day-light sunk, and brought in lowring night
Her shadowy off-spring unsubstantial both,
Privation meer of light and absent day. 400
Our Saviour meek and with untroubl'd mind
After his aerie jaunt, though hurried sore,
Hungry and cold betook him to his rest,
Wherever, under some concourse of shades
Whose branching arms thick intertwin'd might shield 405
From dews and damps of night his shelterd head;
But shelterd slept in vain, for at his head
The Tempter watchd, and soon with ugly dreams
Disturbd his sleep; and either Tropic now
'Gan thunder, and both ends of Heav'n, the Clouds 410
From many a horrid rift abortive pourd
Fierce rain with lightning mixt, water with fire
In ruine reconcil'd: nor slept the winds
Within thir stony caves, but rushd abroad
From the four hinges of the World, and fell 415
On the vext Wilderness, whose tallest Pines,
Though rooted deep as high, and sturdiest Oaks
Bow'd thir Stiff necks, load'n with stormy blasts,
Or torn up sheer: ill wast thou shrouded then,
O patient Son of God, yet onely stoodst 420
Unshak'n; nor yet staid the terror there,
Infernal Ghosts, and Hellish Furies, round
Environd thee, some howld, some yelld, some shriekd,
Some bent at thee thir fiery darts, while thou
Sat'st unappalld in calm and sinless peace. 425
Thus passd the night so foul, till morning fair
Came forth with Pilgrim steps in amice gray;
Who with her radiant finger stilld the roar
Of thunder, chas'd the clouds, and laid the winds,
And grisly Spectres, which the Fiend had rais'd 430
To tempt the Son of God with terrors dire.
And now the Sun with more effectual beams
Had cheard the face of Earth, and dry'd the wet
From drooping plant, or dropping tree; the birds
Who all things now behold more fresh and green, 435
After a night of storm so ruinous,
Cleard up their choicest notes in bush and spray

To gratulate the sweet return of morn;
Nor yet amidst this joy and brightest morn
Was absent, after all his mischief done,   440
The Prince of darkness, glad would also seem
Of this fair change, and to our Saviour came,
Yet with no new device, they all were spent,
Rather by this his last affront resolv'd,
Desperat of better course, to vent his rage,   445
And mad despite to be so oft repelld.
Him walking on a Sunny hill he found,
Backt on the North and West by a thick wood,
Out of the wood he starts in wonted shape;
And in a careless mood thus to him said.   450
    Fair morning yet betides thee Son of God,
After a dismal night; I heard the rack
As Earth and Skie would mingle; but my self
Was distant; and these flaws, though mortals fear them
As dangerous to the pillard frame of Heaven,   455
Or to the Earths dark basis underneath,
Are to the main as inconsiderable,
And harmless, if not wholsom, as a sneeze
To mans less universe, and soon are gone;
Yet as being oft times noxious where they light   460
On man, beast, plant, wastful and turbulent,
Like turbulencies in the affairs of men,
Over whose heads they rore, and seem to point,
They oft fore-signifie and threat'n ill:
This Tempest at this Desert most was bent;   465
Of men at thee, for onely thou here dwell'st.
Did I not tell thee, if thou didst reject
The perfet season offerd with my aid
To win thy destind seat, but wilt prolong
All to the push of Fate, persue thy way   470
Of gaining *Davids* Throne no man knows when,
For both the when and how is no where told,
Thou shalt be what thou art ordaind, no doubt;
For Angels have proclaimd it, but concealing
The time and means: each act is rightliest done,   475
Not when it must, but when it may be best.
.If thou observe not this, be sure to find,

What I foretold thee, many a hard assay
Of dangers, and adversities and pains,
Ere thou of *Israels* Scepter get fast hold;   480
Whereof this ominous night that clos'd thee round,
So many terrors, voices, prodigies
May warn thee, as a sure fore-going sign.
    So talkd he, while the Son of God went on
And staid not, but in brief him answerd thus.   485
    Mee worse then wet thou find'st not; other harm
Those terrors which thou speak'st of, did me none;
I never feard they could, though noising loud
And threatning nigh; what they can do as signs
Betok'ning, or ill boding, I contemn   490
As false portents, not sent from God, but thee;
Who knowing I shall raign past thy preventing,
Obtrud'st thy offerd aid, that I accepting
At least might seem to hold all power of thee,
Ambitious spirit, and wouldst be thought my God,   495
And storm'st refus'd, thinking to terrifie
Mee to thy will; desist, thou art discernd
And toil'st in vain, nor me in vain molest.
    To whom the Fiend now swoln with rage reply'd:
Then hear, O Son of *David*, Virgin-born;   500
For Son of God to me is yet in doubt,
Of the Messiah I have heard foretold
By all the Prophets; of thy birth at length
Announc't by *Gabriel* with the first I knew,
And of the Angelic Song in *Bethlehem* field,   505
On thy birth-night, that sung thee Saviour born.
From that time seldom have I ceast to eye
Thy infancy, thy childhood, and thy youth,
Thy manhood last, though yet in privat bred;
Till at the Ford of *Jordan* whither all   510
Flockd to the Baptist, I among the rest,
Though not to be Baptiz'd, by voice from Heav'n
Heard thee pronounc't the Son of God belov'd.
Thenceforth I thought thee worth my nearer view
And narrower Scrutiny, that I might learn   515
In what degree or meaning thou art calld
The Son of God, which bears no single sense;

The Son of God I also am, or was,
And if I was, I am; relation stands;
All men are Sons of God; yet thee I thought   520
In some respect far higher so declar'd.
Therefore I watchd thy footsteps from that hour,
And followd thee still on to this wast wild;
Where by all best conjectures I collect
Thou art to be my fatal enemy.   525
Good reason then, if I before-hand seek
To understand my Adversary, who
And what he is; his wisdom, power, intent,
By parl, or composition, truce, or league
To win him, or win from him what I can.   530
And opportunity I here have had
To try thee, sift thee, and confess have found thee
Proof against all temptation as a rock
Of Adamant, and as a Center, firm
To th' utmost of meer man both wise and good,   535
Not more; for Honours, Riches, Kingdoms, Glory
Have been before contemnd, and may agen:
Therefore to know what more thou art then man,
Worth naming Son of God by voice from Heav'n,
Another method I must now begin.   540
    So saying he caught him up, and without wing
Of *Hippogrif* bore through the Air sublime
Over the Wilderness and ore the Plain;
Till underneath them fair *Jerusalem*,
The holy City lifted high her Towers,   545
And higher yet the glorious Temple reard
Her pile, farr off appearing like a Mount
Of Alablaster, topt with gold'n Spires:
There on the highest Pinnacle he set
The Son of God; and added thus in scorn: 550
    There stand, if thou wilt stand; to stand upright
Will ask thee skill; I to thy Fathers house
Have brought thee, and highest plac't, highest is best,
Now shew thy Progeny; if not to stand,
Cast thy self down; safely if Son of God: 555
For it is written, He will give command
Concerning thee to his Angels, in thir hands

They shall up lift thee, lest at any time
Thou chance to dash thy foot against a stone.
   To whom thus Jesus: also it is writt'n,   560
Tempt not the Lord thy God; he said and stood.
But Satan smitt'n with amazement fell;
As when Earths Son *Antæus* (to compare
Small things with greatest) in *Irassa* strove
With *Joves Alcides*, and oft foild still rose,   565
Receiving from his mother Earth new strength,
Fresh from his fall, and fiercer grapple joind,
Throttl'd at length in th' Air, expir'd and fell;
So after many a foil the Tempter proud,
Renewing fresh assaults, amidst his pride   570
Fell whence he stood to see his Victor fall.
And as that *Theban* Monster that propos'd
Her riddle, and him, who solv'd it not, devourd;
That once found out and solv'd, for grief and spite
Cast her self headlong from th' *Ismenian* steep,   575
So strook with dread and anguish fell the Fiend,
And to his crew, that sat consulting, brought
Joyless triumphals of his hop't success,
Ruin, and desperation, and dismay,
Who durst so proudly tempt the Son of God.   580
So Satan fell; and strait a fiery Globe
Of Angels on full sail of wing flew nigh,
Who on their plumy Vans receiv'd him soft
From his uneasie station, and upbore
As on a floating couch through the blithe Air,   585
Then in a flowry valley set him down
On a green bank, and set before him spred
A table of Celestial Food, Divine,
Ambrosial, Fruits fetcht from the Tree of Life,
And from the Fount of Life Ambrosial drink,   590
That soon refreshd him wearied, and repaird
What hunger, if aught hunger had impaird,
Or thirst, and as he fed, Angelic Quires
Sung Heav'nly Anthems of his victory
Over temptation, and the Tempter proud.   595
   True Image of the Father, whether thron'd
In the bosom of bliss, and light of light

Conceiving, or remote from Heaven, enshrin'd
In fleshly Tabernacle, and human form,
Wandring the Wilderness, whatever place,   600
Habit, or state, or motion, still expressing
The Son of God, with Godlike force indu'd
Against th' Attempter of thy Fathers Throne,
And Thief of Paradise; him long of old
Thou didst debell, and down from Heaven cast   605
With all his Army, now thou hast aveng'd
Supplanted *Adam*, and by vanquishing
Temptation, hast regaind lost Paradise,
And frustrated the conquest fraudulent:
Hee never more henceforth will dare set foot   610
In Paradise to tempt; his snares are broke:
For though that seat of earthly bliss be faild,
A fairer Paradise is founded now
For *Adam* and his chosen Sons, whom thou
A Saviour art come down to re-install,   615
Where they shall dwell secure, when time shall be
Of Tempter and Temptation without fear.
But thou, Infernal Serpent, shalt not long
Rule in the Clouds; like an Autumnal Starr
Or Lightning thou shalt fall from Heav'n trod down   620
Under his feet: for proof, ere this thou feel'st
Thy wound, yet not thy last and deadliest wound
By this repulse receiv'd, and hold'st in Hell
No triumph; in all her gates *Abaddon* rues
Thy bold attempt; hereafter learn with awe   625
To dread the Son of God: hee all unarmd
Shall chase thee with the terror of his voice
From thy Demoniac holds, possession foul,
Thee and thy Legions, yelling they shall flye,
And beg to hide them in a herd of Swine,   630
Lest he command them down into the deep
Bound, and to torment sent before thir time.
Hail Son of the most High, heir of both Worlds,
Queller of Satan, on thy glorious work
Now enter, and begin to save mankind.   635
    Thus they the Son of God our Saviour meek
Sung Victor, and from Heav'nly Feast refresht

Brought on his way with joy; hee unobserv'd
Home to his Mothers house privat returnd.

THE END

SAMSON
AGONISTES,

A

DRAMATIC POEM.

The Author
JOHN MILTON.

Ariſtot. Poet. Cap. 6.

Τϵαγῳδία μίμησις πϵάξϵως σπυδαίας, &c.

Tragœdia eſt imitatio actionis ſeriæ, &c. Per miſericordiam &
metum perficiens talium affectuum luſtrationem.

LONDON,

Printed by *J. M.* for *John Starkey* at the
Mitre in *Fleetſtreet*, near *Temple-Bar*.
MDCLXXI.

I

Of that sort of Dramatic Poem
which is call'd Tragedy.

TRAGEDY, as it was antiently compos'd, hath been ever held the gravest, moralest, and most profitable of all other Poems: therefore said by *Aristotle* to be of power by raising pity and fear, or terror, to purge the mind of those and such like passions, that is, to temper and reduce them to just measure with a kind of delight, stirr'd up by 5 reading or seeing those passions well imitated. Nor is Nature wanting in her own effects to make good his assertion: for so in Physic things of melancholic hue and quality are us'd against melancholy, sowr against sowr, salt to remove salt humours. Hence Philosophers and other gravest Writers, as *Cicero*, *Plutarch* and others, frequently cite out of Tragic 10 Poets, both to adorn and illustrate thir discourse. The Apostle *Paul* himself thought it not unworthy to insert a verse of *Euripides* into the Text of Holy Scripture, 1 *Cor.* 15. 33. and *Paræus* commenting on the *Revelation*, divides the whole Book as a Tragedy, into Acts distinguisht each by a Chorus of Heavenly Harpings and Song between. Heretofore 15 Men in highest dignity have labour'd not a little to be thought able to compose a Tragedy. Of that honour *Dionysius* the elder was no less ambitious, then before of his attaining to the Tyranny. *Augustus Cæsar* also had begun his *Ajax*, but unable to please his own judgment with what he had begun, left it unfinisht. *Seneca* the Philosopher is by 20 some thought the Author of those Tragedies (at lest the best of them) that go under that name. *Gregory Nazianzen* a Father of the Church, thought it not unbeseeming the sancity of his person to write a Tragedy, which he entitl'd, *Christ suffering*. This is mention'd to vindicate Tragedy from the small esteem, or rather infamy, which in the account 25 of many it undergoes at this day with other common Interludes; hap'ning through the Poets error of intermixing Comic stuff with Tragic sadness and gravity; or introducing trivial and vulgar persons, which by all judicious hath bin counted absurd; and brought in without discretion, corruptly to gratifie the people. And though antient Tragedy 30 use no Prologue, yet using sometimes, in case of self defence, or explanation, that which *Martial* calls an Epistle; in behalf of this Tragedy coming forth after the antient manner, much different from what among us passes for best, thus much before-hand may be Epistl'd; that *Chorus* is here introduc'd after the Greek manner, not antient only but 35

modern, and still in use among the *Italians*. In the modelling therefore
of this Poem, with good reason, the Antients and *Italians* are rather
follow'd, as of much more autority and fame. The measure of Verse
us'd in the Chorus is of all sorts, call'd by the Greeks *Monostrophic*, or
40 rather *Apolelymenon*, without regard had to *Strophe*, *Antistrophe* or *Epod*,
which were a kind of Stanza's fram'd only for the Music, then us'd
with the Chorus that sung; not essential to the Poem, and therefore
not material; or being divided into Stanza's or Pauses, they may be
call'd *Allæostropha*. Division into Act and Scene referring chiefly to the
45 Stage (to which this work never was intended) is here omitted. It
suffices if the whole Drama be found not produc't beyond the fift Act.

Of the style and uniformitie, and that commonly call'd the Plot,
whether intricate or explicit, which is nothing indeed but such
œconomy, or disposition of the fable as may stand best with verisimili-
50 tude and decorum, they only will best judge who are not unacquainted
with *Æschulus*, *Sophocles*, and *Euripides*, the three Tragic Poets unequall'd
yet by any, and the best rule to all who endeavour to write Tragedy.
The circumscription of time wherein the whole Drama begins and
ends, is according to antient rule, and best example, within the space
55 of 24 hours.

THE ARGUMENT

Samson *made Captive, Blind, and now in the Prison at* Gaza, *there to labour as in a common work-house, on a Festival day, in the general cessation from labour, comes forth into the op'n Air, to a place nigh, somewhat retir'd, there to sit a while and bemoan his condition. Where he happ'ns at length to be visited by certain friends and equals of his tribe, which make the Chorus, who seek to* 5 *comfort him what they can; then by his old Father* Manoah, *who endeavours the like, and withall tells him his purpose to procure his liberty by ransom; lastly, that this Feast was proclaim'd by the* Philistins *as a day of Thanksgiving for thir deliverance from the hands of* Samson, *which yet more troubles him.* Manoah *then departs to prosecute his endeavour with the* Philistian *Lords* 10 *for* Samson's *redemption; who in the mean while is visited by other persons; and lastly by a publick Officer to require his coming to the Feast before the Lords and People, to play or shew his strength in thir presence; he at first refuses, dismissing the publick Officer with absolute denyal to come; at length perswaded inwardly that this was from God, he yields to go along with him, who* 15 *came now the second time with great threatnings to fetch him; the Chorus yet remaining on the place,* Manoah *returns full of joyful hope, to procure ere long his Sons deliverance: in the midst of which discourse an Ebrew comes in haste confusedly at first; and afterward more distinctly relating the Catastrophe, what* Samson *had done to the* Philistins, *and by accident to himself; wherewith the* 20 *Tragedy ends.*

The Persons

Samson.
Manoah *the Father of* Samson.
Dalila *his Wife*.
Harapha *of* Gath.
Publick Officer.
Messenger.
Chorus *of* Danites.

The Scene before the Prison in Gaza.

SAMSON AGONISTES

Sams. A LITTLE onward lend thy guiding hand
To these dark steps, a little furder on;
For yonder bank hath choice of Sun or shade;
There I am wont to sit, when any chance
Relieves me from my task of servil toil,   5
Daily in the common Prison else enjoind me,
Where I a Pris'ner chaind, scarce freely draw
The air imprisond also, close and damp,
Unwholsom draught: but here I feel amends,
The breath of Heav'n fresh-blowing, pure and sweet,   10
With day-spring born; here leave me to respire.
This day a solemn Feast the people hold
To *Dagon* thir Sea-Idol, and forbid
Laborious works, unwillingly this rest
Thir Superstition yeilds me; hence with leave   15
Retiring from the popular noise, I seek
This unfrequented place to find some ease;
Ease to the body some, none to the mind
From restless thoughts, that like a deadly swarm
Of Hornets armd, no sooner found alone,   20
But rush upon me thronging, and present
Times past, what once I was, and what am now.
O wherefore was my birth from Heav'n foretold
Twice by an Angel, who at last in sight
Of both my Parents all in flames ascended   25
From off the Altar, where an Off'ring burnd,
As in a fiery column charioting
His Godlike presence, and from some great act
Or benefit reveald to *Abraham*'s race?
Why was my breeding orderd and prescrib'd   30
As of a person separate to God,
Design'd for great exploits; if I must dye
Betray'd, Captiv'd, and both my Eyes put out,
Made of my Enemies the scorn and gaze;
To grind in Brazen Fetters under task   35
With this Heav'n-gifted strength? O glorious strength

Put to the labour of a Beast, debas't
Lower then bondslave! Promise was that I
Should *Israel* from *Philistian* yoke deliver;
Ask for this great Deliverer now, and find him   40
Eyeless in *Gaza* at the Mill with slaves,
Himself in bonds under *Philistian* yoke;
Yet stay, let me not rashly call in doubt
Divine Prediction; what if all foretold
Had been fulfilld but through mine own default;   45
Whom have I to complain of but my self?
Who this high gift of strength committed to me,
In what part lodg'd, how easily bereft me,
Under the Seal of silence could not keep,
But weakly to a woman must reveal it,   50
Orecome with importunity and tears.
O impotence of mind, in body strong!
But what is strength without a double share
Of wisdom, vast, unwieldy, burdensom,
Proudly secure, yet liable to fall   55
By weakest suttleties, not made to rule,
But to subserve where wisdom bears command.
God, when he gave me strength, to shew withall
How slight the gift was, hung it in my Hair.
But peace, I must not quarrel with the will   60
Of highest dispensation, which herein
Haply had ends above my reach to know:
Suffices that to mee strength is my bane,
And proves the sourse of all my miseries;
So many, and so huge, that each apart   65
Would ask a life to wail, but chief of all,
O loss of sight, of thee I most complain!
Blind among enemies, O worse then chains,
Dungeon, or beggery, or decrepit age!
Light the prime work of God to mee is extinct,   70
And all her various objects of delight
Annulld, which might in part my grief have eas'd,
Inferiour to the vilest now become
Of man or worm; the vilest here excell me,
They creep, yet see, I dark in light expos'd   75
To daily fraud, contempt, abuse and wrong,

Within doors, or without, still as a fool,
In power of others, never in my own;
Scarce half I seem to live, dead more then half.
O dark, dark, dark, amid the blaze of noon,   80
Irrecoverably dark, total Eclipse
Without all hope of day!
O first created Beam, and thou great Word,
Let ther be light, and light was over all;
Why am I thus bereav'd thy prime decree?   85
The Sun to me is dark
And silent as the Moon,
When she deserts the night
Hid in her vacant interlunar cave.
Since light so necessary is to life,   90
And almost life itself, if it be true
That light is in the Soul,
She all in every part; why was the sight
To such a tender ball as th' eye confin'd?
So obvious and so easie to be quencht,   95
And not as feeling through all parts diffus'd,
That she might look at will through every pore?
Then had I not bin thus exil'd from light;
As in the land of darkness yet in light,
To live a life half dead, a living death,   100
And buried; but O yet more miserable!
My self, my Sepulcher, a moving Grave,
Buried, yet not exempt
By priviledge of death and burial
From worst of other evils, pains and wrongs,   105
But made hereby obnoxious more
To all the miseries of life,
Life in captivity
Among inhuman foes.
But who are these? for with joint pace I hear   110
The tread of many feet stearing this way;
Perhaps my enemies who come to stare
At my affliction, and perhaps to insult,
Thir daily practice to afflict me more.
  Chor. This, this is hee; softly a while,   115
Let us not break in upon him;

O change beyond report, thought, or belief!
See how he lies at random, carelessly diffus'd,
With languisht head unpropt,
As one past hope, abandond,   120
And by himself giv'n over;
In slavish habit, ill-fitted weeds
Ore worn and soild;
Or do my eyes misrepresent? Can this be hee,
That Heroic, that Renownd,   125
Irresistible *Samson*? whom unarmd
No strength of man, or fiercest wild beast could withstand;
Who tore the Lion, as the Lion tears the Kid,
Ran on embatteld Armies clad in Iron,
And weaponless himself,   130
Made Arms ridiculous, useless the forgery
Of brazen shield and spear, the hammerd Cuirass,
Chalybean temperd steel, and frock of mail
Adamantean Proof;
But safest he who stood aloof,   135
When insupportably his foot advanc't,
In scorn of thir proud arms and warlike tools,
Spurnd them to death by Troops. The bold *Ascalonite*
Fled from his Lion ramp, old Warriors turnd
Thir plated backs under his heel;   140
Or grovling soild thir crested helmets in the dust.
Then with what trivial weapon came to hand,
The Jaw of a dead Ass, his sword of bone,
A thousand fore-skins fell, the flower of *Palestin*
In *Ramath-lechi* famous to this day: 145
Then by main force pulld up, and on his shoulders bore
The Gates of *Azza*, Post, and massie Bar
Up to the Hill by *Hebron*, seat of Giants old,
No journey of a Sabbath day, and loaded so;
Like whom the Gentiles feign to bear up Heav'n.   150
Which shall I first bewail,
Thy Bondage or lost Sight,
Prison within Prison
Inseparably dark?
Thou art become (O worst imprisonment!)   155
The Dungeon of thy self; thy Soul

(Which Men enjoying sight oft without cause complain)
Imprisond now indeed,
In real darkness of the body dwells,
Shut up from outward light   160
To incorporate with gloomy night;
For inward light alas
Puts forth no visual beam.
O mirror of our fickle state,
Since man on earth unparalleld!   165
The rarer thy example stands,
By how much from the top of wondrous glory,
Strongest of mortal men,
To lowest pitch of abject fortune thou art fall'n.
For him I reck'n not in high estate   170
Whom long descent of birth
Or the sphear of fortune raises;
But thee whose strength, while vertue was her mate,
Might have subdu'd the Earth,
Universally crownd with highest praises.   175
  Sam. I hear the sound of words, thir sense the air
Dissolves unjointed ere it reach my ear.
  Chor. He speaks, let us draw nigh. Matchless in might,
The glory late of *Israel*, now the grief;
We come thy friends and neighbours not unknown   180
From *Eshtaol* and *Zora*'s fruitful Vale
To visit or bewail thee, or if better,
Counsel or Consolation we may bring,
Salve to thy Sores; apt words have power to swage
The tumors of a troubl'd mind,   185
And are as Balm to festerd wounds.
  Sam. Your coming, Friends, revives me, for I learn
Now of my own experience, not by talk,
How counterfet a coin they are who friends
Bear in thir Superscription (of the most   190
I would be understood): in prosperous days
They swarm, but in adverse withdraw thir head
Not to be found, though sought. Ye see, O friends,
How many evils have enclos'd me round;
Yet that which was the worst now least afflicts me,   195
Blindness, for had I sight, confus'd with shame,

How could I once look up, or heave the head,
Who like a foolish Pilot have shipwrackt
My Vessel trusted to me from above,
Gloriously riggd; and for a word, a tear,   200
Fool, have divulg'd the secret gift of God
To a deceitful Woman: tell me Friends,
Am I not sung and proverbd for a Fool
In every street, do they not say, how well
Are come upon him his deserts? yet why?   205
Immeasurable strength they might behold
In me, of wisdom nothing more then mean;
This with the other should, at least, have paird,
These two proportiond ill drove me transverse.

   Chor. Tax not divine disposal; wisest Men   210
Have errd, and by bad Women been deceiv'd;
And shall again, pretend they ne're so wise.
Deject not then so overmuch thy self,
Who hast of sorrow thy full load besides;
Yet truth to say, I oft have heard men wonder   215
Why thou shouldst wed *Philistian* women rather
Then of thine own Tribe fairer, or as fair,
At least of thy own Nation, and as noble.

   Sam. The first I saw at *Timna*, and she pleas'd
Mee, not my Parents, that I sought to wed,   220
The daughter of an Infidel: they knew not
That what I motiond was of God; I knew
From intimat impulse, and therefore urg'd
The Marriage on; that by occasion hence
I might begin *Israels* Deliverance,   225
The work to which I was divinely calld;
She proving false, the next I took to Wife
(O that I never had! fond wish too late)
Was in the Vale of *Sorec, Dalila,*
That specious Monster, my accomplisht snare.   230
I thought it lawful from my former act,
And the same end; still watching to oppress
Israels oppressours: of what now I suffer
Shee was not the prime cause, but I my self,
Who vanquisht with a peal of words (O weakness!)   235
Gave up my fort of silence to a Woman.

Chor. In seeking just occasion to provoke
The *Philistine*, thy Countries Enemy,
Thou never wast remiss, I bear thee witness:
Yet *Israel* still serves with all his Sons.   240
    Sam. That fault I take not on me, but transferr
On *Israel*'s Governours, and Heads of Tribes,
Who seeing those great acts which God had done
Singly by mee against thir Conquerours
Acknowledg'd not, or not at all considerd   245
Deliverance offerd: I on th' other side
Us'd no ambition to commend my deeds,
The deeds themselves, though mute, spoke loud the dooer;
But they persisted deaf, and would not seem
To count them things worth notice, till at length   250
Thir Lords the *Philistines* with gatherd powers
Enterd *Judea* seeking mee, who then
Safe to the rock of *Etham* was retir'd,
Not flying, but fore-casting in what place
To set upon them, what advantag'd best;   255
Mean while the men of *Judah* to prevent
The harrass of thir Land, beset me round;
I willingly on some conditions came
Into thir hands, and they as gladly yeild me
To the uncircumcis'd a welcom prey,   260
Bound with two cords; but cords to me were threds
Toucht with the flame: on thir whole Host I flew
Unarmd, and with a trivial weapon felld
Thir choicest youth; they onely liv'd who fled.
Had *Judah* that day joind, or one whole Tribe,   265
They had by this possesst the Towers of *Gath*,
And lorded over them whom now they serve;
But what more oft in Nations grown corrupt,
And by thir vices brought to servitude,
Then to love Bondage more then Liberty,   270
Bondage with ease then strenuous liberty;
And to despise, or envy, or suspect
Whom God hath of his special favour rais'd
As thir Deliverer; if he aught begin,
How frequent to desert him, and at last   275
To heap ingratitude on worthiest deeds!

Chor. Thy words to my remembrance bring
How *Succoth* and the Fort of *Penuel*
Thir great Deliverer contemnd,
The matchless *Gideon* in persuit   280
Of *Madian* and her vanquisht Kings:
And how ingrateful *Ephraim*
Had dealt with *Jephtha*, who by argument,
Not worse then by his shield and spear
Defended *Israel* from the *Ammonite*,   285
Had not his prowess quelld thir pride
In that sore battel when so many dy'd
Without Reprieve adjudg'd to death,
For want of well pronouncing *Shibboleth*.
   Sam. Of such examples add mee to the roul;   290
Mee easily indeed mine may neglect,
But Gods propos'd deliverance not so.
   Chor. Just are the ways of God,
And justifiable to Men;
Unless there be who think not God at all,   295
If any be, they walk obscure;
For of such Doctrin never was ther School,
But the heart of the Fool,
And no man therein Doctor but himself.
   Yet more ther be who doubt his ways not just,   300
As to his own edicts, found contradicting,
Then give the rains to wandring thought,
Regardless of his glories diminution;
Till by thir own perplexities involv'd
They ravel more, still less resolv'd,   305
But never find self-satisfying solution.
   As if they would confine th' interminable,
And tie him to his own prescript,
Who made our Laws to bind us, not himself,
And hath full right to exempt   310
Whom so it pleases him by choice
From National obstriction, without taint
Of sin, or legal debt;
For with his own Laws he can best dispence.
   He would not else who never wanted means,   315
Nor in respect of th' enemy just cause

To set his people free,
Have prompted this Heroic *Nazarite*,
Against his vow of strictest purity,
To seek in marriage that fallacious Bride,   320
Unclean, unchaste.
   Down Reason then, at least vain reasonings down,
Though Reason here averr
That moral verdit quits her of unclean:
Unchaste was subsequent, her stain not his.   325
   But see here comes thy reverend Sire
With careful step, Locks white as doune,
Old *Manoah*: advise
Forthwith how thou oughtst to receive him.
   Sam. Ay me, another inward grief awak't,   330
With mention of that name renews th' assault.
   Man. Brethren and men of *Dan*, for such ye seem,
Though in this uncouth place; if old respect,
As I suppose, towards your once gloried friend,
My Son now Captive, hither hath informd   335
Your younger feet, while mine cast back with age
Came lagging after; say if he be here.
   Chor. As signal now in low dejected state,
As earst in highest, behold him where he lies.
   Man. O miserable change! is this the man,   340
That invincible *Samson*, farr renownd,
The dread of *Israels* foes, who with a strength
Equivalent to Angels walkd thir streets,
None offering fight; who single combatant
Duelld thir Armies rankt in proud array,   345
Himself an Army, now unequal match
To save himself against a coward armd
At one spears length. O ever failing trust
In mortal strength! and oh what not in man
Deceivable and vain! Nay what thing good   350
Pray'd for, but oft'n proves our woe, our bane?
I pray'd for Childern, and thought barrenness
In wedlock a reproach; I gaind a Son,
And such a Son as all Men haild me happy;
Who would be now a Father in my stead?   355
O wherefore did God grant me my request,

And as a blessing with such pomp adornd?
Why are his gifts desirable, to tempt
Our earnest Prayers, then giv'n with solemn hand
As Graces, draw a Scorpions tail behind?   360
For this did th' Angel twice descend? for this
Ordaind thy nurture holy, as of a Plant
Select, and Sacred, Glorious for a while,
The miracle of men: then in an hour
Ensnar'd, assaulted, overcome, led bound,   365
Thy Foes derision, Captive, Poor, and Blind
Into a Dungeon thrust, to work with Slaves?
Alas methinks whom God hath chosen once
To worthiest deeds, if he through frailty err,
He should not so orewhelm, and as a thrall   370
Subject him to so foul indignities,
Be it but for honours sake of former deeds.
   Sam. Appoint not heav'nly disposition, Father,
Nothing of all these evils hath befall'n me
But justly; I my self have brought them on,   375
Sole Author I, sole cause: if aught seem vile,
As vile hath been my folly, who have profan'd
The mystery of God giv'n me under pledge
Of vow, and have betray'd it to a woman,
A *Canaanite*, my faithless enemy.   380
This well I knew, nor was at all surpris'd,
But warnd by oft experience: did not she
Of *Timna* first betray me, and reveal
The secret wrested from me in her highth
Of Nuptial Love profest, carrying it strait   385
To them who had corrupted her, my Spies,
And Rivals? In this other was there found
More Faith? who also in her prime of love,
Spousal embraces, vitiated with Gold,
Though offerd onely, by the sent conceiv'd   390
Her spurious first-born; Treason against me?
Thrice she assay'd with flattering prayers and sighs,
And amorous reproaches to win from me
My capital secret, in what part my strength
Lay stor'd, in what part summd, that she might know: 395
Thrice I deluded her, and turnd to sport

Her importunity, each time perceiving
How op'nly, and with what impudence
She purpos'd to betray me, and (which was worse
Then undissembl'd hate) with what contempt   400
She sought to make me Traitor to my self;
Yet the fourth time, when mustring all her wiles,
With blandisht parlies, feminine assaults,
Tongue-batteries, she surceas'd not day nor night
To storm me over-watcht, and wearied out,   405
At times when men seek most repose and rest,
I yeilded, and unlockd her all my heart,
Who with a grain of manhood well resolv'd
Might easily have shook off all her snares:
But foul effeminacy held me yok't   410
Her Bond-slave; O indignity, O blot
To Honour and Religion! servil mind
Rewarded well with servil punishment!
The base degree to which I now am fall'n,
These rags, this grinding, is not yet so base   415
As was my former servitude, ignoble,
Unmanly, ignominious, infamous,
True slavery, and that blindness worse then this,
That saw not how degeneratly I serv'd.
  Man. I cannot praise thy Marriage choises, Son, 420
Rather approv'd them not; but thou didst plead
Divine impulsion prompting how thou might'st
Find some occasion to infest our Foes.
I state not that; this I am sure; our Foes
Found soon occasion thereby to make thee   425
Thir Captive, and thir triumph; thou the sooner
Temptation found'st, or over-potent charms
To violate the sacred trust of silence
Deposited within thee; which to have kept
Tacit, was in thy power; true; and thou bear'st   430
Anough, and more the burden of that fault;
Bitterly hast thou paid, and still art paying
That rigid score. A worse thing yet remains,
This day the *Philistines* a popular Feast
Here celebrate in *Gaza*; and proclaim   435
Great Pomp, and Sacrifice, and Praises loud

To *Dagon*, as thir God who hath deliverd
Thee *Samson* bound and blind into thir hands,
Them out of thine, who slew'st them many a slain.
So *Dagon* shall be magnifi'd, and God,   440
Besides whom is no God, compar'd with Idols,
Disglorifi'd, blaspheamd and had in scorn
By th' Idolatrous rout amidst thir wine;
Which to have come to pass by means of thee,
Samson, of all thy sufferings think the heaviest,   445
Of all reproach the most with shame that ever
Could have befall'n thee and thy Fathers house.
   Sam. Father, I do acknowledge and confess
That I this honour, I this pomp have brought
To *Dagon*, and advanc't his praises high   450
Among the Heathen round; to God have brought
Dishonour, obloquie, and op't the mouths
Of Idolists, and Atheists; have brought scandal
To *Israel*, diffidence of God, and doubt
In feeble hearts, propense anough before   455
To waver, or fall off and join with Idols;
Which is my chief affliction, shame and sorrow,
The anguish of my Soul, that suffers not
Mine eie to harbour sleep, or thoughts to rest.
This onely hope relieves me, that the strife   460
With mee hath end; all the contest is now
'Twixt God and *Dagon*; *Dagon* hath presum'd,
Mee overthrown, to enter lists with God,
His Deity comparing and preferring
Before the God of *Abraham*. Hee, be sure,   465
Will not connive, or linger, thus provok't,
But will arise and his great name assert:
Dagon must stoop, and shall ere long receive
Such a discomfit, as shall quite despoil him
Of all these boasted Trophies won on me,   470
And with confusion blank his Worshippers.
   Man. With cause this hope relieves thee, and these words
I as a Prophecy receive: for God,
Nothing more certain, will not long deferr
To vindicate the glory of his name   475
Against all competition, nor will long

Endure it, doubtful whether God be Lord,
Or *Dagon*. But for thee what shall be done?
Thou must not in the mean while here forgot
Lie in this miserable loathsom plight 480
Neglected. I already have made way
To some *Philistian* Lords, with whom to treat
About thy ransom: well they may by this
Have satisfi'd thir utmost of revenge
By pains and slaveries, worse then death inflicted 485
On thee, who now no more canst do them harm.
   Sam. Spare that proposal, Father, spare the trouble
Of that sollicitation; let me here,
As I deserve, pay on my punishment;
And expiate, if possible, my crime, 490
Shameful garrulity. To have reveald
Secrets of men, the secrets of a friend,
How hainous had the fact been, how deserving
Contempt, and scorn of all, to be excluded
All friendship, and avoided as a blab, 495
The mark of fool set on his front! But I
Gods counsel have not kept, his holy secret
Presumptuously have publisht impiously,
Weakly at least, and shamefully: A sin
That Gentiles in thir Parables condemn 500
To thir abyss and horrid pains confin'd.
   Man. Be penitent and for thy fault contrite,
But act not in thy own affliction, Son,
Repent the sin, but if the punishment
Thou canst avoid, self-preservation bids; 505
Or th' execution leave to high disposal,
And let another hand, not thine, exact
Thy penal forfeit from thy self; perhaps
God will relent, and quit thee all his debt;
Who evermore approves and more accepts 510
(Best pleas'd with humble and filial submission)
Him who imploring mercy sues for life,
Then who self-rigorous chooses death as due;
Which argues over-just, and self-displeas'd
For self-offence, more then for God offended. 515
Reject not then what offerd means, who knows

But God hath set before us, to return thee
Home to thy countrey and his sacred house,
Where thou mayst bring thy off'rings, to avert
His further ire, with praiers and vows renewd.   520
    Sam. His pardon I implore; but as for life,
To what end should I seek it? when in strength
All mortals I excelld, and great in hopes
With youthful courage and magnanimous thoughts
Of birth from Heav'n foretold and high exploits,   525
Full of divine instinct, after some proof
Of acts indeed heroic, far beyond
The Sons of *Anac*, famous now and blaz'd,
Fearless of danger, like a petty God
I walkd about admir'd of all and dreaded   530
On hostil ground, none daring my affront.
Then swoll'n with pride into the snare I fell
Of fair fallacious looks, venereal trains,
Soft'nd with pleasure and voluptuous life;
At length to lay my head and hallowd pledge   535
Of all my strength in the lascivious lap
Of a deceitful Concubine who shore me
Like a tame Weather, all my precious fleece,
Then turnd me out ridiculous, despoild,
Shav'n, and disarmd among my enemies.   540
    Chor. Desire of wine and all delicious drinks,
Which many a famous Warriour overturns,
Thou couldst repress, nor did the dancing Rubie
Sparkling, out-pow'rd, the flavor, or the smell,
Or taste that cheers the heart of Gods and men,   545
Allure thee from the cool Crystallin stream.
    Sam. Where ever fountain or fresh current flowd
Against the Eastern ray, translucent, pure
With touch ætherial of Heav'ns fiery rod
I drank, from the clear milkie juice allaying   550
Thirst, and refresht; nor envied them the grape
Whose heads that turbulent liquor fills with fumes.
    Chor. O madness, to think use of strongest wines
And strongest drinks our chief support of health,
When God with these forbidd'n made choice to rear   555
His mighty Champion, strong above compare,

Whose drink was onely from the liquid brook.

   Sam. But what availd this temperance, not compleat
Against another object more enticing?
What boots it at one gate to make defence,   560
And at another to let in the foe
Effeminatly vanquisht? by which means,
Now blind, disheart'nd, sham'd, dishonourd, quelld,
To what can I be useful, wherein serve
My Nation, and the work from Heav'n impos'd,   565
But to sit idle on the houshold hearth,
A burdenous drone; to visitants a gaze,
Or pitied object, these redundant locks
Robustious to no purpose clustring down,
Vain monument of strength; till length of years   570
And sedentary numness craze my limbs
To a contemptible old age obscure.
Here rather let me drudge and earn my bread,
Till vermin or the draff of servil food
Consume me, and oft-invocated death   575
Hast'n the welcom end of all my pains.

   Man. Wilt thou then serve the *Philistines* with that gift
Which was expresly giv'n thee to annoy them?
Better at home lie bed-rid, not onely idle,
Inglorious, unimploy'd, with age out-worn.   580
But God who caus'd a fountain at thy prayer
From the dry ground to spring, thy thirst to allay
After the brunt of battel, can as easie
Cause light again within thy eies to spring,
Wherewith to serve him better then thou hast;   585
And I perswade me so; why else this strength
Miraculous yet remaining in those locks?
His might continues in thee not for naught,
Nor shall his wondrous gifts be frustrate thus.

   Sam. All otherwise to mee my thoughts portend,   590
That these dark orbs no more shall treat with light,
Nor th' other light of life continue long,
But yeild to double darkness nigh at hand:
So much I feel my genial spirits droop,
My hopes all flat, nature within me seems   595
In all her functions weary of herself;

My race of glory run, and race of shame,
And I shall shortly be with them that rest.
   Man. Believe not these suggestions which proceed
From anguish of the mind and humours black,   600
That mingle with thy fancy. I however
Must not omit a Fathers timely care
To prosecute the means of thy deliverance
By ransom or how else: mean while be calm,
And healing words from these thy friends admit.   605
   Sam. O that torment should not be confin'd
To the bodies wounds and sores
With maladies innumerable
In heart, head, brest, and reins;
But must secret passage find   610
To th' inmost mind,
There exercise all his fierce accidents,
And on her purest spirits prey,
As on entrails, joints, and limbs,
With answerable pains, but more intense,   615
Though void of corporal sense.
   My griefs not onely pain me
As a lingring disease,
But finding no redress, ferment and rage,
Nor less then wounds immedicable   620
Ranckle, and fester, and gangrene,
To black mortification.
Thoughts my Tormenters armd with deadly stings
Mangle my apprehensive tenderest parts,
Exasperate, exulcerate, and raise   625
Dire inflammation which no cooling herb
Or medcinal liquor can asswage,
Nor breath of Vernal Air from snowy *Alp*.
Sleep hath forsook and giv'n me ore
To deaths benumming Opium as my onely cure.   630
Thence faintings, swounings of despair,
And sense of Heav'ns desertion.
   I was his nursling once and choice delight,
His destind from the womb,
Promisd by Heav'nly message twice descending.   635
Under his special eie

Abstemious I grew up and thriv'd amain;
He led me on to mightiest deeds
Above the nerve of mortal arm
Against th' uncircumcis'd, our enemies.   640
But now hath cast me off as never known,
And to those cruel enemies,
Whom I by his appointment had provok't,
Left me all helpless with th' irreparable loss
Of sight, reserv'd alive to be repeated   645
The subject of thir cruelty, or scorn.
Nor am I in the list of them that hope;
Hopeless are all my evils, all remediless;
This one prayer yet remains, might I be heard,
No long petition, speedy death,   650
The close of all my miseries, and the balm.
   Chor. Many are the sayings of the wise
In ancient and in modern books inrould;
Extolling Patience as the truest fortitude;
And to the bearing well of all calamities,   655
All chances incident to mans frail life
Consolatories writ
With studied argument, and much perswasion sought
Lenient of grief and anxious thought,
But with th' afflicted in his pangs thir sound   660
Little prevails, or rather seems a tune,
Harsh, and of dissonant mood from his complaint,
Unless he feel within
Some sourse of consolation from above;
Secret refreshings, that repair his strength,   665
And fainting spirits uphold.
   God of our Fathers, what is man!
That thou towards him with hand so various,
Or might I say contrarious,
Temperst thy providence through his short course,   670
Not evenly, as thou rul'st
Th' Angelic orders and inferiour creatures mute,
Irrational and brute.
Nor do I name of men the common rout,
That wandring loose about   675
Grow up and perish, as the summer flie,

Heads without name no more rememberd,
But such as thou hast solemnly elected,
With gifts and graces eminently adornd,
To some great work, thy glory,   680
And peoples safety, which in part they effect:
Yet toward these thus dignifi'd, thou oft
Amidst thir highth of noon,
Changest thy countenance, and thy hand with no regard
Of highest favours past   685
From thee on them, or them to thee of service.
    Nor onely dost degrade them, or remit
To life obscur'd, which were a fair dismission,
But throw'st them lower then thou didst exalt them high,
Unseemly falls in human eie,   690
Too grievous for the trespass or omission,
Oft leav'st them to the hostil sword
Of Heathen and prophane, thir carkasses
To dogs and fowls a prey, or else captiv'd:
Or to th' unjust tribunals, under change of times,   695
And condemnation of th' ingrateful multitude.
If these they scape, perhaps in poverty
With sickness and disease thou bow'st them down,
Painful diseases and deformd,
In crude old age;   700
Though not disordinate, yet causless suffring
The punishment of dissolute days, in fine,
Just or unjust, alike seem miserable,
For oft alike, both come to evil end.
    So deal not with this once thy glorious Champion,   705
The Image of thy strength, and mighty minister.
What do I beg? how hast thou dealt already?
Behold him in this state calamitous, and turn
His labours, for thou canst, to peaceful end.
    But who is this, what thing of Sea or Land?   710
Femal of sex it seems,
That so bedeckt, ornate, and gay,
Comes this way sailing
Like a stately Ship
Of *Tarsus*, bound for th' Iles   715
Of *Javan* or *Gadier*

With all her bravery on, and tackle trim,
Sails filld, and streamers waving,
Courted by all the winds that hold them play,
An Amber sent of odorous perfume   720
Her harbinger, a damsel train behind;
Some rich *Philistian* Matron she may seem,
And now at nearer view, no other certain
Then *Dalila* thy wife.

    Sam. My Wife, my Traitress, let her not come near me.   725
    Cho. Yet on she moves, now stands and eies thee fixt,
About t' have spoke, but now, with head declin'd
Like a fair flower surcharg'd with dew, she weeps,
And words addrest seem into tears dissolv'd,
Wetting the borders of her silk'n veil: 730
But now again she makes address to speak.

    Dal. With doubtful feet and wavering resolution
I came, still dreading thy displeasure, *Samson*,
Which to have merited, without excuse
I cannot but acknowledge; yet if tears   735
May expiate (though the fact more evil drew
In the perverse event then I foresaw)
My penance hath not slack'nd, though my pardon
No way assur'd. But conjugal affection
Prevailing over fear, and timerous doubt   740
Hath led me on desirous to behold
Once more thy face, and know of thy estate,
If aught in my ability may serve
To light'n what thou suffer'st, and appease
Thy mind with what amends is in my power,   745
Though late, yet in some part to recompense
My rash but more unfortunat misdeed.

    Sam. Out, out *Hyæna*; these are thy wonted arts,
And arts of every woman false like thee,
To break all faith, all vows, deceive, betray,   750
Then as repentant to submit, beseech,
And reconcilement move with feignd remorse,
Confess, and promise wonders in her change,
Not truly penitent, but chief to try
Her husband, how farr urg'd his patience bears,   755
His vertue or weakness which way to assail:

Then with more cautious and instructed skill
Again transgresses, and again submits;
That wisest and best men full oft beguil'd
With goodness principl'd not to reject   760
The penitent, but ever to forgive,
Are drawn to wear out miserable days,
Entangl'd with a poisnous bosom snake,
If not by quick destruction soon cut off
As I by thee, to Ages an example.   765
      Dal. Yet hear me *Samson*; not that I endeavour
To less'n or extenuate my offence,
But that on th' other side if it be weighd
By it self, with aggravations not surcharg'd,
Or else with just allowance counterpois'd,   770
I may, if possible, thy pardon find
The easier towards me, or thy hatred less.
First granting, as I do, it was a weakness
In me, but incident to all our sex,
Curiosity, inquisitive, importune   775
Of secrets, then with like infirmity
To publish them, both common femal faults:
Was it not weakness also to make known
For importunity, that is for naught,
Wherein consisted all thy strength and safety?   780
To what I did thou shewdst me first the way.
But I to enemies reveald, and should not.
Nor shouldst thou have trusted that to womans frailty:
Ere I to thee, thou to thy self wast cruel.
Let weakness then with weakness come to parl   785
So near related, or the same of kind,
Thine forgive mine; that men may censure thine
The gentler, if severely thou exact not
More strength from mee, then in thy self was found.
And what if Love, which thou interpret'st hate,   790
The jealousie of Love, powerful of sway
In human hearts, nor less in mine towards thee,
Caus'd what I did? I saw thee mutable
Of fancy, feard lest one day thou wouldst leave me
As her at *Timna*, sought by all means therefore   795
How to endear, and hold thee to me firmest:

No better way I saw then by importuning
To learn thy secrets, get into my power
Thy key of strength and safety: thou wilt say,
Why then reveald? I was assur'd by those   800
Who tempted me, that nothing was design'd
Against thee but safe custody, and hold:
That made for mee, I knew that liberty
Would draw thee forth to perilous enterprises,
While I at home sate full of cares and fears   805
Wailing thy absence in my widowd bed;
Here I should still enjoy thee day and night
Mine and Loves prisoner, not the *Philistines*,
Whole to my self, unhazarded abroad,
Fearless at home of partners in my love.   810
These reasons in Loves law have past for good,
Though fond and reasonless to some perhaps;
And Love hath oft, well meaning, wrought much wo,
Yet always pity or pardon hath obtaind.
Be not unlike all others, not austere   815
As thou art strong, inflexible as steel.
If thou in strength all mortals dost exceed,
In uncompassionat anger do not so.
   Sam. How cunningly the sorceress displays
Her own transgressions, to upbraid me mine!   820
That malice not repentance brought thee hither,
By this appears: I gave, thou say'st, th' example,
I led the way; bitter reproach, but true,
I to my self was false ere thou to me,
Such pardon therefore as I give my folly,   825
Take to thy wicked deed: which when thou seest
Impartial, self-severe, inexorable,
Thou wilt renounce thy seeking, and much rather
Confess it feignd, weakness is thy excuse,
And I believe it, weakness to resist   830
Philistian gold: if weakness may excuse,
What Murtherer, what Traitor, Parricide,
Incestuous, Sacrilegious, but may plead it?
All wickedness is weakness: that plea therefore
With God or Man will gain thee no remission.   835
But Love constraind thee; call it furious rage

To satisfie thy lust: Love seeks to have Love;
My love how couldst thou hope, who tookst the way
To raise in me inexpiable hate,
Knowing, as needs I must, by thee betray'd?   840
In vain thou striv'st to cover shame with shame,
Or by evasions thy crime uncoverst more.
   Dal. Since thou determinst weakness for no plea
In man or woman, though to thy own condemning,
Hear what assaults I had, what snares besides,   845
What sieges girt me round, ere I consented;
Which might have aw'd the best resolv'd of men,
The constantest to have yeilded without blame.
It was not gold, as to my charge thou lay'st,
That wrought with me: thou know'st the Magistrates   850
And Princes of my countrey came in person,
Sollicited, commanded, threat'nd, urg'd,
Adjur'd by all the bonds of civil Duty
And of Religion, pressd how just it was,
How honourable, how glorious to entrap   855
A common enemy, who had destroy'd
Such numbers of our Nation: and the Priest
Was not behind, but ever at my ear,
Preaching how meritorious with the gods
It would be to ensnare an irreligious   860
Dishonourer of *Dagon*: what had I
To oppose against such powerful arguments?
Onely my love of thee held long debate;
And combated in silence all these reasons
With hard contest: at length that grounded maxim   865
So rife and celebrated in the mouths
Of wisest men; that to the public good
Privat respects must yeild; with grave autority
Took full possession of me and prevaild;
Vertue, as I thought, truth, duty so enjoining.   870
   Sam. I thought where all thy circling wiles would end;
In feignd Religion, smooth hypocrisie.
But had thy love, still odiously pretended,
Bin, as it ought, sincere, it would have taught thee
Farr other reasonings, brought forth other deeds.   875
I before all the daughters of my Tribe

And of my Nation chose thee from among
My enemies, lov'd thee, as too well thou knew'st,
Too well, unbosomd all my secrets to thee,
Not out of levity, but over-powr'd   880
By thy request, who could deny thee nothing;
Yet now am judg'd an enemy. Why then
Didst thou at first receive me for thy husband?
Then, as since then, thy countries foe profest:
Being once a wife, for mee thou wast to leave   885
Parents and countrey; nor was I their subject,
Nor under their protection but my own,
Thou mine, not theirs: if aught against my life
Thy countrey sought of thee, it sought unjustly,
Against the law of nature, law of nations,   890
No more thy countrey, but an impious crew
Of men conspiring to uphold thir state
By worse then hostil deeds, violating the ends
For which our countrey is a name so dear;
Not therefore to be obeyd. But zeal mov'd thee;   895
To please thy gods thou didst it; gods unable
To acquit themselves and prosecute thir foes
But by ungodly deeds, the contradiction
Of thir own deity, Gods cannot be:
Less therefore to be pleas'd, obeyd, or feard;   900
These false pretexts and varnisht colours failing,
Bare in thy guilt how foul must thou appear!
    Dal. In argument with men a woman ever
Goes by the worse, whatever be her cause.
    Sam. For want of words no doubt, or lack of breath;   905
Witness when I was worried with thy peals.
    Dal. I was a fool, too rash, and quite mistak'n
In what I thought would have succeeded best.
Let me obtain forgiveness of thee, *Samson*,
Afford me place to shew what recompence   910
Towards thee I intend for what I have misdone,
Misguided; onely what remains past cure
Bear not too sensibly, nor still insist
To afflict thy self in vain: though sight be lost,
Life yet hath many solaces, enjoy'd   915
Where other senses want not their delights

At home in leisure and domestic ease,
Exempt from many a care and chance to which
Eye-sight exposes daily men abroad.
I to the Lords will intercede, not doubting   920
Thir favourable ear, that I may fetch thee
From forth this loathsom prison-house, to abide
With me, where my redoubl'd love and care
With nursing diligence, to mee glad office,
May ever tend about thee to old age   925
With all things grateful cheard, and so suppli'd,
That what by mee thou hast lost thou least shalt miss.
    Sam. No, no, of my condition take no care;
It fits not; thou and I long since are twain;
Nor think me so unwary or accurst   930
To bring my feet again into the snare
Where once I have been caught; I know thy trains
Though dearly to my cost, thy ginns, and toils;
Thy fair enchanted cup, and warbling charms
No more on me have power, thir force is nulld,   935
So much of Adders wisdom I have learnt
To fence my ear against thy sorceries.
If in my flower of youth and strength, when all men
Lov'd, honourd, feard me, thou alone could hate me
Thy Husband, slight me, sell me, and forgo me;   940
How wouldst thou use me now, blind, and thereby
Deceiveable, in most things as a child
Helpless, thence easily contemnd, and scornd,
And last neglected? How wouldst thou insult
When I must live uxorious to thy will   945
In perfet thraldom, how again betray me,
Bearing my words and doings to the Lords
To gloss upon, and censuring, frown or smile?
This Gaol I count the house of Liberty
To thine, whose doors my feet shall never enter.   950
    Dal. Let me approach at least, and touch thy hand.
    Sam. Not for thy life, lest fierce remembrance wake
My sudden rage to tear thee joint by joint.
At distance I forgive thee, go with that;
Bewail thy falshood, and the pious works   955
It hath brought forth to make thee memorable

Among illustrious women, faithful wives:
Cherish thy hast'nd widowhood with the gold
Of Matrimonial treason: so farewel.
   Dal. I see thou art implacable, more deaf   960
To prayers, then winds and seas, yet winds to seas
Are reconcil'd at length, and Sea to Shore:
Thy anger, unappeasable, still rages,
Eternal tempest never to be calmd.
Why do I humble thus my self, and suing   965
For peace, reap nothing but repulse and hate?
Bid go with evil omen and the brand
Of infamy upon my name denounc't?
To mix with thy concernments I desist
Henceforth, nor too much disapprove my own.   970
Fame if not double-fac't is double-mouth'd,
And with contrary blast proclaims most deeds,
On both his wings, one black, the other white,
Bears greatest names in his wild aerie flight.
My name perhaps among the Circumcis'd   975
In *Dan*, in *Judah*, and the bordering Tribes,
To all posterity may stand defam'd,
With malediction mentiond, and the blot
Of falshood most unconjugal traduc't.
But in my countrey where I most desire,   980
In *Ecron*, *Gaza*, *Asdod*, and in *Gath*
I shall be nam'd among the famousest
Of Women, sung at solemn festivals,
Living and dead recorded, who to save
Her countrey from a fierce destroyer, chose   985
Above the faith of wedlock-bands, my tomb
With odours visited and annual flowers;
Not less renownd then in Mount *Ephraim*,
Jael, who with inhospitable guile
Smote *Sisera* sleeping through the Temples naild.   990
Nor shall I count it hainous to enjoy
The public marks of honour and reward
Conferrd upon me, for the piety
Which to my countrey I was judg'd to have shewn.
At this who ever envies or repines   995
I leave him to his lot, and like my own.

Chor. She's gone, a manifest Serpent by her sting
Discover'd in the end, till now conceal'd.
   Sam. So let her go, God sent her to debase me,
And aggravate my folly who committed   1000
To such a viper his most sacred trust
Of secresie, my safety, and my life.
   Chor. Yet beauty, though injurious, hath strange power,
After offence returning, to regain
Love once possest, nor can be easily   1005
Repulst, without much inward passion felt
And secret sting of amorous remorse.
   Sam. Love-quarrels oft in pleasing concord end,
Not wedlock-trechery endangering life.
   Chor. It is not vertue, wisdom, valour, wit,   1010
Strength, comliness of shape, or amplest merit
That womans love can win or long inherit;
But what it is, hard is to say,
Harder to hit,
(Which way soever men referr it)   1015
Much like thy riddle, *Samson*, in one day
Or seven, though one should musing sit;
    If any of these or all, the *Timnian* bride
Had not so soon preferr'd
Thy Paranymph, worthless to thee compar'd,   1020
Successour in thy bed,
Nor both so loosly disally'd
Thir nuptials, nor this last so trecherously
Had shorn the fatal harvest of thy head.
Is it for that such outward ornament   1025
Was lavisht on thir Sex, that inward gifts
Were left for hast unfinisht, judgment scant,
Capacity not rais'd to apprehend
Or value what is best
In choice, but oftest to affect the wrong?   1030
Or was too much of self-love mixt,
Of constancy no root infixt,
That either they love nothing, or not long?
    What e're it be, to wisest men and best
Seeming at first all heav'nly under virgin veil,   1035
Soft, modest, meek, demure,

Once joind, the contrary she proves, a thorn
Intestin, farr within defensive arms
A cleaving mischief, in his way to vertue
Adverse and turbulent, or by her charms   1040
Draws him awry enslav'd
With dotage, and his sense deprav'd
To folly and shameful deeds which ruin ends.
What Pilot so expert but needs must wreck
Imbarkt with such a Stears-mate at the Helm?   1045
    Favourd of Heav'n who finds
One vertuous rarely found,
That in domestic good combines:
Happy that house! his way to peace is smooth:
But vertue which breaks through all opposition, 1050
And all temptation can remove,
Most shines and most is acceptable above.
    Therefore Gods universal Law
Gave to the man despotic power
Over his femal in due awe,   1055
Nor from that right to part an hour,
Smile she or lowre:
So shall he least confusion draw
On his whole life, not sway'd
By femal usurpation, nor dismay'd.   1060
    But had we best retire? I see a storm.
    Sam. Fair days have oft contracted wind and rain.
    Chor. But this another kind of tempest brings.
    Sam. Be less abstruse, my riddling days are past.
    Chor. Look now for no inchanting voice, nor fear   1065
The bait of honied words; a rougher tongue
Draws hitherward, I know him by his stride,
The Giant *Harapha* of *Gath*, his look
Hauty as is his pile high-built and proud.
Comes he in peace? what wind hath blown him hither   1070
I less conjecture then when first I saw
The sumptuous *Dalila* floating this way:
His habit carries peace, his brow defiance.
    Sam. Or peace or not, alike to me he comes.
    Chor. His fraught we soon shall know, he now arrives.   1075
    Har. I come not *Samson*, to condole thy chance,

As these perhaps, yet wish it had not been,
Though for no friendly intent. I am of *Gath*,
Men call me *Harapha*, of stock renownd
As *Og* or *Anak* and the *Emims* old   1080
That *Kiriathaim* held, thou knowst me now
If thou at all art known. Much I have heard
Of thy prodigious might and feats performd
Incredible to me, in this displeas'd,
That I was never present on the place   1085
Of those encounters, where we might have tri'd
Each others force in camp or listed field:
And now am come to see of whom such noise
Hath walkt about, and each limb to survey,
If thy appearance answer loud report.   1090
   Sam. The way to know were not to see but taste.
   Har. Dost thou already single me? I thought
Gives and the Mill had tam'd thee. O that fortune
Had brought me to the field where thou art fam'd
To have wrought such wonders with an Asses Jaw;   1095
I should have forc't thee soon wish other arms,
Or left thy carkass where the Ass lay thrown:
So had the glory of Prowess been recoverd
To *Palestine*, won by a *Philistine*
From the unforeskinnd race, of whom thou bear'st   1100
The highest name for valiant Acts; that honour
Certain to have won by mortal duel from thee,
I lose, prevented by thy eyes put out.
   Sam. Boast not of what thou wouldst have done, but do
What then thou wouldst, thou seest it in thy hand.   1105
   Har. To combat with a blind man I disdain,
And thou hast need much washing to be toucht.
   Sam. Such usage as your honourable Lords
Afford me assassinated and betray'd,
Who durst not with thir whole united powers   1110
In fight withstand me single and unarmd,
Nor in the house with chamber Ambushes
Close-banded durst attack me, no not sleeping,
Till they had hir'd a woman with thir gold
Breaking her Marriage Faith to circumvent me.   1115
Therefore without feignd shifts let be assign'd

Some narrow place enclos'd, where sight may give thee,
Or rather flight, no great advantage on me;
Then put on all thy gorgeous arms, thy Helmet
And Brigandine of brass, thy broad Habergeon,   1120
Vant-brass and Greves, and Gauntlet, add thy Spear
A Weavers beam, and seven-times-folded shield,
I onely with an Oak'n staff will meet thee,
And raise such out-cries on thy clatterd Iron,
Which long shall not with-hold mee from thy head,   1125
That in a little time while breath remains thee,
Thou oft shalt wish thy self at *Gath* to boast
Again in safety what thou wouldst have done
To *Samson*, but shalt never see *Gath* more.
   Har. Thou durst not thus disparage glorious arms   1130
Which greatest Heroes have in battel worn,
Thir ornament and safety, had not spells
And black enchantments, some Magicians Art
Armd thee or charmd thee strong, which thou from Heaven
Feigndst at thy birth was giv'n thee in thy hair,   1135
Where strength can least abide, though all thy hairs
Were bristles rang'd like those that ridge the back
Of chaf't wild Boars, or ruffl'd Porcupines.
   Sam. I know no Spells, use no forbidd'n Arts;
My trust is in the living God who gave me   1140
At my Nativity this strength, diffus'd
No less through all my sinews, joints and bones,
Then thine, while I preserv'd these locks unshorn,
The pledge of my unviolated vow.
For proof hereof, if *Dagon* be thy god,   1145
Go to his Temple, invocate his aid
With solemnest devotion, spread before him
How highly it concerns his glory now
To frustrate and dissolve these Magic spells,
Which I to be the power of *Israels* God   1150
Avow, and challenge *Dagon* to the test,
Offering to combat thee his Champion bold,
With th' utmost of his Godhead seconded:
Then thou shalt see, or rather to thy sorrow
Soon feel, whose God is strongest, thine or mine.   1155
   Har. Presume not on thy God, what e're he be,

Thee he regards not, owns not, hath cut off
Quite from his people, and deliverd up
Into thy Enemies hand, permitted them
To put out both thine eyes, and fetterd send thee 1160
Into the common Prison, there to grind
Among the Slaves and Asses thy comrades,
As good for nothing else, no better service
With those thy boist'rous locks, no worthy match
For valour to assail, nor by the sword 1165
Of noble Warriour, so to stain his honour,
But by the Barbers razor best subdu'd.

 Sam. All these indignities, for such they are
From thine, these evils I deserve and more,
Acknowledge them from God inflicted on me 1170
Justly, yet despair not of his final pardon
Whose ear is ever op'n; and his eye
Gracious to re-admit the suppliant;
In confidence whereof I once again
Defie thee to the trial of mortal fight, 1175
By combat to decide whose god is God,
Thine or whom I with *Israels* Sons adore.

 Har. Fair honour that thou dost thy God, in trusting
He will accept thee to defend his cause,
A Murtherer, a Revolter, and a Robber. 1180

 Sam. Tongue-doughtie Giant, how dost thou prove me these?

 Har. Is not thy Nation subject to our Lords?
Thir Magistrates confessd it, when they took thee
As a League-breaker and deliverd bound
Into our hands: for hadst thou not committed 1185
Notorious murder on those thirty men
At *Askalon*, who never did thee harm,
Then like a Robber stripdst them of thir robes?
The *Philistines*, when thou hadst broke the league,
Went up with armed powers thee onely seeking, 1190
To others did no violence nor spoil.

 Sam. Among the Daughters of the *Philistines*
I chose a Wife, which argu'd me no foe;
And in your City held my Nuptial Feast:
But your ill-meaning Politician Lords, 1195
Under pretence of Bridal friends and guests,

Appointed to await me thirty spies,
Who threatning cruel death constraind the bride
To wring from me and tell to them my secret,
That solv'd the riddle which I had propos'd.   1200
When I perceiv'd all set on enmity,
As on my enemies, where ever chanc'd,
I us'd hostility, and took thir spoil
To pay my underminers in thir coin.
My Nation was subjected to your Lords.   1205
It was the force of Conquest; force with force
Is well ejected when the Conquerd can.
But I a privat person, whom my Countrey
As a league-breaker gave up bound, presum'd
Single Rebellion and did Hostil Acts.   1210
I was no privat but a person rais'd
With strength sufficient and command from Heav'n
To free my Countrey; if their servil minds
Mee thir Deliverer sent would not receive,
But to thir Maisters gave me up for naught,   1215
Th' unworthier they; whence to this day they serve.
I was to do my part from Heav'n assign'd,
And had performd it if my known offence
Had not disabl'd me, not all your force:
These shifts refuted, answer thy appellant   1220
Though by his blindness maimd for high attempts,
Who now defies thee thrice to single fight,
As a petty enterprise of small enforce.
　　Har. With thee a Man condemnd, a Slave inrould,
Due by the Law to capital punishment?   1225
To fight with thee no man of arms will deign.
　　Sam. Cam'st thou for this, vain boaster, to survey me,
To descant on my strength, and give thy verdit?
Come nearer, part not hence so slight informd;
But take good heed my hand survey not thee.   1230
　　Har. O *Bääl-zebub*! can my ears unus'd
Hear these dishonours, and not render death?
　　Sam. No man with-holds thee, nothing from thy hand
Fear I incurable; bring up thy van,
My heels are fetterd, but my fist is free.   1235
　　Har. This insolence other kind of answer fits.

Sam. Go baffl'd coward, lest I run upon thee,
Though in these chains, bulk without spirit vast,
And with one buffet lay thy structure low,
Or swing thee in the Air, then dash thee down   1240
To the hazard of thy brains and shatterd sides.

Har. By *Astaroth* ere long thou shalt lament
These braveries in Irons load'n on thee.

Chor. His Giantship is gone somewhat crest-fall'n,
Stalking with less unconsci'nable strides,   1245
And lower looks, but in a sultrie chafe.

Sam. I dread him not, nor all his Giant-brood,
Though Fame divulge him Father of five Sons
All of Gigantic size, *Goliah* chief.

Chor. He will directly to the Lords, I fear,   1250
And with malicious counsel stir them up
Some way or other yet furder to afflict thee.

Sam. He must allege some cause, and offerd fight
Will not dare mention, lest a question rise
Whether he durst accept the offer or not,   1255
And that he durst not plain anough appeard.
Much more affliction then already felt
They cannot well impose, nor I sustain;
If they intend advantage of my labours
The work of many hands, which earns my keeping   1260
With no small profit daily to my owners.
But come what will, my deadliest foe will prove
My speediest friend, by death to rid me hence,
The worst that he can give, to mee the best.
Yet so it may fall out, because thir end   1265
Is hate, not help to me, it may with mine
Draw their own ruin who attempt the deed.

Chor. Oh how comely it is and how reviving
To the Spirits of just men long opprest!
When God into the hands of thir deliverer   1270
Puts invincible might
To quell the mighty of the Earth, th' oppressour,
The brute and boist'rous force of violent men
Hardy and industrious to support
Tyrannic power, but raging to persue   1275
The righteous and all such as honour Truth;

Hee all thir Ammunition
And feats of Warr defeats
With plain Heroic magnitude of mind
And celestial vigour armd,   1280
Thir Armories and Magazins contemns,
Renders them useless, while
With winged expedition
Swift as the lightning glance he executes
His errand on the wicked, who surpris'd   1285
Lose thir defence distracted and amaz'd.
    But patience is more oft the exercise
Of Saints, the trial of thir fortitude,
Making them each his own Deliverer,
And Victor over all   1290
That tyrannie or fortune can inflict;
Either of these is in thy lot,
Samson, with might endu'd
Above the Sons of men; but sight bereav'd
May chance to number thee with those   1295
Whom Patience finally must crown.
This Idols day hath bin to thee no day of rest,
    Labouring thy mind
More then the working day thy hands,
And yet perhaps more trouble is behind.   1300
For I descry this way
Some other tending, in his hand
A Scepter or quaint staff he bears,
Comes on amain, speed in his look.
By his habit I discern him now   1305
A Public Officer, and now at hand.
His message will be short and voluble.
    Off. Ebrews, the Pris'ner *Samson* here I seek.
    Chor. His manacles remark him, there he sits.
    Off. Samson, to thee our Lords thus bid me say;   1310
This day to *Dagon* is a solemn Feast,
With Sacrifices, Triumph, Pomp, and Games;
Thy strength they know surpassing human rate,
And now some public proof thereof require
To honour this great Feast, and great Assembly;   1315

1313 rate] Erratum Ed. 1; Newton 1747: race Edd. 1, 2

Rise therefore with all speed and come along,
Where I will see thee heart'nd and fresh clad
To appear as fits before th' illustrious Lords.

   Sam. Thou knowst I am an *Ebrew*, therefore tell them,
Our Law forbids at thir Religious Rites   1320
My presence; for that cause I cannot come.

   Off. This answer, be assur'd, will not content them.

   Sam. Have they not Sword-players, and ev'ry sort
Of Gymnic Artists, Wrestlers, Riders, Runners,
Juglers and Dancers, Antics, Mummers, Mimics,   1325
But they must pick mee out with shackles tir'd,
And over-labourd at thir publick Mill,
To make them sport with blind activity?
Do they not seek occasion of new quarrels
On my refusal to distress me more,   1330
Or make a game of my calamities?
Return the way thou cam'st, I will not come.

   Off. Regard thy self, this will offend them highly.

   Sam. My self? my conscience and internal peace.
Can they think me so brok'n, so debas'd   1335
With corporal servitude, that my mind ever
Will condescend to such absurd commands?
Although thir drudge, to be thir fool or jester,
And in my midst of sorrow and heart-grief
To shew them feats, and play before thir god,   1340
The worst of all indignities, yet on mee
Joind with extream contempt? I will not come.

   Off. My message was impos'd on me with speed,
Brooks no delay: is this thy resolution?

   Sam. So take it with what speed thy message needs.   1345

   Off. I am sorry what this stoutness will produce.

   Sam. Perhaps thou shalt have cause to sorrow indeed.

   Chor. Consider, *Samson*; matters now are straind
Up to the highth, whether to hold or break;
He's gone, and who knows how he may report   1350
Thy words by adding fuel to the flame?
Expect another message more imperious,
More Lordly thund'ring then thou well wilt bear.

   Sam. Shall I abuse this Consecrated gift

1325 Mimics] Erratum Ed. 1: Mimirs Edd. 1, 2: Mimers Fenton, 1725

Of strength, again returning with my hair   1355
After my great transgression, so requite
Favour renewd, and add a greater sin
By prostituting holy things to Idols;
A *Nazarite* in place abominable
Vaunting my strength in honour to thir *Dagon*?   1360
Besides, how vile, contemptible, ridiculous,
What act more execrably unclean, prophane?
   Chor. Yet with this strength thou serv'st the *Philistines*,
Idolatrous, uncircumcis'd, unclean.
   Sam. Not in thir Idol-worship, but by labour   1365
Honest and lawful to deserve my food
Of those who have me in thir civil power.
   Chor. Where the heart joins not, outward acts defile not.
   Sam. Where outward force constrains, the sentence holds:
But who constrains me to the Temple of *Dagon*,   1370
Not dragging? the *Philistian* Lords command.
Commands are no constraints. If I obey them,
I do it freely; venturing to displease
God for the fear of Man, and Man preferr,
Set God behind: which in his jealousie   1375
Shall never, unrepented, find forgiveness.
Yet that he may dispense with me or thee
Present in Temples at Idolatrous Rites
For some important cause, thou needst not doubt.
   Chor. How thou wilt here come off surmounts my reach.
   Sam. Be of good courage, I begin to feel   1381
Some rouzing motions in me which dispose
To something extraordinary my thoughts.
I with this Messenger will go along,
Nothing to do, be sure, that may dishonour   1385
Our Law, or stain my vow of *Nazarite*.
If there be aught of presage in the mind,
This day will be remarkable in my life
By some great act, or of my days the last.
   Chor. In time thou hast resolv'd, the man returns.   1390
   Off. *Samson*, this second message from our Lords
To thee I am bid say. Art thou our Slave,
Our Captive, at the public Mill our drudge,
And dar'st thou at our sending and command

Dispute thy coming? come without delay;　　　　1395
Or we shall find such Engins to assail
And hamper thee, as thou shalt come of force,
Though thou wert firmlier fast'nd then a rock.
　　Sam. I could be well content to try thir Art,
Which to no few of them would prove pernicious.　　1400
Yet knowing thir advantages too many,
Because they shall not trail me through thir streets
Like a wild Beast, I am content to go.
Maisters commands come with a power resistless
To such as owe them absolute subjection;　　　　1405
And for a life who will not change his purpose?
(So mutable are all the ways of men)
Yet this be sure, in nothing to comply
Scandalous or forbidd'n in our Law.
　　Off. I praise thy resolution, doff these links:　　1410
By this compliance thou wilt win the Lords
To favour, and perhaps to set thee free.
　　Sam. Brethren farewel, your company along
I will not wish, lest it perhaps offend them
To see me girt with Friends; and how the sight　　1415
Of mee as of a common Enemy,
So dreaded once, may now exasperate them
I know not. Lords are Lordliest in thir wine;
And the well-feasted Priest then soonest fir'd
With zeal, if aught Religion seem concernd:　　　1420
No less the people on thir Holy-days
Impetuous, insolent, unquenchable;
Happ'n what may, of mee expect to hear
Nothing dishonourable, impure, unworthy
Our God, our Law, my Nation, or my self,　　　1425
The last of me or no I cannot warrant.
　　Chor. Go, and the Holy One
Of *Israel* be thy guide
To what may serve his glory best, and spread his name
Great among the Heathen round:　　　　　　1430
Send thee the Angel of thy Birth, to stand
Fast by thy side, who from thy Fathers field
Rode up in flames after his message told
Of thy conception, and be now a shield

Of fire; that Spirit that first rushd on thee   1435
In the camp of *Dan*
Be efficacious in thee now at need.
For never was from Heav'n imparted
Measure of strength so great to mortal seed,
As in thy wond'rous actions hath bin seen.   1440
But wherefore comes old *Manoah* in such hast
With youthful steps? much livelier then ere while
He seems: supposing here to find his Son,
Or of him bringing to us some glad news?
   Man. Peace with you brethren; my inducement hither 1445
Was not at present here to find my Son,
By order of the Lords new parted hence
To come and play before them at thir Feast.
I heard all as I came, the City rings
And numbers thither flock, I had no will,   1450
Lest I should see him forc't to things unseemly.
But that which mov'd my coming now, was chiefly
To give ye part with me what hope I have
With good success to work his liberty.
   Chor. That hope would much rejoyce us to partake   1455
With thee; say reverend Sire, we thirst to hear.
   Man. I have attempted one by one the Lords
Either at home, or through the high street passing,
With supplication prone and Fathers tears
To accept of ransom for my Son thir pris'ner;   1460
Some much averse I found and wondrous harsh,
Contemptuous, proud, set on revenge and spite:
That part most reverenc'd *Dagon* and his Priests;
Others more moderat seeming, but thir aim
Privat reward, for which both God and State   1465
They easily would set to sale; a third
More generous farr and civil, who confessd
They had anough reveng'd, having reduc't
Thir foe to misery beneath thir fears,
The rest was magnanimity to remit,   1470
If some convenient ransom were propos'd.
What noise or shout was that? it tore the Skie.
   Chor. Doubtless the people shouting to behold
Thir once great dread, captive, and blind before them,

Or at some proof of strength before them shown.   1475
   Man. His ransom, if my whole inheritance
May compass it, shall willingly be paid
And numberd down: much rather I shall chuse
To live the poorest in my Tribe, then richest,
And he in that calamitous prison left.   1480
No, I am fixt not to part hence without him.
For his redemption all my Patrimony,
If need be, I am ready to forgo
And quit: not wanting him, I shall want nothing.
   Chor. Fathers are wont to lay up for thir Sons,   1485
Thou for thy Son art bent to lay out all;
Sons wont to nurse thir Parents in old age,
Thou in old age car'st how to nurse thy Son,
Made older then thy age through eye-sight lost.
   Man. It shall be my delight to tend his eyes,   1490
And view him sitting in the house, enobl'd
With all those high exploits by him atchiev'd,
And on his shoulders waving down those locks,
That of a Nation armd the strength containd:
And I perswade me God had not permitted   1495
His strength again to grow up with his hair
Garrisond round about him like a Camp
Of faithful Souldiery, were not his purpose
To use him furder yet in some great service,
Not to sit idle with so great a gift   1500
Useless, and thence ridiculous about him.
And since his strength with eye-sight was not lost,
God will restore him eye-sight to his strength.
   Chor. Thy hopes are not ill founded nor seem vain
Of his delivery, and thy joy thereon   1505
Conceiv'd, agreeable to a Fathers love,
In both which we, as next participate.
   Man. I know your friendly minds and . . . . O what noise!
Mercy of Heav'n what hideous noise was that!
Horribly loud unlike the former shout.   1510
   Chor. Noise call you it or universal groan
As if the whole inhabitation perishd;
Blood, death, and deathful deeds are in that noise,
Ruin, destruction at the utmost point.

Man. Of ruin indeed methought I heard the noise,   1515
Oh it continues, they have slain my Son.
Chor. Thy Son is rather slaying them, that outcry
From slaughter of one foe could not ascend.
Man. Some dismal accident it needs must be;
What shall we do, stay here or run and see?   1520
Chor. Best keep together here, lest running thither
We unawares run into dangers mouth.
This evil on the *Philistines* is fall'n,
From whom could else a general cry be heard?
The sufferers then will scarce molest us here,   1525
From other hands we need not much to fear.
What if his eye-sight (for to *Israels* God
Nothing is hard) by miracle restor'd,
He now be dealing dole among his foes,
And over heaps of slaughterd walk his way?   1530
Man. That were a joy presumptuous to be thought.
Chor. Yet God hath wrought things as incredible
For his people of old; what hinders now?
Man. He can I know, but doubt to think he will;
Yet Hope would fain subscribe, and tempts Belief.   1535
A little stay will bring some notice hither.
Chor. Of good or bad so great, of bad the sooner;
For evil news rides post, while good news baits.
And to our wish I see one hither speeding,
An *Ebrew*, as I guess, and of our Tribe.   1540
Mess. O whither shall I run, or which way flie
The sight of this so horrid spectacle
Which earst my eyes beheld and yet behold;
For dire imagination still persues me.
But providence or instinct of nature seems,   1545
Or reason though disturbd, and scarse consulted
To have guided me aright, I know not how,
To thee first reverend *Manoah*, and to these
My Countreymen, whom here I knew remaining,
As at some distance from the place of horrour,   1550
So in the sad event too much concernd.
Man. The accident was loud, and here before thee
With rueful cry, yet what it was we hear not,
No Preface needs, thou seest we long to know.

Mess. It would burst forth, but I recover breath   1555
And sense distract, to know well what I utter.
  Man. Tell us the sum, the circumstance deferr.
  Mess. Gaza yet stands, but all her Sons are fall'n,
All in a moment overwhelmd and fall'n.
  Man. Sad, but thou knowst to *Israelites* not saddest   1560
The desolation of a Hostil City.
  Mess. Feed on that first, there may in grief be surfet.
  Man. Relate by whom. *Mess.* By *Samson.*
        Man. That still less'ns
The sorrow, and converts it nigh to joy.
  Mess. Ah *Manoah* I refrain, too suddenly   1565
To utter what will come at last too soon;
Lest evil tidings with too rude irruption
Hitting thy aged ear should pierce too deep.
  Man. Suspense in news is torture, speak them out.
  Mess. Then take the worst in brief, *Samson* is dead.   1570
  Man. The worst indeed, O all my hopes defeated
To free him hence! but death who sets all free
Hath paid his ransom now and full discharge.
What windy joy this day had I conceiv'd
Hopeful of his Delivery, which now proves   1575
Abortive as the first-born bloom of spring
Nipt with the lagging rear of winters frost.
Yet ere I give the rains to grief, say first,
How dy'd he? death to life is crown or shame.
All by him fell thou say'st, by whom fell hee,   1580
What glorious hand gave *Samson* his deaths wound?
  Mess. Unwounded of his enemies he fell.
  Man. Wearied with slaughter then or how? explain.
  Mess. By his own hands. *Man.* Self-violence? what cause
Brought him so soon at variance with himself   1585
Among his foes? *Mess.* Inevitable cause
At once both to destroy and be destroyd;
The Edifice where all were met to see him
Upon thir heads and on his own he pulld.
  Man. O lastly over-strong against thy self!   1590
A dreadful way thou took'st to thy revenge.
More than anough we know; but while things yet

1571 hopes] Fenton, 1720: hope's Edd. 1, 2

Are in confusion, give us if thou canst,
Eye-witness of what first or last was done,
Relation more particular and distinct.   1595
   Mess. Occasions drew me early to this City,
And as the gates I enterd with Sun-rise,
The morning Trumpets Festival proclaimd
Through each high street: little I had dispatcht
When all abroad was rumourd that this day   1600
Samson should be brought forth to shew the people
Proof of his mighty strength in feats and games;
I sorrowd at his captive state, but minded
Not to be absent at that spectacle.
The building was a spacious Theatre   1605
Half round on two main Pillars vaulted high,
With seats where all the Lords and each degree
Of sort, might sit in order to behold;
The other side was op'n, where the throng
On banks and scaffolds under Skie might stand;   1610
I among these aloof obscurely stood.
The Feast and noon grew high, and Sacrifice
Had filld thir hearts with mirth, high chear, and wine,
When to thir sports they turnd. Immediatly
Was *Samson* as a public servant brought,   1615
In thir state Livery clad; before him Pipes
And Timbrels, on each side went armed guards,
Both horse and foot before him and behind,
Archers, and Slingers, Cataphracts and Spears.
At sight of him the people with a shout   1620
Rifted the Air clamouring thir god with praise,
Who had made thir dreadful enemy thir thrall.
Hee patient but undaunted where they led him,
Came to the place, and what was set before him
Which without help of eye, might be assayd,   1625
To heave, pull, draw, or break, he still performd
All with incredible, stupendious force,
None daring to appear Antagonist.
At length for intermission sake they led him
Between the pillars; he his guide requested   1630
(For so from such as nearer stood we heard)
As over-tir'd to let him lean a while

With both his arms on those two massie Pillars
That to the arched roof gave main support.
He unsuspicious led him; which when *Samson*   1635
Felt in his arms, with head a while enclin'd,
And eyes fast fixt he stood, as one who pray'd,
Or some great matter in his mind revolv'd.
At last with head erect thus cry'd aloud,
Hitherto, Lords, what your commands impos'd   1640
I have performd, as reason was, obeying,
Not without wonder or delight beheld.
Now of my own accord such other tryal
I mean to shew you of my strength, yet greater;
As with amaze shall strike all who behold.   1645
This utterd, straining all his nerves he bowd;
As with the force of winds and waters pent,
When Mountains tremble, those two massie Pillars
With horrible convulsion to and fro,
He tuggd, he shook, till down they came and drew   1650
The whole roof after them, with burst of thunder
Upon the heads of all who sate beneath,
Lords, Ladies, Captains, Councellors, or Priests,
Thir choice nobility and flower, not onely
Of this but each *Philistian* City round   1655
Met from all parts to solemnize this Feast.
Samson with these immixt, inevitably
Pulld down the same destruction on himself;
The vulgar only scap'd who stood without.
    Chor. O dearly-bought revenge, yet glorious!   1660
Living or dying thou hast fulfilld
The work for which thou wast foretold
To *Israel*, and now ly'st victorious
Among thy slain self-killd
Not willingly, but tangl'd in the fold   1665
Of dire necessity, whose law in death conjoind
Thee with thy slaughterd foes in number more
Then all thy life had slain before.
    Semichor. While thir hearts were jocond and sublime,
Drunk with Idolatry, drunk with Wine,   1670
And fat regorg'd of Bulls and Goats,
Chaunting thir Idol, and preferring

Before our living Dread who dwells
In *Silo* his bright Sanctuary:
Among them hee a spirit of phrenzie sent,   1675
Who hurt thir minds,
And urg'd them on with mad desire
To call in hast for thir destroyer;
They onely set on sport and play
Unweetingly importun'd   1680
Thir own destruction to come speedy upon them.
So fond are mortal men
Fall'n into wrauth divine,
As thir own ruin on themselves to invite,
Insensat left, or to sense reprobate,   1685
And with blindness internal strook.
   Semichor. But hee though blind of sight,
Despis'd and thought extinguisht quite,
With inward eyes illuminated
His fierie vertue rouz'd   1690
From under ashes into sudden flame,
And as an ev'ning Dragon came,
Assailant on the perched roosts,
And nests in order rang'd
Of tame villatic Fowl; but as an Eagle   1695
His cloudless thunder bolted on thir heads.
So vertue giv'n for lost,
Deprest, and overthrown, as seemd,
Like that self-begott'n bird
In the *Arabian* woods embost,   1700
That no second knows nor third,
And lay ere while a Holocaust,
From out her ashie womb now teemd
Revives, reflourishes, then vigorous most
When most unactive deemd,   1705
And though her body die, her fame survives,
A secular bird ages of lives.
   Man. Come, come, no time for lamentation now,
Nor much more cause, *Samson* hath quit himself
Like *Samson*, and heroicly hath finisht   1710
A life Heroic, on his Enemies
Fully reveng'd, hath left them years of mourning,

And lamentation to the Sons of *Caphtor*
Through all *Philistian* bounds. To *Israel*
Honour hath left, and freedom, let but them   1715
Find courage to lay hold on this occasion,
To himself and Fathers house eternal fame;
And which is best and happiest yet, all this
With God not parted from him, as was feard,
But favouring and assisting to the end.   1720
Nothing is here for tears, nothing to wail
Or knock the brest, no weakness, no contempt,
Dispraise, or blame, nothing but well and fair,
And what may quiet us in a death so noble.
Let us go find the body where it lies   1725
Sok't in his enemies blood, and from the stream
With lavers pure and cleansing herbs wash off
The clotted gore. I with what speed the while
(*Gaza* is not in plight to say us nay)
Will send for all my kindred, all my friends   1730
To fetch him hence and solemnly attend
With silent obsequie and funeral train
Home to his Fathers house: there will I build him
A Monument, and plant it round with shade
Of Laurel ever green, and branching Palm,   1735
With all his Trophies hung, and Acts inrould
In copious Legend, or sweet Lyric Song.
Thither shall all the valiant youth resort,
And from his memory inflame thir brests
To matchless valour, and adventures high: 1740
The Virgins also shall on feastful days
Visit his Tomb with flowers, onely bewailing
His lot unfortunate in nuptial choice,
From whence captivity and loss of eyes.
    Chor. All is best, though we oft doubt,   1745
What th' unsearchable dispose
Of highest wisdom brings about,
And ever best found in the close.
Oft he seems to hide his face,
But unexpectedly returns   1750
And to his faithful Champion hath in place
Bore witness gloriously; whence *Gaza* mourns

And all that band them to resist
His uncontroulable intent;
His servants hee with new acquist   1755
Of true experience from this great event
With peace and consolation hath dismist,
And calm of mind all passion spent.

THE END

POEMS

OF
Mr. *John* *Milton* ,

BOTH
ENGLISH and LATIN,
Compos'd at feveral times.

Printed by his true Copies.

The SONGS were fet in Mufick by
Mr. HENRY LAWES Gentleman of
the KINGS Chappel, and one
of His MAIESTIES
Private Mufick.

——*Baccare frontem*
Cingite, ne vati noceat mala lingua futuro,
Virgil, Eclog. 7.

Printed and publifh'd according to
ORDER.

LONDON,
Printed by *Ruth Raworth* for *Humphrey Mofeley*,
and are to be fold at the figne of the Princes
Arms in S. *Pauls* Church-yard. 1645

POEMS, &c.

UPON

Several Occasions.

BY

Mr. *JOHN MILTON:*

Both E N G L I S H and L A T I N, &c.
Compofed at feveral times.

With a fmall Tractate of
E D U C A T I O N
To Mr. HARTLIB

LONDON,
Printed for *Tho. Dring* at the *Blew Anchor*
next *Mitre Court* over againft *Fetter
Lane* in *Fleet-ftreet.* 1673.

THE STATIONER
TO THE READER[1]

It is not any private respect of gain, Gentle Reader, for the slightest Pamphlet is now adayes more vendible then the Works of learnedest men; but it is the love I have to our own Language that hath made me diligent to collect, and set forth such Peeces both in Prose and Vers, as may renew the wonted honour and esteem of our English tongue: and it's the worth of these English and Latin Poems, not the flourish of any prefixed encomions that can invite thee to buy them, though these are not without the highest Commendations and Applause of the learnedst Academicks, both domestick and forrein: And amongst those of our own Countrey, the unparallel'd attestation of that renowned Provost of Eaton, Sir Henry Wootton: I know not thy palat how it relishes such dainties, nor how harmonious thy soul is; perhaps more trivial Airs may please thee better. But howsoever thy opinion is spent upon these, that incouragement I have already received from the most ingenious men in their clear and courteous entertainment of Mr. Wallers late choice Peeces, hath once more made me adventure into the World, presenting it with these ever-green, and not to be blasted Laurels. The Authors more peculiar excellency in these studies, was too well known to conceal his Papers, or to keep me from attempting to sollicit them from him. Let the event guide it self which way it will, I shall deserve of the age, by bringing into the Light as true a Birth, as the Muses have brought forth since our famous Spencer wrote; whose Poems in these English ones are as rarely imitated, as sweetly excell'd. Reader if thou art Eagle-eied to censure their worth, I am not fearful to expose them to thy exactest perusal.

Thine to command

HUMPH. MOSELEY.

---

[1] 1645.

POEMS &c. UPON SEVERAL OCCASIONS

On the Morning of CHRISTS Nativity

Compos'd 1629

I

THIS is the Month, and this the happy morn
Wherin the Son of Heav'ns eternal King,
Of wedded Maid, and Virgin Mother born,
Our great redemption from above did bring;
For so the holy sages once did sing,   5
   That he our deadly forfeit should release,
And with his Father work us a perpetual peace.

II

That glorious Form, that Light unsufferable,
And that far-beaming blaze of Majesty,
Wherwith he wont at Heav'ns high Councel-Table,   10
To sit the midst of Trinal Unity,
He laid aside; and here with us to be,
   Forsook the Courts of everlasting Day,
And chose with us a darksom House of mortal Clay.

III

Say Heav'nly Muse, shall not thy sacred vein   15
Afford a present to the Infant God?
Hast thou no vers, no hymn, or solemn strein,
To welcom him to this his new abode,
Now while the Heav'n by the Suns team untrod,
   Hath took no print of the approching light,   20
And all the spangled host keep watch in squadrons bright?

IV

See how from far upon the Eastern rode
The Star-led Wisards haste with odours sweet:
O run, prevent them with thy humble ode,

And lay it lowly at his blessed feet;   25
Have thou the honour first, thy Lord to greet,
　And joyn thy voice unto the Angel Quire,
From out his secret Altar toucht with hallow'd fire.

The Hymn

I

It was the Winter wilde,
While the Heav'n-born-childe,   30
　All meanly wrapt in the rude manger lies;
Nature in aw to him
Had doff't her gawdy trim,
　With her great Master so to sympathize:
It was no season then for her   35
To wanton with the Sun her lusty Paramour.

II

Onely with speeches fair
She woo's the gentle Air
　To hide her guilty front with innocent Snow,
And on her naked shame,   40
Pollute with sinfull blame,
　The Saintly Vail of Maiden white to throw,
Confounded, that her Makers eyes
Should look so neer upon her foul deformities.

III

But he her fears to cease,   45
Sent down the meek-eyd Peace,
　She crown'd with Olive green, came softly sliding
Down through the turning sphear
His ready Harbinger,
　With Turtle wing the amorous clouds dividing,   50
And waving wide her mirtle wand,
She strikes a universall Peace through Sea and Land.

IV

No War, or Battels sound
Was heard the World around:
   The idle spear and shield were high up hung;   55
The hooked Chariot stood
Unstain'd with hostile blood,
   The Trumpet spake not to the armed throng,
And Kings sate still with awfull eye,
As if they surely knew their sovran Lord was by.   60

V

But peacefull was the night
Wherin the Prince of light
   His raign of peace upon the earth began:
The Windes with wonder whist,
Smoothly the waters kist,   65
   Whispering new joyes to the milde Ocean,
Who now hath quite forgot to rave,
While Birds of Calm sit brooding on the charmed wave.

VI

The Stars with deep amaze
Stand fixt in stedfast gaze,   70
   Bending one way their pretious influence,
And will not take their flight,
For all the morning light,
   Or *Lucifer* that often warn'd them thence;
But in their glimmering Orbs did glow,   75
Untill their Lord himself bespake, and bid them go.

VII

And though the shady gloom
Had given day her room,
The Sun himself with-held his wonted speed,
And hid his head for shame,   80
As his inferiour flame,
   The new-enlightn'd world no more should need;
He saw a greater Sun appear
Then his bright Throne, or burning Axletree could bear.

VIII

The Shepherds on the Lawn,   85
Or e're the point of dawn,
  Sate simply chatting in a rustick row;
Full little thought they than,
That the mighty *Pan*
  Was kindly com to live with them below;   90
Perhaps their loves, or els their sheep,
Was all that did their silly thoughts so busie keep.

IX

When such musick sweet
Their hearts and ears did greet,
  As never was by mortall finger strook,   95
Divinely-warbl'd voice
Answering the stringed noise,
  As all their souls in blisfull rapture took:
The Air such pleasure loth to lose,
With thousand echo's still prolongs each heav'nly close.   100

X

Nature that heard such sound
Beneath the hollow round
  Of *Cynthia's* seat, the Airy region thrilling,
Now was almost won
To think her part was don,   105
  And that her raign had here its last fulfilling;
She knew such harmony alone
Could hold all Heav'n and Earth in happier union.

XI

At last surrounds their sight
A Globe of circular light,   110
  That with long beams the shame-fac't night array'd,
The helmed Cherubim
And sworded Seraphim,
  Are seen in glittering ranks with wings displaid,
Harping in loud and solemn quire,   115
With unexpressive notes to Heavens new-born Heir.

116 Heavens] Heav'ns Edd. 1, 2

XII

Such Musick (as 'tis said)
Before was never made,
   But when of old the sons of morning sung,
While the Creator great   120
His constellations set,
   And the well-ballanc't world on hinges hung,
And cast the dark foundations deep,
And bid the weltring waves their oozy channel keep.

XIII

Ring out ye Crystall sphears,   125
Once bless our human ears,
   (If ye have power to touch our senses so)
And let your silver chime
Move in melodious time;
   And let the Base of Heav'ns deep Organ blow,   130
And with your ninefold harmony
Make up full consort to th'Angelike symphony.

XIV

For if such holy Song
Enwrap our fancy long,
   Time will run back, and fetch the age of gold,   135
And speckl'd vanity
Will sicken soon and die,
   And leprous sin will melt from earthly mould,
And Hell it self will pass away,
And leave her dolorous mansions to the peering day.   140

XV

Yea Truth, and Justice then
Will down return to men,
   Orb'd in a Rain-bow; and like glories wearing,
Mercy will sit between,
Thron'd in Celestiall sheen,   145
   With radiant feet the tissued clouds down stearing,
And Heav'n as at som festivall,
Will open wide the Gates of her high Palace Hall.

143–4   Th'enameld Arras of the Rainbow wearing,
And Mercy set between, Ed. 1

XVI

But wisest Fate sayes no,
This must not yet be so,   150
   The Babe lies yet in smiling Infancy,
That on the bitter cross
Must redeem our loss;
   So both himself and us to glorifie:
Yet first to those ychain'd in sleep,   155
The wakefull trump of doom must thunder through the deep,

XVII

With such a horrid clang
As on mount *Sinai* rang
   While the red fire, and smouldring clouds out brake:
The aged Earth agast   160
With terrour of that blast,
   Shall from the surface to the center shake;
When at the worlds last session,
The dreadfull Judge in middle Air shall spread his throne.

XVIII

And then at last our bliss   165
Full and perfet is,
   But now begins; for from this happy day
Th'old Dragon under ground
In straiter limits bound,
   Not half so far casts his usurped sway,   170
And wrath to see his Kingdom fail,
Swindges the scaly Horrour of his foulded tail.

XIX

The Oracles are dumm,
No voice or hideous humm
   Runs through the arched roof in words deceiving.   175
Apollo from his shrine
Can no more divine,
   With hollow shreik the steep of *Delphos* leaving.
No nightly trance, or breathed spell,
Inspire's the pale-ey'd Priest from the prophetic cell.   180

XX

The lonely mountains o're,
And the resounding shore,
   A voice of weeping heard, and loud lament;
From haunted spring, and dale
Edg'd with poplar pale,   185
   The parting Genius is with sighing sent,
With flowre-inwov'n tresses torn
The Nimphs in twilight shade of tangled thickets mourn.

XXI

In consecrated Earth,
And on the holy Hearth,   190
   The *Lars*, and *Lemures* moan with midnight plaint,
In Urns, and Altars round,
A drear, and dying sound
   Affrights the *Flamins* at their service quaint;
And the chill Marble seems to sweat,   195
While each peculiar power forgoes his wonted seat.

XXII

Peor, and *Baalim*,
Forsake their Temples dim,
   With that twise batter'd god of *Palestine*,
And mooned *Ashtaroth*,   200
Heav'ns Queen and Mother both,
   Now sits not girt with Tapers holy shine,
The Libyc *Hammon* shrinks his horn,
In vain the *Tyrian* Maids their wounded *Thamuz* mourn.

XXIII

And sullen *Moloch* fled,   205
Hath left in shadows dred,
   His burning Idol all of blackest hue;
In vain with Cymbals ring,
They call the grisly king,
   In dismall dance about the furnace blue;   210
The brutish gods of *Nile* as fast,
Isis and *Orus*, and the Dog *Anubis* hast.

XXIV

Nor is *Osiris* seen
In *Memphian* Grove, or Green,
   Trampling the unshowr'd Grasse with lowings loud: 215
Nor can he be at rest
Within his sacred chest,
   Naught but profoundest Hell can be his shroud,
In vain with Timbrel'd Anthems dark
The sable-stoled Sorcerers bear his worshipt Ark.   220

XXV

He feels from *Judahs* Land
The dredded Infants hand,
   The rayes of *Bethlehem* blind his dusky eyn;
Nor all the gods beside,
Longer dare abide,   225
   Not *Typhon* huge ending in snaky twine:
Our Babe to shew his Godhead true,
Can in his swadling bands controul the damned crew.

XXVI

So when the Sun in bed,
Curtain'd with cloudy red,   230
   Pillows his chin upon an Orient wave,
The flocking shadows pale,
Troop to th'infernall jail,
   Each fetter'd Ghost slips to his severall grave,
And the yellow-skirted *Fayes*,   235
Fly after the Night-steeds, leaving their Moon-lov'd maze.

XXVII

But see the Virgin blest,
Hath laid her Babe to rest.
   Time is our tedious Song should here have ending:
Heav'ns youngest teemed Star,   240
Hath fixt her polisht Car,
   Her sleeping Lord with Handmaid Lamp attending;
And all about the Courtly Stable,
Bright-harnest Angels sit in order serviceable.

A Paraphrase on *Psalm* 114

This and the following *Psalm* were don
by the Author at fifteen yeers old.

WHEN the blest seed of *Terahs* faithfull Son,
After long toil their liberty had won,
And past from *Pharian* fields to *Canaan* Land,
Led by the strength of the Almighties hand,
Jehovahs wonders were in *Israel* shown,   5
His praise and glory was in *Israel* known.
That saw the troubl'd Sea, and shivering fled,
And sought to hide his froth-becurled head
Low in the earth, *Jordans* clear streams recoil,
As a faint host that hath receiv'd the foil.   10
The high, huge-bellied Mountains skip like Rams
Amongst their Ews, the little Hills like Lambs.
Why fled the Ocean? And why skipt the Mountains?
Why turned *Jordan* toward his Crystall Fountains?
Shake earth, and at the presence be agast   15
Of him that ever was, and ay shall last,
That glassy flouds from rugged rocks can crush,
And make soft rills from fiery flint-stones gush.

Psalm 136

LET us with a gladsom mind
Praise the Lord, for he is kind,
   For his mercies ay endure,
   Ever faithfull, ever sure.

Let us blaze his Name abroad,   5
For of gods he is the God;
   For, &*c*.

O let us his praises tell,
That doth the wrathfull tyrants quell.   10
   For, &*c*.

That with his miracles doth make
Amazed Heav'n and Earth to shake.
   For, &*c*.   15

That by his wisdom did create
The painted Heav'ns so full of state.
   For, *&c.*   19

That did the solid Earth ordain
To rise above the watry plain.
   For, *&c.*

That by his all-commanding might,   25
Did fill the new-made world with light.
   For, *&c.*

And caus'd the Golden-tressed Sun,
All the day long his cours to run.   30
   For, *&c.*

The horned Moon to shine by night,
Amongst her spangled sisters bright.
   For, *&c.*   35

He with his thunder-clasping hand,
Smote the first-born of *Egypt* Land.
   For, *&c.*   39

And in despight of *Pharaoh* fell,
He brought from thence his *Israel*.
   For, *&c.*

The ruddy waves he cleft in twain,   45
Of the *Erythræan* main.
   For, *&c.*

The floods stood still like Walls of Glass,
While the Hebrew Bands did pass.   50
   For, *&c.*

But full soon they did devour
The Tawny King with all his power.
   For, *&c.*   55

His chosen people he did bless
In the wastfull Wildernes.
   For, *&c.*   59

In bloody battel he brought down
Kings of prowess and renown.
   For, *&c.*

He foild bold *Seon* and his host,   65
That rul'd the *Amorrean* coast.
    For, *&c.*

And large-lim'd *Og* he did subdue,
With all his over-hardy crew.   70
    For, *&c.*

And to his servant *Israel*,
He gave their Land therin to dwell.
    For, *&c.*   75

He hath with a piteous eye
Beheld us in our misery.
    For, *&c.*   79

And freed us from the slavery
Of the invading enemy.
    For, *&c.*

All living creatures he doth feed,   85
And with full hand supplies their need.
    For, *&c.*

Let us therfore warble forth
His mighty Majesty and worth.   90
    For, *&c.*

That his mansion hath on high
Above the reach of mortall ey.
    For his mercies ay endure,   95
    Ever faithfull, ever sure.

Anno aetatis 17

On the Death of a fair Infant dying of a Cough

I

O FAIREST flower no sooner blown but blasted,
Soft silken Primrose fading timelesslie,
Summers chief honour if thou hadst out-lasted
Bleak winters force that made thy blossome drie;
For he being amorous on that lovely die   5
   That did thy cheek envermeil, thought to kiss
But kill'd alas, and then bewayl'd his fatal bliss.

II

For since grim Aquilo his charioter
By boisterous rape th' Athenian damsel got,
He thought it toucht his Deitie full neer,   10
If likewise he some fair one wedded not,
Thereby to wipe away th' infamous blot,
  Of long-uncoupled bed, and childless eld,
Which 'mongst the wanton gods a foul reproach was held.

III

So mounting up in ycie-pearled carr,   15
Through middle empire of the freezing aire
He wanderd long, till thee he spy'd from farr,
There ended was his quest, there ceast his care.
Down he descended from his Snow-soft chaire,
  But all unwares with his cold-kind embrace   20
Unhous'd thy Virgin Soul from her fair biding place.

IV

Yet art thou not inglorious in thy fate;
For so *Apollo*, with unweeting hand
Whilome did slay his dearly-loved mate
Young *Hyacinth* born on *Eurotas'* strand,   25
Young *Hyacinth* the pride of *Spartan* land;
  But then transform'd him to a purple flower:
Alack that so to change thee winter had no power.

V

Yet can I not perswade me thou art dead
Or that thy coarse corrupts in earths dark wombe,   30
Or that thy beauties lie in wormie bed,
Hid from the world in a low delved tombe;
Could Heav'n for pittie thee so strictly doom?
  Oh no! for something in thy face did shine
Above mortalitie that shew'd thou wast divine.   35

VI

Resolve me then oh Soul most surely blest
(If so it be that thou these plaints dost hear)
Tell me bright Spirit where e're thou hoverest
Whether above that high first-moving Spheare
Or in the Elisian fields (if such there were.)   40
   Oh say me true if thou wert mortal wight
And why from us so quickly thou didst take thy flight.

VII

Wert thou some Starr which from the ruin'd roofe
Of shak't Olympus by mischance didst fall;
Which carefull *Jove* in natures true behoofe   45
Took up, and in fit place did reinstall?
Or did of late earths Sonnes besiege the wall
   Of sheenie Heav'n, and thou some goddess fled
Amongst us here below to hide thy nectar'd head?

VIII

Or wert thou that just Maid who once before   50
Forsook the hated earth, O tell me sooth
And cam'st again to visit us once more?
Or wert thou Mercy that sweet smiling Youth?
Or that crown'd Matron sage white-robed Truth?
   Or any other of that heav'nly brood   55
Let down in clowdie throne to do the world some good?

IX

Or wert thou of the golden-winged hoast,
Who having clad thy self in human weed,
To earth from thy præfixed seat didst poast,
And after short abode flie back with speed,   60
As if to shew what creatures Heav'n doth breed,
   Thereby to set the hearts of men on fire
To scorn the sordid world, and unto Heav'n aspire.

53 Or wert thou that sweet smiling Youth!] Ed. 2

X

But oh why didst thou not stay here below
To bless us with thy heav'n-lov'd innocence,   65
To slake his wrath whom sin hath made our foe,
To turn Swift-rushing black perdition hence,
Or drive away the slaughtering pestilence,
　　To stand 'twixt us and our deserved smart?
But thou canst best perform that office where thou art.   70

XI

Then thou the mother of so sweet a child
Her false imagin'd loss cease to lament,
And wisely learn to curb thy sorrows wild;
Think what a present thou to God hast sent,
And render him with patience what he lent;   75
　　This if thou do he will an off-spring give,
That till the worlds last-end shall make thy name to live.

Anno Aetatis 19. *At a Vacation Exercise in the Colledge, part* Latin, *part* English. *The* Latin *speeches ended, the* English *thus began*

HAIL native Language, that by sinews weak
Didst move my first endeavouring tongue to speak,
And mad'st imperfect words with childish tripps,
Half unpronounc't, slide through my infant-lipps,
Driving dum silence from the portal dore,   5
Where he had mutely sate two years before:
Here I salute thee and thy pardon ask,
That now I use thee in my latter task:
Small loss it is that thence can come unto thee,
I know my tongue but little Grace can do thee: 10
Thou needst not be ambitious to be first,
Believe me I have thither packt the worst:
And, if it happen as I did forecast,
The daintest dishes shall be serv'd up last.
I pray thee then deny me not thy aide   15
For this same small neglect that I have made:
But haste thee strait to do me once a Pleasure,
And from thy wardrope bring thy chiefest treasure;

Not those new fangled toys, and trimming slight
Which takes our late fantasticks with delight, 20
But cull those richest Robes, and gay'st attire
Which deepest Spirits, and choicest Wits desire:
I have some naked thoughts that rove about
And loudly knock to have their passage out;
And wearie of their place do only stay 25
Till thou hast deck't them in thy best aray;
That so they may without suspect or fears
Fly swiftly to this fair Assembly's ears;
Yet I had rather if I were to chuse,
Thy service in some graver subject use, 30
Such as may make thee search thy coffers round,
Before thou cloath my fancy in fit sound:
Such where the deep transported mind may soare
Above the wheeling poles, and at Heav'ns dore
Look in, and see each blissful Deitie 35
How he before the thunderous throne doth lie,
Listening to what unshorn *Apollo* sings
To th'touch of golden wires, while *Hebe* brings
Immortal Nectar to her Kingly Sire:
Then passing through the Spheres of watchful fire, 40
And mistie Regions of wide air next under,
And hills of Snow and lofts of piled Thunder,
May tell at length how green-ey'd *Neptune* raves,
In Heav'ns defiance mustering all his waves;
Then sing of secret things that came to pass 45
When Beldam Nature in her cradle was;
And last of Kings and Queens and *Hero's* old,
Such as the wise *Demodocus* once told
In solemn Songs at King *Alcinous* feast,
While sad *Ulisses* soul and all the rest 50
Are held with his melodious harmonie
In willing chains and sweet captivitie.
But fie my wandring Muse how thou dost stray!
Expectance calls thee now another way,
Thou know'st it must be now thy only bent 55
To keep in compass of thy Predicament:
Then quick about thy purpos'd buisness come,
That to the next I may resign my Roome.

Then Ens *is represented as Father of the Prædicaments his ten Sons, whereof the*
Eldest stood for Substance *with his Canons, which* Ens *thus speaking, explains.*

Good luck befriend thee Son; for at thy birth
The Faiery Ladies daunc't upon the hearth;   60
Thy drowsie Nurse hath sworn she did them spie
Come tripping to the Room where thou didst lie;
And sweetly singing round about thy Bed
Strew all their blessings on thy sleeping Head.
She heard them give thee this, that thou should'st still   65
From eyes of mortals walk invisible;
Yet there is something that doth force my fear,
For once it was my dismal hap to hear
A *Sybil* old, bow-bent with crooked age,
That far events full wisely could presage,   70
And in Times long and dark Prospective Glass
Fore-saw what future dayes should bring to pass,
Your Son, said she, (nor can you it prevent)
Shall subject be to many an Accident.
O're all his Brethren he shall Reign as King,   75
Yet every one shall make him underling,
And those that cannot live from him asunder
Ungratefully shall strive to keep him under;
In worth and excellence he shall out-go them,
Yet being above them, he shall be below them;   80
From others he shall stand in need of nothing,
Yet on his Brothers shall depend for Cloathing.
To find a Foe it shall not be his hap,
And peace shall lull him in her flowry lap;
Yet shall he live in strife, and at his dore   85
Devouring war shall never cease to roare:
Yea it shall be his natural property
To harbour those that are at enmity.
What power, what force, what mighty spell, if not
Your learned hands, can loose this Gordian knot?   90

The next, Quantity *and* Quality, *spake in Prose, then* Relation *was call'd by his Name.*

Rivers arise; whether thou be the Son,
Of utmost *Tweed*, or *Oose*, or gulphie *Dun*,
Or *Trent*, who like some earth-born Giant spreads

His thirty Armes along the indented Meads,
Or sullen *Mole* that runneth underneath,   95
Or *Severn* swift, guilty of Maidens death,
Or Rockie *Avon*, or of Sedgie *Lee*,
Or Coaly *Tine*, or antient hallowed *Dee*,
Or *Humber* loud that keeps the *Scythians* Name,
Or *Medway* smooth, or Royal Towred *Thame*.   100

The rest was Prose.

The Passion

I

ERE-while of Musick, and Ethereal mirth,
Wherwith the stage of Ayr and Earth did ring,
And joyous news of heav'nly Infants birth,
My muse with Angels did divide to sing;
But headlong joy is ever on the wing,   5
    In Wintry solstice like the shortn'd light
Soon swallow'd up in dark and long out-living night.

II

For now to sorrow must I tune my song,
And set my Harpe to notes of saddest wo,
Which on our dearest Lord did sease ere long,   10
Dangers, and snares, and wrongs, and worse then so,
Which he for us did freely undergo.
    Most perfet *Heroe*, try'd in heaviest plight
Of labours huge and hard, too hard for human wight.

III

He sovran Priest stooping his regall head   15
That dropt with odorous oil down his fair eyes,
Poor fleshly Tabernacle entered,
His starry front low-rooft beneath the skies;
O what a Mask was there, what a disguise!
    Yet more; the stroke of death he must abide,   20
Then lies him meekly down fast by his Brethrens side.

IV

These latter scenes confine my roving vers,
To this Horizon is my *Phoebus* bound;
His Godlike acts, and his temptations fierce,
And former sufferings other where are found;   25
Loud o're the rest *Cremona's* Trump doth sound;
    Me softer airs befit, and softer strings
Of Lute, or Viol still, more apt for mournful things.

V

Befriend me Night best Patroness of grief,
Over the Pole thy thickest mantle throw,   30
And work my flatter'd fancy to belief,
That Heav'n and Earth are colour'd with my wo;
My sorrows are too dark for Day to know:
    The leaves should all be black wheron I write,
And letters where my tears have washt a wannish white.   35

VI

See see the Chariot, and those rushing wheels,
That whirl'd the Prophet up at *Chebar* flood,
My spirit som transporting *Cherub* feels,
To bear me where the Towers of *Salem* stood,
Once glorious Towers, now sunk in guiltles blood;   40
    There doth my soul in holy vision sit
In pensive trance, and anguish, and ecstatick fit.

VII

Mine eye hath found that sad Sepulchral rock
That was the Casket of Heav'ns richest store,
And here though grief my feeble hands up-lock,   45
Yet on the softned Quarry would I score
My plaining vers as lively as before;
    For sure so well instructed are my tears,
That they would fitly fall in order'd Characters.

VIII

Or should I thence hurried on viewles wing,   50
Take up a weeping on the Mountains wilde,
The gentle neighbourhood of grove and spring
Would soon unboosom all thir Echoes milde,
And I (for grief is easily beguild)
  Might think th'infection of my sorrows loud,   55
Had got a race of mourners on som pregnant cloud.

> *This Subject the Author finding to be above the yeers he had,*
> *when he wrote it, and nothing satisfi'd with what was*
> *begun, left it unfinisht.*

On Time

FLY envious *Time*, till thou run out thy race,
Call on the lazy leaden-stepping hours,
Whose speed is but the heavy Plummets pace;
And glut thy self with what thy womb devours,
Which is no more then what is false and vain,   5
And meerly mortal dross;
So little is our loss,
So little is thy gain.
For when as each thing bad thou hast entomb'd,
And last of all, thy greedy self consum'd,   10
Then long Eternity shall greet our bliss
With an individual kiss;
And Joy shall overtake us as a flood,
When every thing that is sincerely good
And perfetly divine,   15
With Truth, and Peace, and Love shall ever shine
About the supreme Throne
Of him, t'whose happy-making sight alone,
When once our heav'nly-guided soul shall clime,
Then all this Earthy grosnes quit,   20
Attir'd with Stars, we shall for ever sit,
  Triumphing over Death, and Chance, and thee O Time.

Upon the Circumcision

YE flaming Powers, and winged Warriours bright,
That erst with Musick, and triumphant song
First heard by happy watchful Shepherds ear,
So sweetly sung your Joy the Clouds along
Through the soft silence of the list'ning night;   5
Now mourn, and if sad share with us to bear
Your fiery essence can distill no tear,
Burn in your sighs, and borrow
Seas wept from our deep sorrow;
He who with all Heav'ns heraldry whileare   10
Enter'd the world, now bleeds to give us ease;
Alas, how soon our sin
  Sore doth begin
    His Infancy to sease!
O more exceeding love or law more just?   15
Just law indeed, but more exceeding love!
For we by rightfull doom remediles
Were lost in death, till he that dwelt above
High thron'd in secret bliss, for us frail dust
Emptied his glory, ev'n to nakednes;   20
And that great Cov'nant which we still transgress
Intirely satisfi'd,
And the full wrath beside
Of vengeful Justice bore for our excess,
And seals obedience first with wounding smart   25
This day, but O ere long
Huge pangs and strong
    Will pierce more neer his heart.

At a solemn Musick

BLEST pair of *Sirens*, pledges of Heav'ns joy,
Sphear-born harmonious Sisters, Voice, and Vers,
Wed your divine sounds, and mixt power employ
Dead things with inbreath'd sense able to pierce,
And to our high-rais'd phantasie present,   5
That undisturbed Song of pure concent,

At a solemn Musick 6 concent] Ed. 2, T.MS.: content Ed. 1

Ay sung before the saphire-colour'd throne
To him that sits theron
With Saintly shout, and solemn Jubily,
Where the bright Seraphim in burning row   10
Their loud up-lifted Angel trumpets blow,
And the Cherubick host in thousand quires
Touch their immortal Harps of golden wires,
With those just Spirits that wear victorious Palms,
Hymns devout and holy Psalms   15
Singing everlastingly;
That we on Earth with undiscording voice
May rightly answer that melodious noise;
As once we did, till disproportion'd sin
Jarr'd against natures chime, and with harsh din   20
Broke the fair musick that all creatures made
To their great Lord, whose love their motion sway'd
In perfet Diapason, whilst they stood
In first obedience, and their state of good.
O may we soon again renew that Song,   25
And keep in tune with Heav'n, till God ere long
To his celestial consort us unite,
To live with him, and sing in endles morn of light.

An Epitaph on the Marchioness of
Winchester

THIS rich Marble doth enterr
The honour'd Wife of *Winchester*,
A Vicounts daughter, an Earls heir,
Besides what her vertues fair
Added to her noble birth,
More then she could own from Earth.   5
Summers three times eight save one
She had told, alas too soon,
After so short time of breath,
To house with darknes, and with death.   10
Yet had the number of her days
Bin as compleat as was her praise,
Nature and fate had had no strife
In giving limit to her life.

Her high birth, and her graces sweet,   15
Quickly found a lover meet;
The Virgin quire for her request
The God that sits at marriage feast;
He at their invoking came
But with a scarce-wel-lighted flame;   20
And in his Garland as he stood,
Ye might discern a Cipress bud.
Once had the early Matrons run
To greet her of a lovely son,
And now with second hope she goes,   25
And calls *Lucina* to her throws;
But whether by mischance or blame
Atropos for *Lucina* came;
And with remorsles cruelty,
Spoil'd at once both fruit and tree: 30
The haples Babe before his birth
Had burial, yet not laid in earth,
And the languisht Mothers Womb
Was not long a living Tomb.
So have I seen som tender slip   35
Sav'd with care from Winters nip,
The pride of her carnation train,
Pluck't up by som unheedy swain,
Who onely thought to crop the flowr
New shot up from vernall showr;   40
But the fair blossom hangs the head
Side-ways as on a dying bed,
And those Pearls of dew she wears,
Prove to be presaging tears
Which the sad morn had let fall   45
On her hast'ning funerall.
Gentle Lady may thy grave
Peace and quiet ever have;
After this thy travail sore
Sweet rest sease thee evermore,   50
That to give the world encrease,
Shortned hast thy own lives lease;

15–24 For MS. version *v.* Commentary, p. 312 *infra*
40 from] Edd. 1, 2 : from a MS.

Here, besides the sorrowing
That thy noble House doth bring,
Here be tears of perfet moan   55
Weept for thee in *Helicon*,
And som Flowers, and som Bays,
For thy Hears to strew the ways,
Sent thee from the banks of *Came*,
Devoted to thy vertuous name;   60
Whilst thou bright Saint high sit'st in glory,
Next her much like to thee in story,
That fair *Syrian* Shepherdess,
Who after yeers of barrennes,
The highly favour'd *Joseph* bore   65
To him that serv'd for her before,
And at her next birth, much like thee,
Through pangs fled to felicity,
Far within the boosom bright
Of blazing Majesty and Light,   70
There with thee, new welcom Saint,
Like fortunes may her soul acquaint,
With thee there clad in radiant sheen,
No Marchioness, but now a Queen.

SONG

On *May* morning

Now the bright morning Star, Dayes harbinger,
Comes dancing from the East, and leads with her
The Flowry *May*, who from her green lap throws
The yellow Cowslip, and the pale Primrose.
  Hail bounteous *May* that dost inspire   5
  Mirth and youth, and warm desire,
  Woods and Groves, are of thy dressing,
  Hill and Dale, doth boast thy blessing.
Thus we salute thee with our early Song,
And welcom thee, and wish thee long.   10

70 Light] Edd. 1, 2 : might MS.

On *Shakespear*. 1630

WHAT needs my *Shakespear* for his honour'd Bones,
The labour of an age in piled Stones,
Or that his hallow'd reliques should be hid
Under a Star-ypointing *Pyramid?*
Dear son of memory, great heir of Fame,   5
What need'st thou such weak witnes of thy name?
Thou in our wonder and astonishment
Hast built thy self a live-long Monument.
For whilst to th' shame of slow-endeavouring art,
Thy easie numbers flow, and that each heart   10
Hath from the leaves of thy unvalu'd Book,
Those Delphick lines with deep impression took,
Then thou our fancy of it self bereaving,
Dost make us Marble with too much conceaving;
And so Sepulcher'd in such pomp dost lie,   15
That Kings for such a Tomb would wish to die.

On the University Carrier

who sickn'd in the time of his vacancy, being forbid to go to *London*, by reason of the Plague

HERE lies old *Hobson*, Death hath broke his girt,
And here alas, hath laid him in the dirt,
Or els the ways being foul, twenty to one,
He's here stuck in a slough, and overthrown.
'Twas such a shifter, that if truth were known,   5
Death was half glad when he had got him down;
For he had any time this ten yeers full,
Dodg'd with him, betwixt *Cambridge* and the Bull.
And surely, Death could never have prevail'd,
Had not his weekly cours of carriage fail'd;   10

On Shakespear. 1630. 1 needs] Edd. 1, 2: neede 1632, 1640: need 1663   4 Star-ypointing]
Edd. 1, 2: starre-ypointing 1632, 1640: starre-ypointed 1632, some copies   6 weak]
Edd. 1, 2: weake 1640: dull 1632, 1663   8 live-long] Edd. 1, 2, 1640: lasting 1632,
1663   10 heart] Edd. 1, 2, 1640: part 1632, 1663
On the University Carrier. 8 Dog'dd him 'twixt Cambridge and the London-Bull 1658

But lately finding him so long at home,
And thinking now his journeys end was come,
And that he had tane up his latest Inne,
In the kind office of a Chamberlin
Shew'd him his room where he must lodge that night,   15
Pull'd off his Boots, and took away the light:
If any ask for him, it shall be sed,
Hobson has supt, and 's newly gon to bed.

Another on the same

HERE lieth one who did most truly prove,
That he could never die while he could move,
So hung his destiny never to rot
While he might still jogg on, and keep his trot,
Made of sphear-metal, never to decay   5
Untill his revolution was at stay.
Time numbers motion, yet (without a crime
'Gainst old truth) motion number'd out his time;
And like an Engin mov'd with wheel and waight,
His principles being ceast, he ended strait.   10
Rest that gives all men life, gave him his death,
And too much breathing put him out of breath;
Nor were it contradiction to affirm
Too long vacation hastned on his term.
Meerly to drive the time away he sickn'd,   15
Fainted, and died, nor would with Ale be quickn'd;
Nay, quoth he, on his swooning bed out-stretch'd,
If I may not carry, sure Ile ne're be fetch'd,
But vow though the cross Doctors all stood hearers,
For one Carrier put down to make six bearers.   20
Ease was his chief disease, and to judge right,
He di'd for heavines that his Cart went light,
His leasure told him that his time was com,
And lack of load, made his life burdensom,
That even to his last breath (ther be that say't)   25
As he were prest to death, he cry'd more waight;

14 In the kind office] Edd. 1, 2: In craftie likenes MS.
Another on the same. v. Commentary, p. 314 *infra*

But had his doings lasted as they were,
He had bin an immortall Carrier.
Obedient to the Moon he spent his date
In cours reciprocal, and had his fate   30
Linkt to the mutual flowing of the Seas,
Yet (strange to think) his wain was his increase:
His Letters are deliver'd all and gon,
Onely remains this superscription.

L'Allegro

HENCE loathed Melancholy
   Of *Cerberus*, and blackest midnight born,
In *Stygian* Cave forlorn
   'Mongst horrid shapes, and shreiks, and sights unholy,
Find out som uncouth cell,   5
   Wher brooding darknes spreads his jealous wings,
And the night-Raven sings;
   There under *Ebon* shades, and low-brow'd Rocks,
As ragged as thy Locks,
   In dark *Cimmerian* desert ever dwell.   10
But com thou Goddes fair and free,
In Heav'n ycleap'd *Euphrosyne*,
And by men, heart-easing Mirth,
Whom lovely *Venus* at a birth
With two sister Graces more   15
To Ivy-crowned *Bacchus* bore;
Or whether (as som Sager sing)
The frolick Wind that breathes the Spring,
Zephir with *Aurora* playing,
As he met her once a Maying,   20
There on Beds of Violets blew,
And fresh-blown Roses washt in dew,
Fill'd her with thee a daughter fair,
So bucksom, blith, and debonair.
Haste thee nymph, and bring with thee   25
Jest and youthful Jollity,
Quips and Cranks, and wanton Wiles,
Nods, and Becks, and Wreathed Smiles,

Such as hang on *Hebe's* cheek,
And love to live in dimple sleek;   30
Sport that wrincled Care derides,
And Laughter holding both his sides.
Com, and trip it as ye go
On the light fantastick toe,
And in thy right hand lead with thee,   35
The Mountain Nymph, sweet Liberty;
And if I give thee honour due,
Mirth, admit me of thy crue
To live with her, and live with thee,
In unreproved pleasures free;   40
To hear the Lark begin his flight,
And singing startle the dull night,
From his watch-towre in the skies,
Till the dappled dawn doth rise;
Then to com in spight of sorrow,   45
And at my window bid good morrow,
Through the Sweet-Briar, or the Vine,
Or the twisted Eglantine.
While the Cock with lively din,
Scatters the rear of darknes thin,   50
And to the stack, or the Barn dore,
Stoutly struts his Dames before,
Oft list'ning how the Hounds and horn,
Chearly rouse the slumbring morn,
From the side of som Hoar Hill,   55
Through the high wood echoing shrill.
Som time walking not unseen
By Hedge-row Elms, on Hillocks green,
Right against the Eastern gate,
Where the great Sun begins his state,   60
Rob'd in flames, and Amber light,
The clouds in thousand Liveries dight,
While the Plowman neer at hand,
Whistles ore the Furrow'd Land,
And the Milkmaid singeth blithe,   65
And the Mower whets his sithe,
And every Shepherd tells his tale

33 ye] Ed. 1 : you Ed. 2

Under the Hawthorn in the dale.
Streit mine eye hath caught new pleasures
Whilst the Lantskip round it measures,   70
Russet Lawns, and Fallows Gray,
Where the nibling flocks do stray,
Mountains on whose barren brest
The labouring clouds do often rest:
Meadows trim with Daisies pide,   75
Shallow Brooks, and Rivers wide.
Towers, and Battlements it sees
Boosom'd high in tufted Trees,
Where perhaps som beauty lies,
The Cynosure of neighbouring eyes.   80
Hard by, a Cottage chimney smokes,
From betwixt two aged Okes,
Where *Corydon* and *Thyrsis* met,
Are at their savory dinner set
Of Hearbs, and other Country Messes,   85
Which the neat-handed *Phillis* dresses;
And then in haste her Bowre she leaves,
With *Thestylis* to bind the Sheaves;
Or if the earlier season lead
To the tann'd Haycock in the Mead,   90
Som times with secure delight
The up-land Hamlets will invite,
When the merry Bells ring round,
And the jocond rebecks sound
To many a youth, and many a maid,   95
Dancing in the Chequer'd shade;
And young and old com forth to play
On a Sunshine Holyday,
Till the live-long day-light fail,
Then to the Spicy Nut-brown Ale,   100
With stories told of many a feat,
How *Faery Mab* the junkets eat,
She was pincht, and pull'd she sed,
And he by Friars Lanthorn led
Tells how the drudging *Goblin* swet,   105
To ern his Cream-bowle duly set,

104 And he by] Ed. 1 : And by the Ed. 2

When in one night, ere glimps of morn,
His shadowy Flale hath thresh'd the Corn
That ten day-labourers could not end,
Then lies him down the Lubbar Fend,   110
And stretch'd out all the Chimney's length,
Basks at the fire his hairy strength;
And Crop-full out of dores he flings,
Ere the first Cock his Mattin rings.
Thus don the Tales, to bed they creep,   115
By whispering Windes soon lull'd asleep.
Towred Cities please us then,
And the busie humm of men,
Where throngs of Knights and Barons bold,
In weeds of Peace high triumphs hold,   120
With store of Ladies, whose bright eies
Rain influence, and judge the prise
Of Wit, or Arms, while both contend
To win her Grace, whom all commend.
There let *Hymen* oft appear   125
In Saffron robe, with Taper clear,
And pomp, and feast, and revelry,
With mask, and antique Pageantry,
Such sights as youthfull Poets dream
On Summer eeves by haunted stream.   130
Then to the well-trod stage anon,
If *Jonsons* learned Sock be on,
Or sweetest *Shakespear* fancies childe,
Warble his native Wood-notes wilde;
And ever against eating Cares,   135
Lap me in soft *Lydian* Aires,
Married to immortal verse
Such as the meeting soul may pierce
In notes, with many a winding bout
Of lincked sweetnes long drawn out,   140
With wanton heed, and giddy cunning,
The melting voice through mazes running;
Untwisting all the chains that ty
The hidden soul of harmony.
That *Orpheus* self may heave his head   145
From golden slumber on a bed

Of heapt *Elysian* flowres, and hear
Such streins as would have won the ear
Of *Pluto*, to have quite set free
His half regain'd *Eurydice*.   150
These delights, if thou canst give,
Mirth with thee, I mean to live.

Il Penseroso

HENCE vain deluding joyes,
   The brood of folly without father bred,
How little you bested,
   Or fill the fixed mind with all your toyes;
Dwell in som idle brain,   5
   And fancies fond with gaudy shapes possess,
As thick and numberless
   As the gay motes that people the Sun Beams,
Or likest hovering dreams
   The fickle Pensioners of *Morpheus* train.   10
But hail thou Goddes, sage and holy,
Hail divinest Melancholy,
Whose Saintly visage is too bright
To hit the Sense of human sight;
And therfore to our weaker view,   15
Ore laid with black staid Wisdoms hue,
Black, but such as in esteem,
Prince *Memnons* sister might beseem,
Or that Starr'd *Ethiope* Queen that strove
To set her beauties praise above   20
The Sea Nymphs, and their powers offended.
Yet thou art higher far descended,
Thee bright-hair'd *Vesta* long of yore,
To solitary *Saturn* bore;
His daughter she (in *Saturns* raign,   25
Such mixture was not held a stain)
Oft in glimmering Bowres, and glades
He met her, and in secret shades
Of woody *Ida's* inmost grove,
While yet there was no fear of *Jove*.   30

Com pensive Nun, devout and pure,
Sober, stedfast, and demure,
All in a robe of darkest grain,
Flowing with majestick train,
And sable stole of *Cipres* Lawn,   35
Over thy decent shoulders drawn.
Com, but keep thy wonted state,
With eev'n step, and musing gate,
And looks commercing with the skies,
Thy rapt soul sitting in thine eyes: 40
There held in holy passion still,
Forget thy self to Marble, till
With a sad Leaden downward cast,
Thou fix them on the earth as fast.
And joyn with thee calm Peace, and Quiet,   45
Spare Fast, that oft with gods doth diet,
And hears the Muses in a ring,
Ay round about *Joves* Altar sing.
And adde to these retired Leasure,
That in trim Gardens takes his pleasure;   50
But first, and chiefest, with thee bring,
Him that yon soars on golden wing,
Guiding the fiery-wheeled throne,
The Cherub Contemplation,
And the mute Silence hist along,   55
'Less *Philomel* will daign a Song,
In her sweetest, saddest plight,
Smoothing the rugged brow of night,
While *Cynthia* checks her Dragon yoke,
Gently o're th'accustom'd Oke;   60
Sweet Bird that shunn'st the noise of folly,
Most musicall, most melancholy!
Thee Chauntress oft the Woods among,
I woo to hear thy Eeven-Song;
And missing thee, I walk unseen   65
On the dry smooth-shaven Green,
To behold the wandring Moon,
Riding neer her highest noon,
Like one that had bin led astray
Through the Heav'ns wide pathles way;   70

And oft, as if her head she bow'd,
Stooping through a fleecy cloud.
Oft on a Plat of rising ground,
I hear the far-off *Curfeu* sound,
Over som wide-water'd shoar,   75
Swinging slow with sullen roar;
Or if the Ayr will not permit,
Som still removed place will fit,
Where glowing Embers through the room
Teach light to counterfeit a gloom,   80
Far from all resort of mirth,
Save the Cricket on the hearth,
Or the Belmans drousie charm,
To bless the dores from nightly harm:
Or let my Lamp at midnight hour,   85
Be seen in som high lonely Towr,
Where I may oft out-watch the *Bear*,
With thrice great *Hermes*, or unsphear
The spirit of *Plato* to unfold
What Worlds, or what vast Regions hold   90
The immortal mind that hath forsook
Her mansion in this fleshly nook:
And of those *Dæmons* that are found
In fire, air, flood, or under ground,
Whose power hath a true consent   95
With Planet, or with Element.
Som time let Gorgeous Tragedy
In Scepter'd Pall com sweeping by,
Presenting *Thebs*, or *Pelops* line,
Or the tale of *Troy* divine.   100
Or what (though rare) of later age,
Ennobled hath the Buskind stage.
But, O sad Virgin, that thy power
Might raise *Musæus* from his bower,
Or bid the soul of *Orpheus* sing   105
Such notes as warbled to the string,
Drew Iron tears down *Pluto's* cheek,
And made Hell grant what Love did seek.
Or call up him that left half told
The story of *Cambuscan* bold,   110

Of *Camball*, and of *Algarsife*,
And who had *Canace* to wife,
That own'd the vertuous Ring and Glass,
And of the wondrous Hors of Brass,
On which the *Tartar* King did ride;   115
And if ought els, great *Bards* beside,
In sage and solemn tunes have sung,
Of Turneys and of Trophies hung;
Of Forests, and inchantments drear,
Where more is meant then meets the ear.   120
Thus Night oft see me in thy pale career,
Till civil-suited Morn appeer,
Not trickt and frounc't as she was wont,
With the Attick Boy to hunt,
But kerchef't in a comly Cloud,   125
While rocking Winds are Piping loud,
Or usher'd with a shower still,
When the gust hath blown his fill,
Ending on the russling Leaves,
With minute drops from off the Eaves.   130
And when the Sun begins to fling
His flaring beams, me Goddes bring
To arched walks of twilight groves,
And shadows brown that *Sylvan* loves
Of Pine, or monumental Oake,   135
Where the rude Ax with heaved stroke,
Was never heard the Nymphs to daunt,
Or fright them from their hallow'd haunt.
There in close covert by som Brook,
Where no profaner eye may look,   140
Hide me from Day's garish eie,
While the Bee with Honied thie,
That at her flowry work doth sing,
And the Waters murmuring
With such consort as they keep,   145
Entice the dewy-feather'd Sleep;
And let som strange mysterious dream,
Wave at his Wings in Airy stream,
Of lively portrature display'd,
Softly on my eye-lids laid.   150

And as I wake, sweet musick breath
Above, about, or underneath,
Sent by som spirit to mortals good,
Or th'unseen Genius of the Wood.
But let my due feet never fail,   155
To walk the studious Cloysters pale,
And love the high embowed Roof,
With antick Pillars massy proof,
And storied Windows richly dight,
Casting a dimm religious light.   160
There let the pealing Organ blow,
To the full voic'd Quire below,
In Service high, and Anthems cleer,
As may with sweetnes, through mine ear,
Dissolve me into extasies,   165
And bring all Heav'n before mine eyes.
And may at last my weary age
Find out the peacefull hermitage,
The Hairy Gown and Mossy Cell,
Where I may sit and rightly spell,   170
Of every Star that Heav'n doth shew,
And every Herb that sips the dew;
Till old experience do attain
To somthing like Prophetic strain.
These pleasures *Melancholy* give,   175
And I with thee will choose to live.

SONNETS

I

O Nightingale, that on yon bloomy Spray
    Warbl'st at eeve, when all the Woods are still,
    Thou with fresh hope the Lovers heart dost fill,
    While the jolly hours lead on propitious *May*,
Thy liquid notes that close the eye of Day,   5
    First heard before the shallow Cuccoo's bill,
    Portend success in love; O if *Jove's* will
    Have linkt that amorous power to thy soft lay,

Now timely sing, ere the rude Bird of Hate
  Foretell my hopeles doom in som Grove ny: 10
  As thou from yeer to yeer hast sung too late
For my relief; yet hadst no reason why:
  Whether the Muse, or Love call thee his mate,
  Both them I serve, and of their train am I.

II

  Donna leggiadra, il cui bel nome honora
    L'herbosa val di Rheno, e il nobil varco,
    Ben è colui d'ogni valore scarco,
    Qual tuo spirto gentil non innamora,
Che dolcemente mostrasi di fuora,   5
    De' suoi atti soavi giamai parco,
    E i don, che son d'Amor saette ed arco,
    Là onde l'alta tua virtù s'infiora.
Quando tu vaga parli, o lieta canti
    Che mover possa duro alpestre legno,   10
    Guardi ciascun a gli occhi, ed a gli orecchi
L'entrata, chi di te si truova indegno;
    Gratia sola di sù gli vaglia, inanti
    Che'l disio amoroso al cuor s'invecchi.

III

Qual in colle aspro, a l' imbrunir di sera,
  L'avezza giovinetta pastorella
  Va bagnando l'herbetta strana e bella,
  Che mal si spande a disusata spera,
Fuor di sua natia alma primavera,   5
  Così Amor meco insù la lingua snella
  Desta il fior novo di strania favella,
  Mentre io di te, vezzosamente altera,
Canto, dal mio buon popol non inteso,
  E'l bel Tamigi cangio col bel Arno.   10
  Amor lo volse, ed io a l'altrui peso
Seppi ch'Amor cosa mai volse indarno.
  Deh! foss'il mio cuor lento e'l duro seno
  A chi pianta dal ciel sì buon terreno.

Canzone

Ridonsi donne e giovani amorosi,
M'accostandosi attorno, e: Perche scrivi,
Perche tu scrivi in lingua ignota e strana
Verseggiando d'amor, e come t'osi?
Dinne, se la tua speme sia mai vana,   5
E de' pensieri lo miglior t'arrivi.
Così mi van burlando. Altri rivi,
Altri lidi t'aspettan, ed altre onde,
Nelle cui verdi sponde
Spuntati ad hor ad hor a la tua chioma   10
L'immortal guiderdon d'eterne frondi:
Perche alle spalle tue soverchia soma?
   Canzon, dirotti, e tu per me rispondi:
Dice mia Donna, e'l suo dir è il mio cuore,
Questa è lingua di çui si vanta Amore.   15

IV

Diodati, e te'l dirò con maraviglia,
  Quel ritroso io, ch'amor spreggiar soléa
  E de' suoi lacci spesso mi ridéa,
  Già caddi, ov'huom dabben talhor s'impiglia.
Nè treccie d'oro, nè guancia vermiglia,   5
  M'abbaglian sì, ma sotto nova idea
  Pellegrina bellezza che'l cuor bea,
  Portamenti alti honesti, e nelle ciglia
Quel sereno fulgor d'amabil nero,
  Parole adorne di lingua più d'una,   10
  E'l cantar che di mezzo l'hemispero
Traviar ben può la faticosa Luna;
  E degli occhi suoi avventa sì gran fuoco
  Che l'incerar gli orecchi mi fia poco.

V

Per certo i bei vostr'occhi, Donna mia,
  Esser non può che non sian lo mio sole,
  Sì mi percuoton forte, come ei suole
  Per l'arene di Libia chi s'invia;

Mentre un caldo vapor (nè senti' pria)   5
  Da quel lato si spinge ove mi duole,
  Che forse amanti nelle lor parole
  Chiaman sospir; io non so che si sia:
Parte rinchiusa, e turbida si cela
  Scossomi il petto, e poi n'uscendo poco,   10
  Quivi d'attorno o s'agghiaccia, o s'ingiela;
Ma quanto a gli occhi giunge a trovar loco
  Tutte le notti a me suol far piovose,
  Finchè mia Alba rivien colma di rose.

VI

Giovane piano, e semplicetto amante,
  Poi che fuggir me stesso in dubbio sono,
  Madonna, a voi del mio cuor l'humil dono
  Farò divoto; io certo a prove tante
L'hebbi fedele, intrepido, costante,   5
  Di pensieri leggiadro, accorto, e buono;
  Quando rugge il gran mondo, e scocca il tuono,
  S'arma di se, e d'intero diamante,
Tanto del forse, e d'invidia sicuro,
  Di timori, e speranze al popol use,   10
  Quanto d'ingegno, e d'alto valor vago,
E di cetra sonora, e delle Muse;
  Sol troverete in tal parte men duro
  Ove Amor mise l'insanabil ago.

VII

How soon hath Time the suttle theef of youth,
  Stoln on his wing my three and twentith yeer!
  My hasting dayes flie on with full career,
  But my late spring no bud or blossom shew'th.
Perhaps my semblance might deceive the truth,   5
  That I to manhood am arriv'd so near,
  And inward ripenes doth much less appear,
  That som more timely-happy spirits indu'th.
Yet be it less or more, or soon or slow,
  It shall be still in strictest measure eev'n,   10

To that same lot, however mean, or high,
Toward which Time leads me, and the will of Heav'n;
    All is, if I have grace to use it so,
    As ever in my great task-Masters eye.

VIII

Captain or Colonel, or Knight in Arms,
    Whose chance on these defenceless dores may sease,
    If deed of honour did thee ever please,
    Guard them, and him within protect from harms,
He can requite thee, for he knows the charms   5
    That call Fame on such gentle acts as these,
    And he can spred thy Name o're Lands and Seas,
    What ever clime the Suns bright circle warms.
Lift not thy spear against the Muses Bowre,
    The great *Emathian* Conqueror bid spare   10
    The house of *Pindarus*, when Temple and Towre
Went to the ground: And the repeated air
    Of sad *Electra's* Poet had the power
    To save th'*Athenian* Walls from ruine bare.

IX

Lady that in the prime of earliest youth,
    Wisely hast shun'd the broad way and the green,
    And with those few art eminently seen,
    That labour up the Hill of heav'nly Truth,
The better part with *Mary* and with *Ruth*,   5
    Chosen thou hast, and they that overween,
    And at thy growing vertues fret their spleen,
    No anger find in thee, but pity and ruth.
Thy care is fixt and zealously attends
    To fill thy odorous Lamp with deeds of light,   10
    And Hope that reaps not shame. Therefore be sure
Thou, when the Bridegroom with his feastfull friends
    Passes to bliss at the mid hour of night,
    Hast gain'd thy entrance, Virgin wise and pure.

VIII. 3] *So Ed.* 2 : If ever deed of honour did thee please, Ed. 1, T.MS.

X

Daughter to that good Earl, once President
  Of *Englands* Counsel, and her Treasury,
  Who liv'd in both, unstain'd with gold or fee,
  And left them both, more in himself content,
Till the sad breaking of that Parlament   5
  Broke him, as that dishonest victory
  At *Chæronéa*, fatal to liberty
  Kill'd with report that Old man eloquent,
Though later born, then to have known the dayes
  Wherin your Father flourisht, yet by you   10
  Madam, me thinks I see him living yet;
So well your words his noble vertues praise,
  That all both judge you to relate them true,
  And to possess them, Honour'd *Margaret*.

XI

A Book was writ of late call'd *Tetrachordon*;
  And wov'n close, both matter, form and stile;
  The Subject new: it walk'd the Town a while,
  Numbring good intellects; now seldom por'd on.
Cries the stall-reader, bless us! what a word on   5
  A title page is this! and some in file
  Stand spelling fals, while one might walk to Mile-
  End Green. Why is it harder Sirs then Gordon,
Colkitto, or Macdonnel, or Galasp?
  Those rugged names to our like mouths grow sleek   10
  That would have made *Quintilian* stare and gasp.
Thy age, like ours, O Soul of Sir *John Cheek*,
  Hated not Learning wors then Toad or Asp;
  When thou taught'st *Cambridge*, and King *Edward* Greek.

XII. *On the same*

I did but prompt the age to quit their cloggs
  By the known rules of antient libertie,
  When strait a barbarous noise environs me
  Of Owles and Cuckoes, Asses, Apes and Doggs.

As when those Hinds that were transform'd to Froggs   5
    Raild at *Latona's* twin-born progenie
    Which after held the Sun and Moon in fee.
    But this is got by casting Pearl to Hoggs;
That bawle for freedom in their senseless mood,
    And still revolt when truth would set them free.   10
    Licence they mean when they cry libertie;
For who loves that, must first be wise and good;
    But from that mark how far they roave we see
    For all this wast of wealth, and loss of blood.

To *Mr*. H. Lawes, *on his Aires*

XIII

Harry whose tuneful and well measur'd Song
    First taught our English Musick how to span
    Words with just note and accent, not to scan
    With *Midas* Ears, committing short and long;
Thy worth and skill exempts thee from the throng,   5
    With praise anough for Envy to look wan;
    To after-age thou shalt be writ the man,
    That with smooth aire couldst humor best our tongue.
Thou honour'st Verse, and Verse must lend her wing
    To honour thee, the Priest of *Phœbus* Quire   10
    That tun'st their happiest lines in Hymn, or Story.
Dante shall give Fame leave to set thee higher
    Then his *Casella*, whom he woo'd to sing,
    Met in the milder shades of Purgatory.

XIV

When Faith and Love which parted from thee never,
    Had ripen'd thy just soul to dwell with God,
    Meekly thou didst resign this earthy load
    Of Death, call'd Life; which us from Life doth sever.
Thy Works and Alms and all thy good Endeavour   5
    Staid not behind, nor in the grave were trod;
    But as Faith pointed with her golden rod,
    Follow'd thee up to joy and bliss for ever.

XIII. 9 lend] 1648, T.MS.: send Ed. 2

Love led them on, and Faith who knew them best
  Thy hand-maids, clad them o're with purple beams   10
  And azure wings, that up they flew so drest,
And spake the truth of thee in glorious Theams
  Before the Judge, who thenceforth bid thee rest
  And drink thy fill of pure immortal streams.

XV

On the Lord Gen. Fairfax *at the seige of* Colchester

Fairfax, whose name in armes through Europe rings
  Filling each mouth with envy, or with praise,
  And all her jealous monarchs with amaze,
  And rumors loud, that daunt remotest kings,
Thy firm unshak'n vertue ever brings   5
  Victory home, though new rebellions raise
  Thir Hydra heads, and the fals North displaies
  Her brok'n league, to impe their serpent wings,
O yet a nobler task awaites thy hand;
  For what can Warr, but endless warr still breed,   10
  Till Truth, and Right from Violence be freed,
And Public Faith cleard from the shamefull brand
  Of Public Fraud. In vain doth Valour bleed
  While Avarice, and Rapine share the land.

XVI

To the Lord Generall Cromwell *May* 1652
On the proposalls of certaine ministers at the Committee for Propagation of the Gospell.

Cromwell, our cheif of men, who through a cloud
  Not of warr onely, but detractions rude,
  Guided by faith and matchless Fortitude
  To peace and truth thy glorious way hast plough'd,
And on the neck of crowned Fortune proud   5
  Hast reard Gods Trophies, and his work pursu'd,
  While *Darwen* stream with blood of Scotts imbru'd,
  And *Dunbarr feild* resounds thy praises loud,

XIV. 12 spake] T.MS.: speak Ed. 2   in] T.MS.: on Ed. 2

And *Worsters* laureat wreath; yet much remaines
   To conquer still; peace hath her victories   10
   No less renownd then warr, new foes arise
Threatning to bind our soules with secular chaines:
   Helpe us to save free Conscience from the paw
   Of hireling wolves whose Gospell is their maw.

XVII

To Sr Henry Vane *the younger*

Vane, young in yeares, but in sage counsell old,
   Then whome a better Senatour nere held
   The helme of *Rome*, when gownes not armes repelld
   The feirce *Epeirot* and the *African* bold,
Whether to settle peace, or to unfold   5
   The drift of hollow states, hard to be spelld,
   Then to advise how warr may best, upheld,
   Move by her two maine nerves, Iron and Gold
In all her equipage; besides to know
   Both spirituall powre and civill, what each meanes   10
   What severs each thou'hast learnt, which few have don.
The bounds of either sword to thee wee ow.
   Therfore on thy firme hand religion leanes
   In peace, and reck'ns thee her eldest son.

On the late *Massacher in* Piemont

XVIII

Avenge O Lord thy slaughter'd Saints, whose bones
   Lie scatter'd on the Alpine mountains cold,
   Ev'n them who kept thy truth so pure of old
   When all our Fathers worship't Stocks and Stones,
Forget not: in thy book record their groanes   5
   Who were thy Sheep and in their antient Fold
   Slayn by the bloody *Piemontese* that roll'd
   Mother with Infant down the Rocks. Their moans
The Vales redoubl'd to the Hills, and they

To Heav'n. Their martyr'd blood and ashes sow   10
   O're all th'*Italian* fields where still doth sway
The triple Tyrant: that from these may grow
   A hunderd-fold, who having learnt thy way
   Early may fly the *Babylonian* wo.

XIX

When I consider how my light is spent,
   Ere half my days, in this dark world and wide,
   And that one Talent which is death to hide,
   Lodg'd with me useless, though my Soul more bent
To serve therewith my Maker, and present   5
   My true account, least he returning chide,
   Doth God exact day-labour, light deny'd,
   I fondly ask; But patience to prevent
That murmur, soon replies, God doth not need
   Either man's work or his own gifts, who best   10
   Bear his milde yoak, they serve him best, his State
Is Kingly. Thousands at his bidding speed
   And post o're Land and Ocean without rest:
   They also serve who only stand and waite.

XX

Lawrence of vertuous Father vertuous Son,
   Now that the Fields are dank, and ways are mire,
   Where shall we sometimes meet, and by the fire
   Help wast a sullen day; what may be won
From the hard Season gaining: time will run   5
   On smoother, till *Favonius* re-inspire
   The frozen earth; and cloath in fresh attire
   The Lillie and Rose, that neither sow'd nor spun.
What neat repast shall feast us, light and choice,
   Of Attick tast, with Wine, whence we may rise   10
   To hear the Lute well toucht, or artfull voice
Warble immortal Notes and *Tuskan* Ayre?
   He who of those delights can judge, and spare
   To interpose them oft, is not unwise.

XXI

Cyriack, whose Grandsire on the Royal Bench
  Of Brittish *Themis*, with no mean applause
  Pronounc't and in his volumes taught our Lawes,
  Which others at their Barr so often wrench:
To day deep thoughts resolve with me to drench   5
  In mirth, that after no repenting drawes;
  Let *Euclid* rest and *Archimedes* pause,
  And what the *Swede* intends, and what the *French*.
To measure life, learn thou betimes, and know
  Toward solid good what leads the nearest way;   10
  For other things mild Heav'n a time ordains,
And disapproves that care, though wise in show,
  That with superfluous burden loads the day,
  And when God sends a cheerful hour, refrains.

XXII

To Mr. Cyriack Skinner *upon his Blindness*

Cyriack, this three years day these eys, though clear
  To outward view, of blemish or of spot;
  Bereft of light thir seeing have forgot,
  Nor to thir idle orbs doth sight appear
Of Sun or Moon or Starre throughout the year,   5
  Or man or woman. Yet I argue not
  Against heavns hand or will, nor bate a jot
  Of heart or hope; but still bear vp and steer
Right onward. What supports me, dost thou ask?
  The conscience, Friend, to have lost them overply'd   10
  In Liberties defence, my noble task,
Of which all Europe talks from side to side.
  This thought might lead me through the worlds vain mask
  Content though blind, had I no better guide.

XXIII

Methought I saw my late espoused Saint
  Brought to me like *Alcestis* from the grave,
  Whom *Joves* great Son to her glad Husband gave,
  Rescu'd from death by force though pale and faint.

XXI. 8 intends] T.MS.: intend Ed. 2   XXII. 12 talks] T.MS.: rings 1694

Mine as whom washt from spot of child-bed taint,   5
  Purification in the old Law did save,
  And such, as yet once more I trust to have
  Full sight of her in Heaven without restraint,
Came vested all in white, pure as her mind:
  Her face was vail'd, yet to my fancied sight,   10
  Love, sweetness, goodness, in her person shin'd
So clear, as in no face with more delight.
  But O as to embrace me she enclin'd,
  I wak'd, she fled, and day brought back my night.

On the new forcers of Conscience under the Long PARLAMENT

Because you have thrown of your Prelate Lord,
  And with stiff Vowes renounc'd his Liturgie
  To seise the widdow'd whore Pluralitie
  From them whose sin ye envi'd, not abhor'd,
Dare ye for this adjure the Civill Sword   5
  To force our Consciences that Christ set free,
  And ride us with a classic Hierarchy
  Taught ye by meer *A. S.* and *Rotherford*?
Men whose Life, Learning, Faith and pure intent
  Would have been held in high esteem with *Paul*   10
  Must now be nam'd and printed Hereticks
By shallow *Edwards* and Scotch what d'ye call:
  But we do hope to find out all your tricks,
  Your plots and packings wors then those of *Trent*,
                That so the Parlament   15
May with their wholsom and preventive Shears
Clip your Phylacteries, though bauk your Ears,
                And succour our just Fears
When they shall read this clearly in your charge
New Presbyter is but *Old Priest* writ Large.   20

The Fifth Ode of Horace. *Lib.* I

Quis multa gracilis te puer in Rosa, *Rendred almost word for word without Rhyme according to the Latin Measure, as near as the Language will permit.*

WHAT slender Youth bedew'd with liquid odours
Courts thee on Roses in some pleasant Cave,
 Pyrrha for whom bind'st thou
 In wreaths thy golden Hair,
Plain in thy neatness; O how oft shall he   5
On Faith and changed Gods complain: and Seas
 Rough with black winds and storms
 Unwonted shall admire:
Who now enjoyes thee credulous, all Gold,
Who always vacant, always amiable   10
 Hopes thee; of flattering gales
 Unmindfull. Hapless they
To whom thou untry'd seem'st fair. Me in my vow'd
Picture the sacred wall declares t' have hung
 My dank and dropping weeds   15
 To the stern God of Sea.

Ad Pyrrham: Ode V

Horatius ex Pyrrhae illecebris tanquam e naufragio enataverat, cujus amore irretitos, affirmat esse miseros.

 Quis multa gracilis te puer in rosa
 Perfusus liquidis urget odoribus,
  Grato, Pyrrha, sub antro?
  Cui flavam religas comam
 Simplex munditie? heu quoties fidem   5
 Mutatosque deos flebit, et aspera
  Nigris aequora ventis
  Emirabitur insolens,
 Qui nunc te fruitur credulus aurea:
 Qui semper vacuam, semper amabilem   10
  Sperat, nescius aurae
  Fallacis. miseri quibus
 Intentata nites. me tabula sacer
 Votiva paries indicat uvida
  Suspendisse potenti   15
  Vestimenta maris Deo.

Arcades.

Part of an entertainment presented to the Countess Dowager of *Darby*
at *Harefield*, by som Noble persons of her Family, who appear
on the Scene in pastoral habit, moving toward the
seat of State, with this Song.

1. SONG

Look Nymphs, and Shepherds look,
What sudden blaze of Majesty
Is that which we from hence descry
Too divine to be mistook:
   This this is she   5
To whom our vows and wishes bend,
Heer our solemn search hath end.

Fame that her high worth to raise,
Seem'd erst so lavish and profuse,
We may justly now accuse   10
Of detraction from her praise,
   Less then half we find exprest,
   Envy bid conceal the rest.

Mark what radiant state she spreds,
In circle round her shining throne,   15
Shooting her beams like silver threds,
This this is she alone,
   Sitting like a Goddes bright,
   In the center of her light.

Might she the wise *Latona* be,   20
Or the towred *Cybele*,
Mother of a hunderd gods;
Juno dare's not give her odds;
   Who had thought this clime had held
   A deity so unparalel'd?   25

As they com forward, the Genius of the Wood appears, and
turning toward them, speaks.

Gen. Stay gentle Swains, for though in this disguise,
I see bright honour sparkle through your eyes,
Of famous *Arcady* ye are, and sprung
Of that renowned flood, so often sung,

Divine *Alpheus*, who by secret sluse,   30
Stole under Seas to meet his *Arethuse*;
And ye the breathing Roses of the Wood,
Fair silver-buskind Nymphs as great and good,
I know this quest of yours, and free intent
Was all in honour and devotion ment   35
To the great Mistres of yon princely shrine,
Whom with low reverence I adore as mine,
And with all helpful service will comply
To furder this nights glad solemnity;
And lead ye where ye may more neer behold   40
What shallow-searching *Fame* hath left untold;
Which I full oft amidst these shades alone
Have sate to wonder at, and gaze upon:
For know by lot from *Jove* I am the powr
Of this fair Wood, and live in Oak'n bowr,   45
To nurse the Saplings tall, and curl the grove
With Ringlets quaint, and wanton windings wove.
And all my Plants I save from nightly ill,
Of noisom winds, and blasting vapours chill.
And from the Boughs brush off the evil dew,   50
And heal the harms of thwarting thunder blew,
Or what the cross dire-looking Planet smites,
Or hurtfull Worm with canker'd venom bites.
When Eev'ning gray doth rise, I fetch my round
Over the mount, and all this hallow'd ground,   55
And early ere the odorous breath of morn
Awakes the slumbring leaves, or tasseld horn
Shakes the high thicket, haste I all about,
Number my ranks, and visit every sprout
With puissant words, and murmurs made to bless,   60
But els in deep of night when drowsines
Hath lockt up mortal sense, then listen I
To the celestial *Sirens* harmony,
That sit upon the nine enfolded Sphears,
And sing to those that hold the vital shears,   65
And turn the Adamantine spindle round,
On which the fate of gods and men is wound.
Such sweet compulsion doth in musick ly,
To lull the daughters of *Necessity*,

And keep unsteddy Nature to her law, 70
And the low world in measur'd motion draw
After the heavenly tune, which none can hear
Of human mould with grosse unpurged ear;
And yet such musick worthiest were to blaze
The peerles height of her immortal praise, 75
Whose lustre leads us, and for her most fit,
If my inferior hand or voice could hit
Inimitable sounds, yet as we go,
What ere the skill of lesser gods can show,
I will assay, her worth to celebrate, 80
And so attend ye toward her glittering state;
Where ye may all that are of noble stemm
Approach, and kiss her sacred vestures hemm.

2. SONG

O're the smooth enameld green
Where no print of step hath been, 85
   Follow me as I sing,
    And touch the warbled string.
Under the shady roof
Of branching Elm Star-proof,
   Follow me, 90
I will bring you where she sits,
Clad in splendor as befits
   Her deity.
Such a rural Queen
All *Arcadia* hath not seen. 95

3. SONG

Nymphs and Shepherds dance no more
   By sandy *Ladons* Lillied banks.
On old *Lycæus* or *Cyllene* hoar,
   Trip no more in twilight ranks,
Though *Erymanth* your loss deplore, 100
   A better soyl shall give ye thanks.
From the stony *Mænalus*,
Bring your Flocks, and live with us,

Here ye shall have greater grace,
To serve the Lady of this place. 105
   Though *Syrinx* your *Pans* Mistres were,
   Yet *Syrinx* well might wait on her.
     Such a rural Queen
   All *Arcadia* hath not seen.

JUSTA
EDOVARDO KING
naufrago,
ab
Amicis mœrentibus,
amoris
&
μνείας χάειν.

Si rectè calculum ponas, ubique naufragium est.
Pet. Arb.

CANTABRIGIÆ:

Apud *Thomam Buck*, & *Rogerum Daniel*, celeberrimæ
Academiæ typographos. 1638.

Lycidas

In this Monody the Author bewails a learned Friend, unfortunatly drown'd
in his Passage from *Chester* on the *Irish* Seas, 1637. And by
occasion foretels the ruine of our corrupted Clergy
then in their height.

YET once more, O ye Laurels, and once more
Ye Myrtles brown, with Ivy never-sear,
I com to pluck your Berries harsh and crude,
And with forc'd fingers rude,
Shatter your leaves before the mellowing year.   5
Bitter constraint, and sad occasion dear,
Compels me to disturb your season due:
For *Lycidas* is dead, dead ere his prime
Young *Lycidas*, and hath not left his peer:
Who would not sing for *Lycidas?* he well knew   10
Himself to sing, and build the lofty rhyme.
He must not flote upon his watry bear
Unwept, and welter to the parching wind,
Without the meed of som melodious tear.

  Begin then, Sisters of the sacred well,   15
That from beneath the seat of *Jove* doth spring,
Begin, and somwhat loudly sweep the string.
Hence with denial vain, and coy excuse,
So may som gentle Muse
With lucky words favour my destin'd Urn,   20
And as he passes turn,
And bid fair peace be to my sable shrowd.
For we were nurst upon the self-same hill,
Fed the same flock, by fountain, shade, and rill.

  Together both, ere the high Lawns appear'd   25
Under the opening eye-lids of the morn,
We drove a field, and both together heard
What time the Gray-fly winds her sultry horn,
Batt'ning our flocks with the fresh dews of night,
Oft till the Star that rose, at Ev'ning, bright   30

10 he well knew] T.MS., 1638ᶜ·, 1638 ᴮ·ᴹ·: he knew] 1638, Edd. 1, 2   26 opening] Edd ·
1, 2 :. glimmering] 1638, T.MS. *orig.*   30 Oft till the ev'n-starre bright] 1638, T.MS.
orig.

Toward Heav'ns descent had slop'd his westering wheel.
Mean while the Rural ditties were not mute,
Temper'd to th'Oaten Flute,
Rough *Satyrs* danc'd, and *Fauns* with clov'n heel,
From the glad sound would not be absent long,   35
And old *Damætas* lov'd to hear our song.

But O the heavy change, now thou art gon,
Now thou art gon, and never must return!
Thee Shepherd, thee the Woods, and desert Caves,
With wilde Thyme and the gadding Vine o'regrown,   40
And all their echoes mourn.
The Willows, and the Hazle Copses green,
Shall now no more be seen,
Fanning their joyous Leaves to thy soft layes.
As killing as the Canker to the Rose,   45
Or Taint-worm to the weanling Herds that graze,
Or Frost to Flowers, that their gay wardrop wear,
When first the White-thorn blows;
Such, *Lycidas*, thy loss to Shepherds ear.

Where were ye Nymphs when the remorseless deep   50
Clos'd o're the head of your lov'd *Lycidas*?
For neither were ye playing on the steep,
Where your old *Bards*, the famous *Druids* ly,
Nor on the shaggy top of *Mona* high,
Nor yet where *Deva* spreads her wisard stream: 55
Ay me, I fondly dream!
Had ye bin there . . . for what could that have don?
What could the Muse her self that *Orpheus* bore,
The Muse her self, for her inchanting son
Whom Universal nature did lament,   60
When by the rout that made the hideous roar,
His goary visage down the stream was sent,
Down the swift *Hebrus* to the *Lesbian* shore.

Alas! What boots it with uncessant care
To tend the homely slighted Shepherds trade,   65
And strictly meditate the thankles Muse,
Were it not better don as others use,
To sport with *Amaryllis* in the shade,

31 burnisht wheel 1638: burnisht weele T.MS. *orig.*   47 wardrop wear] Edd. 1, 2:
wardrobe wear 1638: buttons beare *del.* T.MS.   65 tend] Ed. 1, 1638: end Ed. 2

Or with the tangles of *Neæra's* hair?
Fame is the spur that the clear spirit doth raise   70
(That last infirmity of Noble mind)
To scorn delights, and live laborious dayes;
But the fair Guerdon when we hope to find,
And think to burst out into sudden blaze,
Comes the blind *Fury* with th'abhorred shears,   75
And slits the thin-spun life. But not the praise,
Phœbus repli'd, and touch'd my trembling ears;
Fame is no plant that grows on mortal soil,
Nor in the glistering foil
Set off to th'world, nor in broad rumour lies,   80
But lives and spreds aloft by those pure eyes,
And perfet witnes of all-judging *Jove*;
As he pronounces lastly on each deed,
Of so much fame in Heav'n expect thy meed.

    O Fountain *Arethuse*, and thou honour'd floud,   85
Smooth-sliding *Mincius*, crown'd with vocall reeds,
That strain I heard was of a higher mood:
But now my Oate proceeds,
And listens to the Herald of the Sea
That came in *Neptune's* plea,   90
He ask'd the Waves, and ask'd the Fellon winds,
What hard mishap hath doom'd this gentle swain?
And question'd every gust of rugged wings
That blows from off each beaked Promontory;
They knew not of his story,   95
And sage *Hippotades* their answer brings,
That not a blast was from his dungeon stray'd,
The Ayr was calm, and on the level brine,
Sleek *Panope* with all her sisters play'd.
It was that fatall and perfidious Bark   100
Built in th'eclipse, and rigg'd with curses dark,
That sunk so low that sacred head of thine.

    Next *Camus*, reverend Sire, went footing slow,
His Mantle hairy, and his Bonnet sedge,
Inwrought with figures dim, and on the edge   105
Like to that sanguine flower inscrib'd with woe.
Ah! Who hath reft (quoth he) my dearest pledge?

69 Or with] Edd. 1, 2: Hid in 1638: hid in T.MS.

Last came, and last did go,
The Pilot of the *Galilean* lake,
Two massy Keyes he bore of metals twain,   110
(The Golden opes, the Iron shuts amain)
He shook his Miter'd locks, and stern bespake,
How well could I have spar'd for thee young swain,
Anow of such as for their bellies sake,
Creep and intrude, and climb into the fold?   115
Of other care they little reck'ning make,
Then how to scramble at the shearers feast,
And shove away the worthy bidden guest;
Blind mouthes! that scarce themselves know how to hold
A Sheep-hook, or have learn'd ought els the least   120
That to the faithfull Herdmans art belongs!
What recks it them? What need they? They are sped;
And when they list, their lean and flashy songs
Grate on their scrannel Pipes of wretched straw,
The hungry Sheep look up, and are not fed,   125
But swoln with wind, and the rank mist they draw,
Rot inwardly, and foul contagion spread:
Besides what the grim Woolf with privy paw
Daily devours apace, and nothing sed,
But that two-handed engine at the door,   130
Stands ready to smite once, and smite no more.
     Return *Alpheus*, the dread voice is past,
That shrunk thy streams; Return *Sicilian* Muse,
And call the Vales, and bid them hither cast
Their Bels, and Flourets of a thousand hues.   135
Ye valleys low where the milde whispers use,
Of shades and wanton winds, and gushing brooks,
On whose fresh lap the swart Star sparely looks,
Throw hither all your quaint enameld eyes,
That on the green terf suck the honied showres,   140
And purple all the ground with vernal flowres.
Bring the rathe Primrose that forsaken dies,
The tufted Crow-toe, and pale Gessamine,
The white Pink, and the Pansie freakt with jeat,
The glowing Violet,   145
The Musk-rose, and the well-attir'd Woodbine,

With Cowslips wan that hang the pensive hed,
And every flower that sad embroidery wears:
Bid *Amaranthus* all his beauty shed,
And Daffadillies fill their cups with tears,   150
To strew the Laureat Herse where *Lycid* lies.
For so to interpose a little ease,
Let our frail thoughts dally with false surmise.
Ay me! Whilst thee the shores, and sounding Seas
Wash far away, where ere thy bones are hurld,   155
Whether beyond the stormy *Hebrides*,
Where thou perhaps under the whelming tide
Visit'st the bottom of the monstrous world;
Or whether thou to our moist vows deny'd,
Sleep'st by the fable of *Bellerus* old,   160
Where the great vision of the guarded Mount
Looks toward *Namancos* and *Bayona's* hold;
Look homeward Angel now, and melt with ruth,
And, O ye *Dolphins*, waft the haples youth.
    Weep no more, woful Shepherds weep no more,   165
For *Lycidas* your sorrow is not dead,
Sunk though he be beneath the watry floar,
So sinks the day-star in the Ocean bed,
And yet anon repairs his drooping head,
And tricks his beams, and with new spangled Ore,   170
Flames in the forehead of the morning sky:
So *Lycidas* sunk low, but mounted high,
Through the dear might of him that walk'd the waves;
Where other groves, and other streams along,
With *Nectar* pure his oozy Locks he laves,   175
And hears the unexpressive nuptiall Song,
In the blest Kingdoms meek of joy and love.
There entertain him all the Saints above,
In solemn troops, and sweet Societies
That sing, and singing in their glory move,   180
And wipe the tears for ever from his eyes.
Now *Lycidas* the Shepherds weep no more;
Henceforth thou art the Genius of the shore,
In thy large recompense, and shalt be good
To all that wander in that perilous flood.   185

157 whelming] Edd. 1, 2 : humming 1638, T.MS.

Thus sang the uncouth Swain to th'Okes and rills,
While the still morn went out with Sandals gray,
He touch'd the tender stops of various Quills,
With eager thought warbling his *Dorick* lay:
And now the Sun had stretch'd out all the hills,   190
And now was dropt into the Western bay;
At last he rose, and twitch'd his Mantle blew:
To morrow to fresh Woods, and Pastures new.

A MASKE

PRESENTED

At Ludlow Castle,

1634:

On *Michaelmasse night*, *before the*
RIGHT HONORABLE,

IOHN *Earle of Bridgewater*, *Vicount* BRACKLY,
Lord *Præsident of* WALES, And one of
His MAIESTIES moſt honorable
Privie Counſell.

Eheu quid volui miſero mihi! floribus auſtrum
Perditus ―――――

LONDON

Printed for HYMPHREY ROBINSON,
at the ſigne of the *Three Pidgeons* in
Pauls Church-yard. 1637.

[1] To the Right Honourable, John Lord Vicount Bracly, Son and Heir apparent to the Earl of *Bridgewater, &c.*

MY LORD,

   This Poem, *which receiv'd its first occasion of Birth from your Self, and others of your Noble Family, and much honour from your own Person in the performance, now returns again to make a finall Dedication of it self to you. Although not openly acknowledg'd by the Author, yet it is a legitimate off-spring, so lovely, and so much desired, that the often Copying of it hath tir'd my Pen to give my severall friends satisfaction, and brought me to a necessity of producing it to the publike view; and now to offer it up in all rightfull devotion to those fair Hopes, and rare Endowments of your much-promising Youth, which give a full assurance, to all that know you, of a future excellence. Live sweet Lord to be the honour of your Name, and receive this as your own, from the hands of him, who hath by many favours been long oblig'd to your most honour'd Parents, and as in this representation your attendant* Thyrsis, *so now in all reall expression*

Your faithfull, and most
humble Servant
H. LAWES.

[1] The Copy of a Letter Writt'n By Sir HENRY WOOTTON, To the Author, upon the following Poem

From the Colledge, this 13. *of April,* 1638.

SIR,

   It was a special favour, when you lately bestowed upon me here, the first taste of your acquaintance, though no longer then to make me know that I wanted more time to value it, and to enjoy it rightly; and in truth, if I could then have imagined your farther stay in these parts, which I understood afterwards by Mr. *H.*, I would have been bold in our vulgar phrase to mend my draught (for you left me with an extreme thirst) and to have begged your conversation again, joyntly with your said learned Friend, at a poor meal or two, that we might have banded

---

[1] Omitted in 1673

together som good Authors of the antient time: Among which, I observed you to have been familiar.

Since your going, you have charg'd me with new Obligations, both for a very kinde Letter from you dated the sixth of this Month, and for a dainty peece of entertainment which came therwith. Wherin I should much commend the Tragical part, if the Lyrical did not ravish me with a certain Dorique delicacy in your Songs and Odes, wherunto I must plainly confess to have seen yet nothing parallel in our Language: *Ipsa mollities.* But I must not omit to tell you, that I now onely owe you thanks for intimating unto me (how modestly soever) the true Artificer. For the work it self, I had view'd som good while before, with singular delight, having receiv'd it from our common Friend Mr. *R.* in the very close of the late *R's* Poems, Printed at *Oxford*, wherunto it was added (as I now suppose) that the Accessory might help out the Principal, according to the Art of *Stationers*, and to leave the Reader *Con la bocca dolce.*

Now Sir, concerning your travels, wherin I may chalenge a little more priviledge of Discours with you; I suppose you will not blanch *Paris* in your way; therfore I have been bold to trouble you with a few lines to Mr. *M. B.* whom you shall easily find attending the young Lord *S.* as his Governour, and you may surely receive from him good directions for the shaping of your farther journey into *Italy*, where he did reside by my choice som time for the King, after mine own recess from *Venice*.

I should think that your best Line will be thorow the whole length of *France* to *Marseilles*, and thence by Sea to *Genoa*, whence the passage into *Tuscany* is as Diurnal as a *Gravesend* Barge: I hasten as you do to *Florence*, or *Siena*, the rather to tell you a short story from the interest you have given me in your safety.

At *Siena* I was tabled in the House of one *Alberto Scipioni*, an old *Roman* Courtier in dangerous times, having bin Steward to the *Duca di Pagliano*, who with all his Family were strangled, save this onely man that escap'd by foresight of the Tempest: With him I had often much chat of those affairs; Into which he took pleasure to look back from his Native Harbour; and at my departure toward *Rome* (which had been the center of his experience) I had wonn confidence enough to beg his advice, how I might carry my self securely there, without offence of others, or of mine own conscience. *Signor Arrigo mio* (sayes he) *I pensieri stretti, & il viso sciolto* will go safely over the whole World: Of which *Delphian* Oracle (for so I have found it) your judgement doth need no commentary; and therfore (Sir) I will commit you with it to the best of all securities, Gods dear love, remaining

Your Friend as much at command

as any of longer date,

Henry Wootton.

Postscript.

Sir, *I have expressly sent this my Foot-boy to prevent your departure without som acknowledgement from me of the receipt of your obliging Letter, having myself through som business, I know not how, neglected the ordinary conveyance. In any part where I shall understand you fixed, I shall be glad, and diligent to entertain you with Home-Novelties; even for som fomentation of our friendship, too soon interrupted in the Cradle.*

The Persons

The attendant Spirit afterwards in the habit of *Thyrsis.*
Comus with his crew.
The Lady.
1. Brother.
2. Brother.
Sabrina the Nymph.

The cheif persons which presented, were

The Lord *Bracly,*
Mr. *Thomas Egerton* his Brother,
The Lady *Alice Egerton.*

A MASK

PRESENTED AT LUDLOW-CASTLE

1634 &c.

The first Scene discovers a wilde Wood.

The attendant Spirit descends or enters.

BEFORE the starry threshold of *Joves* Court
My mansion is, where those immortal shapes
Of bright aëreal Spirits live insphear'd
In Regions milde of calm and serene Ayr,
Above the smoak and stirr of this dim spot,   5
Which men call Earth, and with low-thoughted care
Confin'd, and pester'd in this pin-fold here,
Strive to keep up a frail, and Feaverish being
Unmindfull of the crown that Vertue gives
After this mortal change, to her true Servants   10
Amongst the enthron'd gods on Sainted seats.
Yet som there be that by due steps aspire
To lay their just hands on that Golden Key
That ope's the Palace of Eternity:
To such my errand is, and but for such,   15
I would not soil these pure Ambrosial weeds,
With the rank vapours of this Sin-worn mould.
   But to my task. *Neptune* besides the sway
Of every salt Flood, and each ebbing Stream,
Took in by lot 'twixt high, and neather *Jove*,   20
Imperial rule of all the Sea-girt Iles
That like to rich, and various gemms inlay
The unadorned boosom of the Deep,
Which he to grace his tributary gods
By course commits to severall goverment,   25
And gives them leave to wear their Saphire crowns,
And weild their little tridents, but this Ile
The greatest, and the best of all the main
He quarters to his blu-hair'd deities,
And all this tract that fronts the falling Sun   30

A noble Peer of mickle trust, and power
Has in his charge, with temper'd awe to guide
An old, and haughty Nation proud in Arms:
Where his fair off-spring nurs't in Princely lore,
Are coming to attend their Fathers state,   35
And new-entrusted Scepter, but their way
Lies through the perplex't paths of this drear Wood,
The nodding horror of whose shady brows
Threats the forlorn and wandring Passinger.
And here their tender age might suffer perill,   40
But that by quick command from Sovran *Jove*
I was dispatcht for their defence, and guard;
And listen why, for I will tell ye now
What never yet was heard in Tale or Song
From old, or modern Bard in Hall, or Bowr.   45
   Bacchus that first from out the purple Grape,
Crush't the sweet poyson of mis-used Wine,
After the *Tuscan* Mariners transform'd
Coasting the *Tyrrhene* shore, as the winds listed,
On *Circes* Iland fell (who knows not *Circe*   50
The daughter of the Sun? Whose charmed Cup
Whoever tasted, lost his upright shape,
And downward fell into a groveling Swine)
This Nymph that gaz'd upon his clustring locks,
With Ivy berries wreath'd, and his blithe youth,   55
Had by him, ere he parted thence, a Son
Much like his Father, but his Mother more,
Whom therfore she brought up and *Comus* nam'd,
Who ripe, and frolick of his full grown age,
Roaving the *Celtick*, and *Iberian* fields,   60
At last betakes him to this ominous Wood,
And in thick shelter of black shades imbowr'd,
Excells his Mother at her mighty Art,
Offring to every weary Travailer,
His orient liquor in a Crystal Glasse,   65
To quench the drouth of *Phœbus*, which as they taste
(For most do taste through fond intemperate thirst)
Soon as the Potion works, their human count'nance,
Th' express resemblance of the gods, is chang'd
Into som brutish form of Woolf, or Bear,   70

Or Ounce, or Tiger, Hog, or bearded Goat,
All other parts remaining as they were,
And they, so perfet is their misery,
Not once perceive their foul disfigurement,
But boast themselves more comely then before,   75
And all their friends, and native home forget
To roule with pleasure in a sensual stie.
Therfore when any favour'd of high *Jove*,
Chances to passe through this adventrous glade,
Swift as the Sparkle of a glancing Star,   80
I shoot from Heav'n to give him safe convoy,
As now I do: But first I must put off
These my skie robes spun out of *Iris* Wooff,
And take the Weeds and likenes of a Swain,
That to the service of this house belongs,   85
Who with his soft Pipe, and smooth-dittied Song,
Well knows to still the wilde winds when they roar,
And hush the waving Woods, nor of lesse faith,
And in this office of his Mountain watch,
Likeliest, and neerest to the present ayd   90
Of this occasion. But I hear the tread
Of hatefull steps, I must be viewles now.

*Comus enters with a Charming Rod in one hand, his Glass in the other, with him a
rout of Monsters headed like sundry sorts of wilde Beasts, but otherwise like Men and
Women, their Apparel glistring, they com in making a riotous and unruly noise,
with Torches in their hands.*

     Comus. The Star that bids the Shepherd fold,
Now the top of Heav'n doth hold,
And the gilded Car of Day,   95
His glowing Axle doth allay
In the steep *Atlantick* stream,
And the slope Sun his upward beam
Shoots against the dusky Pole,
Pacing toward the other gole   100
Of his Chamber in the East.
Mean while welcom Joy, and Feast,
Midnight shout, and revelry,
Tipsie dance, and Jollity.

Braid your Locks with rosie Twine   105
Dropping odours, dropping Wine.
Rigor now is gon to bed,
And Advice with scrupulous head,
Strict Age, and sowre Severity,
With their grave Saws in slumber ly.   110
We that are of purer fire
Imitate the Starry Quire,
Who in their nightly watchfull Sphears,
Lead in swift round the Months and Years.
The Sounds, and Seas with all their finny drove   115
Now to the Moon in wavering Morrice move,
And on the Tawny Sands and Shelves,
Trip the pert Fairies and the dapper Elves;
By dimpled Brook, and Fountain brim,
The Wood-Nymphs deckt with Daisies trim,   120
Their merry wakes and pastimes keep:
What hath night to do with sleep?
Night hath better sweets to prove,
Venus now wakes, and wak'ns Love.
Com let us our rights begin,   125
'Tis onely day-light that makes Sin
Which these dun shades will ne're report.
Hail Goddesse of Nocturnal sport
Dark vaild *Cotytto*, t'whom the secret flame
Of mid-night Torches burns; mysterious Dame   130
That ne're art call'd, but when the Dragon woom
Of Stygian darknes spets her thickest gloom,
And makes one blot of all the ayr,
Stay thy cloudy Ebon chair,
Wherin thou rid'st with *Hecat'*, and befriend   135
Us thy vow'd Priests, till utmost end
Of all·thy dues be done, and none left out,
Ere the blabbing Eastern scout,
The nice Morn on th' *Indian* steep
From her cabin'd loop hole peep,   140
And to the tel-tale Sun discry
Our conceal'd Solemnity.
Com, knit hands, and beat the ground,
In a light fantastick round.

The Measure.

Break off, break off, I feel the different pace   145
Of som chast footing neer about this ground.
Run to your shrouds, within these Brakes and Trees,
Our number may affright: Som Virgin sure
(For so I can distinguish by mine Art)
Benighted in these Woods. Now to my charms,   150
And to my wily trains, I shall ere long
Be well stock't with as fair a herd as graz'd
About my Mother *Circe.* Thus I hurl
My dazling Spells into the spungy ayr,
Of power to cheat the eye with blear illusion,   155
And give it false presentments, lest the place
And my quaint habits breed astonishment,
And put the Damsel to suspicious flight,
Which must not be, for that's against my course;
I under fair pretence of friendly ends,   160
And well plac't words of glozing courtesie
Baited with reasons not unplausible
Wind me into the easie-hearted man,
And hugg him into snares. When once her eye
Hath met the vertue of this Magick dust,   165
I shall appear som harmles Villager
Whom thrift keeps up about his Country gear,
But here she comes, I fairly step aside
And hearken, if I may, her buisnes here.

The Lady enters.

This way the noise was, if mine ear be true,   170
My best guide now, me thought it was the sound
Of Riot, and ill manag'd Merriment,
Such as the jocond Flute, or gamesom Pipe
Stirs up among the loose unletter'd Hinds,
When for their teeming Flocks, and granges full   175
In wanton dance they praise the bounteous *Pan,*
And thank the gods amiss. I should be loath
To meet the rudenesse, and swill'd insolence
Of such late Wassailers; yet O where els

167 *omitted* Ed. 2   168, 169 *order-inverted* Ed. 2

Shall I inform my unacquainted feet   180
In the blind mazes of this tangl'd Wood?
My Brothers when they saw me wearied out
With this long way, resolving here to lodge
Under the spreading favour of these Pines,
Stept as they se'd to the next Thicket side   185
To bring me Berries, or such cooling fruit
As the kind hospitable Woods provide.
They left me then, when the gray-hooded Eev'n
Like a sad Votarist in Palmers weed
Rose from the hindmost wheels of *Phœbus* wain.   190
But where they are, and why they came not back,
Is now the labour of my thoughts, 'tis likeliest
They had ingag'd their wandring steps too far,
And envious darknes, ere they could return,
Had stole them from me, els O theevish Night   195
Why shouldst thou, but for som fellonious end,
In thy dark lantern thus close up the Stars,
That nature hung in Heav'n, and fill'd their Lamps
With everlasting oil, to give due light
To the misled and lonely Travailer?   200
This is the place, as well as I may guess,
Whence eev'n now the tumult of loud Mirth
Was rife, and perfet in my list'ning ear,
Yet nought but single darknes do I find.
What might this be? A thousand fantasies   205
Begin to throng into my memory
Of calling shapes, and beckning shadows dire,
And airy tongues, that syllable mens names
On Sands, and Shoars, and desert Wildernesses.
These thoughts may startle well, but not astound   210
The vertuous mind, that ever walks attended
By a strong siding champion Conscience. . . .
O welcom pure-ey'd Faith, white-handed Hope,
Thou hovering Angel girt with golden wings,
And thou unblemish't form of Chastity,   215
I see ye visibly, and now beleeve
That he, the Supreme good, t' whom all things ill
Are but as slavish officers of vengeance,

214 hovering] Edd. 1, 2 : flittering 1637, T.MS.

Would send a glistring Guardian if need were
To keep my life and honour unassail'd.   220
Was I deceiv'd, or did a sable cloud
Turn forth her silver lining on the night?
I did not err, there does a sable cloud
Turn forth her silver lining on the night,
And casts a gleam over this tufted Grove.   225
I cannot hallow to my Brothers, but
Such noise as I can make to be heard fardest
Ile venter, for my new enliv'nd spirits
Prompt me; and they perhaps are not far off.

SONG

Sweet Echo, sweetest Nymph that liv'st unseen   230
Within thy airy shell
By slow Meander's *margent green,*
And in the violet-imbroider'd vale
Where the love-lorn Nightingale
Nightly to thee her sad Song mourneth well.   235

Canst thou not tell me of a gentle Pair
That likest thy Narcissus *are?*
O if thou have
Hid them in som flowry Cave,
Tell me but where   240
Sweet Queen of Parly, Daughter of the Sphear,
So maist thou be translated to the skies,
And give resounding grace to all Heav'ns Harmonies.

Com. Can any mortal mixture of Earths mould
Breath such Divine inchanting ravishment?   245
Sure somthing holy lodges in that brest,
And with these raptures moves the vocal air
To testifie his hidd'n residence;
How sweetly did they float upon the wings
Of silence, through the empty-vaulted night   250
At every fall smoothing the Raven doune

243 And give resounding grace] Edd. 1, 2, 1637: and hold a counterpoint T.MS. *del.*: and
hould counterpointe B.MS.

Of darknes till it smil'd: I have oft heard
My Mother *Circe* with the Sirens three,
Amidst the flowry-kirtl'd *Naiades*
Culling their potent hearbs, and balefull drugs,   255
Who as they sung, would take the prison'd soul,
And lap it in *Elysium*, *Scylla* wept,
And chid her barking waves into attention,
And fell *Charybdis* murmur'd soft applause:
Yet they in pleasing slumber lull'd the sense,   260
And in sweet madnes rob'd it of it self,
But such a sacred, and home-felt delight,
Such sober certainty of waking bliss
I never heard till now. Ile speak to her
And she shall be my Queen. Hail forren wonder   265
Whom certain these rough shades did never breed
Unlesse the Goddes that in rurall shrine
Dwell'st here with *Pan*, or *Silvan*, by blest Song
Forbidding every bleak unkindly Fog
To touch the prosperous growth of this tall Wood.   270
     La. Nay gentle Shepherd ill is lost that praise
That is addrest to unattending Ears,
Not any boast of skill, but extreme shift
How to regain my sever'd company
Compell'd me to awake the courteous Echo   275
To give me answer from her mossie Couch.
     Co. What chance good Lady hath bereft you thus?
     La. Dim darknes, and this leavy Labyrinth.
     Co. Could that divide you from neer-ushering guides?
     La. They left me weary on a grassie terf.   280
     Co. By falshood, or discourtesie, or why?
     La. To seek i'th vally som cool friendly Spring.
     Co. And left your fair side all unguarded Lady?
     La. They were but twain, and purpos'd quick return.
     Co. Perhaps fore-stalling night prevented them.   285
     La. How easie my misfortune is to hit!
     Co. Imports their loss, beside the present need?
     La. No less then if I should my brothers loose.
     Co. Were they of manly prime, or youthful bloom?
     La. As smooth as *Hebe's* their unrazor'd lips.   290

252 it] Edd. 1, 2: she 1637, T.MS., B.MS.

Co. Two such I saw, what time the labour'd Oxe
In his loose traces from the furrow came,
And the swink't hedger at his Supper sate;
I saw them under a green mantling vine
That crawls along the side of yon small hill,   295
Plucking ripe clusters from the tender shoots,
Their port was more then human, as they stood;
I took it for a faëry vision
Of som gay creatures of the element
That in the colours of the Rainbow live   300
And play i'th plighted clouds. I was aw-strook,
And as I past, I worshipt; if those you seek
It were a journey like the path to Heav'n,
To help you find them. *La.* Gentle villager
What readiest way would bring me to that place?   305
    Co. Due west it rises from this shrubby point.
    La. To find out that, good Shepherd, I suppose,
In such a scant allowance of Star-light,
Would overtask the best Land-Pilots art,
Without the sure guess of well-practiz'd feet.   310
    Co. I know each lane, and every alley green
Dingle, or bushy dell of this wilde Wood,
And every bosky bourn from side to side
My daily walks and ancient neighbourhood,
And if your stray attendance be yet lodg'd,   315
Or shroud within these limits, I shall know
Ere morrow wake, or the low roosted lark
From her thatch't pallat rowse, if otherwise
I can conduct you Lady to a low
But loyal cottage, where you may be safe   320
Till furder quest'. *La.* Shepherd I take thy word,
And trust thy honest offer'd courtesie,
Which oft is sooner found in lowly sheds
With smoaky rafters, then in tapstry Halls
And Courts of Princes, where it first was nam'd,   325
And yet is most pretended: In a place
Less warranted then this, or less secure
I cannot be, that I should fear to change it.
Eie me blest Providence, and square my triall
To my proportion'd strength. Shepherd lead on. . . .   330

The two Brothers.

Eld. Bro. Unmuffle ye faint Stars, and thou fair **Moon**
That wontst to love the travailers benizon,
Stoop thy pale visage through an amber cloud,
And disinherit *Chaos*, that raigns here
In double night of darknes, and of shades;   335
Or if your influence be quite damm'd up
With black usurping mists, som gentle taper
Though a rush Candle from the wicker hole
Of som clay habitation visit us
With thy long levell'd rule of streaming light,   340
And thou shalt be our star of *Arcady*,
Or *Tyrian* Cynosure. 2. *Bro.* Or if our eyes
Be barr'd that happines, might we but hear
The folded flocks pen'd in their watled cotes,
Or sound of pastoral reed with oaten stops,   345
Or whistle from the Lodge, or village cock
Count the night watches to his feathery Dames,
'Twould be som solace yet, som little chearing
In this close dungeon of innumerous bowes.
But O that haples virgin our lost sister   350
Where may she wander now, whether betake her
From the chill dew, amongst rude burrs and thistles?
Perhaps som cold bank is her boulster now
Or 'gainst the rugged bark of som broad Elm
Leans her unpillow'd head fraught with sad fears.   355
What if in wild amazement, and affright,
Or while we speak within the direfull grasp
Of Savage hunger, or of Savage heat?
    Eld. Bro. Peace brother, be not over-exquisite
To cast the fashion of uncertain evils;   360
For grant they be so, while they rest unknown,
What need a man forestall his date of grief,
And run to meet what he would most avoid?
Or if they be but false alarms of Fear,
How bitter is such self-delusion!   365
I do not think my sister so to seek,

357–9 so fares as did forsaken Proserpine
    when the big wallowing flakes of pitchie clowds
    & darknesse wound her in. 1 Bro. peace brother peace T.MS. *orig.*

Or so unprincipl'd in vertues book,
And the sweet peace that goodnes boosoms ever,
As that the single want of light and noise
(Not being in danger, as I trust she is not)   370
Could stir the constant mood of her calm thoughts,
And put them into mis-becoming plight.
Vertue could see to do what vertue would
By her own radiant light, though Sun and Moon
Were in the flat Sea sunk. And Wisdoms self   375
Oft seeks to sweet retired Solitude,
Where with her best nurse Contemplation
She plumes her feathers, and lets grow her wings
That in the various bussle of resort
Were all to ruffl'd, and somtimes impair'd.   380
He that has light within his own cleer brest
May sit i'th center, and enjoy bright day,
But he that hides a dark soul, and foul thoughts
Benighted walks under the mid-day Sun;
Himself is his own dungeon.
    2. *Bro.* 'Tis most true   385
That musing meditation most affects
The Pensive secrecy of desert cell,
Far from the cheerfull haunt of men, and herds,
And sits as safe as in a Senat house,
For who would rob a Hermit of his Weeds,   390
His few Books, or his Beads, or Maple Dish,
Or do his gray hairs any violence?
But beauty like the fair Hesperian Tree
Laden with blooming gold, had need the guard
Of dragon watch with uninchanted eye,   395
To save her blossoms, and defend her fruit
From the rash hand of bold Incontinence.
You may as well spred out the unsun'd heaps
Of Misers treasure by an out-laws den,
And tell me it is safe, as bid me hope   400
Danger will wink on Opportunity,
And let a single helpless maiden pass
Uninjur'd in this wilde surrounding wast.
Of night, or lonelines it recks me not,
I fear the dred events that dog them both,   405

Lest som ill greeting touch attempt the person
Of our unowned sister.
   Eld. Bro. I do not, brother,
Inferr, as if I thought my sisters state
Secure without all doubt, or controversie:
Yet where an equal poise of hope and fear   410
Does arbitrate th'event, my nature is
That I encline to hope, rather then fear,
And gladly banish squint suspicion.
My sister is not so defenceless left
As you imagine, she has a hidden strength   415
Which you remember not.
   2. Bro. What hidden strength,
Unless the strength of Heav'n, if you mean that?
   Eld. Bro. I mean that too, but yet a hidden strength
Which if Heav'n gave it, may be term'd her own:
'Tis chastity, my brother, chastity: 420
She that has that, is clad in compleat steel,
And like a quiver'd Nymph with Arrows keen
May trace huge Forests, and unharbour'd Heaths,
Infamous Hills, and sandy perilous wildes,
Where through the sacred rayes of Chastity,   425
No savage fierce, Bandite, or mountaneer
Will dare to soyl her Virgin purity,
Yea there, where very desolation dwels
By grots, and caverns shag'd with horrid shades,
She may pass on with unblench't majesty,   430
Be it not don in pride, or in presumption.
Som say no evil thing that walks by night
In fog, or fire, by lake, or moorish fen,
Blew meager Hag, or stubborn unlaid ghost,
That breaks his magick chains at *curfeu* time,   435
No goblin, or swart Faëry of the mine,
Hath hurtfull power o're true virginity.
Do ye beleeve me yet, or shall I call
Antiquity from the old Schools of *Greece*
To testifie the arms of Chastity?   440
Hence had the huntress *Dian* her dred bow
Fair silver-shafted Queen for ever chaste,
Wherwith she tam'd the brinded lioness

And spotted mountain pard, but set at nought
The frivolous bolt of *Cupid*, gods and men   445
Fear'd her stern frown, and she was queen oth' Woods.
What was that snaky-headed *Gorgon* sheild
That wise *Minerva* wore, unconquer'd Virgin,
Wherwith she freez'd her foes to congeal'd stone?
But rigid looks of Chast austerity,   450
And noble grace that dash't brute violence
With sudden adoration, and blank aw.
So dear to Heav'n is Saintly chastity,
That when a soul is found sincerely so,
A thousand liveried Angels lacky her,   455
Driving far off each thing of sin and guilt,
And in cleer dream, and solemn vision
Tell her of things that no gross ear can hear,
Till oft convers with heav'nly habitants
Begin to cast a beam on th'outward shape,   460
The unpolluted temple of the mind,
And turns it by degrees to the souls essence,
Till all be made immortal: but when lust
By unchaste looks, loose gestures, and foul talk,
But most by leud and lavish act of sin,   465
Lets in defilement to the inward parts,
The soul grows clotted by contagion,
Imbodies, and imbrutes, till she quite loose
The divine property of her first being.
Such are those thick and gloomy shadows damp   470
Oft seen in Charnell vaults, and Sepulchers
Lingering, and sitting by a new made grave,
As loath to leave the body that it lov'd,
And link't it self by carnal sensualty
To a degenerate and degraded state.   475
    2. *Bro.* How charming is divine Philosophy!
Not harsh, and crabbed as dull fools suppose,
But musical as is *Apollo's* lute,
And a perpetual feast of nectar'd sweets,
Where no crude surfet raigns. *Eld. Bro.* List, list, I hear   480
Som far off hallow break the silent Air.
    2. *Bro.* Me thought so too; what should it be?

    472 Lingering] Edd. 1, 2: Hovering 1637, hovering T.MS.

Eld. Bro. For certain
Either som one like us night-founder'd here,
Or els som neighbour Wood-man, or at worst,
Som roaving Robber calling to his fellows.   485
    2. *Bro.* Heav'n keep my sister, agen agen and neer,
Best draw, and stand upon our guard.
    Eld. Bro. Ile hallow,
If he be friendly he comes well, if not,
Defence is a good cause, and Heav'n be for us.

The attendant Spirit habited like a Shepherd.

That hallow I should know, what are you? speak;   490
Com not too neer, you fall on iron stakes else.
    Spir. What voice is that? my young Lord? speak agen.
    2. *Bro.* O brother, 'tis my father Shepherd sure.
    Eld. Bro. Thyrsis? Whose artful strains have oft delaid
The huddling brook to hear his madrigal,   495
And sweeten'd every muskrose of the dale,
How cam'st thou here good Swain? hath any ram
Slip't from the fold, or young Kid lost his dam,
Or straggling weather the pen't flock forsook?
How couldst thou find this dark sequester'd nook?   500
    Spir. O my lov'd masters heir, and his next joy,
I came not here on such a trivial toy
As a stray'd Ewe, or to pursue the stealth
Of pilfering Woolf, not all the fleecy wealth
That doth enrich these Downs, is worth a thought   505
To this my errand, and the care it brought.
But O my Virgin Lady, where is she?
How chance she is not in your company?
    Eld. Bro. To tell thee sadly Shepherd, without blame,
Or our neglect, we lost her as we came.   510
    Spir. Ay me unhappy then my fears are true.
    Eld. Bro. What fears good *Thyrsis?* Prethee briefly shew.
    Spir. Ile tell ye, 'tis not vain, or fabulous,
(Though so esteem'd by shallow ignorance)
What the sage Poëts taught by th' heav'nly Muse,   515
Storied of old in high immortal vers
Of dire *Chimera's* and inchanted Iles,

497 Swain?] Edd. 1, 2: shepheard, T.MS., B.MS.

And rifted Rocks whose entrance leads to Hell,
For such there be, but unbelief is blind.
    Within the navil of this hideous Wood,   520
Immur'd in cypress shades a Sorcerer dwels
Of *Bacchus*, and of *Circe* born, great *Comus*,
Deep skill'd in all his mothers witcheries,
And here to every thirsty wanderer,
By sly enticement gives his banefull cup,   525
With many murmurs mixt, whose pleasing poison
The visage quite transforms of him that drinks,
And the inglorious likenes of a beast
Fixes instead, unmoulding reasons mintage
Character'd in the face; this have I learn't   530
Tending my flocks hard by i'th hilly crofts,
That brow this bottom glade, whence night by night
He and his monstrous rout are heard to howl
Like stabl'd wolves, or tigers at their prey,
Doing abhorred rites to *Hecate*   535
In their obscured haunts of inmost bowres.
Yet have they many baits, and guilefull spells
To inveigle and invite th'unwary sense
Of them that pass unweeting by the way.
This evening late by then the chewing flocks   540
Had ta'n their supper on the savoury Herb
Of Knot-grass dew-besprent, and were in fold,
I sate me down to watch upon a bank
With Ivy canopied, and interwove
With flaunting Hony-suckle, and began   545
Wrapt in a pleasing fit of melancholy
To meditate my rural minstrelsie,
Till fancy had her fill, but ere a close
The wonted roar was up amidst the Woods,
And fill'd the Air with barbarous dissonance,   550
At which I ceas't, and listen'd them a while,
Till an unusuall stop of sudden silence
Gave respit to the drowsie frighted steeds
That draw the litter of close-curtain'd sleep.
At last a soft and solemn breathing sound   555
Rose like a steam of rich distill'd Perfumes,
And stole upon the Air, that even Silence

Was took ere she was ware, and wish't she might
Deny her nature, and be never more
Still to be so displac't. I was all eare,   560
And took in strains that might create a soul
Under the ribs of Death, but O ere long
Too well I did perceive it was the voice
Of my most honour'd Lady, your dear sister.
Amaz'd I stood, harrow'd with grief and fear,   565
And O poor hapless Nightingale thought I,
How sweet thou sing'st, how neer the deadly snare!
Then down the Lawns I ran with headlong hast
Through paths, and turnings oft'n trod by day,
Till guided by mine ear I found the place   570
Where that damn'd wisard hid in sly disguise
(For so by certain signes I knew) had met
Already, ere my best speed could prævent,
The aidless innocent Lady his wish't prey,
Who gently ask't if he had seen such two,   575
Supposing him som neighbour villager;
Longer I durst not stay, but soon I guess't
Ye were the two she mean't, with that I sprung
Into swift flight, till I had found you here,
But furder know I not. 2. *Bro.* O night and shades,   580
How are ye joyn'd with hell in triple knot
Against th'unarmed weakness of one Virgin
Alone, and helpless! Is this the confidence
You gave me Brother? *Eld. Bro.* Yes, and keep it still,
Lean on it safely, not a period   585
Shall be unsaid for me: against the threats
Of malice or of sorcery, or that power
Which erring men call Chance, this I hold firm,
Vertue may be assail'd, but never hurt,
Surpriz'd by unjust force, but not enthrall'd,   590
Yea even that which mischief meant most harm,
Shall in the happy trial prove most glory.
But evil on it self shall back recoyl,
And mix no more with goodness, when at last
Gather'd like scum, and setl'd to it self   595
It shall be in eternal restless change
Self-fed, and self-consum'd; if this fail,

The pillar'd firmament is rott'nness,
And earths base built on stubble. But com let's on.
Against th'opposing will and arm of Heav'n   600
May never this just sword be lifted up,
But for that damn'd magician, let him be girt
With all the greisly legions that troop
Under the sooty flag of *Acheron*,
Harpyes and *Hydra's*, or all the monstrous forms   605
'Twixt *Africa* and *Inde*, Ile find him out,
And force him to restore his purchase back,
Or drag him by the curls, to a foul death,
Curs'd as his life.
  Spir. Alas good ventrous youth,
I love thy courage yet, and bold Emprise,   610
But here thy sword can do thee little stead,
Farr other arms, and other weapons must
Be those that quell the might of hellish charms,
He with his bare wand can unthred thy joynts,
And crumble all thy sinews.
  Eld. Bro. Why prethee Shepherd   615
How durst thou then thy self approach so neer
As to make this relation?
  Spir. Care and utmost shifts
How to secure the Lady from surprisal,
Brought to my mind a certain Shepherd Lad
Of small regard to see to, yet well skill'd   620
In every vertuous plant and healing herb
That spreds her verdant leaf to th'morning ray,
He lov'd me well, and oft would beg me sing,
Which when I did, he on the tender grass
Would sit, and hearken even to extasie,   625
And in requitall ope his leather'n scrip,
And shew me simples of a thousand names
Telling their strange and vigorous faculties;
Amongst the rest a small unsightly root,
But of divine effect, he cull'd me out;   630
The leaf was darkish, and had prickles on it,
But in another Countrey, as he said,

605 forms] Edd. 1, 2 : bugs 1637 : buggs T.MS., B.MS. 608–9 to a foul death, Curs'd
as his life] Edd. 1, 2 : and cleave his scalpe Downe to the hipps, 1637, T.MS., B.MS.

Bore a bright golden flowre, but not in this soyl:
Unknown, and like esteem'd, and the dull swayn
Treads on it daily with his clouted shoon, 635
And yet more med'cinal is it then that *Moly*
That *Hermes* once to wise *Ulysses* gave;
He call'd it *Hæmony*, and gave it me,
And bad me keep it as of sovran use
'Gainst all inchantments, mildew blast, or damp 640
Or gastly furies apparition;
I purs't it up, but little reck'ning made,
Till now that this extremity compell'd,
But now I find it true; for by this means
I knew the foul inchanter though disguis'd, 645
Enter'd the very lime-twigs of his spells,
And yet came off: if you have this about you
(As I will give you when we go) you may
Boldly assault the necromancers hall;
Where if he be, with dauntless hardihood, 650
And brandish't blade rush on him, break his glass,
And shed the lushious liquor on the ground,
But sease his wand, though he and his curst crew
Feirce signe of battail make, and menace high,
Or like the sons of *Vulcan* vomit smoak, 655
Yet will they soon retire, if he but shrink.
    Eld. Bro. Thyrsis lead on apace, Ile follow thee,
And som good angel bear a sheild before us.

The Scene changes to a stately Palace, set out with all manner of deliciousness: soft Musick, Tables spred with all dainties. Comus appears with his rabble, and the Lady set in an inchanted Chair, to whom he offers his Glass, which she puts by, and goes about to rise.

    Comus. Nay Lady sit; if I but wave this wand,
Your nervs are all chain'd up in Alablaster, 660
And you a statue; or as *Daphne* was
Root-bound, that fled *Apollo.*
    La. Fool do not boast,
Thou canst not touch the freedom of my minde
With all thy charms, although this corporal rinde
Thou hast immanacl'd, while Heav'n sees good. 665
    Co. Why are you vext Lady? why do you frown?

Here dwel no frowns, nor anger, from these gates
Sorrow flies farr: See here be all the pleasures
That fancy can beget on youthfull thoughts,
When the fresh blood grows lively, and returns   670
Brisk as the *April* buds in Primrose-season.
And first behold this cordial Julep here
That flames, and dances in his crystal bounds
With spirits of balm, and fragrant Syrops mixt.
Not that *Nepenthes* which the wife of *Thone*,   675
In *Egypt* gave to *Jove*-born *Helena*
Is of such power to stir up joy as this,
To life so friendly, or so cool to thirst.
Why should you be so cruel to your self,
And to those dainty limms which nature lent   680
For gentle usage, and soft delicacy?
But you invert the cov'nants of her trust,
And harshly deal like an ill borrower
With that which you receiv'd on other terms,
Scorning the unexempt condition   685
By which all mortal frailty must subsist,
Refreshment after toil, ease after pain,
That have been tir'd all day without repast,
And timely rest have wanted, but fair Virgin
This will restore all soon.
    La. 'Twill not false traitor,   690
'Twill not restore the truth and honesty
That thou hast banish't from thy tongue with lies,
Was this the cottage, and the safe abode
Thou told'st me of? What grim aspects are these,
These ougly-headed Monsters? Mercy guard me!   695
Hence with thy brew'd inchantments, foul deceiver,
Hast thou betrai'd my credulous innocence
With visor'd falshood, and base forgery,
And wouldst thou seek again to trap me here
With lickerish baits fit to ensnare a brute?   700
Were it a draft for *Juno* when she banquets,
I would not taste thy treasonous offer; none
But such as are good men can give good things,
And that which is not good, is not delicious
To a wel-govern'd and wise appetite.   705

Co. O foolishnes of men! that lend their ears
To those budge doctors of the *Stoick* Furr,
And fetch their precepts from the *Cynick* Tub,
Praising the lean and sallow Abstinence.
Wherefore did Nature powre her bounties forth, 710
With such a full and unwithdrawing hand,
Covering the earth with odours, fruits, and flocks,
Thronging the Seas with spawn innumerable,
But all to please, and sate the curious taste?
And set to work millions of spinning Worms, 715
That in their green shops weave the smooth-hair'd silk
To deck her Sons, and that no corner might
Be vacant of her plenty, in her own loyns
She hutch't th'all-worshipt ore, and precious gems
To store her children with; if all the world 720
Should in a pet of temperance feed on Pulse,
Drink the clear stream, and nothing wear but Freize,
Th'all-giver would be unthank't, would be unprais'd,
Not half his riches known, and yet despis'd,
And we should serve him as a grudging master, 725
As a penurious niggard of his wealth,
And live like Natures bastards, not her sons,
Who would be quite surcharg'd with her own weight,
And strangl'd with her waste fertility;
Th'earth cumber'd, and the wing'd air dark't with plumes,
The herds would over-multitude their Lords, 731
The Sea o'refraught would swell, and th'unsought diamonds
Would so emblaze the forhead of the Deep,
And so bestudd with Stars, that they below
Would grow inur'd to light, and com at last 735
To gaze upon the Sun with shameless brows.
List Lady be not coy, and be not cosen'd
With that same vaunted name Virginity,
Beauty is natures coyn, must not be hoorded,
But must be currant, and the good thereof 740
Consists in mutual and partak'n bliss,
Unsavoury in th'injoyment of it self;
If you let slip time, like a neglected rose
It withers on the stalk with languish't head.
Beauty is natures brag, and must be shown 745

In courts, at feasts, and high solemnities
Where most may wonder at the workmanship;
It is for homely features to keep home,
They had their name thence; course complexions
And cheeks of sorry grain will serve to ply   750
The sampler, and to teize the huswifes wooll.
What need a vermeil-tinctur'd lip for that
Love-darting eyes, or tresses like the Morn?
There was another meaning in these gifts,
Think what, and be adviz'd, you are but young yet.   755
   La. I had not thought to have unlockt my lips
In this unhallow'd air, but that this Jugler
Would think to charm my judgement, as mine eyes,
Obtruding false rules pranckt in reasons garb.
I hate when vice can bolt her arguments,   760
And vertue has no tongue to check her pride:
Impostor do not charge most innocent nature,
As if she would her children should be riotous
With her abundance, she good cateress
Means her provision onely to the good   765
That live according to her sober laws,
And holy dictate of spare Temperance:
If every just man that now pines with want
Had but a moderate and beseeming share
Of that which lewdly-pamper'd Luxury   770
Now heaps upon som few with vast excess,
Natures full blessings would be well dispenc't
In unsuperfluous eeven proportion,
And she no whit encomber'd with her store,
And then the giver would be better thank't,   775
His praise due paid, for swinish gluttony
Ne're looks to Heav'n amidst his gorgeous feast,
But with besotted base ingratitude
Cramms, and blasphemes his feeder. Shall I go on?
Or have I said anough? To him that dares   780
Arm his profane tongue with contemptuous words
Against the Sun-clad power of Chastity,
Fain would I somthing say, yet to what end?
Thou hast nor Eare, nor Soul to apprehend
The sublime notion, and high mystery   785

That must be utter'd to unfold the sage
And serious doctrine of Virginity,
And thou art worthy that thou shouldst not know
More happines then this thy present lot.
Enjoy your deer Wit, and gay Rhetorick   790
That hath so well been taught her dazling fence,
Thou art not fit to hear thy self convinc't;
Yet should I try, the uncontrouled worth
Of this pure cause would kindle my rapt spirits
To such a flame of sacred vehemence,   795
That dumb things would be mov'd to sympathize,
And the brute Earth would lend her nerves, and shake,
Till all thy magick structures rear'd so high,
Were shatter'd into heaps o're thy false head.

    Co. She fables not, I feel that I do fear   800
Her words set off by som superior power;
And though not mortal, yet a cold shuddring dew
Dips me all o're, as when the wrath of *Jove*
Speaks thunder, and the chains of *Erebus*
To som of *Saturns* crew. I must dissemble,   805
And try her yet more strongly. Com, no more,
This is meer moral babble, and direct
Against the canon laws of our foundation;
I must not suffer this, yet 'tis but the lees
And setlings of a melancholy blood;   810
But this will cure all streight, one sip of this
Will bathe the drooping spirits in delight
Beyond the bliss of dreams. Be wise, and taste. . . .

*The Brothers rush in with Swords drawn, wrest his Glass out of his hand, and break it
  against the ground; his rout make signe of resistance, but are all driven in; The
  attendant Spirit comes in.*

    Spir. What, have you let the false enchanter scape?
O ye mistook, ye should have snatcht his wand   815
And bound him fast; without his rod revers't,
And backward mutters of dissevering power,
We cannot free the Lady that sits here
In stony fetters fixt, and motionless;
Yet stay, be not disturb'd, now I bethink me,   820
Som other means I have that may be us'd,
       821 that] T.MS., B.MS.: which Edd. 1, 2, 1637

Which once of *Meliboeus* old I learnt
The soothest Shepherd that ere pip't on plains.
　There is a gentle Nymph not farr from hence,
That with moist curb sways the smooth Severn stream,　825
Sabrina is her name, a Virgin pure,
Whilom she was the daughter of *Locrine*,
That had the Scepter from his father *Brute*.
She guiltless damsell flying the mad pursuit
Of her enraged stepdam *Guendolen*,　　　　　　830
Commended her fair innocence to the flood
That stay'd her flight with his cross-flowing course,
The water Nymphs that in the bottom plaid,
Held up their pearled wrists and took her in,
Bearing her straight to aged *Nereus* Hall,　　　　835
Who piteous of her woes, rear'd her lank head,
And gave her to his daughters to imbathe
In nectar'd lavers strew'd with Asphodil,
And through the porch and inlet of each sense
Dropt in Ambrosial Oils till she reviv'd,　　　　　840
And underwent a quick immortal change
Made Goddess of the River; still she retains
Her maid'n gentlenes, and oft at Eeve
Visits the herds along the twilight meadows,
Helping all urchin blasts, and ill luck signes　　　845
That the shrewd medling Elfe delights to make,
Which she with pretious viold liquors heals.
For which the Shepherds at their festivals
Carrol her goodnes lowd in rustick layes,
And throw sweet garland wreaths into her stream　850
Of pancies, pinks, and gaudy Daffadils.
And, as the old Swain said, she can unlock
The clasping charm, and thaw the numming spell,
If she be right invok't in warbled Song,
For maid'nhood she loves, and will be swift　　　855
To aid a Virgin, such as was her self
In hard besetting need, this will I try
And adde the power of som adjuring verse.

SONG

Sabrina fair
   Listen where thou art sitting   860
Under the glassie, cool, translucent wave,
   In twisted braids of Lillies knitting
The loose train of thy amber-dropping hair,
   Listen for dear honours sake,
Goddess of the silver lake,   865
          Listen and save.

Listen and appear to us
In name of great *Oceanus,*
By th'earth-shaking *Neptune's* mace,
And *Tethys* grave majestick pace,   870
By hoary *Nereus* wrincled look,
And the *Carpathian* wisards hook,
By scaly *Tritons* winding shell,
And old sooth-saying *Glaucus* spell,
By *Leucothea's* lovely hands,   875
And her son that rules the strands,
By *Thetis* tinsel-slipper'd feet,
And the Songs of *Sirens* sweet,
By dead *Parthenope's* dear tomb,
And fair *Ligea's* golden comb,   880
Wherwith she sits on diamond rocks
Sleeking her soft alluring locks,
By all the *Nymphs* that nightly dance
Upon thy streams with wily glance,
Rise, rise, and heave thy rosie head   885
From thy coral-pav'n bed,
And bridle in thy headlong wave,
Till thou our summons answer'd have.
          Listen and save.

Sabrina rises, attended by water-Nymphes, and sings.

   By the rushy-fringed bank,   890
Where grows the Willow and the Osier dank,
   My sliding Chariot stayes,
Thick set with Agat, and the azurn sheen
Of Turkis blew, and Emrauld green

That in the channell strayes,   895
Whilst from off the waters fleet
Thus I set my printless feet
O're the Cowslips Velvet head,
   That bends not as I tread,
Gentle swain at thy request   900
   I am here.

   Spir. Goddess dear
We implore thy powerful hand
To undoe the charmed band
Of true Virgin here distrest,   905
Through the force, and through the wile
Of unblest inchanter vile.
   Sab. Shepherd 'tis my office best
To help insnared chastity;
Brightest Lady look on me,   910
Thus I sprinkle on thy brest
Drops that from my fountain pure,
I have kept of pretious cure,
Thrice upon thy fingers tip,
Thrice upon thy rubied lip,   915
Next this marble venom'd seat
Smear'd with gumms of glutenous heat
I touch with chaste palms moist and cold,
Now the spell hath lost his hold;
And I must haste ere morning hour   920
To wait in *Amphitrite*'s bowr.

Sabrina *descends, and the Lady rises out of her seat.*

   Spir. Virgin, daughter of *Locrine*
Sprung of old *Anchises* line,
May thy brimmed waves for this
Their full tribute never miss   925
From a thousand petty rills,
That tumble down the snowy hills:
Summer drouth, or singed air
Never scorch thy tresses fair,
Nor wet *Octobers* torrent flood   930
Thy molten crystal fill with mudd,

May thy billows rowl ashoar
The beryl, and the golden ore,
May thy lofty head be crown'd
With many a tower and terrass round,   935
And here and there thy banks upon
With Groves of myrrhe, and cinnamon.

Com Lady while Heaven lends us grace,
Let us fly this cursed place,
Lest the Sorcerer us intice   940
With som other new device.
Not a waste, or needless sound
Till we com to holier ground,
I shall be your faithfull guide
Through this gloomy covert wide,   945
And not many furlongs thence
Is your Fathers residence,
Where this night are met in state
Many a friend to gratulate
His wish't presence, and beside   950
All the Swains that there abide,
With Jiggs, and rural dance resort,
We shall catch them at their sport,
And our sudden coming there
Will double all their mirth and chere;   955
Com let us haste, the Stars grow high,
But night sits monarch yet in the mid sky.

The Scene changes, presenting Ludlow *Town and the Presidents Castle, then com in*
Countrey-Dancers, after them the attendant Spirit, with the two Brothers and the
Lady.

SONG

Spir. *Back Shepherds, back, anough your play,*
Till next Sun-shine holiday,
Here be without duck or nod   960
Other trippings to be trod
Of lighter toes, and such Court guise
As Mercury *did first devise*
With the mincing Dryades
On the Lawns, and on the Leas.   965

956 grow] Edd. 1, 2, T.MS.²: are 1637, T.MS. *orig.*, B.MS.

This second Song presents them to their father and mother.

> *Noble Lord, and Lady bright,*
> *I have brought ye new delight,*
> *Here behold so goodly grown*
> *Three fair branches of your own,*
> *Heav'n hath timely tri'd their youth,*   970
> *Their faith, their patience, and their truth,*
> *And sent them here through hard assays*
> *With a crown of deathless Praise,*
>   *To triumph in victorious dance*
> *O're sensual Folly, and Intemperance.*   975

> *The dances ended, the Spirit Epiloguizes.*

> *Spir.* To the Ocean now I fly,
> And those happy climes that ly
> Where day never shuts his eye,
> Up in the broad fields of the sky:
> There I suck the liquid ayr   980
> All amidst the Gardens fair
> Of *Hesperus*, and his daughters three
> That sing about the golden tree:
> Along the crisped shades and bowres
> Revels the spruce and jocond Spring,   985
> The Graces, and the rosie-boosom'd Howres,
> Thither all their bounties bring,
> There eternal Summer dwels,
> And West winds, with musky wing
> About the cedar'n alleys fling   990
> *Nard*, and *Cassia*'s balmy smels.
> *Iris* there with humid bow,
> Waters the odorous banks that blow
> Flowers of more mingled hew
> Then her purfl'd scarf can shew,   995
> And drenches with *Elysian* dew
> (List mortals, if your ears be true)
> Beds of *Hyacinth*, and roses
> Where young *Adonis* oft reposes,
> Waxing well of his deep wound   1000

988 There] Erratum Ed. 1, T.MS.¹, B.MS.: That there Edd. 1, 2, 1637: that there T.MS.²

In slumber soft, and on the ground
Sadly sits th'*Assyrian* Queen;
But farr above in spangled sheen
Celestial *Cupid* her fam'd Son advanc't,
Holds his dear *Psyche* sweet intranc't   1005
After her wandring labours long,
Till free consent the gods among
Make her his eternal Bride,
And from her fair unspotted side
Two blissful twins are to be born,   1010
Youth and Joy; so *Jove* hath sworn.
   But now my task is smoothly don,
I can fly, or I can run
Quickly to the green earths end,
Where the bow'd welkin slow doth bend,   1015
And from thence can soar as soon
To the corners of the Moon.
   Mortals that would follow me,
Love vertue, she alone is free,
She can teach ye how to clime   1020
Higher then the Spheary chime;
Or if Vertue feeble were,
Heav'n it self would stoop to her.

THE END

PSAL. I. *Done into Verse*, 1653

BLESS'D is the man who hath not walk'd astray
In counsel of the wicked, and ith'way
Of sinners hath not stood, and in the seat
Of scorners hath not sate. But in the great
Jehovahs Law is ever his delight, 5
And in his Law he studies day and night.
He shall be as a tree which planted grows
By watry streams, and in his season knows
To yield his fruit, and his leaf shall not fall,
And what he takes in hand shall prosper all. 10
Not so the wicked, but as chaff which fann'd
The wind drives, so the wicked shall not stand
In judgment, or abide their tryal then,
Nor sinners in th'assembly of just men.
For the Lord knows th'upright way of the just, 15
And the way of bad men to ruine must.

PSAL. II. *Done* Aug. 8. 1653. *Terzetti*

WHY do the Gentiles tumult, and the Nations
Muse a vain thing, the Kings of th'earth upstand
With power, and Princes in their Congregations
Lay deep their plots together through each Land,
Against the Lord and his Messiah dear. 5
Let us break off, say they, by strength of hand
Their bonds, and cast from us, no more to wear,
Their twisted cords: he who in Heaven doth dwell
Shall laugh, the Lord shall scoff them, then severe
Speak to them in his wrath, and in his fell 10
And fierce ire trouble them; but I saith hee
Anointed have my King (though ye rebell)
On *Sion* my holi' hill. A firm decree
I will declare; the Lord to me hath say'd
Thou art my Son I have begotten thee 15
This day; ask of me, and the grant is made;
As thy possession I on thee bestow
Th'Heathen, and as thy conquest to be sway'd

Earths utmost bounds: them shalt thou bring full low
  With Iron Scepter bruis'd, and them disperse   20
  Like to a potters vessel shiver'd so.
And now be wise at length ye Kings averse,
  Be taught ye Judges of the earth; with fear
  Jehovah serve, and let your joy converse
With trembling; kiss the Son least he appear   25
  In anger and ye perish in the way
  If once his wrath take fire like fuel sere.
Happy all those who have in him their stay.

PSAL. III. Aug. 9. 1653.

When he fled from Absalom

LORD how many are my foes
      How many those
    That in arms against me rise;
      Many are they
    That of my life distrustfully thus say,   5
No help for him in God there lies.
But thou Lord art my shield my glory,
      Thee through my story
    Th'exalter of my head I count;
      Aloud I cry'd   10
  Unto *Jehovah*, he full soon reply'd
And heard me from his holy mount.
I lay and slept, I wak'd again,
      For my sustain
    Was the Lord. Of many millions   15
      The populous rout
  I fear not though incamping round about
They pitch against me their Pavillions.
Rise Lord, save me my God for thou
      Hast smote ere now   20
    On the cheek-bone all my foes,
      Of men abhor'd
  Hast broke the teeth. This help was from the Lord;
Thy blessing on thy people flows.

PSAL. IV. Aug. 10. 1653

ANSWER me when I call
God of my righteousness;
In straights and in distress
Thou didst me disinthrall
And set at large; now spare,   5
  Now pity me, and hear my earnest prai'r.
Great ones how long will ye
My glory have in scorn,
How long be thus forborn
Still to love vanity,   10
To love, to seek, to prize
  Things false and vain and nothing else but lies?
Yet know the Lord hath chose,
Chose to himself a part
The good and meek of heart   15
(For whom to chuse he knows)
Jehovah from on high
  Will hear my voyce what time to him I crie.
Be aw'd, and do not sin,
Speak to your hearts alone,   20
Upon your beds, each one,
And be at peace within.
Offer the offerings just
  Of righteousness and in *Jehovah* trust.
Many there be that say   25
Who yet will shew us good?
Talking like this worlds brood;
But Lord, thus let me pray,
On us lift up the light
  Lift up the favour of thy count'nance bright.   30
Into my heart more joy
And gladness thou hast put
Then when a year of glut
Their stores doth over-cloy
And from their plenteous grounds   35
  With vast increase their corn and wine abounds.
In peace at once will I
Both lay me down and sleep,

For thou alone dost keep
Me safe where e're I lie   40
As in a rocky Cell,
    Thou Lord alone in safety mak'st me dwell.

PSAL. V. Aug. 12. 1653

JEHOVAH to my words give ear
    My meditation waigh,
The voyce of my complaining hear
My King and God, for unto thee I pray.
    Jehovah thou my early voyce   5
    Shalt in the morning hear,
Ith'morning I to thee with choyce
Will rank my Prayers, and watch till thou appear.
    For thou art not a God that takes
    In wickedness delight;   10
Evil with thee no biding makes,
Fools or mad men stand not within thy sight.
    All workers of iniquity
    Thou hat'st; and them unblest
Thou wilt destroy that speak a ly;   15
The bloodi' and guileful man God doth detest.
    But I will in thy mercies dear
    Thy numerous mercies go
Into thy house; I in thy fear
Will towards thy holy temple worship low.   20
    Lord lead me in thy righteousness,
    Lead me because of those
That do observe if I transgress,
Set thy wayes right before, where my step goes.
    For in his faltring mouth unstable   25
    No word is firm or sooth;
Their inside, troubles miserable;
An open grave their throat, their tongue they smooth.
    God, find them guilty, let them fall
    By their own counsels quell'd;   30

Push them in their rebellions all
Still on; for against thee they have rebell'd;
    Then all who trust in thee shall bring
        Their joy, while thou from blame
    Defend'st them, they shall ever sing   35
And shall triumph in thee, who love thy name.
        For thou *Jebovab* wilt be found
            To bless the just man still,
        As with a shield thou wilt surround
Him with thy lasting favour and good will.   40

PSAL. VI. Aug. 13. 1653

Lord in thine anger do not reprehend me
    Nor in thy hot displeasure me correct;
Pity me Lord for I am much deject,
    Am very weak and faint; heal and amend me,
For all my bones, that even with anguish ake,   5
    Are troubled, yea my soul is troubled sore;
And thou O Lord how long? turn Lord, restore
    My soul, O save me for thy goodness sake,
For in death no remembrance is of thee;
    Who in the grave can celebrate thy praise?   10
Wearied I am with sighing out my dayes,
    Nightly my Couch I make a kind of Sea;
My Bed I water with my tears; mine Eie
    Through grief consumes, is waxen old and dark
Ith' mid'st of all mine enemies that mark.   15
    Depart all ye that work iniquitie.
Depart from me, for the voice of my weeping
    The Lord hath heard, the Lord hath heard my prai'r,
My supplication with acceptance fair
    The Lord will own, and have me in his keeping.   20
Mine enemies shall all be blank and dash't
    With much confusion; then grow red with shame,
They shall return in hast the way they came
    And in a moment shall be quite abash't.

PSAL. VII. Aug. 14. 1653

Upon the words of Chush *the* Benjamite
against him

LORD my God to thee I flie,
Save me and secure me under
Thy protection while I crie;
Least as a Lion (and no wonder)
He hast to tear my Soul asunder   5
Tearing and no rescue nigh.

Lord my God if I have thought
Or done this, if wickedness
Be in my hands, if I have wrought
Ill to him that meant me peace,   10
Or to him have render'd less,
And not free'd my foe for naught;

Let th'enemy pursue my soul
And overtake it, let him tread
My life down to the earth and roul   15
In the dust my glory dead,
In the dust and there out spread
Lodge it with dishonour foul.

Rise *Jehovah* in thine ire
Rouze thy self amidst the rage   20
Of my foes that urge like fire;
    And wake for me, their furi'asswage;
Judgment here thou didst ingage
And command which I desire.

So th'assemblies of each Nation   25
Will surround thee, seeking right,
Thence to thy glorious habitation
Return on high and in their sight.
Jehovah judgeth most upright
All people from the worlds foundation.   30

Judge me Lord, be judge in this
According to my righteousness
And the innocence which is
Upon me: cause at length to cease
Of evil men the wickedness   35
And their power that do amiss.

But the just establish fast,
Since thou art the just God that tries
Hearts and reins. On God is cast
My defence, and in him lies   40
In him who both just and wise
Saves th'upright of Heart at last.

God is a just Judge and severe,
And God is every day offended;
If th'unjust will not forbear,   45
His Sword he whets, his Bow hath bended
Already, and for him intended
The tools of death, that waits him near.

(His arrows purposely made he
For them that persecute.) Behold   50
He travels big with vanitie,
Trouble he hath conceav'd of old
As in a womb, and from that mould
Hath at length brought forth a Lie.

He dig'd a pit, and delv'd it deep,   55
And fell into the pit he made;
His mischief that due course doth keep,
Turns on his head, and his ill trade
Of violence will undelay'd
Fall on his crown with ruine steep.   60

Then will I *Jehovahs* praise
According to his justice raise
And sing the Name and Deitie
Of *Jehovah* the most high.

PSAL. VIII. Aug. 14. 1653

O JEHOVAH our Lord how wondrous great
  And glorious is thy name through all the earth!
So as above the Heavens thy praise to set
  Out of the tender mouths of latest bearth,

Out of the mouths of babes and sucklings thou   5
  Hast founded strength because of all thy foes
To stint th'enemy, and slack th'avengers brow
  That bends his rage thy providence to oppose.

When I behold thy Heavens, thy Fingers art,
  The Moon and Starrs which thou so bright hast set,   10
In the pure firmament, then saith my heart,
  O what is man that thou remembrest yet,

And think'st upon him; or of man begot
  That him thou visit'st and of him art found;
Scarce to be less then Gods, thou mad'st his lot,   15
  With honour and with state thou hast him crown'd.

O're the works of thy hand thou mad'st him Lord,
  Thou hast put all under his lordly feet,
All Flocks, and Herds, by thy commanding word,
  All beasts that in the field or forrest meet,   20

Fowl of the Heavens, and Fish that through the wet
  Sea-paths in shoals do slide, and know no dearth.
O *Jehovah* our Lord how wondrous great
  And glorious is thy name through all the earth.

April. 1648. J. M.

*Nine of the Psalms done into Metre, wherein all but
what is in a different Character, are the
very words of the Text, translated
from the Original*

PSAL. LXXX

1 THOU Shepherd that dost Israel *keep*
  Give ear *in time of need,*

Who leadest like a flock of sheep
    Thy loved Josephs seed,
That sitt'st between the Cherubs *bright*   5
    Between their wings out-spread,
Shine forth, *and from thy cloud give light,*
    And on our foes thy dread.

2 In Ephraims view and Benjamins,
    And in Manasse's sight   10
Awake* thy strength, come, and *be seen*   * *Gnorera.*
    To save us by thy might.

3 Turn us again, *thy grace divine*
    To us O God *voutsafe;*
Cause thou thy face on us to shine,   15
    And then we shall be safe.

4 Lord God of Hosts, how long wilt thou,
    How long wilt thou declare
Thy *smoaking wrath, *and angry brow*   * *Gnashanta.*
    Against thy peoples praire.   20

5 Thou feed'st them with the bread of tears,
    Their bread with tears they eat,
And mak'st them *largely drink the tears   * *Shalish.*
    Wherwith their cheeks are wet.

6 A strife thou mak'st us *and a prey*   25
    To every neighbour foe,
Among themselves they *laugh, they *play,   * *Jilgnagu.*
    And *flouts at us they throw.

7 Return us, *and thy grace divine,*
    O God of Hosts *voutsafe,*   30
Cause thou thy face on us to shine,
    And then we shall be safe.

8 A Vine from Ægypt thou hast brought,
    Thy free love made it thine,
And drov'st out Nations *proud and haut*   35
    To plant this *lovely* Vine.

9 Thou did'st prepare for it a place
    And root it deep and fast,
That it *began to grow apace,*
    And fill'd the land *at last.*   40

10 With her *green* shade *that* cover'd *all,*
    The Hills were *over-spread,*

Her Bows as *high as* Cedars tall
   Advanc'd their lofty head.

11 Her branches *on the western side*   45
   Down to the Sea she sent,
   And *upward* to that river *wide*
   Her other branches *went.*

12 Why hast thou laid her Hedges low
   And brok'n down her Fence,   50
   That all may pluck her, as they go,
   With rudest violence?

13 The *tusked* Boar out of the wood
   Up turns it by the roots,
   Wild Beasts there brouze, and make their food   55
   Her Grapes and tender Shoots.

14 Return now, God of Hosts, look down
   From Heav'n, thy Seat divine,
   Behold *us, but without a frown,*
   And visit this *thy* Vine.   60

15 Visit this Vine, which thy right hand
   Hath set, and planted *long,*
   And the young branch, that for thy self
   Thou hast made firm and strong.

16 But now it is consum'd with fire,   65
   And cut *with Axes* down,
   They perish at thy dreadfull ire,
   At thy rebuke and frown.

17 Upon the man of thy right hand
   Let thy *good* hand be *laid,*   70
   Upon the Son of Man, whom thou
   Strong for thyself hast made.

18 So shall we not go back from thee
   To wayes of sin and shame,
   Quick'n us thou, then *gladly* wee   75
   Shall call upon thy Name.
   Return us, *and thy grace divine*
   Lord God of Hosts *voutsafe,*
   Cause thou thy face on us to shine,
   And then we shall be safe.   80

PSAL. LXXXI

1 To God our strength sing loud, *and clear*,
   Sing loud to God *our King*,
To Jacobs God, *that all may hear*
   Loud acclamations ring.

2 Prepare a Hymn, prepare a Song   5
   The Timbrel hither bring,
The *cheerfull* Psaltry bring along
   And Harp *with* pleasant *string*,

3 Blow, *as is wont*, in the new Moon
   With Trumpets *lofty sound*,   10
Th'appointed time, the day wheron
   Our solemn Feast *comes round*.

4 This was a Statute *giv'n of old*
   For Israel *to observe*,
A Law of Jacobs God, *to hold*   15
   From whence they might not swerve.

5 This he a Testimony ordain'd
   In Joseph, *not to change*,
When as he pass'd through Ægypt land;
   The Tongue I heard, was strange.   20

6 From burden, *and from slavish toyle*
   I set his shoulder free;
His hands from pots, *and mirie soyle*
   Deliver'd were *by me*.

7 When trouble did thee sore assaile,   25
   On me then didst thou call,
And I to free thee *did not faile*,
   And led thee out of thrall.

I answer'd thee in *thunder deep   • *Besether ragnam.*
   With clouds encompass'd round;   30
I tri'd thee at the water *steep*
   Of Meriba *renown'd*.

8 Hear O my people, *heark'n well*,
   I testifie to thee
Thou antient flock of Israel,   35
   If thou wilt list to mee,

9 Throughout the land of thy abode
   No alien God shall be

Nor shalt thou to a forein God
  In honour bend thy knee.   40
10 I am the Lord thy God which brought
  Thee out of Ægypt land
Ask large enough, and I, *besought*,
  Will grant thy full demand.
11 And yet my people would not *hear*,   45
  Nor hearken to my voice;
And Israel *whom I lov'd so dear*
  Mislik'd me for his choice.
12 Then did I leave them to their will
  And to their wandring mind;   50
Their own conceits they follow'd still
  Their own devises blind.
13 O that my people would *be wise*
  To serve me *all their daies*,
And O that Israel would *advise*   55
  To walk my *righteous* waies.
14 Then would I soon bring down their foes
  That now so proudly rise,
And turn my hand against *all those*
  That are their enemies.   60
15 Who hate the Lord should *then be fain*
  , *To* bow to him and bend,
But *they, his People, should remain*,
  Their time should have no end.
16 And he would feed them *from the shock*   65
  With flower of finest wheat,
And satisfie them from the rock
  With Honey *for their Meat*.

PSAL. LXXXII

1 GOD in the *great *assembly stands   • *Bagnadath-el.*
  Of Kings and lordly States,
Among the gods† on both his hands   † *Bekerev.*
  He judges and debates.
2 How long will ye *pervert the right   • *Tish-phetu* 5
  With *judgment false and wrong   *gnavel.*
Favouring the wicked *by your might*,

Who thence grow bold and strong?

3 *Regard the *weak and fatherless,   • *Shiphtu-dal.*
   *Dispatch the *poor mans cause,   10
And †raise the man in deep distress
   By †just and equal Lawes.   † *Hatzdiku.*

4 Defend the poor and desolate,
   And rescue from the hands
Of wicked men the low estate   15
   Of him *that help demands.*

5 They know not nor will understand,
   In darkness they walk on,
The Earths foundations all are *mov'd   • *Jimmotu.*
   And *out of order gon.   20

6 I said that ye were Gods, yea all
   The Sons of God most high,
7 But ye shall die like men, and fall
   As other Princes *die.*

8 Rise God, *judge thou the earth *in might*,   25
   This *wicked* earth *redress,   • *Shiphta.*
For thou art he who shalt by right
   The Nations all possess.

PSAL. LXXXIII

1 Be not thou silent *now at length*
   O God hold not thy peace,
Sit not thou still O God *of strength,*
   We cry and do not cease.

2 For lo thy *furious* foes *now* *swell   5
   And *storm outrageously,   • *Jehemajun.*
And they that hate thee *proud and fell*
   Exalt their heads full hie.

3 Against thy people they †contrive   † *Jagnarimu.*
   †Their Plots and Counsels deep,   † *Sod.*   10
*Them to ensnare they chiefly strive   • *Jithjagnatsu gnal.*
   *Whom thou dost hide and keep.   • *Tsephuneca.*

4 Còme let us cut them off, say they,
   Till they no Nation be,
That Israels name for ever may   15
   Be lost in memory.

5 For they consult †with all their might,   † *Lev jachdau.*
   And all as one in mind
Themselves against thee they unite
   And in firm union bind.   20
6 The tents of Edom, and the brood
   Of *scornful* Ishmael,
Moab, with them of Hagars blood
   That in the Desart dwell,
7 Gebal and Ammon *there conspire,*   25
   And *hateful* Amalec,
The Philistims, and they of Tyre
   Whose bounds the Sea doth check.
8 With them *great* Asshur also bands
   And doth confirm the knot,   30
All these have lent their armed hands
   To aid the Sons of Lot.
9 Do to them as to Midian *bold*
   That wasted all the Coast,
To Sisera, and as *is told*   35
   Thou didst to Jabins *boast,*
When at the brook of Kishon *old*
   They were repulst and slain,
10 At Endor quite cut off, and rowl'd
   As dung upon the plain.   40
11 As Zeb and Oreb evil sped
   So let their Princes speed,
As Zeba, and Zalmunna *bled*
   So let their Princes *bleed.*
12 *For they amidst their pride* have said   45
   By right now shall we seize
†Gods houses, and *will now invade*   † *Neoth Elohim*
   †Their stately Palaces.   *bears both.*
13 My God, oh make them as a wheel
   No quiet let them find,   50
Giddy and *restless* let *them reel*
   Like stubble from the wind.
14 As *when* an *aged* wood takes fire
   Which on a sudden straies,
The *greedy* flame runs hier and hier   55
   Till all the mountains blaze,

15 So with thy whirlwind them pursue,
 And with thy tempest chase;
16 *And till they *yield thee honour due,   * *They seek thy*
 Lord fill with shame their face.   *name.* Heb.
17 Asham'd and troubl'd let them be,   61
 Troubl'd and sham'd for ever,
 Ever confounded, and so die
  With shame, *and scape it never.*
18 Then shall they know that thou whose name 65
 Jehovah is alone,
 Art the most high, *and thou the same*
 O're all the earth *art one.*

PSAL. LXXXIV

1 How lovely are thy dwellings fair!
 O Lord of Hoasts, how dear
 The *pleasant* Tabernacles are!
  Where thou do'st dwell so near.
2 My Soul doth long and almost die   5
 Thy Courts O Lord to see,
 My heart and flesh aloud do crie,
  O living God, for thee.
3 There ev'n the Sparrow *freed from wrong*
 Hath found a house of *rest*,   10
 The Swallow there, to lay her young
 Hath built her *brooding* nest,
 Ev'n *by* thy Altars Lord of Hoasts
  They find their safe abode,
 And home they fly from round the Coasts 15
  Toward thee, My King, my God.
4 Happy, who in thy house reside
 Where thee they ever praise,
5 Happy, whose strength in thee doth bide,
 And in their hearts thy waies.   20
6 They pass through Baca's *thirstie* Vale,
  That dry and barren ground
 As through a fruitfull watry Dale
  Where Springs and Showrs abound.
7 They journey on from strength to strength 25

With joy and gladsom cheer
Till all before *our* God *at length*
In Sion do appear.

8 Lord God of Hoasts hear *now* my praier
O Jacobs God give ear,   30
9 Thou God our shield look on the face
Of thy anointed *dear*.
10 For one day in thy Courts *to be*
Is better, *and more blest*
Then *in the joyes of Vanity*,   35
A thousand daies *at best*.
I in the temple of my God
Had rather keep a dore,
Then dwell in Tents, *and rich abode*
With Sin *for evermore*.   40
11 For God the Lord both Sun and Shield
Gives grace and glory *bright*,
No good from them shall be with-held
Whose waies are just and right.
12 Lord *God* of Hoasts *that raign'st on high*,   45
That man is *truly* blest
Who *only* on thee doth relie,
And in thee only rest.

PSAL. LXXXV

1 THY Land to favour graciously
Thou hast not Lord been slack,
Thou hast from *hard* Captivity
Returned Jacob back.
2 Th'iniquity thou didst forgive   5
That wrought thy people woe,
And all their Sin, *that did thee grieve*
Hast hid *where none shall know*.
3 Thine anger all thou hadst remov'd,
And *calmly* didst return   10
From thy †fierce wrath which we had prov'd   † Heb. *The*
Far worse then fire to burn.   *burning*
                                                          heat of thy
                                                          wrath.
4 God of our saving health and peace,
Turn us, and us restore,

Thine indignation cause to cease   15
　　Toward us, *and chide no more.*
5 Wilt thou be angry without end,
　　For ever angry thus
　Wilt thou thy frowning ire extend
　　From age to age on us?   20
6 Wilt thou not *turn, and *hear our voice*   * Heb. *Turn to*
　And us again *revive,   *quicken us.*
　That so thy people may rejoyce
　　By thee preserv'd alive.
7 Cause us to see thy goodness Lord,   25
　　To us thy mercy shew,
　Thy saving health to us afford
　　And life in us renew.
8 *And now* what God the Lord will speak
　　I will *go strait and* hear,   30
　For to his people he speaks peace
　　And to his Saints *full dear,*
　To his dear Saints he will speak peace,
　　But let them never more
　Return to folly, *but surcease*   35
　　To trespass as before.
9 Surely to such as do him fear
　　Salvation is at hand
　And glory shall *ere long appear*
　　To dwell within our Land.   40
10 Mercy and Truth *that long were miss'd*
　　Now *joyfully* are met,
　Sweet Peace and Righteousness have kiss'd
　　And hand in hand are set.
11 Truth from the earth *like to a flowr*   45
　　Shall bud and blossom *then,*
　And Justice from her heavenly bowr
　　Look down *on mortal men.*
12 The Lord will also then bestow
　　Whatever thing is good,   50
　Our Land shall forth in plenty throw
　　Her fruits *to be our food.*
13 Before him Righteousness shall go
　　His Royal Harbinger,

Then *will he come, and not be slow
His footsteps cannot err.

* Heb. *He will
set his steps
to the way.*

PSAL. LXXXVI

1 THY *gracious* ear, O Lord, encline,
  O hear me *I thee pray*,
For I am poor, and almost pine
  With need, *and sad decay.*

2 Preserve my soul, for †I have trod
  Thy waies, and love the just,
Save thou thy servant O my God
  Who *still* in thee doth trust.

† Heb. *I am good,
loving, a doer of
good and holy
things.*

3 Pitty me Lord for daily thee
  I call; 4 O make rejoyce
Thy Servants Soul; for Lord to thee
  I lift my soul *and voice,*

10

5 For thou art good, thou Lord art prone
  To pardon, thou to all
Art full of mercy, thou *alone*
  To them that on thee call.

15

6 Unto my supplication Lord
  Give ear, and to the crie
Of my *incessant* praiers afford
  Thy hearing graciously.

20

7 I in the day of my distress
  Will call on thee *for aid;*
For thou wilt *grant* me *free access*
  And answer, *what I pray'd.*

8 Like thee among the gods is none
  O Lord, nor any works
Of all that other gods have done
  Like to thy *glorious* works.

25

9 The Nations all whom thou hast made
  Shall come, *and all shall frame*
To bow them low before thee Lord,
  And glorifie thy name.

30

10 For great thou art, and wonders great
  By thy strong hand are done,
Thou *in thy everlasting Seat*

35

Remainest God alone.
11 Teach me O Lord thy way *most right,*
   I in thy truth will bide,
   To fear thy name my heart unite
   So shall it never slide.   40
12 Thee will I praise O Lord my God
   Thee honour, and adore
   With my whole heart, and blaze abroad
   Thy name for ever more.
13 For great thy mercy is toward me,   45
   And thou hast free'd my Soul
   Eev'n from the lowest Hell set free
   From deepest darkness foul.
14 O God the proud against me rise
   And violent men are met   50
   To seek my life, and in their eyes
   No fear of thee have set.
15 But thou Lord art the God most mild
   Readiest thy grace to shew,
   Slow to be angry, and *art stil'd*   55
   Most mercifull, most true.
16 O turn to me *thy face at length,*
   And me have mercy on,
   Unto thy servant give thy strength,
   And save thy hand-maids Son.   60
17 Some sign of good to me afford
   And let my foes *then* see
   And be asham'd, because thou Lord
   Do'st help and comfort me.

PSAL. LXXXVII

 1 AMONG the holy Mountains *high*
   Is his foundation fast,
   There Seated in his Sanctuary,
   His Temple there is plac't.
 2 Sions *fair* Gates the Lord loves more   5
   Then all the dwellings *faire*
   Of Jacobs *Land, though there be store,*
   And all within his care.

3 City of God, most glorious things
    Of thee *abroad* are spoke;   10
4 I mention Egypt, *where proud Kings
    Did our forefathers yoke,*
  I mention Babel to my friends,
    Philistia *full of scorn,*
  And Tyre with Ethiops *utmost ends,*   15
    Lo this man there was born:
5 But *twise that praise shall in our ear*
    Be said of Sion *last*
  This and this man was born in her,
    High God shall fix her fast.   20
6 The Lord shall write it in a Scrowle
    That ne're shall be out-worn
  When he the Nations doth enrowle
    That this man there was born.
7 Both they who sing, and they who dance   25
    With sacred Songs are there,
  In thee *fresh brooks, and soft streams glance
    And* all my fountains *clear.*

PSAL. LXXXVIII

1 LORD God that dost me save and keep,
    All day to thee I cry;
  And all night long, before thee *weep,*
    Before thee *prostrate lie.*
2 Into thy presence let my praier   5
    With sighs devout ascend
  And to my cries, that *ceaseless are,*
    Thine ear with favour bend.
3 For cloy'd with woes and trouble store
    Surcharg'd my Soul doth lie,   10
  My life *at death's uncherful dore*
    Unto the grave draws nigh.
4 Reck'n'd I am with them that pass
    Down to the *dismal* pit,
  I am a *man, but weak alas   * Heb. *A man
    And for that name unfit.   without manly
                                            strength.*

5 From life discharg'd and parted quite
    Among the dead *to sleep,*
And like the slain *in bloody fight*
    That in the grave lie *deep,*   20
Whom thou rememberest no more,
    Dost never more regard;
Them from thy hand deliver'd o're
    Deaths hideous house hath barr'd.

6 Thou in the lowest pit *profound*   25
    Hast set me *all forlorn,*
Where thickest darkness *hovers round,*
    In horrid deeps *to mourn.*

7 Thy wrath *from which no shelter saves*
    Full sore doth press on me;   30
    Thou break'st upon me all thy waves,   * *The* Heb.
    And all thy waves break me.   *bears both.*

8 Thou dost my friends from me estrange,
    And mak'st me odious,
Me to them odious, *for they change,*   35
    And I here pent up thus.

9 Through sorrow, and affliction great
    Mine eye grows dim and dead,
Lord all the day I thee entreat,
    My hands to thee I spread.   40

10 Wilt thou do wonders on the dead,
    Shall the deceas'd arise
And praise thee *from their loathsom bed*
    With pale and hollow eyes?

11 Shall they thy loving kindness tell   45
    On whom the grave *hath hold,*
Or they *who* in perdition *dwell*
    Thy faithfulness *unfold?*

12 In darkness can thy mighty *hand*
    Or wondrous acts be known,   50
Thy justice in the *gloomy* land
    Of *dark* oblivion?

13 But I to thee O Lord do cry
    Ere yet my life be spent,
And *up to thee* my praier *doth hie*   55
    Each morn, and thee prevent.

14 Why wilt thou Lord my soul forsake,
  And hide thy face from me,

15 That am already bruis'd, and †shake   † Heb. *Prae Con-*
  With terror sent from thee;   *cussione.*
  Bruz'd, and afflicted and *so low*   60
  As ready to expire,
  While I thy terrors undergo
  Astonish'd with thine ire.

16 Thy fierce wrath over me doth flow   65
  Thy threatnings cut me through.

17 All day they round about me go,
  Like waves they me persue.

18 Lover and friend thou hast remov'd
  And sever'd from me far.   70
  They *fly me now* whom I have lov'd,
  And as in darkness are.

FINIS.

Passages translated into English verse in the Prose Works

[FROM *Of Reformation . . . in England*, 1641]

Ah *Constantine*, of how much ill was cause
Not thy Conversion, but those rich demaines
That the first wealthy *Pope* receiv'd of thee.

DANTE, Inf. xix. 115.

Founded in chast and humble Povertie,
'Gainst them that rais'd thee dost thou lift thy horn,
Impudent whoore, where hast thou plac'd thy hope?
In thy Adulterers, or thy ill got wealth?
Another *Constantine* comes not in hast.

PETRARCA, Son. 108.

And to be short, at last his guid him brings
Into a goodly valley, where he sees
A mighty masse of things strangely confus'd,
Things that on earth were lost, or were abus'd.

.   .   .   .   .   .

Then past hee to a flowry Mountaine greene,
Which once smelt sweet, now stinks as odiously;
This was that gift (if you the truth will have)
That *Constantine* to good *Sylvestro* gave.

ARIOSTO, Orl. Fur. xxxiv. 80.

[FROM *Reason of Church Government*, 1641]

When I dye, let the Earth be roul'd in flames.

[FROM *Apology for Smectymnuus*, 1642]

. . . laughing to teach the truth
What hinders? as some teachers give to Boyes
Junkets and knacks, that they may learne apace.

HORACE, Sat. I. i. 24.

. . . Jesting decides great things
Stronglier, and better oft than earnest can.

Ibid., I. x. 14.

'Tis you that say it, not I: you do the deeds,
And your ungodly deeds finde me the words.

SOPHOCLES, *Elec.* 624.

[FROM *Areopagitica*, 1644]

This is true Liberty when free-born men
Having to advise the public may speak free,
Which he who can, and will, deserv's high praise;
Who neither can nor will, may hold his peace;
What can be juster in a State then this?

EURIPIDES, *Supp.* 438.

[FROM *Tetrachordon*, 1645]

Whom doe we count a good man, whom but he
Who keepes the laws and statutes of the Senate,
Who judges in great suits and controversies,
Whose witnesse and opinion winnes the cause?
But his own house, and the whole neighbourhood
See his foule inside through his whited skin.

HORACE, *Ep.* I. xvi. 40.

[FROM *The Tenure of Kings and Magistrates*, 1649]

There can be slaine
No sacrifice to God more acceptable
Than an unjust and wicked king.

SENECA, *Herc. Fur.* 922.

[FROM *History of Britain*, 1670]

Brutus *thus addresses* Diana *in the country of* Leogecia.

Goddess of Shades, and Huntress, who at will
Walk'st on the rowling Sphear, and through the deep,
On thy third Reigne the Earth look now, and tell
What Land, what Seat 'of rest thou bidst me seek,
What certain Seat, where I may worship thee
For aye, with Temples vow'd, and Virgin quires.

To whom sleeping before the altar, Diana *in a Vision that night thus answer'd.*

    Brutus far to the West, in th'Ocean wide
Beyond the Realm of *Gaul*, a Land there lies,
Sea-girt it lies, where Giants dwelt of old,
Now void, it fitts thy People; thether bend
Thy course, there shalt thou find a lasting seat,
There to thy Sons another *Troy* shall rise,
And *Kings* be born of thee, whose dredded might
Shall aw the World, and conquer Nations bold.

Geoffrey of Monmouth.

Low in a mead of Kine under a Thorn,
Of head bereft li'th poor *Kenelm* King-born.

Matthew of Westminster.

Joannis Miltoni

LONDINENSIS

POEMATA.

Quorum pleraque· intra
Annum ætatis Vigesimum
Conscripsit.

Nunc primum Edita.

LONDINI,
Typis *R. R.* Prostant ad Insignia Principis,
in Cœmeterio D. *Pauli*, apud *Humphredum*
Moseley. 1 6 4 5.

HÆC quæ sequuntur de Authore testimonia, tametsi ipse intelligebat non tam de se quàm supra se esse dicta, eò quòd preclaro ingenio viri, nec non amici ita fere solent laudare, ut omnia suis potius virtutibus, quàm veritati congruentia nimis cupidè affingant, noluit tamen horum egregiam in se voluntatem non esse notam; Cum alii præsertim ut id faceret magnopere suaderent. Dum enim nimiæ laudis invidiam totis ab se viribus amolitur, sibique quod plus æquo est non attributum esse mavult, judicium interim hominum cordatorum atque illustrium quin summo sibi honori ducat, negare non potest.

Joannes Baptista Mansus, Marchio Villensis Neapolitanus ad Joannem Miltonium Anglum

UT mens, forma, decor, facies, mos, si pietas sic,
Non Anglus, verùm herclè Angelus ipse fores.

Ad Joannem Miltonem Anglum triplici poeseos laureâ coronandum Græcâ nimirum, Latinâ, atque Hetruscâ, Epigramma Joannis Salsilli Romani

CEDE Meles, cedat depressa Mincius urna;
Sebetus Tassum desinat usque loqui;
At Thamesis victor cunctis ferat altior undas,
Nam per te, Milto, par tribus unus erit.

Ad Joannem Miltonum

GRÆCIA Mæonidem, jactet sibi Roma Maronem,
Anglia Miltonum jactat utrique parem.

Selvaggi.

Al Signor Gio. Miltoni Nobile Inglese

ODE

ERGIMI all' Etra, ò Clio,
Perche di stelle intreccierò corona,
Non più del Biondo Dio
La Fronde eterna in Pindo, e in Elicona;
Diensi a merto maggior, maggiori i fregi,   5
A celeste virtù celesti pregi.

Non può del tempo edace
Rimaner preda eterno alto valore,
Non può l'oblio rapace
Furar dalle memorie eccelso onore;   10
Su l'arco di mia cetra un dardo forte
Virtù m'adatti, e ferirò la Morte.

Del Ocean profondo
Cinta dagli ampi gorghi Anglia risiede
Separata dal mondo,   15
Però che il suo valor l'umano eccede:
Questa feconda sà produrre Eroi,
Ch' hanno a ragion del sovruman tra noi.

Alla virtù sbandita
Danno nei petti lor fido ricetto,   20
Quella gli è sol gradita,
Perche in lei san trovar gioia, e diletto;
Ridillo tu, Giovanni, e mostra in tanto
Con tua vera virtù, vero il mio Canto.

Lungi dal Patrio lido   25
Spinse Zeusi l'industre ardente brama,
Ch' udìo d'Helena il grido
Con aurea tromba rimbombar la fama,
E per poterla effigiare al paro
Dalle più belle Idee trasse il più raro.   30

Così l'Ape Ingegnosa
Trae con industria il suo liquor pregiato
Dal giglio e dalla rosa,
E quanti vaghi fiori ornano il prato;
Formano un dolce suon diverse Chorde,   35
Fan varie voci melodia concorde.

Di bella gloria amante,
Milton, dal Ciel natío per varie parti
Le peregrine piante
Volgesti a ricercar scienze, ed arti;   40
Del Gallo regnator vedesti i Regni,
E dell'Italia ancor gl'Eroi più degni.

Fabro quasi divino,
Sol virtù rintracciando, il tuo pensiero
Vide in ogni confino   45
Chi di nobil valor calca il sentiero;
L'ottimo dal miglior dopo scegliea
Per fabbricar d'ogni virtù l'Idea.

Quanti nacquero in Flora
O in lei del parlar Tosco appreser l'arte,   50
La cui memoria onora
Il mondo fatta eterna in dotte carte,
Volesti ricercar per tuo tesoro,
E parlasti con lor nell' opre loro.

Nell' altera Babelle   55
Per te il parlar confuse Giove in vano,
Che per varie favelle
Di se stessa trofeo cadde su'l piano:
Ch' ode oltr' all' Anglia il suo più degno Idioma
Spagna, Francia, Toscana, e Grecia e Roma.   60

I più profondi arcani
Ch' occulta la Natura e in cielo e in terra,
Ch'a Ingegni sovrumani
Troppo avara tal'hor gli chiude, e serra,
Chiaramente conosci, e giungi al fine   65
Della mor[t]al virtude al gran confine.

Non batta il Tempo l'ale,
Fermisi immoto, e in un ferminsi gl'anni,
Che di virtù immortale
Scorron di troppo ingiuriosi ai danni;   70
Chè s'opre degne di Poema o storia
Furon già, l'hai presenti alla memoria.

Dammi tua dolce Cetra
Se vuoi ch'io dica del tuo dolce canto,
Ch' inalzandoti all' Etra   75
Di farti huomo celeste ottiene il vanto;
Il Tamigi il dirà che gl' è concesso
Per te suo cigno pareggiar Permesso.

Io che in riva del Arno
Tento spiegar tuo merto alto, e preclaro,   80
So che fatico indarno,
E ad ammirar, non a lodarlo imparo;
Freno dunque la lingua, e ascolto il core
Che ti prende a lodar con lo stupore.

Del sig. Antonio Francini gentilhuomo
Fiorentino.

JOANNI MILTONI

LONDINIENSI

Juveni Patria, virtutibus eximio,

*VIRO qui multa peregrinatione, studio cuncta orbis terrarum loca perspexit, ut
novus Vlysses omnia ubique ab omnibus apprehenderet.* 5

*Polyglotto, in cujus ore linguæ jam deperditæ sic reviviscunt, ut idiomata omnia
sint in ejus laudibus infacunda; Et jure ea percallet ut admirationes & plausus
populorum ab propria sapientia excitatos, intelligat.*

*Illi, cujus animi dotes corporisque, sensus ad admirationem commovent, & per
ipsam motum cuique auferunt; cujus opera ad plausus hortantur, sed venustate* 10
vocem laudatoribus adimunt.

*Cui in Memoria totus Orbis: In intellectu Sapientia: in voluntate ardor
gloriæ: in ore Eloquentia: Harmonicos celestium Sphærarum sonitus Astro-
nomia Duce audienti, Characteres mirabilium naturæ per quos Dei magnitudo
describitur magistra Philosophia legenti; Antiquitatum latebras, vetustatis* 15
*excidia, eruditionis ambages comite assidua autorum Lectione exquirenti,
restauranti, percurrenti. At cur nitor in arduum? Illi in cujus virtutibus
evulgandis ora Famæ non sufficiant, nec hominum stupor in laudandis satis est,
Reverentiæ & amoris ergo hoc ejus meritis debitum admirationis tributum offert
Carolus Datus Patricius Florentinus,* 20

Tanto homini servus, tantæ virtutis amator.

2 Londiniensi Ed. 1 : Londinensi Ed. 2
4 terrarum Ed. 2 : terrararum Ed. 1
10 venustate Ed. 2 : Vastitate Ed. 1

ELEGIARUM
Liber primus.
Elegia prima ad *Carolum Diodatum*.

TANDEM, chare, tuæ mihi pervenere tabellæ,
 Pertulit & voces nuntia charta tuas,
Pertulit occiduâ Devæ Cestrensis ab orâ
 Vergivium prono quà petit amne salum.
Multùm crede juvat terras aluisse remotas   5
 Pectus amans nostri, tamque fidele caput,
Quòdque mihi lepidum tellus longinqua sodalem
 Debet, at unde brevi reddere jussa velit.
Me tenet urbs refluâ quam Thamesis alluit undâ,
 Meque nec invitum patria dulcis habet.   10
Jam nec arundiferum mihi cura revisere Camum,
 Nec dudum vetiti me laris angit amor.
Nuda nec arva placent, umbrasque negantia molles,
 Quàm male Phœbicolis convenit ille locus!
Nec duri libet usque minas perferre magistri   15
 Cæteraque ingenio non subeunda meo,
Si sit hoc exilium patrios adiisse penates,
 Et vacuum curis otia grata sequi,
Non ego vel profugi nomen, sortemve recuso,
 Lætus & exilii conditione fruor.   20
O utinam vates nunquam graviora tulisset
 Ille Tomitano flebilis exul agro;
Non tunc Jonio quicquam cessisset Homero
 Neve foret victo laus tibi prima, Maro.
Tempora nam licet hîc placidis dare libera Musis,   25
 Et totum rapiunt me mea vita libri.
Excipit hinc fessum sinuosi pompa theatri,
 Et vocat ad plausus garrula scena suos.
Seu catus auditur senior, seu prodigus hæres,
 Seu procus, aut positâ casside miles adest,   30
Sive decennali fœcundus lite patronus
 Detonat inculto barbara verba foro,
Sæpe vafer gnato succurrit servus amanti,

Et nasum rigidi fallit ubique Patris;
Sæpe novos illic virgo mirata calores   35
   Quid sit amor nescit, dum quoque nescit, amat.
Sive cruentatum furiosa Tragœdia sceptrum
   Quassat, & effusis crinibus ora rotat,
Et dolet, & specto, juvat & spectasse dolendo,
   Interdum & lacrymis dulcis amaror inest: 40
Seu puer infelix indelibata reliquit
   Gaudia, & abrupto flendus amore cadit,
Seu ferus e tenebris iterat Styga criminis ultor
   Conscia funereo pectora torre movens,
Seu mæret Pelopeia domus, seu nobilis Ili,   45
   Aut luit incestos aula Creontis avos.
Sed neque sub tecto semper nec in urbe latemus,
   Irrita nec nobis tempora veris eunt.
Nos quoque lucus habet vicinâ consitus ulmo
   Atque suburbani nobilis umbra loci.   50
Sæpius hic blandas spirantia sydera flammas
   Virgineos videas præteriisse choros.
Ah quoties dignæ stupui miracula formæ
   Quæ posset senium vel reparare Iovis;
Ah quoties vidi superantia lumina gemmas,   55
   Atque faces quotquot volvit uterque polus;
Collaque bis vivi Pelopis quæ brachia vincant,
   Quæque fluit puro nectare tincta via,
Et decus eximium frontis, tremulosque capillos,
   Aurea quæ fallax retia tendit Amor;   60
Pellacesque genas, ad quas hyacinthina sordet
   Purpura, & ipse tui floris, Adoni, rubor.
Cedite laudatæ toties Heroides olim,
   Et quæcunque vagum cepit amica Jovem.
Cedite Achæmeniæ turritâ fronte puellæ,   65
   Et quot Susa colunt, Memnoniamque Ninon.
Vos etiam Danaæ fasces submittite Nymphæ,
   Et vos Iliacæ, Romuleæque nurus.
Nec Pompeianas Tarpëia Musa columnas
   Jactet, & Ausoniis plena theatra stolis.   70
Gloria Virginibus debetur prima Britannis,
   Extera, sat tibi sit, fœmina, posse sequi.
Tuque urbs Dardaniis Londinum structa colonis

Turrigerum latè conspicienda caput,
Tu nimium felix intra tua mœnia claudis   75
 Quicquid formosi pendulus orbis habet.
Non tibi tot cælo scintillant astra sereno
 Endymioneæ turba ministra deæ,
Quot tibi conspicuæ formáque auróque puellæ
 Per medias radiant turba videnda vias.   80
Creditur huc geminis venisse invecta columbis
 Alma pharetrigero milite cincta Venus,
Huic Cnidon, & riguas Simoentis flumine valles,
 Huic Paphon, & roseam posthabitura Cypron.
Ast ego, dum pueri sinit indulgentia cæci,   85
 Mœnia quàm subitò linquere fausta paro;
Et vitare procul malefidæ infamia Circes
 Atria, divini Molyos usus ope.
Stat quoque juncosas Cami remeare paludes,
 Atque iterum raucæ murmur adire Scholæ.   90
Interea fidi parvum cape munus amici,
 Paucaque in alternos verba coacta modos.

Elegia secunda, Anno ætatis 17

In obitum Præconis Academici Cantabrigiensis

TE, qui conspicuus baculo fulgente solebas
 Palladium toties ore ciere gregem,
Ultima præconum præconem te quoque sæva
 Mors rapit, officio nec favet ipsa suo.
Candidiora licet fuerint tibi tempora plumis   5
 Sub quibus accipimus delituisse Jovem,
O dignus tamen Hæmonio juvenescere succo,
 Dignus in Æsonios vivere posse dies,
Dignus quem Stygiis medicâ revocaret ab undis
 Arte Coronides, sæpe rogante dea.   10
Tu si jussus eras acies accire togatas,
 Et celer a Phœbo nuntius ire tuo,
Talis in Iliacâ stabat Cyllenius aula
 Alipes, æthereâ missus ab arce Patris.
Talis & Eurybates ante ora furentis Achillei   15
 Rettulit Atridæ jussa severa ducis.
Magna sepulchrorum regina, satelles Averni

Sæva nimis Musis, Palladi sæva nimis,
Quin illos rapias qui pondus inutile terræ
   Turba quidem est telis ista petenda tuis.   20
Vestibus hunc igitur pullis, Academia, luge,
   Et madeant lachrymis nigra feretra tuis.
Fundat & ipsa modos querebunda Elegëia tristes,
   Personet & totis nænia mœsta scholis.

Elegia tertia, Anno ætatis 17

In obitum Præsulis Wintoniensis

Mœstus eram, & tacitus nullo comitante sedebam,
   Hærebantque animo tristia plura meo,
Protinus en subiit funestæ cladis imago
   Fecit in Angliaco quam Libitina solo;
Dum procerum ingressa est splendentes marmore turres   5
   Dira sepulchrali mors metuenda face;
Pulsavitque auro gravidos & jaspide muros,
   Nec metuit satrapum sternere falce greges.
Tunc memini clarique ducis, fratrisque verendi
   Intempestivis ossa cremata rogis.   10
Et memini Heroum quos vidit ad æthera raptos,
   Flevit & amissos Belgia tota duces.
At te præcipuè luxi, dignissime præsul,
   Wintoniæque olim gloria magna tuæ;
Delicui fletu, & tristi sic ore querebar,   15
   Mors fera Tartareo diva secunda Jovi,
Nonne satis quod sylva tuas persentiat iras,
   Et quod in herbosos jus tibi detur agros,
Quodque afflata tuo marcescant lilia tabo,
   Et crocus, & pulchræ Cypridi sacra rosa,   20
Nec sinis ut semper fluvio contermina quercus
   Miretur lapsus prætereuntis aquæ?
Et tibi succumbit liquido quæ plurima caelo
   Evehitur pennis quamlibet augur avis,
Et quæ mille nigris errant animalia sylvis,   25
   Et quod alunt mutum Proteos antra pecus.
Invida, tanta tibi cum sit concessa potestas,
   Quid juvat humanâ tingere cæde manus?

19 terræ? *Keightley*: terræ, Edd. 1, 2

Nobileque in pectus certas acuisse sagittas,
    Semideamque animam sede fugâsse suâ?   30
Talia dum lacrymans alto sub pectore volvo,
    Roscidus occiduis Hesperus exit aquis,
Et Tartessiaco submerserat æquore currum
    Phœbus ab eöo littore mensus iter.
Nec mora, membra cavo posui refovenda cubili,   35
    Condiderant oculos noxque soporque meos:
Cum mihi visus eram lato spatiarier agro,
    Heu nequit ingenium visa referre meum.
Illic puniceâ radiabant omnia luce,
    Ut matutino cum juga sole rubent.   40
Ac veluti cum pandit opes Thaumantia proles,
    Vestitu nituit multicolore solum.
Non dea tam variis ornavit floribus hortos
    Alcinoi, Zephyro Chloris amata levi.
Flumina vernantes lambunt argentea campos,   45
    Ditior Hesperio flavet arena Tago.
Serpit odoriferas per opes levis aura Favoni,
    Aura sub innumeris humida nata rosis.
Talis in extremis terræ Gangetidis oris
    Luciferi regis fingitur esse domus.   50
Ipse racemiferis dum densas vitibus umbras
    Et pellucentes miror ubique locos,
Ecce mihi subito præsul Wintonius astat,
    Sydereum nitido fulsit in ore jubar;
Vestis ad auratos defluxit candida talos,   55
    Infula divinum cinxerat alba caput.
Dumque senex tali incedit venerandus amictu,
    Intremuit læto florea terra sono.
Agmina gemmatis plaudunt cælestia pennis,
    Pura triumphali personat æthra tubâ.   60
Quisque novum amplexu comitem cantuque salutat,
    Hosque aliquis placido misit ab ore sonos;
Nate veni, & patrii felix cape gaudia regni,
    Semper ab hinc duro, nate, labore vaca.
Dixit, & aligeræ tetigerunt nablia turmæ,   65
    At mihi cum tenebris aurea pulsa quies.
Flebam turbatos Cephaleiâ pellice somnos,
    Talia contingant somnia sæpe mihi.

Elegia quarta. Anno ætatis 18

Ad Thomam Junium præceptorem
suum apud mercatores Anglicos Hamburgæ
agentes Pastoris munere fungentem

CURRE per immensum subitò, mea littera, pontum,
    I, pete Teutonicos læve per æquor agros,
Segnes rumpe moras, & nil, precor, obstet eunti,
    Et festinantis nil remoretur iter.
Ipse ego Sicanio frænantem carcere ventos   5
    Æolon, & virides sollicitabo Deos;
Cæruleamque suis comitatam Dorida Nymphis,
    Ut tibi dent placidam per sua regna viam.
At tu, si poteris, celeres tibi sume jugales,
    Vecta quibus Colchis fugit ab ore viri;   10
Aut queis Triptolemus Scythicas devenit in oras
    Gratus Eleusinâ missus ab urbe puer.
Atque ubi Germanas flavere videbis arenas
    Ditis ad Hamburgæ mœnia flecte gradum,
Dicitur occiso quæ ducere nomen ab Hamâ,   15
    Cimbrica quem fertur clava dedisse neci.
Vivit ibi antiquæ clarus pietatis honore
    Præsul Christicolas pascere doctus oves;
Ille quidem est animæ plusquam pars altera nostræ,
    Dimidio vitæ vivere cogor ego.   20
Hei mihi quot pelagi, quot montes interjecti
    Me faciunt aliâ parte carere mei!
Charior ille mihi quam tu, doctissime Graium,
    Cliniadi, pronepos qui Telamonis erat;
Quámque Stagirites generoso magnus alumno,   25
    Quem peperit Libyco Chaonis alma Jovi.
Qualis Amyntorides, qualis Philyrëius Heros
    Myrmidonum regi, talis & ille mihi.
Primus ego Aonios illo præeunte recessus
    Lustrabam, & bifidi sacra vireta jugi,   30
Pieriosque hausi latices, Clioque favente,
    Castalio sparsi læta ter ora mero.
Flammeus at signum ter viderat arietis Æthon,
    Jnduxitque auro lanea terga novo,

Bisque novo terram sparsisti, Chlori, senilem   35
  Gramine, bisque tuas abstulit Auster opes:
Necdum ejus licuit mihi lumina pascere vultu,
  Aut linguæ dulces aure bibisse sonos.
Vade igitur, cursuque Eurum præverte sonorum,
  Quàm sit opus monitis res docet, ipsa vides.   40
Invenies dulci cum conjuge forte sedentem,
  Mulcentem gremio pignora chara suo,
Forsitan aut veterum prælarga volumina patrum
  Versantem, aut veri biblia sacra Dei,
Cælestive animas saturantem rore tenellas,   45
  Grande salutiferæ religionis opus.
Utque solet, multam sit dicere cura salutem,
  Dicere quam decuit, si modo adesset, herum.
Hæc quoque paulum oculos in humum defixa modestos,
  Verba verecundo sis memor ore loqui: 50
Hæc tibi, si teneris vacat inter prælia Musis,
  Mittit ab Angliaco littore fida manus.
Accipe sinceram, quamvis sit sera, salutem
  Fiat & hoc ipso gratior illa tibi.
Sera quidem, sed vera fuit, quam casta recepit   55
  Icaris a lento Penelopeia viro.
Aft ego quid volui manifestum tollere crimen,
  Ipse quod ex omni parte levare nequit?
Arguitur tardus meritò, noxamque fatetur,
  Et pudet officium deseruisse suum.   60
Tu modò da veniam fasso, veniamque roganti,
  Crimina diminui, quæ patuere, solent.
Non ferus in pavidos rictus diducit hiantes,
  Vulnifico pronos nec rapit ungue leo.
Sæpe sarissiferi crudelia pectora Thracis   65
  Supplicis ad mœstas delicuere preces.
Extensæque manus avertunt fulminis ictus,
  Placat & iratos hostia parva Deos.
Jamque diu scripsisse tibi fuit impetus illi,
  Neve moras ultra ducere passus Amor.   70
Nam vaga Fama refert, heu nuntia vera malorum!
  In tibi finitimis bella tumere locis,
Teque tuàmque urbem truculento milite cingi,

57 nequit? Newton: nequit. Edd. 1, 2

Et jam Saxonicos arma parasse duces.
Te circum latè campos populatur Enyo,   75
    Et sata carne virum jam cruor arva rigat.
Germanisque suum concessit Thracia Martem,
    Illuc Odrysios Mars pater egit equos.
Perpetuóque comans jam deflorescit oliva,
    Fugit & ærisonam Diva perosa tubam,   80
Fugit io terris, & jam non ultima virgo
    Creditur ad superas justa volasse domos.
Te tamen intereà belli circumsonat horror,
    Vivis & ignoto solus inópsque solo;
Et, tibi quam patrii non exhibuere penates   85
    Sede peregrinâ quæris egenus opem.
Patria dura parens, & saxis sævior albis
    Spumea quæ pulsat littoris unda tui,
Siccine te decet innocuos exponere fætus,
    Siccine in externam ferrea cogis humum,   90
Et sinis ut terris quærant alimenta remotis
    Quos tibi prospiciens miserat ipse Deus,
Et qui læta ferunt de cælo nuntia, quique
    Quæ via post cineres ducat ad astra, docent?
Digna quidem Stygiis quæ vivas clausa tenebris,   95
    Æternâque animæ digna perire fame!
Haud aliter vates terræ Thesbitidis olim
    Pressit inassueto devia tesqua pede,
Desertasque Arabum salebras, dum regis Achabi
    Effugit atque tuas, Sidoni dira, manus.   100
Talis & horrisono laceratus membra flagello,
    Paulus ab Æmathiâ pellitur urbe Cilix.
Piscosæque ipsum Gergessæ civis Jësum
    Finibus ingratus jussit abire suis.
At tu sume animos, nec spes cadat anxia curis   105
    Nec tua concutiat decolor ossa metus.
Sis etenim quamvis fulgentibus obsitus armis,
    Intententque tibi millia tela necem,
At nullis vel inerme latus violabitur armis,
    Deque tuo cuspis nulla cruore bibet.   110
Namque eris ipse Dei radiante sub ægide tutus,
    Ille tibi custos, & pugil ille tibi;
Ille Sionææ qui tot sub mœnibus arcis

Assyrios fudit nocte silente viros;
Inque fugam vertit quos in Samaritidas oras   115
   Misit ab antiquis prisca Damascus agris,
Terruit & densas pavido cum rege cohortes,
   Aere dum vacuo buccina clara sonat,
Cornea pulvereum dum verberat ungula campum,
   Currus arenosam dum quatit actus humum,   120
Auditurque hinnitus equorum ad bella ruentûm,
   Et strepitus ferri, murmuraque alta virûm.
Et tu (quod superest miseris) sperare memento,
   Et tua magnanimo pectore vince mala.
Nec dubites quandoque frui melioribus annis,   125
   Atque iterum patrios posse videre lares.

Elegia quinta, Anno ætatis 20

In adventum veris

IN se perpetuo Tempus revolubile gyro
   Jam revocat Zephyros vere tepente novos.
Induiturque brevem Tellus reparata juventam,
   Jamque soluta gelu dulce virescit humus.
Fallor? an & nobis redeunt in carmina vires,   5
   Ingeniumque mihi munere veris adest?
Munere veris adest, iterumque vigescit ab illo
   (Quis putet?) atque aliquod jam sibi poscit opus.
Castalis ante oculos, bifidumque cacumen oberrat,
   Et mihi Pyrenen somnia nocte ferunt.   10
Concitaque arcano fervent mihi pectora motu,
   Et furor, & sonitus me sacer intùs agit.
Delius ipse venit, video Penëide lauro
   Implicitos crines, Delius ipse venit.
Jam mihi mens liquidi raptatur in ardua cœli,   15
   Perque vagas nubes corpore liber eo.
Perque umbras, perque antra feror penetralia vatum,
   Et mihi fana patent interiora Deûm.
Intuiturque animus toto quid agatur Olympo,
   Nec fugiunt oculos Tartara cæca meos.   20
Quid tam grande sonat distento spiritus ore?

8 putet? Tickell: putet Edd. 1, 2

Quid parit hæc rabies, quid sacer iste furor?
Ver mihi, quod dedit ingenium, cantabitur illo;
  Profuerint isto reddita dona modo.
Jam, Philomela, tuos foliis adoperta novellis   25
  Instituis modulos, dum silet omne nemus.
Urbe ego, tu sylvâ simul incipiamus utrique,
  Et simul adventum veris uterque canat.
Veris io rediere vices, celebremus honores
  Veris, & hoc subeat Musa perennis opus,   30
Jam sol Æthiopas fugiens Tithoniaque arva,
  Flectit ad Arctöas aurea lora plagas.
Est breve noctis iter, brevis est mora noctis opacæ,
  Horrida cum tenebris exulat illa suis.
Jamque Lycaonius plaustrum cæleste Boötes   35
  Non longâ sequitur fessus ut ante viâ,
Nunc etiam solitas circum Jovis atria toto
  Excubias agitant sydera rara polo.
Nam dolus & cædes, & vis cum nocte recessit,
  Neve Giganteum Dii timuere scelus.   40
Forte aliquis scopuli recubans in vertice pastor,
  Roscida cum primo sole rubescit humus,
Hac, ait, hac certè caruisti nocte puellâ,
  Phœbe, tuâ, celeres quæ retineret equos.
Læta suas repetit sylvas, pharetramque resumit   45
  Cynthia, Luciferas ut videt alta rotas,
Et tenues ponens radios gaudere videtur
  Officium fieri tam breve fratris ope.
Desere, Phœbus ait, thalamos, Aurora, seniles,
  Quid juvat effœto procubuisse toro?   50
Te manet Æolides viridi venator in herba,
  Surge, tuos ignes altus Hymettus habet.
Flava verecundo dea crimen in ore fatetur,
  Et matutinos ocyus urget equos.
Exuit invisam Tellus rediviva senectam,   55
  Et cupit amplexus, Phœbe, subire tuos;
Et cupit, & digna est, quid enim formosius illâ,
  Pandit ut omniferos luxuriosa sinus,
Atque Arabum spirat messes, & ab ore venusto
  Mitia cum Paphiis fundit amoma rosis?   60

30 perennis Ed. 2: quotannis Ed. 1   60 rosis? *scripsi*: rosis. Edd. 1, 2

Ecce coronatur sacro frons ardua luco,
    Cingit ut Idæam pinea turris Opim;
Et vario madidos intexit flore capillos,
    Floribus & visa est posse placere suis.
Floribus effusós ut erat redimita capillos   65
    Tænario placuit diva Sicana Deo.
Aspice, Phœbe, tibi faciles hortantur amores,
    Mellitasque movent flamina verna preces.
Cinnameâ Zephyrus leve plaudit odorifer alâ,
    Blanditiasque tibi ferre videntur aves.   70
Nec sine dote tuos temeraria quærit amores
    Terra, nec optatos poscit egena toros;
Alma salutiferum medicos tibi gramen in usus
    Præbet, & hinc titulos adjuvat ipsa tuos.
Quòd si te pretium, si te fulgentia tangunt   75
    Munera, (muneribus sæpe coemptus Amor)
Illa tibi ostentat quascunque sub æquore vasto,
    Et superinjectis montibus abdit opes.
Ah quoties cum tu clivoso fessus Olympo
    In vespertinas præcipitaris aquas,   80
Cur te, inquit, cursu languentem, Phœbe, diurno
    Hesperiis recipit cærula mater aquis?
Quid tibi cum Tethy? Quid cum Tartesside lymphâ,
    Dia quid immundo perluis ora salo?
Frigora, Phœbe, meâ melius captabis in umbrâ,   85
    Huc ades, ardentes imbue rore comas.
Mollior egelidâ veniet tibi somnus in herbâ,
    Huc ades, & gremio lumina pone meo.
Quáque jaces circum mulcebit lene susúrrans
    Aura per humentes corpora fusa rosas.   90
Nec me (crede·mihi) terrent Semelëia fata,
    Nec Phäetontéo fumidus axis equo;
Cum tu, Phœbe, tuo sapientius uteris igni,
    Huc ades & gremio lumina pone meo.
Sic Tellus lasciva suos suspirat amores;   95
    Matris in exemplum cætera turba ruunt.
Nunc etenim toto currit vagus orbe Cupido,
    Languentesque fovet solis ab igne faces.

82 cærula Warton: Cærula Edd. 1, 2

Insonuere novis lethalia cornua nervis,
   Triste micant ferro tela corusca novo.   100
Jamque vel invictam tentat superasse Dianam,
   Quæque sedet sacro Vesta pudica foco.
Ipsa senescentem reparat Venus annua formam,
   Atque iterum tepido creditur orta mari.
Marmoreas juvenes clamant Hymenææ per urbes,   105
   Littus io Hymen, & cava saxa sonant.
Cultior ille venit tunicâque decentior aptâ,
   Puniceum redolet vestis odora crocum.
Egrediturque frequens ad amœni gaudia veris
   Virgineos auro cincta puella sinus.   110
Votum est cuique suum, votum est tamen omnibus unum,
   Ut sibi quem cupiat, det Cytherea virum.
Nunc quoque septenâ modulatur arundine pastor,
   Et sua quæ jungat carmina Phyllis habet.
Navita nocturno placat sua sydera cantu,   115
   Delphinasque leves ad vada summa vocat.
Jupiter ipse alto cum conjuge ludit Olympo,
   Convocat & famulos ad sua festa Deos.
Nunc etiam Sátyri cum sera crepuscula surgunt,
   Pervolitant celeri florea rura choro,   120
Sylvanusque suâ Cyparissi fronde revinctus,
   Semicaperque Deus, semideusque caper.
Quæque sub arboribus Dryades latuere vetustis
   Per juga, per solos expatiantur agros.
Per sata luxuriat fruticetaque Mænalius Pan,   125
   Vix Cybele mater, vix sibi tuta Ceres,
Atque aliquam cupidus prædatur Oreada Faunus,
   Consulit in trepidos dum sibi Nympha pedes,
Jamque latet, latitansque cupit male tecta videri,
   Et fugit, & fugiens pervelit ipsa capi.   130
Dii quoque non dubitant cælo præponere sylvas,
   Et sua quisque sibi numina lucus habet.
Et sua quisque diu sibi numina lucus habeto,
   Nec vos arboreâ, dii, precor ite domo.
Te referant miseris te, Jupiter, aurea terris   135
   Sæcla, quid ad nimbos aspera tela redis?
Tu saltem lentè rapidos age, Phœbe, jugales

110 Virgineos Ed. 3 : Virgineas Edd. 1, 2

Quà potes, & sensim tempora veris eant.
Brumaque productas tardè ferat hispida noctes,
Ingruat & nostro serior umbra polo.   140

Elegia sexta.

Ad Carolum Diodatum ruri commorantem

*Qui cum idibus Decemb. scripsisset, & sua carmina excusari postulasset si
solito minus essent bona, quòd inter lautitias quibus erat ab amicis exceptus,
haud satis felicem operam Musis dare se posse affirmabat, hunc habuit
responsum.*

MITTO tibi sanam non pleno ventre salutem,
    Quâ tu distento forte carere potes.
At tua quid nostram prolectat Musa camœnam,
    Nec sinit optatas posse sequi tenebras?
Carmine scire velis quàm te redamémque colámque,   5
    Crede mihi vix hoc carmine scire queas.
Nam neque noster amor modulis includitur arctis,
    Nec venit ad claudos integer ipse pedes.
Quàm bene solennes epulas, hilaremque Decembrim
    Festaque cœlifugam quæ coluere Deum,   10
Deliciasque refers, hyberni gaudia ruris,
    Haustaque per lepidos Gallica musta focos.
Quid quereris refugam vino dapibusque poesin?
    Carmen amat Bacchum, Carmina Bacchus amat.
Nec puduit Phœbum virides gestasse corymbos,   15
    Atque hederam lauro præposuisse suæ.
Sæpius Aoniis clamavit collibus Euœ
    Mista Thyonêo turba novena choro.
Naso Corrallæis mala carmina misit ab agris:
    Non illic epulæ non sata vitis erat.   20
Quid nisi vina, rosasque racemiferumque Lyæum
    Cantavit brevibus Tëia Musa modis?
Pindaricosque inflat numeros Teumesius Euan,
    Et redolet sumptum pagina quæque merum;
Dum gravis everso currus crepat axe supinus,   25
    Et volat Eléo pulvere fuscus eques.
Quadrimoque madens Lyricen Romanus Jaccho
    Dulce canit Glyceran, flavicomamque Chloen.

Jam quoque lauta tibi generoso mensa paratu,
    Mentis alit vires, ingeniumque fovet.   30
Massica fœcundam despumant pocula venam,
    Fundis & ex ipso condita metra cado.
Addimus his artes, fusumque per intima Phœbum
    Corda, favent uni Bacchus, Apollo, Ceres.
Scilicet haud mirum tam dulcia carmina per te   35
    Numine composito tres peperisse Deos.
Nunc quoque Thressa tibi cælato barbitos auro
    Insonat argutâ molliter icta manu;
Auditurque chelys suspensa tapetia circum,
    Virgineos tremulâ quæ regat arte pedes.   40
Illa tuas saltem teneant spectacula Musas,
    Et revocent, quantum crapula pellit iners.
Crede mihi dum psallit ebur, comitataque plectrum
    Implet odoratos festa chorea tholos,
Percipies tacitum per pectora serpere Phœbum,   45
    Quale repentinus permeat ossa calor,
Perque puellares oculos digitumque sonantem
    Irruet in totos lapsa Thalia sinus.
Namque Elegia levis multorum cura deorum est,
    Et vocat ad numeros quemlibet illa suos;   50
Liber adest elegis, Eratoque, Ceresque, Venusque,
    Et cum purpureâ matre tenellus Amor.
Talibus inde licent convivia larga poetis,
    Sæpius & veteri commaduisse mero.
At qui bella refert, & adulto sub Jove cælum,   55
    Heroasque pios, semideosque duces,
Et nunc sancta canit superum consulta deorum,
    Nunc latrata fero regna profunda cane,
Ille quidem parcè Samii pro more magistri
    Vivat, & innocuos præbeat herba cibos;   60
Stet prope fagineo pellucida lympha catillo,
    Sobriaque è puro pocula fonte bibat.
Additur huic scelerisque vacans, & casta juventus,
    Et rigidi mores, & sine labe manus.
Qualis veste nitens sacrâ, & lustralibus undis   65
    Surgis ad infensos augur iture Deos.
Hoc ritu vixisse ferunt post rapta sagacem
    Lumina Tiresian, Ogygiumque Linon,

Et lare devoto profugum Calchanta, senemque
    Orpheon edomitis sola per antra feris;   70
Sic dapis exiguus, sic rivi potor Homerus
    Dulichium vexit per freta longa virum,
Et per monstrificam Perseiæ Phœbados aulam,
    Et vada fœmineis insidiosa sonis,
Perque tuas, rex ime, domos, ubi sanguine nigro   75
    Dicitur umbrarum detinuisse greges.
Diis etenim sacer est vates, divûmque sacerdos,
    Spirat & occultum pectus, & ora Jovem.
At tu siquid agam, scitabere (si modò saltem
    Esse putas tanti noscere siquid agam)   80
Paciferum canimus cælesti semine regem,
    Faustaque sacratis sæcula pacta libris,
Vagitumque Dei, & stabulantem paupere tecto
    Qui suprema suo cum patre regna colit;
Stelliparumque polum, modulantesque æthere turmas,   85
    Et subitò elisos ad sua fana Deos.
Dona quidem dedimus Christi natalibus illa,
    Illa sub auroram lux mihi prima tulit.
Te quoque pressa manent patriis meditata cicutis,
    Tu mihi, cui recitem, judicis instar eris.   90

Elegia septima, Anno ætatis undevigesimo

NONDUM blanda tuas leges, Amathusia, norâm,
    Et Paphio vacuum pectus ab igne fuit.
Sæpe cupidineas, puerilia tela, sagittas,
    Atque tuum sprevi maxime, numen, Amor.
Tu puer imbelles, dixi, transfige columbas,   5
    Conveniunt tenero mollia bella duci.
Aut de passeribus tumidos age, parve, triumphos,
    Hæc sunt militiæ digna trophæa tuæ.
In genus humanum quid inania dirigis arma?
    Non valet in fortes ista pharetra viros.   10
Non tulit hoc Cyprius, (neque enim Deus ullus ad iras
    Promptior) & duplici jam ferus igne calet.
Ver erat, & summæ radians per culmina villæ
    Attulerat primam lux tibi, Maie, diem:

2 fuit Ed. 3 : suit Edd. 1, 2

At mihi adhuc refugam quærebant lumina noctem 15
    Nec matutinum sustinuere jubar.
Astat Amor lecto, pictis Amor impiger alis,
    Prodidit astantem mota pharetra Deum:
Prodidit & facies, & dulce minantis ocelli,
    Et quicquid puero, dignum & Amore fuit. 20
Talis in æterno juvenis Sigeius Olympo
    Miscet amatori pocula plena Jovi;
Aut qui formosas pellexit ad oscula nymphas
    Thiodamantæus Naiade raptus Hylas;
Addideratque iras, sed & has decuisse putares, 25
    Addideratque truces, nec sine felle minas.
Et miser exemplo sapuisses tutiùs, inquit,
    Nunc mea quid possit dextera testis eris.
Inter & expertos vires numerabere nostras,
    Et faciam vero per tua damna fidem. 30
Ipse ego, si nescis, strato Pythone superbum
    Edomui Phœbum, cessit & ille mihi;
Et quoties meminit Peneidos, ipse fatetur
    Certiùs & graviùs tela nocere mea.
Me nequit adductum curvare peritiùs arcum, 35
    Qui post terga solet vincere Parthus eques.
Cydoniusque mihi cedit venator, & ille
    Inscius uxori qui necis author erat.
Est etiam nobis ingens quoque victus Orion,
    Herculeæque manus, Herculeusque comes. 40
Jupiter ipse licet sua fulmina torqueat in me,
    Hærebunt lateri spicula nostra Jovis.
Cætera quæ dubitas meliùs mea tela docebunt,
    Et tua non leviter corda petenda mihi.
Nec te, stulte, tuæ poterunt defendere Musæ, 45
    Nec tibi Phœbæus porriget anguis opem.
Dixit, & aurato quatiens mucrone sagittam,
    Evolat in tepidos Cypridos ille sinus.
At mihi risuro tonuit ferus ore minaci,
    Et mihi de puero non metus ullus erat. 50
Et modò quà nostri spatiantur in urbe Quirites
    Et modò villarum proxima rura placent.
Turba frequens, faciéque simillima turba dearum

21 æterno Ed. 2 : aererno Ed. 1

Splendida per medias itque reditque vias.
Auctaque luce dies gemino fulgore coruscat,   55
    Fallor? an & radios hinc quoque Phœbus habet?
Hæc ego non fugi spectacula grata severus,
    Impetus & quò me fert juvenilis, agor.
Lumina luminibus malè providus obvia misi,
    Neve oculos potui continuisse meos.   60
Unam forte aliis supereminuisse notabam,
    Principium nostri lux erat illa mali.
Sic Venus optaret mortalibus ipsa videri,
    Sic regina Deûm conspicienda fuit.
Hanc memor objecit nobis malus ille Cupido,   65
    Solus & hos nobis texuit antè dolos.
Nec procul ipse vafer latuit, multæque sagittæ,
    Et facis a tergo grande pependit onus.
Nec mora, nunc ciliis hæsit, nunc virginis ori,
    Insilit hinc labiis, insidet inde genis: 70
Et quascunque agilis partes jaculator oberrat,
    Hei mihi, mille locis pectus inerme ferit.
Protinus insoliti subierunt corda furores,
    Uror amans intùs, flammaque totus eram.
Interea misero quæ jam mihi sola placebat,   75
    Ablata est oculis non reditura meis.
Ast ego progredior tacitè querebundus, & excors,
    Et dubius volui sæpe referre pedem.
Findor, & hæc remanet, sequitur pars altera votum,
    Raptaque tàm subitò gaudia flere juvat.   80
Sic dolet amissum proles Junonia cœlum,
    Inter Lemniacos præcipitata focos.
Talis & abreptum solem respexit, ad Orcum
    Vectus ab attonitis Amphiaraus equis.
Quid faciam infelix, & luctu victus? amores   85
    Nec licet inceptos ponere, neve sequi.
O utinam spectare semel mihi detur amatos
    Vultus, & coram tristia verba loqui;
Forsitan & duro non est adamante creata,
    Forte nec ad nostras surdeat illa preces.   90
Crede mihi nullus sic infeliciter arsit,
    Ponar in exemplo primus & unus ego.

56 habet? Warton: habet. Edd. 1, 2   85 victus? Newton: victus. Edd. 1, 2

Parce precor teneri cum sis Deus ales amoris,
  Pugnent officio nec tua facta tuo.
Jam tuus O certè est mihi formidabilis arcus,   95
  Nate deâ, jaculis nec minus igne potens:
Et tua fumabunt nostris altaria donis,
  Solus & in superis tu mihi summus eris.
Deme meos tandem, verùm nec deme furores,
  Nescio cur, miser est suaviter omnis amans: 100
Tu modo da facilis, posthæc mea siqua futura est,
  Cuspis amaturos figat ut una duos.

HÆC ego mente olim lævâ, studioque supino
  Nequitiæ posui vana trophæa meæ.
Scilicet abreptum sic me malus impulit error,
  Indocilisque ætas prava magistra fuit.
Donec Socraticos umbrosa Academia rivos   5
  Præbuit, admissum dedocuitque jugum.
Protinus extinctis ex illo tempore flammis,
  Cincta rigent multo pectora nostra gelu.
Unde suis frigus metuit puer ipse Sagittis,
  Et Diomedéam vim timet ipsa Venus.   10

In proditionem Bombardicam

CUM simul in regem nuper satrapasque Britannos
  Ausus es infandum, perfide Fauxe, nefas,
Fallor? an & mitis voluisti ex parte videri,
  Et pensare malâ cum pietate scelus;
Scilicet hos alti missurus ad atria cæli,   5
  Sulphureo curru flammivolisque rotis:
Qualiter ille feris caput inviolabile Parcis
  Liquit Jördanios turbine raptus agros.

In eandem

SICCINE tentasti cælo donâsse Jäcobum
  Quæ septemgemino Bellua monte lates?
Ni meliora tuum poterit dare munera numen,
  Parce precor donis insidiosa tuis.

Ille quidem sine te consortia serus adivit   5
  Astra, nec inferni pulveris usus ope.
Sic potiùs fœdos in cælum pelle cucullos,
  Et quot habet brutos Roma profana Deos.
Namque hac aut aliâ nisi quemque adjuveris arte,
  Crede mihi cæli vix bene scandet iter.   10

In eandem

PURGATOREM animæ derisit Jäcobus ignem,
  Et sine quo superûm non adeunda domus.
Frenduit hoc trinâ monstrum Latiale coronâ
  Movit & horrificùm cornua dena minax.
Et nec inultus ait, temnes mea sacra, Britanne,   5
  Supplicium spretâ relligione dabis.
Et si stelligeras unquam penetraveris arces,
  Non nisi per flammas triste patebit iter.
O quàm funesto cecinisti proxima vero,
  Verbaque ponderibus vix caritura suis!   10
Nam prope Tartareo sublime rotatus ab igni
  Ibat ad æthereas umbra perusta plagas.

In eandem

QUEM modò Roma suis devoverat impia diris,
  Et Styge damnarât Tænarioque sinu,
Hunc vice mutatâ jam tollere gestit ad astra,
  Et cupit ad superos evehere usque Deos.

In inventorem Bombardæ

JAPETIONIDEM laudavit cæca vetustas,
  Qui tulit æetheream solis ab axe facem;
At mihi major erit, qui lurida creditur arma,
  Et trifidum fulmen surripuisse Jovi.

Ad Leonoram Romæ canentem

ANGELUS unicuique suus (sic credite gentes)
  Obtigit æthereis ales ab ordinibus.
Quid mirum, Leonora, tibi si gloria major?
  Nam tua præsentem vox sonat ipsa Deum.
Aut Deus, aut vacui certè mens tertia cœli   5
  Per tua secretò guttura serpit agens;
Serpit agens, facilisque docet mortalia corda
  Sensim immortali assuescere posse sono.
Quòd si cuncta quidem Deus est, per cunctaque fusus,
  In te unâ loquitur, cætera mutus habet.   10

Ad eandem

ALTERA Torquatum cepit Leonora Poëtam,
  Cujus ab insano cessit amore furens.
Ah miser ille tuo quantò feliciùs ævo
  Perditus, & propter te, Leonora, foret!
Et te Pieriâ sensisset voce canentem   5
  Aurea maternæ fila movere lyræ!
Quamvis Dircæo torsisset lumina Pentheo
  Sævior, aut totus desipuisset iners,
Tu tamen errantes cæcâ vertigine sensus
  Voce eadem poteras composuisse tuâ;   10
Et poteras ægro spirans sub corde quietem
  Flexanimo cantu restituisse sibi.

Ad eandem

CREDULA quid liquidam Sirena, Neapoli, jactas,
  Claraque Parthenopes fana Achelöiados,
Littoreamque tuâ defunctam Naiada ripâ
  Corpora Chalcidico sacra dedisse rogo?
Illa quidem vivitque, & amœnâ Tibridis undâ   5
  Mutavit rauci murmura Pausilipi.
Illic Romulidûm studiis ornata secundis,
  Atque homines cantu detinet atque Deos.

Ad eandem (Altera Torquatum) 5 canentem Ed. 1, Ed. 2 Errata: canentam Ed. 2
8 desipuisset Ed. 2 Errata, Ed. 3 : desipuiisset Ed. 1 : desipulisset Ed. 2

Apologus de Rustico & Hero

RUSTICUS ex malo sapidissima poma quotannis
  Legit, & urbano lecta dedit Domino:
Hic incredibili fructûs dulcedine captus
  Malum ipsam in proprias transtulit areolas.
Hactenus illa ferax, sed longo debilis ævo,   5
  Mota solo assueto, protinùs aret iners.
Quod tandem ut patuit Domino, spe lusus inani,
  Damnavit celeres in sua damna manus.
Atque ait, Heu quantò satius fuit illa Coloni
  (Parva licet) grato dona tulisse animo!   10
Possem Ego avaritiam frœnare, gulamque voracem:
  Nunc periere mihi & fœtus & ipsa parens.

ELEGIARUM FINIS

Apologus de Rustico et Hero *add. in* Ed. 2

SYLVARUM LIBER

Anno ætatis 16. In obitum
Procancellarii medici

PARÉRE fati discite legibus,
Manusque Parcæ jam date supplices,
   Qui pendulum telluris orbem
      Jäpeti colitis nepotes.

Vos si relicto mors vaga Tænaro   5
Semel vocârit flebilis, heu moræ
   Tentantur incassùm dolique;
      Per tenebras Stygis ire certum est.

Si destinatam pellere dextera
Mortem valeret, non ferus Hercules   10
   Nessi venenatus cruore
      Æmathiâ jacuisset Oetâ.

Nec fraude turpi Palladis invidæ
Vidisset occisum Ilion Hectora, aut
   Quem larva Pelidis peremit   15
      Ense Locro, Jove lacrymante.

Si triste fatum verba Hecatëia
Fugare possint, Telegoni parens
   Vixisset infamis, potentique
      Ægiali soror usa virgâ.   20

Numenque trinum fallere si queant
Artes medentûm, ignotaque gramina,
   Non gnarus herbarum Machaon
      Eurypyli cecidisset hastâ.

Læsisset & nec te, Philyreie,   25
Sagitta echidnæ perlita sanguine,
   Nec tela te fulmenque avitum
      Cæse puer genitricis alvo.

Tuque O alumno major Apolline,
Gentis togatæ cui regimen datum,   30
   Frondosa quem nunc Cirrha luget,
      Et mediis Helicon in undis,

Jam præfuisses Palladio gregi

Lætus, superstes, nec sine gloria,
   Nec puppe lustrasses Charontis   35
      Horribiles barathri recessus.
At fila rupit Persephone tua
Irata, cum te viderit artibus
   Succoque pollenti tot atris
      Faucibus eripuisse mortis.   40
Colende præses, membra precor tua
Molli quiescant cespite, & ex tuo
   Crescant rosæ, calthæque busto,
      Purpureoque hyacinthus ore.
Sit mite de te judicium Æaci,   45
Subrideatque Ennæa Proserpina,
   Interque felices perennis
      Elysio spatiere campo.

In quintum Novembris, Anno
ætatis 17

JAM pius extremâ veniens Jäcobus ab arcto
Teucrigenas populos, latéque patentia regna
Albionum tenuit, jamque inviolabile fœdus
Sceptra Caledoniis conjunxerat Anglica Scotis:
Pacificusque novo felix divesque sedebat   5
In solio, occultique doli securus & hostis:
Cum ferus ignifluo regnans Acheronte tyrannus,
Eumenidum pater, æthereo vagus exul Olympo,
Forte per immensum terrarum erraverat orbem,
Dinumerans sceleris socios, vernasque fideles,   10
Participes regni post funera mœsta futuros;
Hic tempestates medio ciet aëre diras,
Illic unanimes odium struit inter amicos,
Armat & invictas in mutua viscera gentes;
Regnaque olivifera vertit florentia pace,   15
Et quoscunque videt puræ virtutis amantes,
Hos cupit adjicere imperio, fraudumque magister
Tentat inaccessum sceleri corrumpere pectus,
Insidiasque locat tacitas, cassesque latentes

46 Ennæa *scripsi*: Ætnæa Edd. 1, 2

Tendit, ut incautos rapiat, ceu Caspia Tigris 20
Insequitur trepidam deserta per avia prædam
Nocte sub illuni, & somno nictantibus astris.
Talibus infestat populos Summanus & urbes
Cinctus cæruleæ fumanti turbine flammæ.
Jamque fluentisonis albentia rupibus arva 25
Apparent, & terra Deo dilecta marino,
Cui nomen dederat quondam Neptunia proles
Amphitryoniaden qui non dubitavit atrocem
Æquore tranato furiali poscere bello,
Ante expugnatæ crudelia sæcula Troiæ. 30
 At simul hanc opibusque & festâ pace beatam
Aspicit, & pingues donis Cerealibus agros,
Quodque magis doluit, venerantem numina veri
Sancta Dei populum, tandem suspiria rupit
Tartareos ignes & luridum olentia sulphur. 35
Qualia Trinacriâ trux ab Jove clausus in Ætna
Efflat tabifico monstrosus ab ore Tiphœus.
Ignescunt oculi, stridetque adamantinus ordo
Dentis, ut armorum fragor, ictaque cuspide cuspis.
Atque pererrato solum hoc lacrymabile mundo 40
Inveni, dixit, gens hæc mihi sola rebellis,
Contemtrixque jugi, nostrâque potentior arte.
Illa tamen, mea si quicquam tentamina possunt,
Non feret hoc impune diu, non ibit inulta.
Hactenus; & piceis liquido natat aëre pennis; 45
Quà volat, adversi præcursant agmine venti,
Densantur nubes, & crebra tonitrua fulgent.
 Jamque pruinosas velox superaverat alpes,
Et tenet Ausoniæ fines; à parte sinistrâ
Nimbifer Appenninus erat, priscique Sabini, 50
Dextra veneficiis infamis Hetruria, nec non
Te furtiva, Tibris, Thetidi videt oscula dantem;
Hinc Mavortigenæ consistit in arce Quirini.
Reddiderant dubiam jam sera crepuscula lucem,
Cum circumgreditur totam Tricoronifer urbem, 55
Panificosque Deos portat, scapulisque virorum
Evehitur, præeunt summisso poplite reges,

20 ceu Warton: seu Edd. 1, 2
38 adamantius Ed. 2: Adamantinus Ed. 2 Errata 45 natat Ed. 2: Natat Ed. 2 Errata

Et mendicantum series longissima fratrum;
Cereaque in manibus gestant funalia cæci,
Cimmeriis nati in tenebris, vitamque trahentes.   60
Templa dein multis subeunt lucentia tædis
(Vesper erat sacer iste Petro) fremitúsque canentum
Sæpe tholos implet vacuos, & inane locorum.
Qualiter exululat Bromius, Bromiique caterva,
Orgia cantantes in Echionio Aracyntho,   65
Dum tremit attonitus vitreis Asopus in undis,
Et procul ipse cavâ responsat rupe Cithæron.
    His igitur tandem solenni more peractis,
Nox senis amplexus Erebi taciturna reliquit,
Præcipitesque impellit equos stimulante flagello,   70
Captum oculis Typhlonta, Melanchætemque ferocem,
Atque Acherontæo prognatam patre Siopen
Torpidam, & hirsutis horrentem Phrica capillis.
Interea regum domitor, Phlegetontius hæres,
Ingreditur thalamos (neque enim secretus adulter   75
Producit steriles molli sine pellice noctes);
At vix compositos somnus claudebat ocellos,
Cum niger umbrarum dominus, rectorque silentum,
Prædatorque hominum falsâ sub imagine tectus
Astitit, assumptis micuerunt tempora canis,   80
Barba sinus promissa tegit, cineracea longo
Syrmate verrit humum vestis, pendetque cucullus
Vertice de raso, & ne quicquam desit ad artes,
Cannabeo lumbos constrinxit fune salaces,
Tarda fenestratis figens vestigia calceis.   85
Talis, uti fama est, vastâ Franciscus eremo
Tetra vagabatur solus per lustra ferarum,
Sylvestrique tulit genti pia verba salutis
Impius, atque lupos domuit, Lybicosque leones.
    Subdolus at tali Serpens velatus amictu   90
Solvit in has fallax ora execrantia voces;
Dormis, nate? Etiamne tuos sopor opprimit artus?
Immemor O fidei, pecorumque oblite tuorum,
Dum cathedram, venerande, tuam, diademaque triplex
Ridet Hyperboreo gens barbara nata sub axe,   95
Dumque pharetrati spernunt tua jura Britanni;
Surge, age, surge piger, Latius quem Cæsar adorat,

Cui reserata patet convexi janua cæli,
Turgentes animos, & fastus frange procaces,
Sacrilegique sciant, tua quid maledictio possit,   100
Et quid Apostolicæ possit custodia clavis;
Et memor Hesperiæ disjectam ulciscere classem,
Mersaque Iberorum lato vexilla profundo,
Sanctorumque cruci tot corpora fixa probrosæ,
Thermodoontéa nuper regnante puella.   105
At tu si tenero mavis torpescere lecto
Crescentesque negas hosti contundere vires,
Tyrrhenum implebit numeroso milite Pontum,
Signaque Aventino ponet fulgentia colle:
Relliquias veterum franget, flammisque cremabit,   110
Sacraque calcabit pedibus tua colla profanis,
Cujus gaudebant soleïs dare basia reges.
Nec tamen hunc bellis & aperto Marte lacesses,
Irritus ille labor, tu callidus utere fraude,
Quælibet hæreticis disponere retia fas est;   115
Jamque ad consilium extremis rex magnus ab oris
Patricios vocat, & procerum de stirpe creatos,
Grandævosque patres trabeâ, canisque verendos;
Hos tu membratim poteris conspergere in auras,
Atque dare in cineres, nitrati pulveris igne   120
Ædibus injecto, quà convenere, sub imis.
Protinus ipse igitur quoscumque habet Anglia fidos
Propositi, factique mone : quisquámne tuorum
Audebit summi non jussa facessere Papæ?
Perculsosque metu subito, casumque stupentes   125
Invadat vel Gallus atrox, vel sævus Iberus.
Sæcula sic illic tandem Mariana redibunt,
Tuque in belligeros iterum dominaberis Anglos.
Et nequid timeas, divos divasque secundas
Accipe, quotque tuis celebrantur numina fastis.   130
Dixit & adscitos ponens malefidus amictus
Fugit ad infandam, regnum illætabile, Lethen.
　　Jam rosea Eoas pandens Tithonia portas
Vestit inauratas redeunti lumine terras;
Mæstaque adhuc nigri deplorans funera nati   135

110 Relliquias Ed. 1 : Relliquas Ed. 2 : Relliquias Ed. 2 Errata　　124 Papæ? Newton :
Papae. Edd. 1, 2　　125 casumque Ed. 2 : casuque Ed. 1

Irrigat ambrosiis montana cacumina guttis;
Cum somnos pepulit stellatæ janitor aulæ,
Nocturnos visus & somnia grata revolvens.
   Est locus æternâ septus caligine noctis
Vasta ruinosi quondam fundamina tecti,   140
Nunc torvi spelunca Phoni, Prodotæque bilinguis
Effera quos uno peperit Discordia partu.
Hic inter cæmenta jacent praeruptaque saxa,
Ossa inhumata virûm, & trajecta cadavera ferro;
Hic Dolus intortis semper sedet ater ocellis,   145
Jurgiaque, & stimulis armata Calumnia fauces,
Et Furor, atque viæ moriendi mille videntur
Et Timor, exanguisque locum circumvolat Horror,
Perpetuoque leves per muta silentia Manes
Exululant, tellus & sanguine conscia stagnat.   150
Ipsi etiam pavidi latitant penetralibus antri
Et Phonos, & Prodotes, nulloque sequente per antrum,
Antrum horrens, scopulosum, atrum feralibus umbris,
Diffugiunt sontes, & retrò lumina vortunt;
Hos pugiles Romæ per sæcula longa fideles   155
Evocat antistes Babylonius, atque ita fatur.
Finibus occiduis circumfusum incolit æquor
Gens exosa mihi, prudens natura negavit
Indignam penitùs nostro conjungere mundo;
Illuc, sic jubeo, celeri contendite gressu,   160
Tartareoque leves difflentur pulvere in auras
Et rex & pariter satrapæ, scelerata propago:
Et quotquot fidei caluere cupidine veræ
Consilii socios adhibete, operisque ministros.
·Finierat, rigidi cupidè paruere gemelli.   165
   Interea longo flectens curvamine cælos
Despicit æthereâ dominus qui fulgurat arce,
Vanaque perversæ ridet conamina turbæ,
Atque sui causam populi volet ipse tueri.
   Esse ferunt spatium, quà distat ab Aside terra   170
Fertilis Europe, & spectat Mareotidas undas;
Hic turris posita est Titanidos ardua Famæ
Ærea, lata, sonans, rutilis vicinior astris

---

143 praeruptaque Ed. 2 : semifractaque Ed. 1   149–50 Manes Exululat, Ed. 2 : Manes
Exululat Ed. 2 Errata

Quàm superimpositum vel Athos vel Pelion Ossæ.
Mille fores aditusque patent, totidemque fenestræ,   175
Amplaque per tenues translucent atria muros;
Excitat hic varios plebs agglomerata susurros;
Qualiter instrepitant circum mulctralia bombis
Agmina muscarum, aut texto per ovilia junco,
Dum Canis æstivum cœli petit ardua culmen.   180
Ipsa quidem summâ sedet ultrix matris in arce,
Auribus innumeris cinctum caput eminet olli,
Queis sonitum exiguum trahit, atque levissima captat
Murmura, ab extremis patuli confinibus orbis.
Nec tot, Aristoride servator inique juvencæ   185
Isidos, immiti volvebas lumina vultu,
Lumina non unquam tacito nutantia somno,
Lumina subjectas late spectantia terras.
Istis illa solet loca luce carentia sæpe
Perlustrare, etiam radianti impervia soli.   190
Millenisque loquax auditaque visaque linguis
Cuilibet effundit temeraria, veráque mendax
Nunc minuit, modò confictis sermonibus auget.
Sed tamen a nostro meruisti carmine laudes
Fama, bonum quo non aliud veracius ullum,   195
Nobis digna cani, nec te memorasse pigebit
Carmine tam longo, servati scilicet Angli
Officiis, vaga diva, tuis, tibi reddimus æqua.
Te Deus æternos motu qui temperat ignes,
Fulmine præmisso alloquitur, terrâque tremente: 200
Fama siles? an te latet impia Papistarum
Conjurata cohors in meque meosque Britannos,
Et nova sceptrigero cædes meditata Jäcobo?
Nec plura, illa statim sensit mandata Tonantis,
Et satis antè fugax stridentes induit alas,   205
Induit & variis exilia corpora plumis;
Dextra tubam gestat Temesæo ex ære sonoram.
Nec mora, jam pennis cedentes remigat auras,
Atque parum est cursu celeres prævertere nubes,
Jam ventos, jam solis equos post terga reliquit: 210
Et primò Angliacas solito de more per urbes
Ambiguas voces, incertaque murmura spargit,
Mox arguta dolos, & detestabile vulgat

Proditionis opus, nec non facta horrida dictu,
Authoresque addit sceleris, nec garrula cæcis   215
Insidiis loca structa silet; stupuere relatis,
Et pariter juvenes, pariter tremuere puellæ,
Effætique senes pariter, tantæque ruinæ
Sensus ad ætatem subitò penetraverat omnem.
Attamen interea populi miserescit ab alto   220
Ætthereus pater, & crudelibus obstitit ausis
Papicolûm; capti pœnas raptantur ad acres;
At pia thura Deo, & grati solvuntur honores;
Compita læta focis genialibus omnia fumant;
Turba choros juvenilis agit: Quintoque Novembris   225
Nulla Dies toto occurrit celebratior anno.

Anno ætatis 17. In obitum
Præsulis Eliensis

ADHUC madentes rore squalebant genæ,
    Et sicca nondum lumina
Adhuc liquentis imbre turgebant salis,
    Quem nuper effudi pius,
Dum mæsta charo justa persolvi rogo   5
    Wintoniensis præsulis;
Cum centilinguis Fama (proh semper mali
    Cladisque vera nuntia)   ·
Spargit per urbes divitis Britanniæ,
    Populosque Neptuno satos,   10
Cessisse morti, & ferreis sororibus
    Te generis humani decus,
Qui rex sacrorum illâ fuisti in insulâ
    Quæ nomen Anguillæ tenet.
Tunc inquietum pectus ira protinus   15
    Ebulliebat fervidâ,
Tumulis potentem sæpe devovens deam:
    Nec vota Naso in Ibida
Concepit alto diriora pectore,
    Graiusque vates parciùs   20
Turpem Lycambis execratus est dolum,
    Sponsamque Neobolen suam.

At ecce diras ipse dum fundo graves,
　Et imprecor neci necem,
Audisse tales videor attonitus sonos　　　　25
　Leni, sub aurâ, flamine:
Cæcos furores pone, pone vitream
　Bilemque & irritas minas,
Quid temerè violas non nocenda numina,
　Subitoque ad iras percita?　　　　　　30
Non est, ut arbitraris elusus miser,
　Mors atra Noctis filia,
Erebóve patre creta, sive Erinnye,
　Vastóve nata sub Chao:
Ast illa cælo missa stellato, Dei　　　　35
　Messes ubique colligit;
Animasque mole carneâ reconditas
　In lucem & auras evocat:
Ut cum fugaces excitant Horæ diem
　Themidos Jovisque filiæ;　　　　　40
Et sempiterni ducit ad vultus patris;
　At justa raptat impios
Sub regna furvi luctuosa Tartari,
　Sedesque subterraneas.
Hanc ut vocàntem lætus audivi, citò　　　45
　Fœdum reliqui carcerem,
Volatilesque faustus inter milites
　Ad astra sublimis feror:
Vates ut olim raptus ad cœlum senex
　Auriga currus ignei,　　　　　　50
Non me Boötis terruere lucidi
　Sarraca tarda frigore, aut
Formidolosi Scorpionis brachia,
　Non ensis Orion tuus.
Prætervolavi fulgidi solis globum,　　　55
　Longéque sub pedibus deam
Vidi triformem, dum coercebat suos
　Frænis dracones aureis.
Erraticorum syderum per ordines,
　Per lacteas vehor plagas,　　　　60
Velocitatem sæpe miratus novam,

30 percita? Ed. 3 : percita. Edd. 1, 2

    Donec nitentes ad fores
Ventum est Olympi, & regiam Crystallinam, &
    Stratum smaragdis Atrium.
Sed hic tacebo, nam quis effari queat   65
    Oriundus humano patre
Amœnitates illius loci? mihi
    Sat est in æternum frui.

Naturam non pati senium

HEU quàm perpetuis erroribus acta fatiscit
Avia mens hominum, tenebrisque immersa profundis
Œdipodioniam volvit sub pectore noctem!
Quæ vesana suis, metiri facta deorum
Audet, & incisas leges adamante perenni   5
Assimilare suis nulloque solubile sæclo
Consilium fati perituris alligat horis.
    Ergone marcescet sulcantibus obsita rugis
Naturæ facies, & rerum publica mater
Omniparum contracta uterum sterilescet ab ævo?   10
Et se fassa senem malè certis passibus ibit
Sidereum tremebunda caput? num tetra vetustas
Annorumque æterna fames, squalórque situsque
Sidera vexabunt? an & insatiabile Tempus
Esuriet Cælum, rapietque in viscera patrem?   15
Heu, potuitne suas imprudens Jupiter arces
Hoc contra munisse nefas, & Temporis isto
Exemisse malo, gyrosque dedisse perennes?
Ergo erit ut quandoque sono dilapsa tremendo
Convexi tabulata ruant, atque obvius ictu   20
Stridat uterque polus, superâque ut Olympius aulâ
Decidat, horribilisque retectâ Gorgone Pallas;
Qualis in Ægæam proles Junonia Lemnon
Deturbata sacro cecidit de limine cæli.
Tu quoque, Phœbe, tui casus imitabere nati   25
Præcipiti curru, subitáque ferere ruinâ
Pronus, & extinctâ fumabit lampade Nereus,
Et dabit attonito feralia sibila ponto.
Tunc etiam aërei divulsis sedibus Hæmi

Dissultabit apex, imoque allisa barathro 30
Terrebunt Stygium dejecta Ceraunia Ditem
In superos quibus usus erat, fraternaque bella.
   At Pater omnipotens fundatis fortius astris
Consuluit rerum summæ, certoque peregit
Pondere fatorum lances, atque ordine summo 35
Singula perpetuum jussit servare tenorem.
Volvitur hinc lapsu mundi rota prima diurno;
Raptat & ambitos sociâ vertigine cælos.
Tardior haud solito Saturnus, & acer ut olim
Fulmineùm rutilat cristatâ casside Mavors. 40
Floridus æternùm Phœbus juvenile coruscat,
Nec fovet effœtas loca per declivia terras
Devexo temone Deus; sed semper amicá
Luce potens eadem currit per signa rotarum.
Surgit odoratis pariter formosus ab Indis 45
Æthereum pecus albenti qui cogit Olympo
Mane vocans, & serus agens in pascua cæli,
Temporis & gemino dispertit regna colore.
Fulget, obitque vices alterno Delia cornu,
Cæruleumque ignem paribus complectitur ulnis. 50
Nec variant elementa fidem, solitóque fragore
Lurida perculsas jaculantur fulmina rupes.
Nec per inane furit leviori murmure Corus,
Stringit & armiferos æquali horrore Gelonos
Trux Aquilo, spiratque hyemem, nimbosque volutat. 55
Utque solet, Siculi diverberat ima Pelori
Rex maris, & raucâ circumstrepit æquora conchâ
Oceani Tubicen, nec vastâ mole minorem
Ægæona ferunt dorso Balearica cete.
Sed neque, Terra, tibi sæcli vigor ille vetusti 60
Priscus abest, servatque suum Narcissus odorem,
Et puer ille suum tenet & puer ille decorem
Phœbe, tuusque, &, Cypri, tuus, nec ditior olim
Terra datum sceleri celavit montibus aurum
Conscia, vel sub aquis gemmas. Sic denique in ævum 65
Ibit cunctarum series justissima rerum,
Donec flamma orbem populabitur ultima, latè
Circumplexa polos, & vasti culmina cæli;
Ingentique rogo flagrabit machina mundi.

De Idea Platonica quemadmodum
Aristoteles intellexit

DICITE, sacrorum præsides nemorum deæ,
Tuque O noveni perbeata numinis
Memoria mater, quæque in immenso procul
Antro recumbis otiosa Æternitas,
Monumenta servans, & ratas leges Jovis,   5
Cælique fastos atque ephemeridas Deûm,
Quis ille primus cujus ex imagine
Natura sollers finxit humanum genus,
Æternus, incorruptus, æquævus polo,
Unusque & universus, exemplar Dei?   10
Haud ille Palladis gemellus innubæ
Interna proles insidet menti Jovis;
Sed quamlibet natura sit communior,
Tamen seorsùs extat ad morem unius,
Et, mira, certo stringitur spatio loci;   15
Seu sempiternus ille syderum comes
Cæli pererrat ordines decemplicis,
Citimúmve terris incolit Lunæ globum:
Sive inter animas corpus adituras sedens
Obliviosas torpet ad Lethes aquas: 20
Sive in remotâ forte terrarum plagâ
Incedit ingens hominis archetypus gigas,
Et diis tremendus erigit celsum caput
Atlante major portitore syderum.
Non cui profundum cæcitas lumen dedit   25
Dircæus augur vidit hunc alto sinu;
Non hunc silenti nocte Plëiones nepos
Vatum sagaci præpes ostendit choro;
Non hunc sacerdos novit Assyrius, licet
Longos vetusti commemoret atavos Nini,   30
Priscumque Belon, inclytumque Osiridem.
Non ille trino gloriosus nomine
Ter magnus Hermes (ut sit arcani sciens)
Talem reliquit Isidis cultoribus.
At tu perenne ruris Academi decus   35
(Hæc monstra si tu primus induxti scholis)
Jam jam pöetas urbis exules tuæ

Revocabis, ipse fabulator maximus,
Aut institutor ipse migrabis foras.

Ad Patrem

NUNC mea Pierios cupiam per pectora fontes
Irriguas torquere vias, totumque per ora
Volvere laxatum gemino de vertice rivum;
Ut tenues oblita sonos audacibus alis
Surgat in officium venerandi Musa parentis.   5
Hoc utcunque tibi gratum, pater optime, carmen
Exiguum meditatur opus, nec novimus ipsi
Aptiùs à nobis quæ possint munera donis
Respondere tuis, quamvis nec maxima possint
Respondere tuis, nedum ut par gratia donis   10
Esse queat, vacuis quæ redditur arida verbis.
Sed tamen hæc nostros ostendit pagina census,
Et quod habemus opum chartâ numeravimus istâ,
Quæ mihi sunt nullæ, nisi quas dedit aurea Clio,
Quas mihi semoto somni peperere sub antro,   15
Et nemoris laureta sacri Parnassides umbræ.
  Nec tu vatis opus divinum despice carmen,
Quo nihil æthereos ortus, & semina cæli,
Nil magis humanam commendat origine mentem,
Sancta Promethéæ retinens vestigia flammæ.   20
Carmen amant superi, tremebundaque Tartara carmen
Ima ciere valet, divosque ligare profundos,
Et triplici duros Manes adamante coercet.
Carmine sepositi retegunt arcana futuri
Phœbades, & tremulæ pallentes ora Sibyllæ;   25
Carmina sacrificus sollennes pangit ad aras,
Aurea seu sternit motantem cornua taurum;
Seu cùm fata sagax fumantibus abdita fibris
Consulit, & tepidis Parcam scrutatur in extis.
Nos etiam patrium tunc cum repetemus Olympum,   30
Æternæque moræ stabunt immobilis ævi,
Ibimus auratis per cæli templa coronis,
Dulcia suaviloquo sociantes carmina plectro,
Astra quibus, geminique poli convexa sonabunt.
Spiritus & rapidos qui circinat igneus orbes,   35
Nunc quoque sydereis intercinit ipse choreis

Immortale melos, & inenarrabile carmen;
Torrida dum rutilus compescit sibila serpens,
Demissoque ferox gladio mansuescit Orion;
Stellarum nec sentit onus Maurusius Atlas.   40
Carmina regales epulas ornare solebant,
Cum nondum luxus, vastæque immensa vorago
Nota gulæ, & modico spumabat cœna Lyæo.
Tum de more sedens festa ad convivia vates
Æsculeâ intonsos redimitus ab arbore crines,   45
Heroumque actus, imitandaque gesta canebat,
Et chaos, & positi latè fundamina mundi,
Reptantesque Deos, & alentes numina glandes,
Et nondum Ætnæo quæsitum fulmen ab antro.
Denique quid vocis modulamen inane juvabit,   50
Verborum sensusque vacans, numerique loquacis?
Silvestres decet iste choros, non Orphea cantus,
Qui tenuit fluvios & quercubus addidit aures
Carmine, non citharâ, simulachraque functa canendo
Compulit in lacrymas; habet has à carmine laudes.   55
   Nec tu perge precor sacras contemnere Musas,
Nec vanas inopesque puta, quarum ipse peritus
Munere, mille sonos numeros componis ad aptos,
Millibus & vocem modulis variare canoram
Doctus, Arionii meritò sis nominis hæres.   60
Nunc tibi quid mirum, si me genuisse poëtam
Contigerit, charo si tam propè sanguine juncti
Cognatas artes, studiumque affine sequamur?
Ipse volens Phœbus se dispertire duobus,
Altera dona mihi, dedit altera dona parenti,   65
Dividuumque Deum genitorque puerque tenemus.
   Tu tamen ut simules teneras odisse camœnas,
Non odisse reor, neque enim, pater, ire jubebas
Quà via lata patet, quà pronior area lucri,
Certaque condendi fulget spes aurea nummi: 70
Nec rapis ad leges, malè custoditaque gentis
Jura, nec insulsis damnas clamoribus aures.
Sed magis excultam cupiens ditescere mentem,
Me procul urbano strepitu, secessibus altis
Abductum Aoniæ jucunda per otia ripæ   75

63 sequamur? *scripsi*: sequamur: Edd. 1, 2

Phœbæo lateri comitem sinis ire beatum.
Officium chari taceo commune parentis,
Me poscunt majora, tuo pater optime sumptu
Cum mihi Romuleæ patuit facundia linguæ,
Et Latii veneres, & quæ Jovis ora decebant   80
Grandia magniloquis elata vocabula Graiis,
Addere suasisti quos jactat Gallia flores,
Et quam degeneri novus Italus ore loquelam
Fundit, Barbaricos testatus voce tumultus,
Quæque Palæstinus loquitur mysteria vates.   85
Denique quicquid habet cælum, subjectaque cœlo
Terra parens, terræque & cœlo interfluus aer,
Quicquid & unda tegit, pontique agitabile marmor,
Per te nosse licet, per te, si nosse libebit.
Dimotàque venit spectanda scientia nube,   90
Nudaque conspicuos inclinat ad oscula vultus,
Ni fugisse velim, ni sit libâsse molestum.
　　I nunc, confer opes quisquis malesanus avitas
Austriaci gazas, Perüanaque regna præoptas.
Quæ potuit majora pater tribuisse, vel ipse   95
Jupiter, excepto, donâsset ut omnia, cœlo?
Non potiora dedit, quamvis & tuta fuissent,
Publica qui juveni commisit lumina nato
Atque Hyperionios currus, & fræna diei,
Et circùm undantem radiatâ luce tiaram.   100
Ergo ego jam doctæ pars quamlibet ima catervæ
Victrices hederas inter, laurosque sedebo,
Jamque nec obscurus populo miscebor inerti,
Vitabuntque oculos vestigia nostra profanos.
Este procul, vigiles curæ, procul este, querelæ,   105
Invidiæque acies transverso tortilis hirquo,
Sæva nec anguiferos extende, Calumnia, rictus;
In me triste nihil fœdissima turba potestis,
Nec vestri sum juris ego; securaque tutus
Pectora, vipereo gradiar sublimis ab ictu.   110
　　At tibi, chare pater, postquam non æqua merenti
Posse referre datur, nec dona rependere factis,
Sit memorâsse satis, repetitaque munera grato
Percensere animo, fidæque reponere menti.
　　Et vos, O nostri, juvenilia carmina, lusus,   115

Si modo perpetuos sperare audebitis annos,
Et domini superesse rogo, lucemque tueri,
Nec spisso rapient oblivia nigra sub Orco,
Forsitan has laudes, decantatumque parentis
Nomen, ad exemplum, sero servabitis ævo.   120

Psalm 114

Ἰσραὴλ ὅτε παῖδες, ὅτ' ἀγλαὰ φῦλ' Ἰακώβου
Αἰγύπτιον λίπε δῆμον, ἀπεχθέα, βαρβαρόφωνον,
Δὴ τότε μοῦνον ἔην ὅσιον γένος υἷες Ἰούδα.
Ἐν δὲ θεὸς λαοῖσι μέγα κρείων βασίλευεν.
Εἶδε καὶ ἐντροπάδην φύγαδ' ἐρρώησε θάλασσα   5
Κύματι εἰλυμένη ῥοθίῳ, ὁ δ' ἄρ' ἐστυφελίχθη
Ἱρὸς Ἰορδάνης ποτὶ ἀργυροειδέα πηγήν.
Ἐκ δ' ὄρεα σκαρθμοῖσιν ἀπειρέσια κλονέοντο,
Ὡς κριοὶ σφριγόωντες ἐϋτραφερῷ ἐν ἀλωῇ.
Βαιότεραι δ' ἅμα πᾶσαι ἀνασκίρτησαν ἐρίπναι,   10
Οἷα παραὶ σύριγγι φίλῃ ὑπὸ μητέρι ἄρνες.
Τίπτε σύ γ' αἰνὰ θάλασσα πέλωρ φύγαδ' ἐρρώησας;
Κύματι εἰλυμένη ῥοθίῳ; τί δ' ἄρ' ἐστυφελίχθης
Ἱρὸς Ἰορδάνη ποτὶ ἀργυροειδέα πηγήν;
Τίπτ' ὄρεα σκαρθμοῖσιν ἀπειρέσια κλονέεσθε   15
Ὡς κριοὶ σφριγόωντες ἐϋτραφερῷ ἐν ἀλωῇ;
Βαιότεραι τί δ' ἄρ' ὑμμὲς ἀνασκιρτήσατ' ἐρίπναι,
Οἷα παραὶ σύριγγι φίλῃ ὑπὸ μητέρι ἄρνες;
Σείεο γαῖα τρέουσα θεὸν μεγάλ' ἐκκτυπέοντα
Γαῖα θεὸν τρείουσ' ὕπατον σέβας Ἰσσακίδαο   20
Ὅς τε καὶ ἐκ σπιλάδων ποταμοὺς χέε μορμύροντας,
Κρήνηντ' ἀέναον πέτρης ἀπὸ δακρυοέσσης.

*Philosophus ad regem quendam qui eum ignotum & insontem
inter reos forte captum inscius damnaverat, τὴν ἐπὶ θανάτῳ
πορευόμενος hæc subito misit*

Ὦ ἄνα εἰ ὀλέσῃς με τὸν ἔννομον, οὐδέ τιν' ἀνδρῶν
Δεινὸν ὅλως δράσαντα, σοφώτατον ἴθι κάρηνον
Ῥηϊδίως ἀφέλοιο, τὸ δ' ὕστερον αὖθι νοήσεις,

19 ἐκκτυπέοντα G. S. Gordon: ἐκτυπέοντα Edd. 1, 2

Μὰψ αὔτως δ'ἄρ' ἔπειτα χρόνῳ μάλα πολλὸν ὀδύρῃ
Τοιόνδ' ἐκ πόλεως περιώνυμον ἄλκαρ ὀλέσσας.   5

In Effigiei Ejus Sculptorem

Ἀμαθεῖ γεγράφθαι χειρὶ τήνδε μὲν εἰκόνα
Φαίης τάχ' ἂν πρὸς εἶδος αὐτοφυὲς βλέπων,
Τὸν δ' ἐκτυπωτὸν οὐκ ἐπιγνόντες, φίλοι,
Γελᾶτε φαύλου δυσμίμημα ζωγράφου.

Ad Salsillum poetam Romanum
ægrotantem
SCAZONTES.

O MUSA gressum quæ volens trahis claudum,
Vulcanioque tarda gaudes incessu,
Nec sentis illud in loco minus gratum,
Quàm cùm decentes flava Dëiope suras
Alternat aureum ante Junonis lectum,   5
Adesdum & hæc s'is verba pauca Salsillo
Refer, camœna nostra cui tantum est cordi,
Quamque ille magnis prætulit immeritò divis.
Hæc ergo alumnus ille Londini Milto,
Diebus hisce qui suum linquens nidum   10
Polique tractum, (pessimus ubi ventorum,
Insanientis impotensque pulmonis
Pernix anhela sub Jove exercet flabra)
Venit feraces Itali soli ad glebas,
Visum superbâ cognitas urbes famâ   15
Virosque doctæque indolem juventutis,
Tibi optat idem hic fausta multa, Salsille,
Habitumque fesso corpori penitus sanum;
Cui nunc profunda bilis infestat renes,
Præcordiisque fixa damnosum spirat.   20.
Nec id pepercit impia quòd tu Romano
Tam cultus ore Lesbium condis melos.
O dulce divûm munus, O salus Hebes
Germana! Tuque, Phœbe, morborum terror
Pythone cæso, sive tu magis Pæan   25
Libenter audis, hic tuus sacerdos est.

(Philosophus ad Regem)   4 μαψιδίως δ' ἄρ' ἔπειτα χρόνῳ μάλα πολλὸν ὀδύρῃ Ed. 2
5 τοιόνδ' Burney : τοῖον δ' Edd. 1, 2

Querceta Fauni, vosque rore vinoso
Colles benigni, mitis Euandri sedes,
Siquid salubre vallibus frondet vestris,
Levamen ægro ferte certatim vati.   30
Sic ille charis redditus rursùm Musis
Vicina dulci prata mulcebit cantu.
Ipse inter atros emirabitur lucos
Numa, ubi beatum degit otium æternum,
Suam reclivis semper Ægeriam spectans.   35
Tumidusque & ipse Tibris hinc delinitus
Spei favebit annuæ colonorum:
Nec in sepulchris ibit obsessum reges
Nimiùm sinistro laxus irruens loro:
Sed fræna melius temperabit undarum,   40
Adusque curvi salsa regna Portumni.

Mansus

Joannes Baptista Mansus Marchio Villensis vir ingenii laude, tum literarum
studio, nec non & bellicâ virtute apud Italos clarus in primis est. Ad quem
Torquati Tassi dialogus extat de Amicitiâ scriptus; erat enim Tassi amicis-
simus; ab quo etiam inter Campaniæ principes celebratur, in illo poemate cui
titulus Gerusalemme conquistata, lib. 20.

Fra cavalier magnanimi, è cortesi
Risplende il Manso——

Is authorem Neapoli commorantem summâ benevolentiâ prosecutus est, multaque ei
detulit humanitatis officia. Ad hunc itaque hospes ille antequam ab eâ urbe
discederet, ut ne ingratum se ostenderet, hoc carmen misit.

HÆC quoque, Manse, tuæ meditantur carmina laudi
Pierides, tibi, Manse, choro notissime Phœbi,
Quandoquidem ille alium haud æquo est dignatus honore,
Post Galli cineres, & Mecænatis Hetrusci.
Tu quoque si nostræ tantùm valet aura Camœnæ,   5
Victrices hederas inter, laurosque sedebis.
Te pridem magno felix concordia Tasso
Junxit, & æternis inscripsit nomina chartis,
Mox tibi dulciloquum non inscia Musa Marinum
Tradidit, ille tuum dici se gaudet alumnum,   10
Dum canit Assyrios divûm prolixus amores;

Mollis & Ausonias stupefecit carmine nymphas.
Ille itidem moriens tibi soli debita vates
Ossa tibi soli, supremaque vota reliquit.
Nec manes pietas tua chara fefellit amici,   15
Vidimus arridentem operoso ex ære poetam.
Nec satis hoc visum est in utrumque, & nec pia cessant
Officia in tumulo, cupis integros rapere Orco,
Quà potes, atque avidas Parcarum eludere leges:
Amborum genus, & variâ sub sorte peractam   20
Describis vitam, moresque, & dona Minervæ;
Æmulus illius Mycalen qui natus ad altam
Rettulit Æolii vitam facundus Homeri.
Ergo ego te Cliûs & magni nomine Phœbi,
Manse pater, jubeo longum salvere per ævum   25
Missus Hyperboreo juvenis peregrinus ab axe.
Nec tu longinquam bonus aspernabere Musam,
Quæ nuper gelidâ vix enutrita sub Arcto
Imprudens Italas ausa est volitare per urbes.
Nos etiam in nostro modulantes flumine cygnos   30
Credimus obscuras noctis sensisse per umbras,
Quà Thamesis latè puris argenteus urnis
Oceani glaucos perfundit gurgite crines.
Quin & in has quondam pervenit Tityrus oras.
Sed neque nos genus incultum, nec inutile Phœbo,   35
Quà plaga septeno mundi sulcata Trione
Brumalem patitur longâ sub nocte Boöten.
Nos etiam colimus Phœbum, nos munera Phœbo
Flaventes spicas, & lutea mala canistris,
Halantemque crocum (perhibet nisi vana vetustas)   40
Misimus, & lectas Druidum de gente choreas.
(Gens Druides antiqua sacris operata deorum
Heroum laudes imitandaque gesta canebant)
Hinc quoties festo cingunt altaria cantu
Delo in herbosâ Graiæ de more puellæ   45
Carminibus lætis memorant Corineïda Loxo,
Fatidicamque Upin, cum flavicomâ Hecaërge
Nuda Caledonio variatas pectora fuco.
Fortunate senex, ergo quacunque per orbem
Torquati decus, & nomen celebrabitur ingens,   50
Claraque perpetui succrescet fama Marini,

Tu quoque in ora frequens venies plausumque virorum,
Et parili carpes iter immortale volatu.
Dicetur tum sponte tuos habitasse penates
Cynthius, & famulas venisse ad limina Musas: 55
At non sponte domum tamen idem, & regis adivit
Rura Pheretiadæ cælo fugitivus Apollo;
Ille licet magnum Alciden susceperat hospes;
Tantùm ubi clamosos placuit vitare bubulcos,
Nobile mansueti cessit Chironis in antrum,   60
Irriguos inter saltus frondosaque tecta
Peneium prope rivum: ibi sæpe sub ilice nigrâ
Ad citharæ strepitum blandâ prece victus amici
Exilii duros lenibat voce labores.
Tum neque ripa suo, barathro nec fixa sub imo,   65
Saxa stetere loco, nutat Trachinia rupes,
Nec sentit solitas, immania pondera, silvas,
Emotæque suis properant de collibus orni,
Mulcenturque novo maculosi carmine lynces.
Diis dilecte senex, te Jupiter æquus oportet   70
Nascentem, & miti lustrarit lumine Phœbus,
Atlantisque nepos; neque enim nisi charus ab ortu
Diis superis poterit magno favisse poetæ.
Hinc longæva tibi lento sub flore senectus
Vernat, & Æsonios lucratur vivida fusos,   75
Nondum deciduos servans tibi frontis honores,
Ingeniumque vigens, & adultum mentis acumen.
O mihi si mea sors talem concedat amicum
Phœbæos decorâsse viros qui tam bene norit,
Si quando indigenas revocabo in carmina reges,   80
Arturumque etiam sub terris bella moventem;
Aut dicam invictæ sociali fœdere mensæ,
Magnanimos Heroas, & (O modo spiritus adsit)
Frangam Saxonicas Britonum sub Marte phalanges.
Tandem ubi non tacitæ permensus tempora vitæ,   85
Annorumque satur cineri sua jura relinquam,
Ille mihi lecto madidis astaret ocellis,
Astanti sat erit si dicam sim tibi curæ;
Ille meos artus liventi morte solutos
Curaret parvâ componi molliter urnâ.   90
Foristan & nostros ducat de marmore vultus,

Nectens aut Paphiâ myrti aut Parnasside lauri
Fronde comas, at ego securâ pace quiescam.
Tum quoque, si qua fides, si præmia certa bonorum,
Ipse ego cælicolûm semotus in æthera divûm,   95
Quò labor & mens pura vehunt, atque ignea virtus,
Secreti hæc aliquâ mundi de parte videbo
(Quantum fata sinunt) & totâ mente serenùm
Ridens purpureo suffundar lumine vultus
Et simul æthereo plaudam mihi lætus Olympo.   100

EPITAPHIUM
DAMONIS.

ARGUMENTUM.

THYRSIS & Damon ejusdem viciniæ Pastores, eadem studia sequuti a
pueritiâ amici erant, ut qui plurimùm. Thyrsis animi causâ profectus
peregrè de obitu Damonis nuncium accepit. Domum postea reversus,
& rem ita esse comperto, se, suamque solitudinem hoc carmine de-
plorat. Damonis autem sub personâ hîc intelligitur Carolus Deodatus ex
urbe Hetruriæ Luca paterno genere oriundus, cætera Anglus; ingenio,
doctrina, clarissimisque cæteris virtutibus, dum viveret, juvenis
egregius.

EPITAPHIUM
DAMONIS.

HIMERIDES nymphæ (nam vos & Daphnin & Hylan,
Et plorata diu meministis fata Bionis)
Dicite Sicelicum Thamesina per oppida carmen:
Quas miser effudit voces, quæ murmura Thyrsis,
Et quibus assiduis exercuit antra querelis,   5
Fluminaque, fontesque vagos, nemorumque recessus,
Dum sibi præreptum queritur Damona, neque altam
Luctibus exemit noctem loca sola pererrans.
Et jam bis viridi surgebat culmus arista,
Et totidem flavas numerabant horrea messes,   10
Ex quo summa dies tulerat Damona sub umbras,
Nec dum aderat Thyrsis, pastorem scilicet illum
Dulcis amor Musæ Thusca retinebat in urbe.
Ast ubi mens expleta domum, pecorisque relicti
Cura vocat, simul assuetâ sedítque sub ulmo,   15
Tum vero amissum tum denique sentit amicum,
Cœpit & immensum sic exonerare dolorem.
    Ite domum impasti, domino jam non vacat, agni.
Hei mihi! quæ terris, quæ dicam numina cœlo,
Postquam te immiti rapuerunt funere, Damon?   20
Siccine nos linquis, tua sic sine nomine virtus
Ibit, & obscuris numero fociabitur umbris?

20 Damon? *scripsi*: Damon; Edd. 1, 2

At non ille, animas virgâ qui dividit aureâ,
Ista velit, dignumque tui te ducat in agmen,
Ignavumque procul pecus arceat omne silentum.   25
   Ite domum impasti, domino jam non vacat, agni.
Quicquid erit, certè nisi me lupus antè videbit,
Indeplorato non comminuere sepulcro,
Constabitque tuus tibi honos, longúmque vigebit
Inter pastores, illi tibi vota secundo   30
Solvere post Daphnin, post Daphnin dicere laudes
Gaudebunt, dum rura Pales, dum Faunus amabit:
Si quid id est, priscamque fidem coluisse, piúmque,
Palladiásque artes, sociúmque habuisse canorum.
   Ite domum impasti, domino jam non vacat, agni.   35
Hæc tibi certa manent, tibi erunt hæc præmia, Damon,
At mihi quid tandem fiet modò? quis mihi fidus
Hærebit lateri comes, ut tu sæpe solebas
Frigoribus duris, & per loca fœta pruinis,
Aut rapido sub sole, siti morientibus herbis?   40
Sive opus in magnos fuit eminùs ire leones
Aut avidos terrere lupos præsepibus altis;
Quis fando sopire diem, cantuque solebit?
   Ite domum impasti, domino jam non vacat, agni.
Pectora cui credam? quis me lenire docebit   45
Mordaces cùras, quis longam fallere noctem
Dulcibus alloquiis, grato cùm sibilat igni
Molle pyrum, & nucibus strepitat focus, at malus auster
Miscet cuncta foris, & desuper intonat ulmo.
   Ite domum impasti, domino jam non vacat, agni.   50
Aut æstate, dies medio dum vertitur axe,
Cum Pan æsculeâ somnum capit abditus umbrâ,
Et repetunt sub aquis sibi nota sedilia nymphæ,
Pastoresque latent, stertit sub sepe colonus,
Quis mihi blanditiásque tuas, quis tum mihi risus,   55
Cecropiosque sales referet, cultosque lepores?
   Ite domum impasti, domino jam non vacat, agni.
At jam solus agros, jam pascua solus oberro,
Sicubi ramosæ densantur vallibus umbræ,
Hic serum expecto, supra caput imber & Eurus   60
Triste sonant, fractæque agitata crepuscula silvæ.
   Ite domum impasti, domino jam non vacat, agni.

Heu quàm culta mihi priùs arva procacibus herbis
Involvuntur, & ipsa situ seges alta fatiscit!
Innuba neglecto marcescit & uva racemo,   65
Nec myrteta juvant; ovium quoque tædet, at illæ
Mœrent, inque suum convertunt ora magistrum.
　　Ite domum impasti, domino jam non vacat, agni.
Tityrus ad corylos vocat, Alphesibœus ad ornos,
Ad salices Aegon, ad flumina pulcher Amyntas,   70
Hîc gelidi fontes, hîc illita gramina musco,
Hîc Zephyri, hîc placidas interstrepit arbutus undas;
Ista canunt surdo, frutices ego nactus abibam.
　　Ite domum impasti, domino jam non vacat, agni.
Mopsus ad hæc, nam me redeuntem forte notârat   75
(Et callebat avium linguas, & sydera Mopsus)
Thyrsi quid hoc? dixit, quæ te coquit improba bilis?
Aut te perdit amor, aut te malè fascinat astrum,
Saturni grave sæpe fuit pastoribus astrum,
Intimaque obliquo figit præcordia plumbo.   80
　　Ite domum impasti, domino jam non vacat, agni.
Mirantur nymphæ, & quid ⟨de⟩ te, Thyrsi, futurum est?
Quid tibi vis? ajunt, non hæc solet esse juventæ
Nubila frons, oculique truces, vultusque severi,
Illa choros, lususque leves, & semper amorem   85
Jure petit, bis ille miser qui serus amavit.
　　Ite domum impasti, domino jam non vacat, agni.
Venit Hyas, Dryopéque, & filia Baucidis Aegle
Docta modos, citharæque sciens, sed perdita fastu,
Venit Idumanii Chloris vicina fluenti;   90
Nil me blanditiæ, nil me solantia verba,
Nil me, si quid adest, movet, aut spes ulla futuri.
　　Ite domum impasti, domino jam non vacat, agni.
Hei mihi quam similes ludunt per prata juvenci,
Omnes unanimi secum sibi lege sodales,   95
Nec magis hunc alio quisquam secernit amicum
De grege, sic densi veniunt ad pabula thoes,
Inque vicem hirsuti paribus junguntur onagri;
Lex eadem pelagi, deserto in littore Proteus
Agmina Phocarum numerat, vilisque volucrum   100
Passer habet semper quicum sit, & omnia circum

82 de te *scripsi*: te Edd. 1, 2

Farra libens volitet, serò sua tecta revisens,
Quem si fors letho objecit, seu milvus adunco
Fata tulit rostro, seu stravit arundine fossor,
Protinus ille alium socio petit inde volatu.   105
Nos durum genus, & diris exercita fatis
Gens homines aliena animis, & pectore discors,
Vix sibi quisque parem de millibus invenit unum,
Aut si sors dederit tandem non aspera votis,
Illum inopina dies quâ non speraveris horâ   110
Surripit, æternum linquens in sæcula damnum.
   Ite domum impasti, domino jam non vacat, agni.
Heu quis me ignotas traxit vagus error in oras
Ire per aëreas rupes, Alpemque nivosam!
Ecquid erat tanti Romam vidisse sepultam,   115
Quamvis illa foret, qualem dum viseret olim,
Tityrus ipse suas & oves & rura reliquit,
Ut te tam dulci possem caruisse sodale,
Possem tot maria alta, tot interponere montes,
Tot sylvas, tot saxa tibi, fluviosque sonantes?   120
Ah certè extremùm licuisset tangere dextram,
Et bene compositos placidè morientis ocellos,
Et dixisse vale, nostri memor ibis ad astra.
   Ite domum impasti, domino jam non vacat, agni.
Quamquam etiam vestri nunquam meminisse pigebit,   125
Pastores Thusci, Musis operata juventus,
Hic Charis, atque Lepos; & Thuscus tu quoque Damon,
Antiquâ genus unde petis Lucumonis ab urbe.
O ego quantus eram, gelidi cum stratus ad Arni
Murmura, populeumque nemus, quà mollior herba,   130
Carpere nunc violas, nunc summas carpere myrtos,
Et potui Lycidæ certantem audire Menalcam.
Ipse etiam tentare ausus sum, nec puto multùm
Displicui, nam sunt & apud me munera vestra
Fiscellæ, calathique & cerea vincla cicutæ,   135
Quin & nostra suas docuerunt nomina fagos
Et Datus, & Francinus, erant & vocibus ambo
Et studiis noti, Lydorum sanguinis ambo.
   Ite domum impasti, domino jam non vacat, agni.
Hæc mihi tum læto dictabat roscida luna,   140

.137 Datus *scripsi*: Datis Edd. 1, 2

Dum solus teneros claudebam cratibus hœdos.
Ah quoties dixi, cùm te cinis ater habebat,
Nunc canit, aut lepori nunc tendit retia Damon,
Vimina nunc texit, varios sibi quod sit in usus;
Et quæ tum facili sperabam mente futura   145
Arripui voto levis, & præsentia finxi,
Heus bone numquid agis? nisi te quid forte retardat,
Imus? & argutâ paulùm recubamus in umbra,
Aut ad aquas Colni, aut ubi jugera Cassibelauni?
Tu mihi percurres medicos, tua gramina, succos,   150
Helleborûmque, humilésque crocos, foliûmque hyacinthi,
Quasque habet ista palus herbas, artesque medentûm.
Ah pereant herbæ, pereant artesque medentûm,
Gramina postquam ipsi nil profecere magistro.
Ipse etiam, nam nescio quid mihi grande sonabat   155
Fistula, ab undecimâ jam lux est altera nocte,
Et tum forte novis admôram labra cicutis,
Dissiluere tamen rupta compage, nec ultra
Ferre graves potuere sonos, dubito quoque ne sim
Turgidulus, tamen & referam, vos cedite silvæ.   160
   Ite domum impasti, domino jam non vacat, agni.
Ipse ego Dardanias Rutupina per æquora puppes
Dicam, & Pandrasidos regnum vetus Inogeniæ,
Brennúmque Arviragúmque duces, priscúmque Belinum,
Et tandem Armoricos Britonum sub lege colonos;   165
Tum gravidam Arturo fatali fraude Jögernen,
Mendaces vultus, assumptáque Gorlöis arma,
Merlini dolus. O mihi tum si vita supersit,
Tu procul annosa pendebis fistula pinu
Multùm oblita mihi, aut patriis mutata camœnis   170
Brittonicum strides, quid enim? omnia non licet uni
Non sperasse uni licet omnia, mi satis ampla
Merces, & mihi grande decus (sim ignotus in ævum
Tum licet, externo penitúsque inglorius orbi)
Si me flava comas legat Usa, & potor Alauni,   175
Vorticibúsque frequens Abra, & nemus omne Treantæ,
Et Thamesis meus ante omnes, & fusca metallis
Tamara, & extremis me discant Orcades undis.
   Ite domum impasti, domino jam non vacat, agni.
Hæc tibi servabam lentâ sub cortice lauri,   180

Hæc, & plura simul, tum quæ mihi pocula Mansus,
Mansus Chalcidicæ non ultima gloria ripæ
Bina dedit, mirum artis opus, mirandus & ipse,
Et circùm gemino cælaverat argumento:
In medio rubri maris unda, & odoriferum ver,   185
Littora longa Arabum, & sudantes balsama silvæ,
Has inter Phœnix divina avis, unica terris
Cæruleùm fulgens diversicoloribus alis
Auroram vitreis surgentem respicit undis.
Parte alia polus omnipatens, & magnus Olympus,   190
Quis putet? hic quoque Amor, pictæque in nube pharetræ,
Arma corusca faces, & spicula tincta pyropo;
Nec tenues animas, pectúsque ignobile vulgi
Hinc ferit, at circùm flammantia lumina torquens
Semper in erectum spargit sua tela per orbes   195
Impiger, & pronos nunquam collimat ad ictus,
Hinc mentes ardere sacræ, formæque deorum.
    Tu quoque in his, nec me fallit spes lubrica, Damon,
Tu quoque in his certè es, nam quò tua dulcis abiret
Sanctáque simplicitas, nam quò tua candida virtus?   200
Nec te Lethæo fas quæsivisse sub orco,
Nec tibi conveniunt lacrymæ, nec flebimus ultrà,
Ite procul lacrymæ, purum colit æthera Damon,
Æthera purus habet, pluvium pede reppulit arcum;
Heroúmque animas inter, divósque perennes,   205
Æthereos haurit latices & gaudia potat
Ore Sacro. Quin tu cœli post jura recepta
Dexter ades, placidúsque fave quicúnque vocaris,
Seu tu noster eris Damon, sive æquior audis
Diodotus, quo te divino nomine cuncti   210
Cœlicolæ norint, sylvísque vocabere Damon.
Quòd tibi purpureus pudor, & sine labe juventus
Grata fuit, quòd nulla tori libata voluptas,
En etiam tibi virginei servantur honores;
Ipse caput nitidum cinctus rutilante corona,   215
Letáque frondentis gestans umbracula palmæ
Æternùm perages immortales hymenæos;
Cantus ubi, choreisque furit lyra mista beatis,
Festa Sionæo bacchantur & Orgia Thyrso.

(ADDED IN 1673)

Ad *Joannem Rousium* Oxoniensis Academiæ Bibliothecarium

De libro Poematum amisso, quem ille sibi denuo mitti postulabat, ut cum aliis nostris in Bibliotheca publica reponeret, Ode.[1]

Strophe 1

GEMELLE cultu simplici gaudens liber,
Fronde licet geminâ,
Munditiéque nitens non operosâ,
Quam manus attulit
Juvenilis olim,   5
Seduli tamen haud nimis Poetæ;
Dum vagus Ausonias nunc per umbras
Nunc Britannica per vireta lusit
Insons populi, barbitóque devius
Indulsit patrio, mox itidem pectine Daunio   10
Longinquum intonuit melos
Vicinis, & humum vix tetigit pede;

Antistrophe

Quis te, parve liber, quis te fratribus
Subduxit reliquis dolo?
Cum tu missus ab urbe,   15
Docto jugiter obsecrante amico,
Illustre tendebas iter
Thamesis ad incunabula
Cærulei patris,
Fontes ubi limpidi   20
Aonidum, thyasusque sacer
Orbi notus per immensos
Temporum lapsus redeunte cœlo,
Celeberque futurus in ævum;

Note under title: Ode Ed. 2 : Ode. Joannis Miltoni MS. Bodl.   2 Fronte Warton *conj.* :
Fronde MS. Bodl., Ed. 2   6 Seduli ... nimis *scripsi* : Sedula ... nimii MS. Bodl., Ed. 2

Strophe 2

Modò quis deus, aut editus deo   25
Pristinam gentis miseratus indolem
(Si satis noxas luimus priores
Mollique luxu degener otium)
Tollat nefandos civium tumultus,
Almaque revocet studia sanctus   30
Et relegatas sine sede Musas
Jam penè totis finibus Angligenûm;
Immundasque volucres
Unguibus imminentes
Figat Apollineâ pharetrâ,   35
Phinéamque abigat pestem procul amne Pegaséo.

Antistrophe

Quin tu, libelle, nuntii licet malâ
Fide, vel oscitantiâ
Semel erraveris agmine fratrum,
Seu quis te teneat specus,   40
Seu qua te latebra, forsan unde vili
Callo teréris institoris insulsi,
Lætare felix, en iterum tibi
Spes nova fulget posse profundam
Fugere Lethen, vehique Superam   45
In Jovis aulam remige pennâ;

Strophe 3

Nam te Roüsius sui
Optat peculî, numeróque justo
Sibi pollicitum queritur abesse,
Rogatque venias ille cujus inclyta   50
Sunt data virûm monumenta curæ:
Téque adytis etiam sacris
Voluit reponi quibus & ipse præsidet
Æternorum operum custos fidelis,
Quæstorque gazæ nobilioris,   55
Quàm cui præfuit Iön
Clarus Erechtheides
Opulenta dei per templa parentis

Fulvosque tripodas, donaque Delphica
Iŏn Actæa genitus Creusâ.   60

Antistrophe

Ergo tu visere lucos
Musarum ibis amœnos,
Diamque Phœbi rursus ibis in domum
Oxoniâ quam valle colit
Delo posthabitâ,   65
Bifidóque Parnassi jugo:
Ibis honestus,
Postquam egregiam tu quoque sortem
Nactus abis, dextri prece sollicitatus amici.
Illic legéris inter alta nomina   70
Authorum, Graiæ simul & Latinæ
Antiqua gentis lumina, & verum decus.

Epodos

Vos tandem haud vacui mei labores,
Quicquid hoc sterile fudit ingenium,
Jam serò placidam sperare jubeo   75
Perfunctam invidiâ requiem, sedesque beatas
Quas bonus Hermes
Et tutela dabit solers Roüsi,
Quò neque lingua procax vulgi penetrabit, atque longè
Turba legentum prava facesset;   80
At ultimi nepotes,
Et cordatior ætas
Judicia rebus æquiora forsitan
Adhibebit integro sinu.
Tum livore sepulto,   85
Si quid meremur sana posteritas sciet
Roüsio favente.

Ode tribus constat Strophis, totidémque Antistrophis unâ demum epodo clausis, quas, tametsi omnes nec versuum numero, nec certis ubique colis exactè respondeant, ita tamen secuimus, commodè legendi potius, quam ad antiquos concinendi modos rationem spectantes. Alioquin hoc genus rectiùs fortasse dici monostrophicum debuerat. Metra partim sunt κατὰ σχέσιν, partim ἀπολελυμένα. Phaleucia quæ sunt, spondæum tertio loco bis admittunt, quod idem in secundo loco Catullus ad libitum fecit.

(FROM *Defensio pro populo anglicano*, 1651)

In Salmasii Hundredam

QUIS expedivit Salmasio suam Hundredam,
Picamque docuit verba nostra conari?
Magister artis venter, et Jacobei
Centum exulantis viscera marsupii regis,
Quod si dolosi spes refulserit nummi,   5
Ipse, Antichristi modo qui primatum Papæ
Minatus uno est dissipare sufflatu,
Cantabit ultro Cardinalitium melos.

(FROM *Defensio secunda*, 1654)

In Salmasium

GAUDETE scombri, et quicquid est piscium salo,
Qui frigida hyeme incolitis algentes freta!
Vestrum misertus ille Salmasius Eques
Bonus, amicire nuditatem cogitat;
Chartæque largus, apparat papyrinos   5
Vobis cucullos, præferentes Claudii
Insignia, nomenque et decus, Salmasii:
Gestetis ut per omne cetarium forum
Equitis clientes, scriniis mungentium
Cubito virorum, et capsulis, gratissimos.   10

(FROM *Defensio secunda*, 1654)

GALLI ex concubitu gravidam te, Pontia, Mori
Quis bene moratam morigeramque neget?

(FROM MILTON'S COMMONPLACE BOOK)

(*c.* 1628)

[i]

Carmina Elegiaca

Surge, age surge, leves, iam convenit, excute somnos,
    Lux oritur, tepidi fulcra relinque tori;
Iam canit excubitor gallus, prænuncius ales
    Solis, et invigilans ad sua quemque vocat;
Flammiger Eois Titan caput exerit undis,   5
    Et spargit nitidum læta per arva iubar;
Daulias argutum modulatur ab ilice carmen,
    Edit et excultos mitis alauda modos;
Iam rosa fragrantes spirat silvestris odores,
    Iam redolent violæ luxuriatque seges;   10
Ecce novo campos Zephyritis gramine vestit
    Fertilis, et vitreo rore madescit humus;
Segnes invenias molli vix talia lecto,
    Cum premat imbellis lumina fessa sopor;
Illic languentes abrumpunt somnia somnos,   15
    Et turbant animum tristia multa tuum;
Illic tabifici generantur semina morbi—
    Qui pote torpentem posse valere virum?
Surge, age surge, leves, iam convenit, excute somnos,
    Lux oritur, tepidi fulcra relinque tori.   20

[ii]

    Ignavus satrapam dedecet inclytum
    Somnus qui populo multifido præest.
    Dum Dauni veteris filius armiger
    Stratus purpureo procubuit thoro
    Audax Eurialus, Nisus et impiger   5
    Invasere cati nocte sub horrida
    Torpentes Rutilos castraque Volscia:
    Hinc cædes oritur clamor et absonus . . .

TABLE OF ABBREVIATIONS
USED IN THE TEXTUAL COMMENTARY, ETC.

MILTON'S MANUSCRIPTS OR MANUSCRIPT CORRECTIONS

T.MS.   Trinity College Manuscript, Trin. Coll. Camb. R. 34.

B.MS.   The Bridgwater Manuscript of *A Mask* (*Comus*).

Pforz.   Corrections written into the copy of *A Mask* (*Comus*), 1637, in the Pforzheimer Collection.

MILTON'S POEMS

Arc.   *Arcades.*

Com.   *Comus, A Mask.*

D.F.I.   *Death of a Fair Infant.*

Hymn.   *Hymn on the Morning of Christ's Nativity.*

Il Pens.   *Il Penseroso.*

L'All.   *L'Allegro.*

Lyc.   *Lycidas.*

P.L.   *Paradise Lost.*   *P.R.*   *Paradise Regain'd.*

S.A.   *Samson Agonistes.*

P.R. and S.A. Ed. 1 edition of 1671.

P.R. and S.A. Ed. 2 edition of 1680.

Poems, &c. Ed. 1 edition of 1645.

Poems, &c. Ed. 2 edition of 1673.

S.M.   *At a Solemn Musick.*

MILTON'S EDITORS

Birch   Thomas Birch. Preface to *A Complete Collection of the Historical, Political and Miscellaneous Works of John Milton,* 1734.

Dalton   *Comus, a Mask, Now adapted to the Stage* by Dr. Dalton. 1738.

Dunster   C. Dunster: *Considerations on Milton's Early Reading,* 1800.

Fenton   Elijah Fenton. ed. *Par. Reg., Sams. Agon.,* and *Poems,* 1725.

Keightley   T. Keightley. ed. *The Poems of John Milton,* 1859.

Newton   Thomas Newton. ed. *Par. Reg., Sams. Agon.,* and *Poems,* with Notes by Various Authors, 1752.

Peck   Francis Peck. *New Memoirs of the Life and Poetical Works of John Milton,* 1740.

Smart   John S. Smart. ed. *The Sonnets of Milton,* 1921.

Tickell   Thomas Tickell. ed. *The Poetical Works of John Milton* for J. Tonson, 1720.

Todd   Henry John Todd. ed. *Comus, a Mask,* 1798. *The Poetical Works of John Milton,* 1801–26.

Warton   Thomas Warton. ed. *Poems on Several Occasions,* 1785 and 1791.

Wright or *W. A. W.* William Aldis Wright. ed. *The Poetical Works of John Milton,* 1903.

TEXTUAL COMMENTARY

PARADISE REGAIN'D AND SAMSON AGONISTES

For an account of the first editions of these poems and of the history of their printing *vide* Introduction, p. x *supra*, and Appendix, p. 370 *infra*.

PARADISE REGAIN'D

BOOK I

1 ere] e're Edd. 1, 2. I have corrected *e're* to *ere* (= before) throughout *P.R.* and *S.A.*: *ere* is Milton's spelling throughout *P.L.* with few exceptions: he reserves *e're* for the contraction of *ever*.

4 tri'd] Edd. 1, 2. Milton uses this spelling in preterite and past participle forms when *i* is long (cf. *glorifi'd*, *P.R.* iii. 113; *satisfi'd*, *S.A.* 484) reserving the spelling *-ied* for words where the syllable is short, as in *Accompanied*, l. 300 *infra*. I have carried out this distinction in *P.R.* and *S.A.* Cf. note on l. 414 *infra*.

11 th' undoubted] the undoubted Edd. 1, 2. But Milton intended to indicate, for the metrical reading of the line, the elision of *the* before a vowel. Cf. *th' exalted*, l. 36 *infra* and *S.A.*, l. 1272:

> To quell the mighty of the Earth, th' oppressour.

Edd. 1, 2. Throughout these texts I have corrected *the* to *th'* where elision is intended, as in *P.L. v.* Vol. I, p. xi.

19 then] Ed. 1: than Ed. 2. *Then* is Milton's spelling for this preposition. *v.* Word-List, Vol. I. In *P.R.* and *S.A. than* is substituted in Ed. 2 for *then* of Ed. 1 throughout.

20 Heav'ns] Heavens Edd. 1, 2. *v.* note to l. 30 *infra*.

30 Heav'n] Heaven Edd. 1, 2: but cf. *Heav'n* at l. 32 *infra*. Milton evidently meant to carry out the distinction he made in *P.L.* between *heav'n* monosyllable and *heaven* disyllable. Cf. note to l. 78 *infra*. He made the same distinction between *eev'n* and *even*. Cf. Vol. I, pp. xii, xiii.

Op'nd] open'd Edd. 1, 2. I have throughout adopted Milton's spelling of sonant *'n* as in *happ'ns* i. 334.

34 World] world Edd. 1, 2. I follow Milton's usage in *P.L.* in printing *World* with initial capital when it means *this world*. Cf. 'That brought into this World a world of woe', *P.L.* ix. 11.

36 Thunder-strook] Thunder-struck Edd. 1, 2. But cf. *strook*, *P.R.* iv. 576. I have adopted the spelling *strook* for *struck* as in *P.L. v.* Word-List, Vol. I.

44 ancient] Edd. 1, 2. This is Milton's spelling throughout *P.L.* and in his MSS. *Antient* occurs eight times in *P.R.* and *S.A.* Edd. 1, 2. I have printed *ancient* throughout.

55 head:] Newton: head, Edd. 1, 2.

62 being] being. Edd. 1, 2: being, 1705, Newton: being 1747. Erratum Ed. 1 directs 'after *being* no stop'. There is a careful list of Errata for *P.R.* and *S.A.* at the end of Ed. 1, *v.* p. 370 *infra*, but Ed. 2 has in no case followed the directions. Peck in his *New Memoirs of the Life and Poetical Works of Milton*, 1740, gives a list of the errata; and most of the corrections were made in 1747; all in Newton's edition of 1752.

65 Woman] Ed. 2: woman Ed. 1.
    born:] Newton: born, Edd. 1, 2.

75 thir] their Edd. 1, 2. The printer has not been consistent in carrying out Milton's distinction between *thir* (unemphatic) and *their* (emphatic): but in two places he has corrected *their* to *thir* in accordance with Milton's practice, *v.* note to iv. 424 *infra*, and to *S.A.* 1183. The spelling *thir* preponderates in *P.R.* and *S.A.* and I have corrected *their* to *thir* where necessary throughout, and in one place *thir* to *their*, *v.* iii. 55 and note.

78 Heaven] Edd. 1, 2. I have retained Milton's spelling which indicates Heaven as disyllable here before the caesura. Cf. Vol. I, p. 284.

80 reverence;] reverence, Edd. 1, 2. Here as in l. 82 Milton's practice requires semicolon. *v.* Vol. I, Introd., p. xxi.

82 Dores;] Wright: Dores, Edd. 1, 2.

84 Sovran] Sov'raign Edd. 1, 2. *Sovran* is Milton's spelling. *v.* note to *Com.* 41.
    heard] Ed. 1: hear Ed. 2.

87 Hee] He Edd. 1, 2. I have printed the word according to Milton's spelling for emphasis. ' "He who obtains the monarchy of Heaven": Obtains means here *obtains by conquest*: Satan being the speaker, it is a word of much force. It implies usurpation. It should be noted that *He* is in this place sneeringly emphatic.' Dunster.

115 *Adams*] *Adam*'s Edd. 1, 2. Milton spelt proper names in the possessive case without apostrophe. *v.* Introd., Vol. I, p. xii. I have followed his practice throughout my text of *P.R.* and *S.A.* The Printer of 1680 (Ed. 2) occasionally gives Milton's spelling, as in *Davids*, *P.R.* iii. 153, 159, *Israels*, *S.A.* 1527.

116 Hells] Hell's Edd. 1, 2. I follow Milton's practice in *P.L.* *v.* Introd., Vol. I, p. xii and note 1.

120 steps,] steps; Edd. 1, 2.

122 Man] Ed. 2: man Ed. 1.

137 Then toldst] Edd. 1, 2: Thou toldst Keightley *conj.* 'The sense, which he intends here is plainly "*Thou told'st her*", etc., so that *told'st* is used here as equivalent to the Latin *dixisti* with its pronominal nominative understood.' Dunster. For a similar omission of the pronoun *v.* l. 221 *infra*.

144 suttlety] subtlety Edd. 1, 2. *suttlety* and *suttle* are Milton's spellings. *v.* Vol. I, Introd., pp. x and xvi.

151 femal] female Edd. 1, 2. But cf. 'Femal of sex', *S.A.* 711 and *v.* Word-List, Vol. I. *Femal* is Milton's spelling, and I have adopted it throughout *P.R.* and *S.A.*

162 World] world Edd. 1, 2.

166 perfet] perfect Edd. 1, 2. Milton spells the word *perfet* at iv. 468 and in *S.A.* 946, and this is his chosen spelling. *v.* Word-List, Vol. I, and Introd., p. xi, *supra*.

181 naught] nought Edd. 1, 2. The word is always spelt *naught* in *P.L.*, in *P.R.* elsewhere, and in *S.A.* with one exception.

182 and Vigils] in Vigils Sympson *conj.* But the sense is quite clear: a Vigil was a service on the eve of a holy day. Dr. Johnson quotes in his *Dictionary*
    'The rivals call my muse another way
     To sing their Vigils for the ensuing day.' *Dryden.*

189 leading,] 1747, Newton: leading; Edd. 1, 2.

207 red] read Edd. 1, 2. Milton seems to have distinguished *red* (preterite) from *read* (present). Cf. *P.L.* ii. 422 and note on i. 798. I have carried out this distinction.

226 subdue] erratum Ed. 1: destroy. Edd. 1, 2. The correction was made in 1747.
    onely] only Edd. 1, 2. I have adopted throughout Milton's spelling of *onely*.

237 men;] men, Edd. 1, 2.

241 should] Ed. 1: shall Ed. 2.

247 laist] lais't Edd. 1, 2.

254 thee] Ed. 1: the Ed. 2.

264 eev'n] even Edd. 1, 2. *v.* note to l. 30 *supra*.

271 knew] Ed. 1: new Ed. 2.

274 hee] he Edd. 1, 2. I have given emphatic *hee* here and in iii. 433, and likewise *mee* in ll. 276, 277, 278 where Edd. 1, 2 read *me*.

289 Autority] Authority Edd. 1, 2. *Autority* is Milton's spelling. *v.* Word-List, Vol. I, and I have adopted it throughout these texts.

294 our] Ed. 1: out Ed. 2.

297 markt] mark'd Edd. 1, 2. I have preserved throughout the text of *P.R.* and *S.A.* Milton's distinction between the preterite in *-d* and the past participle in *-t*. *v.* Introd., Vol. I, p. xxx, and p. ix, *supra*.

298 human] humane Edd. 1, 2. Milton distinguished by spelling (*v.* Vol. I, Introd., p. xxix) *húman* from *humáne* and I have followed suit: the printer has not been consistent here.

307 one Cave] some cave Meadowcourt and Jortin *conj.*

320 utterd] utt'red Edd. 1, 2: utter'd Ed. 3. *Entred, wandred, utt'red* are the printer's spellings. Milton spells *enterd, wanderd,* &c., both in the MS. and

printed text of *P.L.*, and in some places these spellings survive in the texts of 1671. *v. S.A.* 246, *offerd,* and 252, *enterd.* I have adopted Milton's spelling in *erd* throughout these texts.

323–5 Caravan, . . . droughth?] Edd. 1, 2: Caravan? . . . droughth. Tickell.

324 dropd] dropt Edd. 1, 2. The verb is preterite. *v.* note to l. 297 *supra.*

339 stubs] shrubs Thyer *conj.*, but Milton means stalks which have been cut down. *v. O.E.D.*

353 *Elijah*] *Eliah* Edd. 1, 2. I have adopted the spelling which Milton uses at ii. 268 and 277.

373 demurring] erratum Ed. 1; 1720: demuring Edd. 1, 2. For Milton's spelling cf. *preferring S.A.* 464 Ed. 1, and Introd., Vol. I, p. xxx.

400 Nearer] erratum Ed. 1: Never Edd. 1, 2. Correction was made by Fenton in 1730 (Keightley).

410 Heavens] Ed. 1: Heav'ns Ed. 2. Possibly a disyllable, allowing for extra metrical syllable at the caesura. So also *Heaven* in l. 416 *infra.* The printer does not respect Milton's distinction (*Heav'n* monosyllable: *Heaven* disyllable) as carefully as did the printer of *P.L.*

414 emptied . . . unpitied] Ed. 2: emptyed . . . unpityed Ed. 1. Cf. note to l. 4 *supra.*

  shunnd] shun'd Edd. 1, 2, a wrong spelling, since according to Milton's code the apostrophe would indicate that the preceding vowel was long. *v.* Introd., Vol. I, p. xi, note 5.

417 Imparts] erratum Ed. 1: Imports Edd. 1, 2. The right reading was restored in 1747.

421 Heav'ns] Ed. 2: Heaven's Ed. 1.

428 hunderd] hundred Edd. 1, 2: but at iii. 287 the spelling is *hunderd,* Milton's undoubted form: *v.* Vol. I, note to *P.L.* i. 709 and Word-List.

455 shalt] Ed. 1: shall Ed. 2.

463 an] Ed. 1: and Ed. 2.

470 wrested] Ed. 3: rested Edd. 1, 2, but *wrested,* the word in this sense, *S.A.,* 384 and *P.L.* xi. 503.

472 truth,] truth; Edd. 1, 2.

478 Truth] truth Edd. 1, 2. But *Truth* is here personified. *v.* ll. 481–2 'to hear / Her dictates . . .'.

490 voutsaf'd] vouchsaf'd Edd. 1, 2. I have adopted Milton's spelling. *v.* Word-List, Vol. I.

500 wing] Ed. 1: wings Ed. 2.

BOOK II

16 *Thisbite*] Milton uses the Latin form of the word — *Thesbites,* in the Vulgate. The Hebrew form is better rendered in *Tishbite* of the Authorized Version. *v.* Todd's note to this line (edition of 1826, vol. iv, p. 75).

25 Creek,] Creek; Edd. 1, 2.

30 what high] Ed. 1: that high Ed. 2.

31 fall'n;] fall'n, Edd. 1, 2.

34 truth:] truth, Edd. 1, 2.

47 thee;] thee, Edd. 1, 2.

48 yoke:] yoke, Edd. 1, 2.

63 calm;] Edd. 1, 2. This use of the semicolon marking a break in speech is not modern. *v.* Vol. I, p. xxi, note 6.

86 lookd] look't Ed. 1: look'd Ed. 2. *v.* note to i. 297 *supra.*

99 buisness] business Edd. 1, 2. For M.'s spelling *v.* note to *Com.* 169.

106 past] pass'd Edd. 1, 2. Milton's spelling *past* for the participle is found at *P.R.* iii. 294, *S.A.* 22, 685, &c., as generally in *P.L.*

127 risen] ris'n Edd. 1, 2. But the word is here a disyllable, and Milton's spelling must therefore be *risen.* In *P.L.* as it happens the word is always a monosyllable. *v.* Vol. I, p. xxvii.

who] Ed. 1: whom Ed. 2.

128 then] *om.* Edd. 1, 2: inserted in Errata Ed. 1. Tickell 1720 inserts *than.*

131 tasted him] = tested, made trial of him. Cf. *S.A.* 1091, 'The way to know were not to see but taste.' Todd quotes translation of Boccaccio, 1620: 'He began to taste his pulse.'

134 Wives] this is a usual form in Milton's day for the possessive singular.

136 If he be Man . . . side at least,] Edd. 1, 2: If he be Man . . . side, at least Dunster.

179 False-titl'd] False titl'd Edd. 1, 2.

189 scapes] = escapades, used in this sense by Shakespeare.

228 oftest] Edd. 1, 2: often Ed. 3.

232 wide] Ed. 1: wild Ed. 2. cf. *Com.* 403, note.

240 Persons] Ed. 2: persons Ed. 1.

259 Mee] Ed. 1: Me Ed. 2.

268 Ev'n] Even Edd. 1, 2. I have followed Milton's practice in *P.L.* in the spelling of *Even* followed by *and.* Cf. *P.L.* vii. 550.

279 Harald] Herald Edd. 1, 2. *Harald* is Milton's spelling. *v.* Word-List, Vol. I.

283 dream;] dream, Edd. 1, 2.

309 *Nebaioth,* son of Ishmael, seems to be put by mistake for Ishmael, who was Hagar's son.

he] Edd. 1, 2: here 1705. This reading, *here,* has been adopted by some editors, but I think the recurrence of the word at l. 311 puts it out of court.

313 *Thebez*] erratum Ed. 1; 1747, Newton: *Thebes* Ed. 1, 2. Cf. note to *P.L.* i. 578, Vol. I. Blakeney emends *Thisbe.* According to Keightley: 'it should be Thisbe: Thebez was in Ephraim'.

336 honour:] honour, Edd. 1, 2.

341 pil'd] erratum Ed. 1: pill'd Edd. 1, 2. The correction was made in 1705.

353 Hylas;] *Hylas,* Edd. 1, 2.

357 th' *Hesperides*] Ed. 1: the *Hesperides* Ed. 2.

363 pipes,] pipes Edd. 1, 2.

370 pure;] pure, Edd. 1, 2.

371 knowledge works,] erratum Ed. 1: knowledge, works Edd. 1, 2: knowledge works Ed. 3.

393 seest;] seest, Edd. 1, 2.

404 importune] Pronounced with stress on second syllable. Cf. Spenser, *Faerie Queene*, I. xii. 16: 'And often blame the too importune fate.'

405 persu'd] pursu'd Edd. 1, 2. M.'s spelling was *persu'd* as in i. 195 *supra*.

409 yeilds] yields Edd. 1, 2. *yeilds* is Milton's spelling. *v.* Word-List, Vol. I.

447 those] 'He probably dictated *these*'. Keightley.

486 oftest] often Landor *conj.*

BOOK III

15 brest] breast Edd. 1, 2: *brest* elsewhere in *P.R.* and *S.A.* 609, and in *P.L.* passim.

51 praise;] praise Edd. 1, 2.

52 what,] what; Edd. 1, 2.

55 their . . . their] thir . . . thir Edd. 1, 2. I have printed *their*, the emphatic form (= of them) which Milton used in this construction. Cf. *P.L.* ii. 362:

> this place may lie expos'd
> The utmost border of his kingdom left
> To their defence who hold it

and *v.* note to *P.L.* i. 383.

56 disprais'd] Edd. 1, 2: dispis'd 1705, Tickell and Fenton. The right reading, noted by Peck, was restored in 1747.

122 Word] word Edd. 1, 2. This word should be spelt here with initial capital as in *S.A.* 83:

> O first created Beam, and thou great Word,

and in *P.L.* v. 836:

> by whom
> As by his Word the mighty Father made
> All things . . .

Cf. Introd., Vol. I, p. xiv.

127 is] Ed. 1: it Ed. 2.

130 that,] that Edd. 1, 2: what Ed. 3.

151 the seeking] Ed. 1: their seeking Ed. 2. The right reading was restored in 1747.

158 *Roman*] Ed. 2: Roman Ed. 1.

227 linger'st] Ed. 1: lingrest Ed. 2.

238 insight] 1747: in sight Edd. 1, 2.

241 loth] Ed. 1 (state 2), Ed. 2: loah Ed. 1 (state. 1). In *P.L.* the word is spelt alternatively *loath* and *loth*.

287 hunderd] Ed. 1: hundred Ed. 2. *v.* note to i. 428 *supra*.

292 *Ctesiphon*] Fenton: *Tesiphon* Edd. 1, 2. But the right form is *Ctesiphon*, as in l. 300 *infra*.

309 half-moons] Ed. 2: half moons Ed. 1.

316 *Candaor*] Ed. 1: *Gandaor* Ed. 2.

324 showers] erratum Ed. 1; shower Edd. 1, 2: show'rs 1747.

343 *Paynim*] *v. Panim* in Word-List, Vol. I. Cf. Florio's *Worlde of Wordes*: Pagano, *a pagan, a painim, an infidell*.

351 sight] Ed. 2: fight Ed. 1.

355 means;] means, Ed. 1: means Ed. 2.

357 wert] Ed. 2: wer't Ed. 1.

377 Ten sons] Edd. 1, 2, &c.: Eight sons Dunster *conj.*

378 *Israel,*] *Israel* Edd. 1, 2.

393 World] Ed. 2: world Ed. 1.

397 fardest] farthest Edd. 1, 2. I have respected Milton's preference in spelling *fardest* in *P.L.* and *furder* in *P.L.* and *S.A.*

BOOK IV

12 salve] Ed. 1: save Ed. 2.

25 Western] Ed. 2: western Ed. 1.

30 th' earth] Ed. 2: the earth Ed. 1. Cf. note to i. 11 *supra*.

33 of whose banks] Edd. 1, 2: off whose banks Masson.

41 multipli'd] multiply'd Ed. 1: multiplied Ed. 2. *v.* note to i. 4 *supra*.

56 gods] Edd. 1, 2: God Newton. Cf. note to *S.A.* 1176.

71, 75 Ile] Isle Edd. 1, 2. Milton's spelling is *Ile, Iland. v.* note to *P.L.* i. 205.

92 Iland] Island Edd. 1, 2.

102 victor] victor, Edd. 1, 2. Erratum Ed. 1 directs 'no stop after victor'. Newton made the correction.

108 be] Ed. 1: he Ed. 2.

127 expell] Ed. 2: expel Ed. 1. Milton doubled the final consonant in the stressed syllable. *v.* Introd., Vol. I, p. xxx.

128 withall] Ed. 2: withal Ed. 1. *v.* note to l. 127 *supra*.

129 Expell] Ed. 2: Expel Ed. 1.

157 the difficult] thee difficult Jortin *conj.*

186 supream] supreme Ed. 1: Supreme Ed. 2. Milton spells *supream* when the stress falls on the second syllable, *supreme* when it falls on the first. *v.* Word-List, Vol. I.

217 wast] Tickell, 1720: was Edd. 1, 2.

218 Rabbi's] Rabbies Edd. 1, 2. *v.* note to i. 4 *supra*.

227, 229 Gentiles] *Gentiles* Edd. 1, 2, but elsewhere in *P.R.* and *P.L.* always printed in Roman type.

230 mean'st;] Tickell: mean'st, Edd. 1, 2.

270 th' Arsenal] the Arsenal Edd. 1, 2: the Arsenals Meadowcourt.

288 ought] aught Edd. 1, 2. Milton distinguishes *ought* the verb from *aught* meaning *anything*.

299 hee] he Edd. 1, 2. ' "He" is here contemptuously emphatical.' Dunster.

303 Equal] Edd. 1, 2: Equals Newton *conj.*

424 thir] most copies Ed. 1; and Ed. 2: their a few copies Ed. 1. *thir* is the right form, unemphatic, introduced here as a correction of the press.

452 rack] wrack Newton. But *rack* was used in Milton's day in the sense of a rush of wind, a gale, a storm. *v. O.E.D.* Cf. *P.L.* iv. 994.

497 Mee] Ed. 1: Me Ed. 2.
    will; desist, thou] Ed. 1 (state 2), Ed. 2: will desist; thou Ed. 1 (state 1).

502 have] Edd. 1, 2: had Dunster *conj.*

517 sense] Ed. 2: sence Ed. 1.

548 Alablaster] Alabaster Edd. 1, 2. Milton spells in the manner of his day *alablaster. v. P.L.* and Word-List, Vol. I.

549 Pinnacle] Ed. 2: Pinacle Ed. 1.

565 *Alcides,*] Ed. 1 (state 2), Ed. 2: *Alcides* Ed. 1 (state 1).

589 Tree of Life] Ed. 2: tree of life Ed. 1.

590 Fount of Life] fount of Life Ed. 2.

596 Father,] Tickell: Father Edd. 1, 2.

598 Conceiving,] Ed. 1 (state 2), Ed. 2: Conceiving Ed. 1 (state 1).

608 hast] Edd. 1, 2: hath Ed. 3: *hast* was noted as *corrigendum* by Peck, 1740, and was restored to the text in 1747.

615 re-install,] Tickell, 1720: re-install Edd. 1, 2.

633 Worlds] Ed. 2: worlds Ed. 1.

SAMSON AGONISTES

Of that sort of Dramatic Poem which is call'd Tragedy

45 omitted.] Edd. 1, 2 make the paragraph end here, whereas clearly it should end at 'fift Act'. l. 46.

46 fift Act.] fift Act, Edd. 1, 2.

47 Of the style] of the style Edd. 1, 2. I print with new paragraph which must have been Milton's intention.

50 decorum,] decorum; Edd. 1, 2. The punctuation here was part of the original muddle: *v.* notes *supra*.

The Argument

6 Manoah] Manoa Edd. 1, 2. *v.* note to l. 328 of the text *infra*. I have generalized the Hebrew form.

Samson Agonistes

2 furder] further Edd. 1, 2. *v.* note to *P.R.* iii. 397.

5 servil] servile Edd. 1, 2. Milton spells *servil* at ll. 412 and 574, and I adopt his spelling here as in *P.L. v.* Word-List, Vol. I.

7 Pris'ner] Prisoner Edd. 1, 2. But the word is a disyllable here and should be spelt *pris'ner* as at l. 1308 and l. 1460. *v.* also note on l. 808 *infra* and on l. 1460. *v.* Introd., Vol. I, p. xxvi.

17 ease;] ease, Ed. 1. Milton uses semicolon in this position.

23 Heav'n] Heaven Edd. 1, 2. *v.* note to *P.R.* i. 30.

33 Captiv'd] as in l. 694 accented on second syllable: so Spenser *F.Q.* ii. 4. 16, 'Thus when as *Guyon Furor* had captiv'd.'

41 Eyeless in Gaza at the mill with slaves] 'There ought to be commas after *eyeless*, after *Gaza*, and after *mill*.' Landor. Milton has left the reader to read the line aright.

45 default;] default, Edd. 1, 2.

62 Haply] Happ'ly Edd. 1, 2. *Haply* in the sense of *perhaps* is spelt thus in *P.L.* i. 203, &c.

63 mee] me Edd. 1, 2. I have adopted throughout Milton's distinction between *mee* emphatic and *me* unemphatic.

69 or decrepit] Ed. 1: decrepit Ed. 2.

84 ther] there Edd. 1, 2. I follow Milton's spelling of the unemphatic form of *there*. Cf. *P.L.* vii. 243, 'Let ther be light'.

115 hee] he Edd. 1, 2. I follow Milton's practice here and elsewhere in spelling *hee* where the word demands emphasis.

123 Ore worn] O're worn Edd. 1, 2. I have adopted Milton's spelling of *Ore* (= *over*) as in *P.L.*

126 Irresistible] erratum Ed. 1; 1705: irresistable Edd. 1, 2.

136 advanc't] Edd. 1, 2. This is the past participle, with final -*t*. The preterite would be *advanc'd*.

157 complain] erratum Ed. 1; Peck, 1747, Newton: complain'd Edd. 1, 2.

177 ere] e're Ed. 1: er'e Ed. 2. Milton's spelling is *ere*. *v.* note to *P.R.* i. 1 *supra*.

178 speaks] Ed. 1: speak Ed. 2: spake Ed. 3. Newton notes, 'He speaks] We have followed Milton's own edition; most of the others have it *He spake*.'

184 Sores;] Sores, Edd. 1, 2.

189 counterfet] counterfeit Edd. 1, 2. *v.* Word-List, Vol. I.

191 understood):] understood) Edd. 1, 2.

193 Ye Ed. 2: Yee Ed. 1.

210 disposal;] disposal, Ed. 1: disposal Ed. 2.

216 women] Ed. 1: Woman Ed. 2.

222 motiond] motion'd erratum Ed. 1; Peck, 1747, Newton: mention'd Edd. 1, 2. Milton uses the word in the sense of *advise*, *propose*, as in *P.L.* ix. 229: 'Well hast thou motiond, well thy thoughts imployd.'

234 Shee] She Edd. 1, 2. Milton would use the emphatic form of the pronoun here, in antithesis to *I my self. v.* Vol. I, Introd., pp. xxxii–xxxiii.

244 mee] me Edd. 1, 2. Cf. note to l. 234 *supra.*

276 deeds!] deeds? Edd. 1, 2. For the printer's mistaken use of ? for ! *v.* Vol. I, Introd., p. xxii and notes to ll. 496, 820, and 902 *infra.*

290 roul;] roul, Edd. 1, 2.

297 ther] there Edd. 1, 2. *v.* note to l. 300 *infra.*

300 ther be] there be Edd. 1, 2. I have printed the unemphatic form of the word *ther* according to Milton's usage, cf. l. 84 *supra* and note.

323 averr] aver Edd. 1, 2. I adopt Milton's spelling to represent the stressed second syllable. *v.* Vol. I, Introd., p. xxx.

328 *Manoah*] Edd. 1, 2. This spelling renders the Hebrew form: I have altered *Manoa* to *Manoah* in other places.

354 And such] Erratum Ed. 1; Peck, Jortin *conj.*, 1747, Newton: Such Edd. 1, 2.

362 Plant] Plant; Edd. 1, 2.

390 sent] Edd. 1, 2. Milton's spelling of *scent* as in l. 720, and in *P.L. v.* Word-List, Vol. I.

401 sought] Edd. 1, 2; Newton: thought 1705.

405 out,] Newton: out. Edd. 1, 2.

424 I state not that] *O.E.D.* gives this as a single instance of a use of the word *state* in the meaning (queried) of *assign a value to, give an opinion upon*: it is in this sense allied to a well-recognized meaning, *give a rank or position to.* Cf. Burnet, *History of our own Time*: 'The two religions, popish and protestant were so equally stated in his mind, that a few grains of loyalty . . . turned the balance with him.' Manoah appears to be saying impatiently, 'I attach no particular value to that . . .'

431 Anough] Enough Edd. 1, 2. Milton's spelling is *anough* as at ll. 455, 1468, and 1592 *infra.*

474 deferr] defer Edd. 1, 2. *v.* note to l. 323 *supra.*

496–7   The mark of fool set on his front ?
             But I God's counsel have not kept, his holy secret Edd. 1, 2.
In Tonson's edition, 1713, the lines were first divided rightly. Interrogation mark has been used for exclamation mark Edd. 1, 2. *v.* note to l. 276 *supra.*

535 hallowd] hallow'd Ed. 1; 1747: hollow Ed. 2.

545 heart of Gods and men] Ed. 1: . . . and Men 1747, Newton: hearts of God or Men Ed. 2, and other editions.

548 pure] pure. Edd. 1, 2.

555 forbidd'n] Ed. 2: forbid'n Ed. 1.

612 There] Edd. 1, 2: These 1713.

627 medcinal] Edd. 1, 2: medicinal Ed. 3. *Medcinal* is Milton's spelling: the second syllable is elided as in *Com.* (1645), l. 636:
             And yet more med'cinal is it then that Moly.
In *Com.* (1637) and in both MSS. it is spelt *med'cinall* in this line.

653 inrould] enroll'd Edd. 1, 2. I have adopted Milton's spelling in *P.L.*, xii.
   523. Cf. *rowl* in Word-List, Vol. I, and note *roul* l. 290, *supra*.
656 life] erratum Ed. 1: life. Edd. 1, 2: life: 1720: life, Newton.
658 sought] Edd. 1, 2: fraught Warburton *conj*.
660 But with] erratum Ed. 1; Peck, Newton: But to Edd. 1, 2: But 1720.
711 Femal] Ed. 1: Female Ed. 2. *v*. note to *P.R.* i. 151 *supra*.
715 Iles] Isles Edd. 1, 2. *v*. note to *P.R.* iv. 71, 75.
720 sent] Ed. 1: scent Ed. 2. *v*. note to l. 390 *supra*.
729 seem into tears] Edd. 1, 2; Newton: seem tears 1705.
734 without excuse] without excuse, Edd. 1, 2. 'The comma should be
   expunged after excuse, else the sentence is ambiguous.' Landor.
742 estate,] estate. Edd. 1, 2.
783 frailty:] Wright: frailty Edd. 1, 2.
808 prisoner] Possibly Milton allows for an extra syllable at the caesura.
   v. note to l. 7 *supra* and Introd., Vol. I, p. xxvi.
819 sorceress] Ed. 1: sorserer Ed. 2: sorseress Ed. 3.
820 mine!] mine? Edd. 1, 2. *v*. note to l. 276 *supra*.
842 Or] Edd. 1, 2: For 1705.
864 these] Edd. 1, 2; Newton: their 1705.
883 receive] Ed. 2: reccive Ed. 1. One of the few places where Ed. 2 corrects
   a mechanical error.
902 appear!] appear? Edd. 1, 2. *v*. note to l. 276 *supra*.
905 breath;] breath, Edd. 1, 2.
939 could] Ed. 1: couldst Ed. 2. The subjunctive is intended.
973 the other] th' other Edd. 1, 2. Cf. note to *P.R.* i. 11. The metre requires
   the here.
974 wild] Edd. 1, 2: wide Jortin *conj*.
987 flowers;] Wright: flowers. Edd. 1, 2.
1000 folly who] Ed. 1: folly, who Ed. 2. Milton's principle is to omit comma
   before a restrictive or defining relative clause.
1033 nothing,] Edd. 1, 2. Some copies of Ed. 1 read *nothing* without comma.
1038 farr] far Edd. 1, 2; 1705, Newton: war 1713.
1045 Imbarkt] Embarqu'd Edd. 1, 2. I have adopted Milton's spelling in
   P.L. xi. 753. For the spelling *embarqu'd*, cf. *attaque* l. 1113, *infra*, and note.
   These French spellings are not Milton's.
1055, 1060 femal] female Edd. 1, 2. *v*. note to l. 711 *supra*.
1060 nor] Ed. 1: or Ed. 2.
1061 retire? . . . storm.] Fenton: Retire, . . . storm? Edd. 1, 2.
1069 Hauty] Haughty Edd. 1, 2. *Hauty* seems to be Milton's spelling. *v*.
   Word-List, Vol. I.
   as is ,his] Edd. 1, 2, Newton: as is 1705: as his Peck: as is a 1720.
1075 fraught] 'The freight or fraught of a ship.' Cotgrave. Meadowcroft's
   emendation *freight* is unnecessary.

1078 *Gath,*] Ed. 1 (state 2), Ed. 2; *Gath* Ed. 1 (state 1).

1081 *Kiriathaim*] Ed. 1: *Kariathaim* Ed. 2.

1086 encounters,] Ed. 1 (state 2), Ed. 2: encounters Ed. 1 (state 1).

1092 me?] Ed. 2: me; Ed. 1.

1093 thee.] Ed. 2: thee; Ed. 1 (state 1): thee? Ed. 1 (state 2). Ed. 2 here clears up a muddle.

1096 wish] Edd. 1, 2: with 1720, Tickell, on no authority.

1101 Acts;] Acts, Edd. 1, 2.

1109 assassinated] *O.E.D.* gives an obsolete use of *assassinate* 'to endeavour to kill by treacherous violence'. Dr. Johnson quotes this instance from *S.A.* in his *Dictionary* under *assassinate* 2: 'To waylay, to take by treachery. This meaning is perhaps peculiar to Milton.'

1113 attack] attaque Edd. 1, 2. *v.* note to l. 1045 *supra*.

1121 add] Ed. 1: and Ed. 2, and successive editions. The correct reading was restored in 1747.

1125 mee] Ed. 1: me Ed. 2.

1127 shalt] Ed. 1: shall Ed. 2.

1158 deliverd] delivered Edd. 1, 2: deliver'd 1705.

1162 comrades] Accented on the second syllable. Cf. *Henry IV, Pt. I*, IV. i, 'And his comrádes that daff'd the world aside'. Newton.

1176 god is God] some copies Ed. 1 (state 2), and Ed. 2: god is god other copies Ed. 1 (state 1). This is clearly a correction made as the book went through the press: cf. Milton's translation of Psalm 136, l. 6, p. 121 *supra*, 'For of gods he is the God', and note to *Hymn*, l. 224.

1181 Tongue-doughtie] Ed. 2: Tongue-doubtie Ed. 1. Clearly a mistake of amanuensis or printer.

1183 Thir] some copies Ed. 1 (state 2), and Ed. 2: *Their* other copies Ed. 1 (state 1). *Thir* unstressed is clearly a correction. For another correction on the same page, signature N4, *v.* note on l. 1176 *supra*.

1214 thir Ed. 2: their Ed. 1.

1215 naught] nought Edd. 1, 2. *v.* note to *P.R.* i. 181.

1218 my known Edd. 1, 2: mine own *conj.* Sampson.

1224 inrould] enrol'd Edd. 1, 2. *v.* note to l. 653 *supra*.

1231 *Bääl-zebub*] Baal-zebub Edd. 1, 2. Here *Baal* must clearly be pronounced as two syllables, with accent on the first as in Hebrew: contrast the pronunciation of *Bëëlzebúb* (nearer the Greek rendering), *P.L.* i. 81, &c.

1248 divulge] erratum Ed. 1; Peck, 1747, Newton: divulg'd Edd. 1, 2.

1251 malicious] as *P.L.*, ix. 253: malitious Edd. 1, 2.

1264 mee] me Edd. 1, 2. A clear use of the emphatic pronoun.

1267 their] thir Edd. 1, 2. In this position, where the pronoun is antecedent to the relative, Milton spells *their*. *v.* note to *P.R.* iii. 55 *supra*.

1291 inflict;] inflict, Edd. 1, 2.

1306 hand.] Ed. 1: hand, Ed. 2.

1313 rate] erratum Ed. 1; Peck, 1747, Newton: race Edd. 1, 2.

1325 Mimics] erratum Ed. 1; Peck, 1747, Newton: Mimirs Edd. 1, 2: Mimers Fenton, 1725. Dr. Johnson, accepting Fenton's reading, quotes this line in his *Dictionary*, as illustration of '*Mimer*: a mimick or buffoon.'

1337 commands?] Ed. 1 (state 2), Ed. 2: commands. Ed. 1 (state 1).

1340 feats,] Ed. 1 (state 2), Ed. 2: feats Ed. 1 (state 1).

1369 holds:] holds no stop Edd. 1, 2.

1373 freely;] Ed. 1: freely, Ed. 2. A difficult sentence, in which Ed. 1's punctuation gives the better reading.

1387. aught] Ed. 1: ought Ed. 2.

1398 wert] Ed. 1: art Ed. 2.

1431 Send thee the] Ed. 1, Peck, 1747, Newton: Send the Ed. 2: Send th' 1720.

1432 thy side] Ed. 1: the side Ed. 2.

1440 bin seen] been seen Edd. 1, 2. *bin* is Milton's spelling and pronunciation. *been seen* is an impossible collocation.

1453 ye] Edd. 1, 2: you Ed. 3.

1460 pris'ner;] pris'ner, Ed. 1: pris'oner, Ed. 2. Here and in the rest of this sentence I have revised the punctuation on Milton's principles. *v.* Introd., Vol. I, pp. xx, xxi.

1462 spite:] spite; Edd. 1, 2.

1463 Priests;] Priests, Ed. 1: priests, Ed. 2.

1466 sale;] sale, Edd. 1, 2.

1488 Son,] Ed. 2: Son. Ed. 1.

1495 had] Ed. 1, 1747, Newton: hath Ed. 2.

1512 perishd;] perish'd, Edd. 1, 2.

1527-35 What if . . . Belief] Ed. 2: *om.* Ed. 1 but inserted as *Omissa* at the end of the book.

1537 Of good . . . the sooner] Ed. 2: *om.* Ed. 1 but inserted as *Omissa*.

1544 persues] Ed. 1: pursues Ed. 2. *persue* is Milton's spelling. *v.* Word-List, Vol. I.

1548 thee] Ed. 1: the Ed. 2.

1552 here] erratum Ed. 1; Peck, 1747, Newton: heard Edd. 1, 2.

1571 hopes defeated] 1720, 1747: hope's Edd. 1, 2, 1725, Newton.

1580 hee] he Edd. 1, 2.

1605 spacious] Ed. 1: specious Ed. 2.

1606 Half round] Ed. 1: Half-round Ed. 2.

1608 behold;] behold, Edd. 1, 2.

1623 Hee] He Edd. 1, 2.

1627 stupendious] Edd. 1, 2, the form used by Milton in *P.L.* x. 351. It appears from the examples collected that *stupendious* was the form generally used until the end of the seventeenth century. *v. O.E.D.* Tickell, 1720, reads *stupendous* here.

1635 unsuspicious] Ed. 2: unsuspitious Ed. 1.

1642 Not] Ed. 1: Nor Ed. 2.

1649 convulsion] Edd. 1, 2; 1747, Newton: confusion 1705 and several editions.

1650 shook,] Ed. 1, 1720, Peck, 1647, Newton: took, Ed. 2 and several editions.

1669 jocond] jocund Edd. 1, 2. *jocond* is Milton's spelling in *P.L.*, *Com.*, and *L'All.*

1683 wrauth] wrath Edd. 1, 2. I print *wrauth* here as Milton's considered spelling in *P.L.*

1700 embost] this must be the past participle of the Middle English verb *embose*; cf. Chaucer, *Dethe of Blanche*, l. 352:

> how the hert had upon lengthe
> So much embosed.

The meaning is to take shelter in a wood, and is equivalent to *imbosk*. Cf. Milton, *Reformation . . . in England*, 'They seek the dark, the bushy, the tangled forest, they would imbósk.'

1713 *Caphtor*] Ed. 1, Peck, 1747, Newton: *Chaphtor* Ed. 2 and several editions.

1728 the while] Ed. 1: thee while Ed. 2.

1754 intent;] intent, Edd. 1, 2.

1755 servants] Edd. 1, 2; Newton: servant Ed. 3 and most of the editions before Newton.

POEMS, ETC., UPON SEVERAL OCCASIONS

The Stationer to the Reader, p. 112.

Humphrey Moseley's prefatory Note to the edition of 1645, Ed. 1, was naturally not reprinted in 1673 by Thomas Dring, the publisher of the revised edition, Ed. 2.

6 the flourish of any prefixed *encomions*] There are none prefixed to the English Poems as a whole, but in Ed. 1 there are two letters introductory to *Comus* (*v.* pp. 173-5 *supra*), and in Edd. 1, 2 four *testimonia* to the Latin Poems from Italian admirers, viz. three Epigrams in Latin, and an Ode in Italian (*v.* pp. 232-4 *supra*).

9 attestation of that renowned Provost of *Eaton*] *v.* p. 173 *supra*.

14 Mr. *Wallers* late choice Peeces] Humphrey Moseley was a publisher who reckoned himself a judge of good literature, and prided himself on his enterprise in publishing it. For his hand in the publication of Edmund Waller's poems in 1645, and for his Prefaces and Epistles Dedicatory, *v.* the article on Humphrey Moseley in *Proceedings of the Oxford Bibliographical Society*, vol. ii, part ii, 1928.

On the Morning of Christ's Nativity

First printed in 1645, Ed. 1: composed, as the heading suggests, on 25 December 1629.

2 Wherin] Ed. 1: Wherein Ed. 2.

3 Of wedded Maid, and Virgin Mother born,] Edd. 1, 2. Cf. l. 197, 'Peor, and Baalim'. The placing of the comma before *and* and *or* is a convention followed in printed books of the time, and is a convention adopted by Milton in his early period. Cf. note on *On Time*, l. 3 (p. 308) *infra*; and *Com.* 428 'By Grots, and Caverns shag'd with horrid shades'. The comma is found in Milton's holograph in T.MS., and in all three printed editions in his lifetime. Sometimes the comma before *and* or *or* is felt to have metrical function but often not. Cf. note to l. 53 *infra*.

10 Wherwith] Ed. 1: Wherewith Ed. 2.

15 Say Heav'nly Muse,] Edd. 1, 2. The comma left out before vocative, common in contemporary printing, is usual in Milton's text. Cf. l. 125 *infra* and note to *Com.* 265.

17 vers] Ed. 1: verse Ed. 2.] The spelling *vers* is characteristic: Milton tends to eschew idle *e* in this position.

18 welcom] Ed. 1: welcome Ed. 2.

23 sweet:] Ed. 1: sweet, Ed. 2.

36 the Sun her lusty Paramour] The comma left out before phrase in apposition is a feature of Milton's punctuation. Cf. ll. 48–49 *infra*.

37 Onely] Ed. 1: Only Ed. 2. *v.* Word-List, Vol. I.

53 No War, or Battels sound] The comma before *or* perhaps has a metrical function.

 Battels] Ed. 2: Battails Ed. 1. Milton spells the word *Battel* in his MSS. and throughout *P.L.*

60 sovran] Edd. 1, 2. Cf. note to *Com.* 41.

62 Wherin] Ed. 1: Wherein Ed. 2.

64 Windes] Ed. 1: Winds Ed. 2.

86 Or e're] Or ere Edd. 1, 2. The phrase descends from 'Ere ever'. Milton distinguished *ere* (= before) from *e're* (= ever). *v.* note to *P.R.* i. 1.

90 com] Ed. 1: come Ed. 2.

91 els] Ed. 1: else Ed. 2.

96 Divinely-warbl'd] Ed. 2: Divinely-warbled Ed. 1.

98 blisfull] Ed. 1: blissful Ed. 2. The MS. of *P.L.*, Book I, l. 5, reads *blisfull*.

105 don] Ed. 1: done Ed. 2.

116 Heavens] Heav'ns Edd. 1, 2. I have printed *Heavens* since the word is here, as nowhere else in the volume of 1645, a disyllable. For Milton's useful distinction by spelling carried out in *P.L. v.* Vol. I, Introd., p. xii and Word-List.

120 great] Edd. 2, 3: Great Ed. 1.

126 human] Ed. 1: humane Ed. 2. Cf. note to *P.R.* i. 298 *supra*.

143–4 *app. crit.*] I adopt the revised text of 1673, Ed. 2. The alteration of the text in 1673 is one of the few significant revisions that show Milton's hand: 'an emendation of Milton's riper genius.' Warton.

156 deep,] Ed. 1: deep. Ed. 2.

166 perfet] Ed. 2: perfect Ed. 1. *perfet* is Milton's spelling. Ed. 2 again corrects *perfect* to *perfet* in *S.M.* 23. *Lyc.* 82 has *perfet* Edd. 1, 2.

171 wrath] Ed. 1: wroth Ed. 2. In T.MS. *Upon the Circumcision*, l. 23, he first writes *wrauth*, deletes it, and substitutes *wrath*. But in later years he insists on the form *wrauth*. *v.* Vol. I, Word-List, and note to *S.A.* 1683.

180 Inspire's] Ed. 1: Inspires Ed. 2.

185 pale,] Ed. 2: pale. Ed. 1.

207 hue;] Ed. 2: hue, Ed. 1.

210 blue;] Ed. 2: blue, Ed. 1.

221 *Judahs*] *Juda's* Ed. 2: *Juda's* Ed. 1. Milton used no apostrophe for the possessive case, except when the word ended in a vowel. He spells *Judah* thus in *P.L.*, and preponderantly in *P.R.* and *S.A.* taken together. For the spelling of the possessive form cf. *Jehovahs*, Ps. i. 5 and note, p. 362 *infra*.

224 gods] Ed. 1: Gods Ed. 2. It is characteristic of Milton to reserve the spelling *God* with capital letter for the God of the Christian religion. Cf. note to *S.A.* 1176. He has spelt *gods of Nile* thus in l. 211 *supra*.

231 wave,] Ed. 2: wave. Ed. 1. Cf. note to l. 185 above.

239 ending:] Ed. 2: ending, Ed. 1.

240–1 Star, Hath fixt] The comma after *Star* has metrical function and flies in the face of grammar: this again is a feature often to be observed in contemporary punctuation.

241 Car,] Ed. 2: Car. Ed. 1.

242 attending;] attending: Ed. 2: attending. Ed. 1. I attend here, and in l. 239 *supra*, to Milton's distinct use of colon and semicolon. *v.* Vol. I, Introd., p. xxi.

A Paraphrase on Psalm 114

First printed 1645, Ed. 1.

This (the title is significant) and the rendering of Psalm 136 which follows, both done when Milton was a schoolboy, are far from being close translations from the Hebrew: they are free paraphrases influenced by George Buchanan's famous Latin version: *Psalmorum Davidis Paraphrasis Poetica*, first published in 1566, and frequently republished.

1 *Terahs*] *Terah's* Edd. 1, 2. *v.* note to *Psalm* i. 5, p. 362 *infra*.

3 *Pharian*] *Pharus*, the island, is used in Latin as the poetical name for Egypt. Cf. Buchanan's opening lines in his paraphrase of this psalm:

> Quum domus Isacidum patrias remearet ad oras
> Barbarasque invisa linqueret aura Phari . . .

5 *Jehovahs*] *Jehovah's* Edd. 1, 2. *v.* notes to l. 1 *supra* and to *Psalm* i. 5, p. 362, *infra.*
7 troubl'd] Ed. 1: troubled Ed. 2.
14 Crystall] Ed. 1: Chrystal Ed. 2. *v.* Word-List, Vol. I.

Psalm 136

First printed 1645, Ed. 1.
7 For, *&c.*] Ed. 1: For his, *&c.* Ed. 2. Neither Ed. 1 nor Ed. 2 is consistent throughout the poem in the abbreviated version of this line. Since the differences are due to the compositors' carelessness I have ignored them and printed For, *&c.* throughout.
10 That doth the wrathfull tyrants quell] Milton follows Buchanan: *Cui domini rerum submittunt sceptra tyranni.* The Hebrew has simply 'Lord of Lords'.
10, 13, 17, 21, 25 That] Ed. 1: Who Ed. 2.
42 *Pharaoh*] *Pharao*: Edd. 1, 2. *Pharaoh* is the Hebrew form, which Milton uses in *P.L.* i. 342 both in MS. and Ed. 1.
45–50 Milton must have remembered Spenser's lines, quoted by his schoolmaster, Alexander Gill, in his *Logonomia Anglica*, as example of periphrasis:

> That bloud-red billows like a walled front
> On either side disparted with his rod,
> Till that his army dry-foot through them yod. *F.Q.* I. x. 53.

49 floods] Ed. 1: flouds Ed. 2. Milton used both spellings. *v.* Word-List, Vol. I.
58 Wildernes] Ed. 1: Wilderness Ed. 2. Milton's chosen spelling in these word-endings seems to have been *-nes* and *-les*. *v.* Vol. I, Introd., p. xxxiii.
61 battel] Ed. 2: battail Ed. 1. Cf. note *supra*, *Hymn*, 53.
65–66. *Seon* and *Amorrean* correspond to Latin forms used by Buchanan: the Hebrew forms would be *Sihon* and *'Emori*.
73 servant] Ed. 1: Servant Ed. 2.
74 therin] Ed. 1: therein Ed. 2.
82 enemy] Ed. 2: enimy Ed. 1.
89 therfore] Ed. 1: therefore Ed. 2.
94 ey.] Ed. 1: eye. Ed. 2.

On the Death of a fair Infant dying of a Cough

First printed 1673, Ed. 2, composed *Anno aetatis 17*, and placed after the two Psalms 'don at fifteen years old'. Milton keeps the chronological order of composition in this volume, unless he has special reason for another arrangement: for instance he places first *On the morning of Christ's Nativity* since it is the best, though not the earliest, of his Juvenilia, and *A Mask* (*Comus*) last, though earlier in date than *Lycidas*, because, of all the poems written before 1645, it clearly deserves pride of place. (On the same principle Wordsworth placed *Ode. Intimations of Immortality* last in the collective edition of his *Poetical Works*.)

12 infamous] Milton accents the word on the second syllable with the vowel long as in Latin. Cf. *Com.* 424 and Spenser, *F.Q.* III. vi. 13, 'with fowle infamous blot'.

25 *Eurotas'*] Newton, 1753: *Eurota's* Ed. 2.

27 flower:] Newton: flower Ed. 2: flower, Ed. 3.

34 Oh no!] Oh no? Ed. 2. For the erroneous interchange of ! and ? *v.* note to *S.A.* 276 *supra,* and Vol. I, Introd., p. xxii.

49 head?] head. Ed. 2.

53 Or wert thou Mercy that sweet smiling Youth?] Or wert thou that sweet smiling Youth! Ed. 2. Warton notes that in this line 'a disyllable word is wanting, which probably fell out at the press. The late Mr. John Heskin of Christ Church, Oxford . . . proposed in a periodical Miscellany which appeared about the year 1750, and with the utmost probability, to insert *Mercy*. For as he observed, Mercy is not only most aptly represented as a sweet-smiling Youth, that is of the age most susceptible of the tender passions, but Mercy is joined with Justice and Truth in the Ode on the Nativity, St. XV. Doctor Newton has omitted the name of the author of this conjecture, and gives the reasons for it as his own.' Cf. also Psalm lxxxv. 10 and Milton's translation, p. 220, l. 41, *supra,* where Mercy and Truth are again linked.

54 crown'd] Ed. 3: cown'd Ed. 2.

56 good?] good. Ed. 2.

58 human] humane Ed. 2. *v.* note to *Hymn,* l. 126.

69 smart?] Newton: smart Ed. 2: smart; Ed. 3.

At a Vacation Exercise in the Colledge

This poem was part of an academic exercise delivered by Milton after the end of the summer term, 1628 (*v.* the heading: Anno Aetatis 19). It followed the Latin Prolusion of Exercise VI (*v. Prolusiones Oratoriae* 1674). This English portion was first printed in Ed. 2, 1673, placed between *The fifth Ode of Horace. Lib. 1. English'd,* and *On the new forcers of Conscience*; but according to the Errata it 'should have come at the end of the Elegie', and there I have placed it. *v.* note to 'On the Death of a fair Infant'.

10 thee:] Ed. 3, Newton: thee Ed. 2.

14 daintest] Ed. 2: daintiest Ed. 3. *daintest* is Spenser's form.

19 trimming] triming Ed. 2. Milton would have spelt with double *m* to denote short vowel in the first syllable. Cf. *brimming, P.L.* iv. 336, and *brimmed, Com.* 924.

36 thunderous] Ed. 2: Thunderer's Jortin *conj.*

40 Spheres] Ed. 3: Spherse Ed. 2. This must be a printer's error.

57 buisness] business Ed. 2. For Milton's spelling, which I adopt here, *v. Com.* 169 note, and Word-List, Vol. I.

66 invisible;] Ed. 3: invisible, Ed. 2.

71 Times] times Ed. 2.

98 hallowed] 1720: hollowed Ed. 2.

The Passion

First printed 1645, Ed. 1.

2 Wherwith] Ed. 1: Wherewith Ed. 2.

10 ere] e're Edd. 1, 2. Milton distinguish'd *ere* = before, from *e're* contraction of *ever. v.* P.R. i. 1 note, and *Hymn,* l. 86 and note *supra.*

13 perfet] perfect Edd. 1, 2. *v.* Word-List, Vol. I, and note to *Hymn,* 166, *supra.* I adopt Milton's spelling of *perfet,* since it clearly indicates his pronunciation of the word.

15 sovran] sov'ran Edd. 1, 2. Cf. note to *Com.* 41.

22 latter] Ed. 1: latest Ed. 2.

23 bound;] 1720: bound, Edd. 1, 2.

24 acts,] 1752: acts; Edd. 1, 2. In some copies of Ed. 1 the stop looks like a comma.

29 Night] 1720: night Edd. 1, 2.

33 Day] day Edd. 1, 2.

53 thir] Ed. 1: their Ed. 2. Milton had begun to write *thir* (unemphatic) for *their* at the time when he prepared *Poems &c.,* 1645, for the press (*v.* Introd., Vol. I, pp. xvi, xviii), but he has not troubled to insist on his printer's adopting this form in that volume. This is the single instance in Ed. 1: there are none in Ed. 2.

On Time

First printed 1645, Ed. 1. In T.MS. f. 8 in Milton's earlier hand: he first wrote as heading *set on a clock case* but later struck this out and wrote *On Time.* (The handwriting betrays the sequence: in the first heading he is using the Greek ε of his earlier hand, in the second his characteristic English *e,* which he began to use in 1637-8. *v.* note to *Lyc.,* 58-63 *infra.*) A version of the poem, shorter by two lines, which may be copied from an earlier draft, is found in a manuscript collection of the early seventeenth century in the Bodleian: MS. Ashmole 36, 37, f. 22. I quote this as MS. Bodl. The heading in this manuscript is *Upon a Clocke Case or Dyall.*

1 *Time*] Edd. 1, 2: Time T.MS.: time MS. Bodl.

2 stepping] Edd. 1, 2: sleepinge MS. Bodl.

hours] Edd. 1, 2: howres T.MS.: howers MS. Bodl.

3 pace;] Edd. 1, 2: pace, MS. Bodl. T.MS. has no punctuation in the whole poem except in ll. 16 and 22, which are punctuated as printed text, with commas before *and.*

4 devours,] Edd. 1, 2: devours; MS. Bodl.

10 all,] Ed. 1: all Ed. 2.

15 perfetly] perfectly Edd. 1, 2. Milton's spelling is *perfet, perfetly*. *v.* note to *Hymn*, l. 166.

16 Truth] trueth MS. Bodl.

17 supreme throne] Milton distinguished by spelling *súpreme* with accent on first syllable (cf. *Com.* 217, 'That he, the Supreme good . . .') from *supréam* with accent on second syllable (cf. *P.L.* v. 667, 'the Throne supream').

17–22 MS. Bodl. gives a shortened and carelessly copied version of these lines from what is possibly an early draft:

> About your supreame Throwne
> Of him whose happy makeinge sight, alone
> Shall heape our days with everlastinge store
> When death and Chance, and thou O tyme shall be noe more.

In the first of these lines *your* is a slip for *the*.

Upon the Circumcision

First printed 1645, Ed. 1. In T.MS. f. 8 immediately after *On Time*: the handwriting is of the early period.

10 whileare] Ed. 1: whilear Ed. 2, spelt as an eye-rhyme.

13–14 In T.MS. first written as one line, but in Milton's later hand in the margin they are divided as in the printed text.

23 wrath] Edd. 1, 2: wrauth *corr. to* wrath T.MS. Cf. note to *Hymn*, l. 171 *supra*.

27–28 In T.MS. first written as one line, but later divided, as ll. 13–14.

28 Will] shall *alt. to* will *in margin* T.MS.

    neer] near Ed. 2.

At a solemn Musick

First printed 1645, Ed. 1. In T.MS. ff. 4 and 5 there are three drafts of this poem in his earlier hand, the first two much worked over, and finally struck out: the first with title *Song* (MS.¹); the second with no title (MS.²); the third a fair copy, headed in his later hand *At a solemn Music* (MS.³). The page of the first draft is very much torn.

The second draft is as follows (I give variants of the first draft at the foot of the page, and line numbers of the printed text in square brackets):

> Blest paire of Sirens pledges of heavens joy
> Spheare-borne harmonious sisters, Voice & Verse,
> Mixe yoᵣ choise chords, & happiest sounds employ   wed yoʳ
> [4] dead things wᵗʰ inbreath'd sense able to peirce   divine sounds
>   & mixt power employ

    3 [3] [Wed your di]vine power & joint force employ

       as
    and ~~whilst~~ yor equall raptures temper'd sweet
    in high misterious *~~holie~~ spousall meet   * happie
    snatch us from earth a while
    ūs of our selves & *~~home-bred~~ woes beguile   * native
   [5] and to our *high-rays'd Phantasie praesent   ~~up-ray'sd~~
10   that undisturbed song of pure concent   * high-rays'd
    ay sung before the saphire-colour'd throne
    to him that sits thereon
    wth saintly shout, & solemne jubilie
   [10] wh̶e̶re the bright Seraphim in *~~tripled~~ row   * burning
        uplifted
15 thire ~~high-lifted~~ loud ~~arch~~ angell trumpets blow
    and the Cherubick hoast in thousand quires
    touch thire immortall harps of golden wires
    wth those just spirits that weare the *blooming palmes * blooming
                   or victorious
   [15] hymnes devout & *sacred psalmes   * holie
20   singing everlastingly
    ~~while all the starrie rounds & arches blue~~
    ~~resound & eccho Hallelu~~
    on earth
   [17] that wee ʌ wth undiscording ~~hart &~~ voice
   [18] may rightly answere that melodious noise
25   by leaving out those harsh *~~chromatiek~~ jarres * ill sounding
    of clamorous Sin that all our musick marres
    & in our lives & in our song
   [26] may keepe in tune wth heaven, till God ere long
    to his celestiall consort us unite
30   to live & sing wth him in endlesse morne of light.

[The last eight lines are rewritten at the bottom of this draft in a form which
corresponds to the text of MS.[3] and Edd. 1, 2, except for lines 19–20 of the
printed text which here first ran:

    as once wee could, till disproportion'd Sin
    drown'd nature's chime & with tumultuous din]

 9 [5] . . . Fancies then present
 13 [9] [wth uni]versa[ll shout] & solemne crie
 14 [10] [there where] the sera[phim in] princely row
 15 [11] [th]ire loud ~~un[jarring?] trumpets blow~~ loud symphonie of silver trumpets blow
    and the youth[ful cher]ubim sweet winged squires
    Heavns henshmen in ten thous[and qui]res   * blooming
    wth those just [spirits] that weare the *fresh greene palmes victorious
 21 whilst all the frame [*alt. to* the whole frame] of heaven and arches blue [*in the margin* whilst
all the starrie frame]
 23 [17] that wee below may learne wth hart & voice
  [18] rightly to answere that melodious noise
    by leaving out those harsh chromatick jarres
    of sin that all our musick marres
 30 [28] To live & sing wth him in *ever-endlesse life   * ever-glorious
                   * uneclipsed
            where day dwells w^{thout} night
            in { endlesse } morne of light
             { cloudlesse } birth
            in never parting light.

6 concent] Ed. 2, MSS. 1–3: content Ed. 1: consent Ed. 3. In Milton's presenta-
tion copy of Ed. 1 to the Bodleian (Arch. G. f. 17) *content* is corrected in
ink to *concent*. It is certain that *concent*, a singing together, a harmony, is
what Milton meant. Cf. Richard Hughes, *A Special Help to Orthographie*,
1643: 'He gave his *consent* to have a *concent* of musick.'
8 theron] Ed. 1: thereon Ed. 2.
11 In T.MS. the line underwent significant changes. In MS.¹ there is a tear
in the paper. I read '[th]ire loud unj[arring] trumpets blow', which is
replaced quite clearly by 'loud symphonie of trumpets blow', with *silver*, as
an afterthought, inserted before *trumpets*. In MS.² the line originally ran
'high-lifted loud arch-angell trumpets blow', which was altered to 'thire
loud uplifted angell trumpets blow'. The 'uplifted angel-trumpets' suggest
some picture or sculpture (to me the famous bronze gate of the Baptistery
in Florence).
16/17 These lines (21–22 of MS.²), finally rejected, are again interesting to
follow through their evolution in MS.¹ and MS.². Again he is pursuing a
visual image that haunts him from some pictorial representation of heaven
with its 'starrie frame' and 'arches blue'.
18 *et seq*. In MS.¹ and MS.² he writes after l. 18 the following line, afterwards
significantly rejected.

> by leaving out those harsh chromatick jarres
> (chromatick *altered to* ill sounding MS.²)

For Milton's liking for technical musical terms and his rejection of them
in the interest of poetic decorum compare *Com*. 243, where in the song to
Eccho he changes 'hold a counterpoint' to 'give resounding grace'.
23 perfet] Ed. 2: perfect Ed. 1. *v*. note to *Hymn*, l. 166.

An Epitaph on the Marchioness of Winchester

The first known publication was in 1645, Ed. 1, but Todd and subsequent
editors have noticed a manuscript version in a collection in the British
Museum, Sloane MS. 1446 (ff. 37*b*, 38) headed 'On the Marchionesse of
Winchester who died in childbedd Ap. 15. 1631'; with the ascription at the
end 'Jo. Milton of Chr. Coll. Camb.' Warton writes: 'I have been told that
there was a Cambridge collection of verses on her death, among which
Milton's elegiack ode first appeared. But I have never seen it.' *The Topo-
grapher*, 1789, vol. i, first noticed the Sloane MS. version, *v*. W. R. Parker
(*M.L.R*., Oct. 1949), who has found no such collection of elegies as Warton
mentions. The Sloane MS. is written in two hands, probably towards the
middle of the seventeenth century. Milton's poem stands in the first part
among a number of poems by Christ Church (Oxford) men, such as Corbett,
Strode, and Henry King: this is presumably why Milton is designated 'of
Chr. Coll. Cambridge'.

The MS. has one important variant, which may suggest that it follows an early version of the poem, afterwards revised by Milton for publication in Ed. 1. *v.* note to ll. 15–24 *infra.*

15–24   Seaven times had the yeerlie starre
                         in everie signe sett upp his carr
                         Since for her they did request
                         the god that sits at marriage feast
                         when first the earlie Matrons runne
                         to greete her of her lovelie sonne;   MS.

22 Cipress] Ed. 1: Cypress Ed. 2.
40 from] Edd. 1, 2: from a MS.
43 she] Edd. 1, 2: it MS.
47 thy] Edd. 1, 2: the MS.
49 travail] Ed. 1: travel Ed. 2: travell MS.
50 sease] Edd. 1, 2: ceaze MS.
52 lives] possessive case of *life.* Cf. *Wives,* for *wife's,* P.R. ii. 134 and note *supra.*
     lease;] Ed. 2: lease, Ed. 1.
53 Here,] Ed. 2: Here Ed. 1.
57–60 This reference to tributes from Cambridge gives some colour to Warton's remark, quoted above, about Cambridge elegies.
64 barrennes] Ed. 1: barrenness Ed. 2.
67 birth,] birth Edd. 1, 2. MS. brackets (much like thee).
70 Light] might MS., a possible reading, but more probably a copyist's error.

Song. On May morning

First printed 1645, Ed. 1.
6 youth,] Ed. 1: youth Ed. 2.
7 Groves,] Ed. 1: Groves Ed. 2.
8 Dale,] Ed. 1: Dale Ed. 2.
6–8 In these lines the placing of commas before *and* and between nominative and verb is in the manner of Milton's punctuation in *Poems,* &c. Ed. 1; I therefore let them stand. *v.* Introd., *supra,* p. xii.

On Shakespear. 1630

First printed 1632, anonymously, in the Second Folio of Shakespeare under the title 'An Epitaph on the admirable Dramaticke Poet, W. Shakespeare'; again in Shakespeare, *Poems* 1640, with the initials J. M.; and anonymously in the Third Folio Shakespeare, 1663. It first appeared in Milton's own works in *Poems &c.,* 1645, Ed. 1. It will be noted that the text of 1640 agrees rather with Milton's own text than with the Folio versions. For a close analysis and summary of the bibliographical differences between states of the Second Folio printing (there are three states) *v.* W. B. Todd in *Studies in Bibliography,* Univ. of Virginia, vol. v.

1 honour'd] Edd. 1, 2, 1632 (states 1 and 2), 1640, 1663: honor'd 1632 (state 3).

4 Star-ypointing] Edd. 1, 2: starre-ypointing 1632 (states 1 and 3), 1640: Starre-ypointing 1663: starre-ypointed 1632 (state 2). Sir Edwin Durning Lawrence (*Notes and Queries,* 11th Series) found in these variants in copies of F2, 1632, a signal to the uninitiated that Bacon wrote Shakespeare's plays. He argued that a pyramid with a star on its apex, *starre-ypointed,* signified a Beacon (pronounced Bacon, as in 'Bacon, great Beacon of the State') and assumed that 'the leaves so printed . . . were issued only to those to whom Bacon's secrets were entrusted'. This preposterous suggestion is suitably dealt with by R. Metcalf-Smith in *Lehigh University Publications,* vol. ii, no. 3, 1928. Mr. W. B. Todd in the article cited above has established the order of the three states of the page on which Milton's lines were printed in 1632, and has shown that the reading *starre-y-pointing* is found in the first state.

6 need'st] Edd. 1, 2, 1663: needst 1632: needs 1640.

   weak] Edd. 1, 2: weake 1640: dull 1632, 1663.

   witnes] Ed. 1: witness Ed. 2: witnesse 1632, 1640, 1663.

9 endeavouring] Edd. 1, 2, 1632 (state 3), 1663: endevouring 1632 (states 1 and 2), 1640.

12 took,] Edd. 1, 2: tooke: 1632 (state 2): tooke 1632 (states 1, 3): took 1663: tooke. 1640.

13 it] Edd. 1, 2: her 1632, 1663: our 1640.

15 dost] Edd. 1, 2, 1632, 1663: doth 1640.

On the University Carrier

First printed by Milton in 1645, Ed. 1.

Hobson died 1 Jan. 1630. For the proverbial phrase 'Hobson's choice' *v. The Spectator,* No. 509. This and the following poem are the only poems of Milton which won contemporary popularity. Both are found in a Book of Jests, *Wit Restor'd,* 1658, and the second also in *The Banquet of Jests,* 1640 (reprinted 1657), in each case without the author's name. A manuscript version of the present poem has been found in the Folger Shakespeare Library, Washington, D.C., of the approximate date 1640–50, possibly earlier. *v.* G. Blakemore Evans, *M.L.N.,* Mar. 1942. The only important variant is in l. 14. *v. infra.*

2 And] Ed. 2: A Ed. 1. This *A* is corrected in ink to *And* in the copy of Ed. 1 which Milton presented to the Bodleian Library.

7 this] Edd. 1, 2: those MS.

14 In the kind office] Edd. 1, 2: Death in the likenesse 1658: In craftie likenes MS. The MS. variant shows a clever hand, but the reading of Ed. 1 is more in keeping with Milton's whole meaning and tone in the poem.

Another on the same

First printed in *Banquet of Jests*, 1640, and subsequently in *Wit Restor'd*, 1658. *v.* note to preceding poem. Milton's own version was first printed in 1645, Ed. 1. Two MS. versions have been found: one in the Bodleian, MS. Malone 21, a miscellany which Malone dates 1644 *circa* (B.MS.), the other in the Huntington Library, California, MS. H.M. 116 (H.MS.). *v.* G. B. Evans, *M.L.N.*, Mar. 1942. B.MS. has the heading 'On Hobson the Cambridge carrier who died in the vacancy of his carriage by reason of the sicknesse then hott at Cambridge'.

1 Here lieth one] Edd. 1, 2, 1658: Here Hobson lyes MSS., 1640.
2 could move] Edd. 1, 2, B.MS., 1658: did move H.MS., 1640.
5 sphear-metal] spheare-mettall MSS.: spheares mettall 1640.
6 revolution] Edd. 1, 2, B.MS.: resolution H.MS., 1640, 1658.
     was at] made of 1658.
7 without a] Edd. 1, 2, MSS., 1658: without all 1640.
8 'Gainst old truth] Edd. 1, 2, MSS., 1658: Gainst truth, 'twas 1640.
     time;] Ed. 1: time: Ed. 2, 1640.
9 an Engin] some Engine MSS., 1640, 1658.
     wheel] wheels 1640: wheeles 1658.
10 being] once 1658.
     strait.] B.MS.: strait, Edd. 1, 2.
11 all men] Edd. 1, 2, MSS., 1858: all us 1640.
12 breath;] Ed. 2: breath. Ed. 1.
13–26 *om.* 1658.
15–20 *om.* B.MS., 1640.
21 his chief disease . . . right] Edd. 1, 2, 1640: his disease . . . aright MSS.
25–26 *om.* B.MS., 1640.
27 But] Edd. 1, 2: For 1640, 1658.
29–end, *om.* 1658.
30 and had his fate] Edd. 1, 2, 1640: and in his fate B.MS.: and his fate H.MS.
31 Linkt] Linct 1640: Like MSS.
     flowing] flowings B.MS.
32 increase:] disease 1640.
33 deliver'd all and gon] deliver'd, all are gon H.MS.

L'Allegro

First printed 1645, Ed. 1.
3 forlorn] Ed. 1: forlorn. Ed. 2.
6 Wher] Ed. 1: Where Ed. 2. Milton tends to use *Wher* when the word is unstressed, *Where* when stressed.
     darknes] Ed. 1: darkness Ed. 2.
11 Goddes] Ed. 1: Goddess Ed. 2.
17 Sager] Edd. 1, 2: Sages Tickell, 1720.

18 Spring,] Ed. 1: Spring. Ed. 2.

33 ye] Ed. 1: you Ed. 2. Cf. Word-list, Vol. I.

53 horn,] Ed. 1: Horn Ed. 2.

60 Where] Ed. 2: Wher Ed. 1.

61 Rob'd Ed. 1: Roab'd Ed. 2.

62 dight,] Ed. 2: dight. Ed. 1.

75 pide] Edd. 1, 2: pied Newton, 1752. *Pide* is a common spelling in the 17th century: Milton, or his printer, preferred it, to match the rhyme-word *wide*.

79 Where] Wher Edd. 1, 2.

91 Som] Ed. 1: Some Ed. 2: as frequently.

108 Corn] Ed. 1: Corn, Ed. 2.

110 Fend,] Fend. Edd. 1, 2. Milton elsewhere spells *Fiend*. The pronunciation seems to have varied between *Feend* and *Fend*. Spenser rhymes *feend* with *weend* and *end* F.*Q*. III. viii. 41, and with *attend* and *spend* III. vii. 32.

116 Windes] Ed. 1: Winds Ed. 2.

122 prise] Ed. 1: prise, Ed. 2.

124 commend.] Ed. 1: commend, Ed. 2.

134 wilde;] wilde, Edd. 1, 2.

140 sweetnes] Ed. 1: sweetness Ed. 2.

Il Penseroso

First printed 1645, Ed. 1.

5 som] Ed. 1: some Ed. 2.

11 Goddes,] Ed. 1: Goddess, Ed. 2; *so also in* l. 132.

15 therfore] Ed. 1: therefore Ed. 2.

16 hue,] Ed. 3: hue. Edd. 1, 2.

21 offended.] Ed. 1: offended, Ed. 2.

49 Leasure,] leasure, Ed. 1: leasure; Ed. 2.

57 In] Ed. 2: Id Ed. 1. *corr. to* In *with pen in many copies.*

64 Eeven-Song] eeven Song Ed. 1: Even-Song Ed. 2.

75 som] Ed. 1: some Ed. 2; *so also in* l. 139.

81 mirth,] Ed. 1: mirth. Ed. 2. In several places Ed. 2 prints period mistakenly where Ed. 1 has comma. I have not thought it necessary to record them further.

88 unsphear] Ed. 1: unsphear. Ed. 2.

120 ear.] Ed. 1: ear, Ed. 2.

121 Night] night Edd. 1, 2.

125 kerchef't] Cherchef't Edd. 1, 2. No such form as *cherchef't* is traceable: the initial consonant must be hard *c* or *k*.

140 profaner] Ed. 1: prophaner Ed. 2.

156 pale,] Ed. 1: pale. Ed. 2.

170 spell,] Ed. 1: spell Ed. 2.

SONNETS

Milton clearly arranged his Sonnets in chronological order, I to X in Ed. 1 (for the Italian sonnets II to VI, *v.* notes p. 317 *infra*) and also the later sonnets, XI to XXIII, in Ed. 2, though here he omitted for political reasons four sonnets, XV, XVI, XVII, and XXII (*v. infra*), which appear in their right order in T.MS. I have adopted for the whole series his own order in Ed. 2, introducing in their place in the scheme, with the aid of T.MS., the sonnets which he first intended for, and then withheld from, publication. These sonnets, arranged in preparation for Ed. 2, are clearly numbered in T.MS., where, however, a page is missing which must have contained Sonnets XVIII, XIX, XX, and part of XXI: the last page holds the latter part of XXI, together with XXII and XXIII. The numbering in the MS. is as follows:

11. I did but prompt the age . . .
12. A book was writt of late . . .
13. Harry whose tunefull & well measur'd Song
14. When Faith & Love . . .
15. Fairfax whos name in armes . . .
16. Cromwell, our chief of men . . .
17. Vane, young in yeares . . .

The page is missing that contained

18. Avenge O lord . . .
19. When I consider how my light is spent
20. Lawrence of vertuous Father . . .
21. Cyriack whose Grandsire . . . ll. 1–4

The last page contains

21. (from l. 5) Cyriack whose Grandsire . . .
22. Cyriack this three years day . . .
23. Methought I saw my late espoused saint

For the placing of the extended Sonnet 'On the new forcers of Conscience' *vide* note *infra*, p. 327.

I. 'O Nightingale, that on yon bloomy Spray'

First printed 1645, Ed. 1: not in T.MS.
6 bill,] bill Edd. 1, 2.
10 ny] Edd. 1, 2. The spelling is clearly dictated by the liking for eye-rhyme.
11 yeer . . . yeer] Ed. 1: year . . . year Ed. 2.
12 why:] why, Edd. 1, 2.

II–VI

The following notes on the Italian Poems are by Mr. John Purves.

The Italian sonnets printed first in 1645, Ed. 1, are not in T.MS. It is now generally accepted that these poems belong to an early period of Milton's poetical life, and were probably all composed before the Sonnet on his twenty-third year. This is suggested by the position they occupy in the edition of 1645, and supported indirectly, as regards Sonnet III and the so-called *Canzone*, by the words of the poems themselves. It is remarkable that the clear indication there given that the poet was writing not in Italy but in an environment where the language of these poems was *ignota e strana* remained so long ignored. Hence the repeated attempts to associate this group of poems with places and persons Milton had known in Italy, and its tentative ascription to the years 1638–9, a view accepted by Mark Pattison and most of the early editors of the Sonnets. Masson, too, though obviously in two minds over the question, also came down finally on the same side. It was left, however, to an Italian student, Ettore Allodoli, in his *Giovanni Milton e l'Italia* (Prato, 1907), to pronounce definitely for an early date, possibly much before 1638, and to suggest that the poems had been written 'per una signora italiana forse emiliana, da Milton veduta o conosciuta a Londra, se pure non è una persona immaginaria'. Some years later two American scholars, D. H. Stevens and J. H. Hanford, also concluded for an early date,[1] and the same view was reached independently by the late Dr. J. S. Smart in *The Sonnets of Milton* (Glasgow, 1921), and developed in one of the fullest studies we have of the Italian poems. By a more careful scrutiny of Milton's words Smart also recognized that the lady addressed in the first of these poems was not merely *emiliana* but herself *Emilia* by name,[2] and that the *nobil varco* (l. 2) was none other than that of the Rubicon, 'the most famous ford in the world'—two entirely convincing interpretations. By emphasizing the personal element in these poems he was able also to claim, with reason, that they had never received their due place in Milton's biography, and by the fullness of his illustrations was able to show more adequately than previous writers the nature of his debt to Italian poetry. Another scholar, Mr. F. T. Prince, in *The Italian Element in Milton's Verse* has since carried Dr. Smart's researches a stage further, and has shown how Milton's practice in his Italian poems affected his English sonnets.

The few Italian poems composed in England in Elizabethan and Jacobean times were usually either occasional sonnets such as those exchanged between Elizabeth and Mary Queen of Scots, or commendatory sonnets such as those by Matthew Gwinne prefixed to Florio's *Montaigne* and *A Worlde*

---

[1] In *Modern Philology*, xvii (1919), pp. 25 ff., and xviii, pp. 475 ff. Hanford's suggestion that the Italian poems belong to the same period as the Seventh Elegy, written 'at the age of 19', has much to be said for it. Cf. Son. IV, ll. 1–4 and *Elegia Septima*, ll. 1–4.

[2] Keightley (*Poems of J.M.*, vol. i, p. 149 n. 1) seems to have had an inkling of this. 'He [Milton]', he writes, 'may only mean her own Christian name.

of Wordes under the designation of 'Il Candido'. Other examples are the sonnets contributed by Walter Quin to *Coryat's Crudities* and Joshua Sylvester's *Lachrymae Lachrymarum*, and the same author's tributes to James I and to Charles I on the occasion of his marriage. But such compositions are mere *tours de force*, and have little that is personal or distinctive about them. Milton's Italian poems, on the other hand, despite the metrical and stylistic defects to which Italian critics have drawn attention, had clearly a more serious purpose. The fact that they were incorporated among his sonnets in English suggests that he wished them to be judged on their literary merits, as forming an integral part of his work.

Sonnet II

1 *leggiadra,*] *leggiadra* Edd. 1, 2.   3 *Ben*] *Bene* Ed. 2.   5 *mostrasi*] *mostra si* Edd. 1, 2.   *fuora,*] *fuora* Edd.   6 *De'*] *De* Edd. 1, 2.   *suoi*] *sui* Ed. 2. 7 *E i don,*] *E i don'*, Edd. 1, 2. *i don(i)* are the gifts and graces which accompany the lady's gentle looks (*atti soavi*). These lines, as Smart noted (*op. cit.*, p. 145), 'are no more than a texture of Petrarchian fancies, closely woven together'—too closely, in fact, to submit to a regular syntax.   *Amor*] *amor* Edd. 1, 2. *arco,*] *arco.* Ed. 2.   8 *Là onde*] *La onde* Edd. 1, 2.   *virtù*] *virtu* Ed. 2. 12 *chi*, in place of the simple relative *che*, reinforces the *ciascun* of l. 11.   13 *sù*] *su* Ed. 2.

Sonnet III

1 *a l'imbrunir*] *al imbrunir* Edd. 1, 2.   *sera,*] *sera* Edd. 1, 2.   2 *avezza*, more correctly *avvezza*, has given rise to some conjecture. The adj., or syncopated p.p., derives from *avvezzare*, to accustom; to bring up (Prov. *avesar*, Spanish and Portuguese *avezar*), and seems here to mean 'at home, brought up there' (Smart). Keightley quoted similar instances from Tasso and Ariosto, but the usage is not common.   3 *bella,*] *bella* Edd. 1, 2.   4 *spera,*] *spera* Edd. 1, 2.   5 *natìa*] *natia* Ed. 2.   6 *Amor*] *amor* Ed. 2.   *insù*] *insu* Ed. 2.   9 *inteso,*] *inteso* Edd. 1, 2.   10 Here the hendecasyllable, like others in these poems, has an English rather than an Italian cadence.   12 *Amor*] *amor* Ed. 2.   14 *sì*] *si* Edd. 1, 2. This sonnet, like Sonnets IV and V, ends with a rhyming couplet, *rima baciata*. That such sonnets, though uncommon in Italy, were not unorthodox, was shown by the late Professor W. Ll. Bullock in his article on 'The First French Sonnets' (*Modern Language Notes*, xxxix, 1924).

Canzone

Technically, this is not a *canzone*, but merely a *canzone*-stanza, with a *commiato* or *congedo* of three lines. Carducci (*Primi Saggi*, p. 457), quoting the whole poem, assented to the judgement of Eugenio Camerini that it was 'vaghissima, se non tutto irreprensibile', adding on his own account 'l'ultimo verso potrebbe sonare non indegnamente tra alcuni della Vita Nuova'.

1 *amorosi,*] *amorosi* Edd. 1, 2.   2 *e: Perche*] *e perche* Edd. 1, 2. In contemporary
texts reported speech is generally introduced merely by a colon.   4 *amor* is
here given a lower-case letter, as in Edd. 1, 2, since it does not seem to be
personified. But there is much doubt as to the practice in this respect of con-
temporary Italian texts. The key, however, seems to be given by the line in
the Prologue to Tasso's *Aminta* (ed. Aldo, 1583, p. 19): 'Se io, che son l'Amor,
d'amor m'intendo.'   6 *de'*] *de* Edd. 1, 2.   *t'arrivi.*] *t'arrivi,* Edd. 1, 2.   7
Così] *Cosi* Edd. *burlando.*] *burlando,* Edd. 1, 2. This seems to refer particularly
to the preceding lines; a fuller stop than a comma is therefore called for.
The jest is at the poet's writing in Italian, while his true gifts are for English
poetry (ll. 7–11). *Altri rivi,*] *altri rivi* Edd. 1, 2.   8 *onde,*] *onde* Edd. 1, 2.
10 *Spùntati* would indicate the correct accentuation, but no change has been
here made in the text.   *ad hor ad hor*] *ad hor, ad hor* Edd. 1, 2.   11 *frondi:*]
frondi Edd. 1, 2.   13 *Canzon,*] *Canzon* Edd. 1, 2.   *rispondi:*] *rispondi*
Edd. 1, 2.   14 *dir*] *dir,* Edd. 1, 2.   *è*] *e* Edd. 2.   *cuore,*] *cuore* Edd. 1, 2.
15 *è*] *e* Edd. 2.

Sonnet IV

1 *dirò*] *diro* Ed. 2.   2 *io,*] *io* Edd. 1, 2.   Preceded by elision or syn-
aloepha.   *soléa*] *solea* Ed. 2.   3 *de'*] *de* Edd. 1, 2.   *ridéa,*] *ridéa* Ed. 1; *ridea*
Ed. 2.   4 *Già*] *Gia* Edd. 1, 2.   5 *Nè . . . nè*] *Ne . . . ne* Edd. 1, 2.   *vermiglia,*]
vermiglia Edd. 1, 2.   6 *sì*] *si* Ed. 2.   10 *più*] *piu* Edd. 1, 2.   11 *hemispero*
more correctly *hemisphero,* as in Florio (mod. *emisfero*).   12 *può*] *puo* Ed. 2.
Luna;] *Luna,* Edd. 1, 2.   13 *sì*] *si* Edd. 1, 2.

Sonnet V

1 *occhi,*] *occhi* Ed. 1.   *mia,*] *mia* Edd. 1, 2.   2 *può*] *puo* Edd. 1, 2.   *sian*]
fian Ed. 2.   *sole,*] *sole* Edd. 1, 2.   3 *Sì*] *Si* Edd. 1, 2.   4 *s'invia;*] *s'invia*
Edd. 1, 2.   5 *nè*] *ne* Edd. 1, 2.   *senti'*] *sentì* Ed. 1; *senti* Ed. 2.   10 *Scossomi*]
Scosso mi Edd. 1, 2.   *poco,*] *poco* Edd. 1, 2.   12 *a trovar*] *e trovar* Ed. 2.
13 *piovose,*] *piovose* Edd. 1, 2.

Sonnet VI

This is the most original and personal of the Italian sonnets, and there
is good recent Italian opinion that it is also the most successful both for its
literary and linguistic qualities. The young scholar Guido di Pino writes
'Questo è certo il migliore dei sonetti: quello in cui l'ispirazione riesce a
superare il gioco letterario che c'è sempre in queste poesie in lingua stra-
niera. Linguisticamente questo sonetto mi pare il più sicuro e sciolto di
tutti. Ci sento un piglio cavalcantiano.' Wordsworth, too, seems to have
recognized its individual character when he chose it for translation in his
recently recovered version. See *The Poetical Works of W. W.*, ed. E. de Selin-
court and Helen Darbishire, vol. iii, p. 577.

1 *amante,*] *amante* Edd. 1, 2.   2 *in dubbio*] *indubbio* Ed. 2.   3 *Madonna,*]

Madonna Edd. 1, 2.   4 *Farò*] *Faro* Ed. 2.   6 *Di*] *De* Edd. 1, 2.   8 *e d'intero*] *e* omitted Ed. 2.   *diamante*] Cf. *Elegia septima*, 89–90:

> Forsitan et duro non est adamante creata,
> Forte nec ad nostras surdeat illa preces!

10 *use,*] *use* Edd. 1, 2.   12 *Muse;*] *muse:* Edd. 1, 2.   14 *Amor*] *amor* Ed. 2. Keightley pointed out ·that Milton 'seems to have had here before him Tasso's sonnet *Rose, che l'arte invidiosa ammira*', in which that poet speaks of Love as *Ape novella . . . con troppo acut'ago* (*Rime*, 1583, Parte seconda, p. 11).

VII. 'How soon hath Time the suttle theef of youth'

First printed 1645, Ed. 1. In T.MS. it appears on f. 6 in Milton's hand at the end of the first draft of a letter in prose to a friend who had rebuked him for his secluded scholar's life. Milton was born on 9 Dec. 1608, so the sonnet was probably written after 9 Dec. 1632.[1] Between Sonnet I and Sonnet VII Milton places the Italian poems, evidently because this is where they stand chronologically. *v.* Notes *supra*, p. 317.

1 suttle] This characteristic spelling is in T.MS. as well as Edd. 1, 2.
2 Stoln] Ed. 1: Soln Ed. 2: Stolne T.MS.
   twentith] Ed. 1, T.MS.: twentieth Ed. 2.
11 mean,] Ed. 1: mean Ed. 2.
14 task-Masters] task Masters Edd. 1, 2: task-Maisters T.MS.

VIII. 'Captain or Colonel, or Knight in Arms'

First printed 1645, Ed. 1. In T.MS. f. 9 there is a copy of this sonnet not numbered, and not in Milton's hand. It is headed 'On his dore when yᵉ Citty expected an assault'. Milton has struck this out and has substituted in his own hand 'When the assault was intended to yᵉ Citty'. The date of the intended assault was November, 1642.
3 *app. crit.*] If deed of honour did thee ever please, Ed. 2: If ever deed of honour did thee please, Ed. 1, T.MS. I take this to be a considered change made by Milton.

IX. 'Lady that in the prime of earliest youth'

First printed 1645, Ed. 1. This sonnet written in Milton's hand, not numbered, follows the preceding sonnet VIII in T.MS. f. 9, and is followed by X also in his own hand. Its date must be intermediate between the two.
5 with *Ruth,*] Ed. 2, T.MS.: the *Ruth*, Ed. 1.

[1] *v.* 'Some Problems in the Chronology of Milton's Early Poems', by W. R. Parker, *R.E.S.*, July 1935.

7 growing vertues] Edd. 1, 2. In T.MS. f. 9 Milton first wrote *blooming vertues*, corrected *blooming* to *prospering*, striking out *s* of *vertues*, and finally wrote *growing vertues*.

 their] Edd. 1, 2: thir T.MS. Milton was beginning in the early forties to use the spelling *thir* for unemphatic *their*. *v.* Vol. I, p. xvi, and note to *The Passion*, p. 308, *supra*.

8 ruth] the rhyme with *Ruth*, the same word in sound, but with different sense, is in accordance with contemporary practice. Newton gives parallel instances in Spenser's *F.Q.* I. vi. 39, VI. vi. 38. Milton had found the same usage in Italian poetry.

13 In T.MS. Milton first wrote

opens the dore of Bliss, that howre of night,

deleted it, and wrote

passes to bliss at yᵉ midd watch of night,

and finally altered *watch* to *howr*.

X. 'Daughter to that good Earl, once President'

First printed 1645, Ed. 1. In T.MS. f. 9 this sonnet, not numbered, is written in Milton's hand, and headed 'To yᵉ Lady Margaret Ley'.

3 liv'd in] Edd. 1, 2: left them, *altered to text* T.MS.

 fee,] Ed. 1: fee. Ed. 2.

5 Parlament] Edd. 1, 2, T.MS. This is Milton's spelling of the word in his prose works *passim*.

8 Kill'd] Ed. 2: Kil'd Ed. 1.

10 you] Ed. 1: you, Ed. 2.

XI. 'A Book was writ of late call'd *Tetrachordon*'

First printed 1673, Ed. 2. A first draft of this sonnet (MS.[1]) appears in Milton's hand, numbered 12, in T.MS. f. 47. On f. 46 there is a fair copy (MS.[2]) again numbered 12, preceded by a copy of Sonnet XII, here numbered 11, 'I did but prompt . . . .' These two sonnets, which he finally printed in reverse order, are headed as follows: '*On the detraccon which followed upon my writing certaine treatises*', with the note: *these sonnets follow yᵉ 10 in yᵉ printed booke*. The 'certaine treatises' would be 'The Doctrine and Discipline of Divorce', 1643, 'Tetrachordon' and 'Colasterion', 1645. From this point the transcription of Sonnets in T.MS. has the additional interest that, whilst some of them are in Milton's hand with his corrections, all have been arranged and numbered, some copied, by his different amanuenses, for the edition of 1673, Ed. 2, where they follow immediately Sonnets I to X of *Poems, &c.*, 1645, Ed. 1.

1 A Book was writ] A Book was was writ Ed. 2: I writt a book MS.[1] *orig.*, *altered to* A booke was writt

2 wov'n close] Ed. 2, MSS.[1, 2]: weav'd it *deleted* MS.[1]

3 The Subject new: it walk'd] Ed. 2, MS.²: It went off well about MS.¹ *orig.*
4 good intellects; now] Ed. 2: good witts; but now is MS.¹ *orig.*
8 is it] T.MS., errata Ed. 2, Newton: is Ed. 2.
9 Colkitto] T.MS., errata Ed. 2: Coliktto Ed. 2.
10 rugged] Ed. 2, MS.²: barbarous MS.¹ *orig.*, *altered to* rough-hewn, *then to* rugged.

    our like mouths] cf. Spenser, *Hymne of Heavenly Love*, 116, 'He made by love out of his owne like mould.'

XII. On the same. 'I did but prompt the age to quit their cloggs'

First printed 1673, Ed. 2. *Vide* note on preceding sonnet. Of this also there is a first draft in Milton's hand in T.MS. f. 43 (MS.¹) numbered 11.

1 their] Ed. 2: thir MS.¹: *v.* note on Sonnet IX, l. 7 *supra.*
4 Cuckoes] Ed. 2: buzzards MS.¹
9 their] Ed. 2: thir MS.¹
    senseless] senseles, T.MS.: senceless Ed. 2.
10 And still revolt when truth would set them free] Ed. 2: And hate the truth wherby they should be free MS.¹ *orig.*

XIII. '*Harry* whose tuneful and well measur'd Song'

First printed in 1648 in *Choice Psalms put into Musick for three voices*, *v. infra*: next in 1673, Milton's *Poems, &c.*, Ed. 2. There are three copies in T.MS.: a rough draft in Milton's hand (MS.¹), a fair copy in his hand (MS.²), both on f. 43; finally a fair copy by an amanuensis (MS.³) on f. 45.

To MS.¹ Milton has written the heading *To my freind Mr. Hen. Laws Feb. 9. 1645.* The amanuensis has headed MS.² and also MS.³ *To Mr Hen. Laws on the publishing of his Aires*, and has afterwards in his fair copy (MS.³) deleted the words *the publishing of*. The sonnet was first published in 1648 in *Choice Psalms put into Musick for three voices* under the heading *To my friend Mr. Henry Lawes.* The *Ayres* were not published till 1653. The first draft (MS.¹) is as follows (I omit the revisions):

    Harry whose tunefull & well-measur'd song
      first taught our English Music how to span
      words with just notes wᶜʰ till then us'd to scan
      with Midas eares, committing short & long
    Thy worth & skill exempts thee from the throng   5
      and gives thee praise above the pipe of Pan;
      to after age thou shalt be writt a man
      that didst reform thy art, the cheif among
    Thou honourst vers, & vers must lend her wing
      to honour thee, the Preist of Phoebus quire   10
      that tun'st thir happiest lines in hymn or story
    Fame by the Tuscan's leav, shall set thee higher
      then old Casella whom Dante woo'd to sing
      met in the milder shades of Purgatory.

3 Words . . . scan] words with just notes wch till then us'd to scan MS.¹ *altered to* when most were wont to scan: finally in the margin the version of the printed text is written.

4 committing] Ed. 1, T.MS. first draft: *misjoyning* is written in the margin. Dr. Johnson defines one sense of *commit*, 'to place in a state of hostility or incongruity: a latinism', and gives as illustration this passage from Milton's sonnet.

5 worth] first written in MS.¹, then deleted and *wit* substituted, and rejected.

6 *v.* first draft *supra.*
    anough] MSS.¹⁻³: enough Ed. 2. *anough* is Milton's characteristic spelling.

7 after-age] MS.² and MS.³: after age Ed. 2, MS.¹
    the man] Ed. 2, 1648, MS.²֝,³: a man MS.¹

8 *v.* first draft *supra.*
    aire] aires MS.² *orig.*
    tongue] tongu Ed. 2.

9 lend] 1648, MSS.¹⁻³: send Ed. 2. I adopt the reading of the three manuscript versions.

11 their] Ed. 2: thir MS.¹ and MS.²: theire MS.³
    Story] 1648 has a marginal note to this word: 'The story of Ariadne set by him in Music.'

12–13 *v.* first draft *supra.*

13 sing,] 1648: sing Ed. 2.

XIV. 'When Faith and Love which parted from thee never'

First printed 1673, Ed. 2. There are three drafts in T.MS., first a rough draft (MS.¹) in Milton's hand, secondly a fair copy (MS.²) on the same page (f. 44) in his hand, numbered 14, and finally a copy (MS.³) on the next page by an amanuensis, also numbered 14. The first draft is as follows (I omit the revisions):

> On ye religious memorie of Mrs Catharine Thomason
> my Christian freind deceas'd [16 *del.*] Decem. 1646.

[This should probably read 'Decem. 1646.' The '16' written before 'Decem.' was probably the beginning of 1646: he changed his mind and put in the month, Decem., before 1646. *v.* Smart, p. 81.]

> When Faith & Love, that parted from thee never,
> Had rip'n'd thy just soul to dwell with God,
> Meekly thou didst resigne this earthy clod
> Of flesh & sin, wch man from heav'n doth sever.
> Thy Works, & Almes, and all thy good Endeavor   5
> Strait follow'd thee the path that Saints have trod
> Still as they journey'd from this dark abode
> Up to ye Realm of peace & Joy for ever,

Faith who led on ye way, & knew them best
thy handmaids, clad them o're with purple beames   10
and azure wings, thence up they flew so drest
And spake the truth of thee in glorious theames
before the Judge, who thenceforth bidd thee rest,
and drink thy fill of pure immortal streames.

For the identity of Mrs. Thomason *v.* Smart, pp. 78–82.

4 from Life] from blis MS.³ *orig.*

6–8 *v.* first draft *supra.*

9 In MS.¹ (*v. supra*) Milton altered this line to

Faith shew'd the way and shee who saw them best

which is the first reading of MS.² (altered to text).

12 spake] MSS.¹⁻³: speak Ed. 2.

in] MS.¹,², Milton's holograph: on Ed. 2 and MS.³, amanuensis's fair
copy. In adopting this reading I accept Grierson's suggestion (*T.L.S.*,
25 June 1923) that *Theams* is here a musical term. *v. O.E.D.*: 'Theme *Mus.*
The principal melody. . . .' It would be unlike Milton to let this admired
Christian soul enter Heaven without the accompaniment of glorious music.

XV. *On the Lord. Gen.* Fairfax *at the seige of Colchester*

Not in Edd. 1, 2, first printed 1694, first included in Milton's Poetical Works
by Tonson, 1713.

This and the two following sonnets with Sonnet XXII were not published
in Ed. 2, although they appear numbered 15, 16, 17, and 22 in T.MS., clearly
in the order in which Milton first intended them to stand. But he changed his
mind; they are omitted in 1673. Edward Phillips printed them in corrupt
text in 1694 at the end of his Life of Milton prefixed to the *Letters of State*;
XVII had appeared in *The Life and Death of Sir H. Vane* by G. Sikes in 1662.
John Aubrey noted: 'Mr. John Milton made two admirable panegyricks as
to sublimitie of witt, one on Oliver Cromwel, and the other on Thomas,
Lord Fairfax, both which his nephew Mr. Philip hath. But he hath hung back
these two years as to imparting copies to me for the collection of mine with
you. . . . Were they made in commendation of the devill, 'twere all one to me:
'tis the ὕψος that I looke after' (*Brief Lives*, ed. A. Clark, p. 70). Warton, who
bases his text on T.MS., notes: 'They are quoted by Toland in his Life of
Milton, 1698. Tonson omitted them in his editions of 1695, 1705. But,
growing less offensive by time, they appear in his edition of 1713. The Cam-
bridge manuscript happily corrects many of their vitiated readings. They
were the favourites of the republicans long after the restoration: it was some
consolation to an exterminated party, to have such good poetry remaining
on their side of the question. These four Sonnets, being frequently tran-
scribed, or repeated from memory, became extremely incorrect: their faults
were implicitly preserved by Tonson, and afterwards continued without
examination by Tickell and Fenton.'

For these sonnets I take T.MS. as the basis of my text: this sonnet on f. 47 is in Milton's own hand.

The siege of Colchester lasted from 15 June to 28 August 1648.

2 Filling each mouth] T.MS.: And fills all Mouths 1694.

4 that] T.MS.: which 1694.

5 unshak'n vertue] T.MS.: unshaken Valour 1694. The spelling of T.MS. with '*n* for sonant *n* is Milton's spelling, cf. *brok'n*, l. 8 *infra*.

6 though] T.MS.: while 1694.

7 Thir Hydra heads] T.MS.: Their Hydra-heads 1694.

8 brok'n league] T.MS.: broken League 1694.

    their] T.MS.: her 1694. Cf. l. 7 above, where *thir* is unemphatic; it is possible that *their* here indicates emphasis.

10 Warr, but endless warr] T.MS.: War, but Acts of War 1694.

11 Truth, and Right] T.MS.: injur'd Truth 1694.

12 Public Faith cleard from the shamefull brand] T.MS.: publick Faith be rescu'd from the Brand 1694.

14 share] T.MS.: shares 1694.

XVI. *To the Lord Generall* Cromwell *May* 1652

First printed 1694 (*v.* note to preceding Sonnet XV). The copy in T.MS. f. 47, numbered 16, is in the hand of an amanuensis.

1 who] T.MS.: that 1694.

    cloud] T.MS.: Croud 1694.

2 warr onely] T.MS.: War only 1694.

    detractions] T.MS.: distractions 1694.

5–6 And Fought God's Battels, and his Work pursu'd,] 1694. l. 5 of the text is omitted.

7 *Darwen* stream] T.MS.: *Darwent* Streams 1694. The *Darwen* or *Derwen* is a small river near Preston in Lancashire, mentioned by Camden; and there Cromwell routed the Scotch army under Duke Hamilton in August 1648.

    imbru'd,] T.MS.: imbru'd; 1694.

8 resounds] T.MS.: resound 1694.

9 And *Worsters* laureat wreath] And twentie battels more T.MS. *orig. corrected to* text. The scribe, evidently by mistake, first struck out *Dunbarr feild*, l. 8, and wrote above it *Worsters laureat wreath*.

11 No less renownd then] T.MS.: No less than those of 1694.

    arise] aries T.MS. The amanuensis offers an eye-rhyme.

12 soules with] T.MS.: Souls in 1694.

XVII. *To S^r* Henry Vane *the younger*

First published in *The Life and Death of Sir Henry Vane* by G. Sikes, 1662, where we are told that 'a learned Gentleman' who composed the sonnet sent a copy to Sir Henry Vane on 3 July 1652. Printed again in 1694. In T.MS. f. 48 it is numbered 17, is in the hand of an amanuensis, and follows the Sonnet to Cromwell, numbered 16.

1 counsell] T.MS.: counsells T.MS. *orig.*: counsel 1662: Councels 1694.

4 Epeirot] 1662: Epeirote T.MS. *orig. corr. to* text: Epirote 1694.

6 drift] 1662: drifts T.MS. *orig. corr. to* text.

7 Then] And T.MS. *orig.*

    best, upheld] T.MS., 1662: best be upheld 1694.

8 Move by] T.MS. 1662: Move on T.MS. *orig.*: Mann'd by 1694.

9–11 The first draft in T.MS. reads

besides to know

What powre the Church & what the civill meanes

Thou teachest best, which few have ever don

Milton must then have dictated to his amanuensis his second thoughts:

besides to know

Both spirituall power and civill what [it *del.*] each meanes

Thou hast learnt well, a praise which few have won.

Lastly he dictated the final form of the last line as it stands in the text.

11 severs] T.MS. 1662: serves 1694.

13 firme] 1662, 1694: right *corr. to* firme T.MS.

14 In peace, and reck'ns thee] T.MS., 1662: And reckons thee in chief 1694.

XVIII. *On the late Massacher in* Piemont

First printed 1673, Ed. 2. Not in T.MS. *v.* p. 316 *supra*. The date of the massacre was 24 April 1655.

10 sow] Errata Ed. 2, Ed. 3: so Ed. 2.

13 hundred-fold] hunder'd-fold Ed. 2. *hunderd* is Milton's spelling. *v. Arcades*, 21, and Word-List, Vol. I.

XIX. 'When I consider how my light is spent'

First printed 1673, Ed. 2. Not in T.MS. *v.* p. 316 *supra*.

2 Ere] E're Ed. 2. Milton distinguished *ere = before* from *e're* contraction of *ever*: *v.* note to *P.R.* i. 1.

XX. '*Lawrence* of vertuous Father vertuous Son'

First printed 1673, Ed. 2. Not in T.MS. *v.* p. 316 *supra*.

Heading in 1713, Ed. 5: 'To Mr Lawrence, Son of the President of Cromwell's Council.' Smart shows that the son addressed is Edward Lawrence.

7 cloath] Ed. 3: cloth Ed. 2. The vowel sound is long, and Milton spells the word *cloath* in *Vacation Exercise*, 32, and in *P.L.* x. 219.

13 and] And Ed. 2.

XXI. 'Cyriack, whose Grandsire on the Royal Bench'

First printed 1673, Ed. 2. The transcript in T.MS. f. 49 is in the hand of John Phillips and begins at l. 5. The first four lines must have been on the missing page, *v*. p. 316 *supra*. Immediately following this sonnet is the second sonnet addressed to Cyriack Skinner, and it is numbered 22.

XXII. *To Mr* Cyriack Skinner *upon his Blindness*

First printed 1694. T.MS. f. 49 in John Phillips's hand. The date of composition would be 1655: Milton was totally blind in 1652.

3 light] T.MS.: Sight 1694.
    thir] their T.MS., the *e* struck out. J. Phillips was the amanuensis who consistently adopted Milton's spelling *thir* for *their* unstressed. *v*. my *Early Lives of Milton*, Introd.
4 sight] T.MS.: day 1694.
5 Of] T.MS.: Or 1694.
7 heavns] T.MS.: Gods T.MS. *orig*.: Heaven's 1694.
8 bear up and] T.MS., 1694: attend to T.MS. *orig*.
9 Right onward] T.MS., 1694: Uphillward T.MS. *orig*.
11 Liberties] 1694: libertyes T.MS.
12 talks] T.MS.: rings 1694.
13 the worlds] T.MS.: this World's 1694.

XXIII. 'Methought I saw my late espoused Saint'

First printed 1673, Ed. 2. In T.MS. f. 50, where it is placed last of the sonnets and numbered 23. It is in a very neat formal hand which I do not find elsewhere in the MS. It has been assumed that the sonnet refers to Milton's second wife, Katharine Woodcock, who died in February 1658. Elijah Fenton in his 'life' of Milton 1725 is the first biographer to say that this sonnet 'does honour to her memory'. Thereafter his statement was accepted by Thomas Birch, Francis Peck, and Bishop Newton, and has remained unchallenged till Mr. W. R. Parker in *R.E.S.*, vol. xxi, July 1945, put forward the contention that the sonnet commemorates Milton's first wife, Mary Powell, who died in 1652. His arguments have some cogency, but in default of specific evidence I incline to hold to the traditional ascription, particularly since the dates support it. Milton places it last in the order of the Sonnets, after the Sonnet to Cyriack Skinner, written in 1655 three years after the total failure of his sight.
13 enclin'd,] T.MS.: enclin'd Ed. 2.

On the new forcers of Conscience under the Long Parlament

First printed in 1673, Ed. 2, where it appears, perhaps by a mistake of the printer, between *At a Vacation Exercise in the Colledge* (*v*. note to this poem,

p. 307) and *Arcades*. In T.MS. it appears, with the heading *On the forcers of Conscience* (in the hand of the amanuensis who wrote copies of the Sonnets to Vane and Cromwell), on f. 48 immediately after Sonnet XXII, to Vane, but its place in the order first planned by Milton for Ed. 2 is clearly indicated both here, where the amanuensis has written beside the heading *to come in as is directed in the leafe before*, and on f. 47, where Milton has written in the margin immediately before Sonnet XV on Fairfax, *on ye forcers of Conscience to come in heer*. Milton's first idea was plainly a chronological order. Later he decided not to place the poem among the Sonnets. In form it corresponds with the Italian *sonetto caudato*, a form to which the satiric purpose was appropriate. I have placed it after the Sonnets, but without a number. (It has no number in T.MS.)

Long Parlament] T.MS.: *Long Parliament* Ed. 2. *v.* note to l. 15 *infra*.

1 of] Ed. 2: off T.MS. The two forms were used as alternatives as late as the 17th century.

3 widdow'd] Ed. 2: vacant T.MS. *corr. to* text.

6 our] Ed. 2: the T.MS. *corr. to* text.

7 classic] *v.* Dr. Johnson's *Dictionary* under *classick, classical*. 3. Relating to the order and rules of Presbyterian assemblies: 'We perceive it [presbyterian government] aspiring to be a compulsive power upon all without exception in parochial, *classical*, and provincial hierarchies.' Milton, *Observ. Art. of Peace betw. E. of Orm. and Irish*.

12 shallow] Ed. 2: hare-braind T.MS. *corr. to* text.

14 packings] T.MS.: packing Ed. 2.

15 Parlament] T.MS.: Parliament Ed. 2. *Parlament* is Milton's chosen spelling. *v.* note to Sonnet X. 5.

17 Clip your Phylacteries, though bauk your Ears] Cropp yee as close as marginall P——s ears T.MS. *orig.*: the reference is to William Prynne, 'whose ears were cropped close in the pillory, and who was fond of ostentatiously loading the margins of his voluminous books with a parade of authorities'. T. Warton.

bauk] Errata *to* Ed. 2: bauke T.MS.: bank Ed. 2.

19 they] Ed. 2: you *corr. to* they T.MS.

20 Large] Ed. 2: at large *corr. to* text T.MS.

THE FIFTH ODE OF HORACE. Lib. I

First printed in 1673, Ed. 2, and placed immediately after the Sonnets. This gives no positive indication of its date, though negatively it would suggest that, since he did not include it among his Juvenilia in the first group, he wished it to be considered as one of his mature poems, near in date perhaps to *Arcades*, which follows. (For the placing of *At a Vacation Exercise* among the Juvenilia *v.* note *supra*, p. 307.)

Ad Pyrrham

5 *munditie*] The accepted text of Horace here reads *mundities*, but the reading *munditie* is given by John Bond in his edition of Horace, first published in 1606, and many times reprinted.

ARCADES

First printed 1645, Ed. 1.

This portion of a Mask is the first entry in T.MS., occupying ff. 1–3, the first two pages a good deal mutilated. It is altogether in Milton's early hand. *Arcades.* Part of an entertainment . . . with this Song] Part of a Maske. T.MS. *orig.* In his later hand Milton has written in the title: '*Arcades.* Part of an Entertainment at . . .'. The paper is here cut away. The date of the performance at Harefield is not known: 1632 or 1633 would be likely dates.

1 Looke nymphs & shepherds looke heere ends our quest since at last o^r eyes are blest T.MS. *orig. deleted.*

2 Majesty] Ed. 2: majesty Ed. 1.

10–11   now seemes guiltie of abuse
               and detraction from her praise T.MS. *orig. alt. to* text.

12 we find] she hath T.MS. *orig. alt. to* we find.

13 conceal] her hide T.MS. *orig. alt. to* conceale.

18 Sitting] seated T.MS. *orig. alt. to* sitting.

22 hunderd] Ed. 1: hundred Ed. 2, T.MS. For Milton's spelling of this word *v.* Word-List, Vol. I.

23 *Juno*] Juno T.MS. *orig.* altered to Ceres, which is struck out and *Juno* restored by underlining.

24 had] would have T.MS. *orig. alt. to* text.

25/26 stage direction.] As they offer to come forward the Genius of the wood rises and turning towards them speakes. T.MS. *orig.*

28 ye] Edd. 1, 2: you T.MS.

39 furder] T.MS.: further Edd. 1, 2. For Milton's spelling of this word *v. Com.* 580 and Word-List, Vol. I.

40 ye . . . ye] Edd. 1, 2: you . . . you T.MS.
   neer] Ed. 1: neere T.MS.: near Ed. 2.

41 What shallow-searching *Fame*] Edd. 1, 2: those virtues wch dull Fame T.MS. *orig. alt. to* text.

44 am the powr] Edd. 1, 2. The MS. is torn here but Warton reads 'have the power', 'have' altered to 'am'.

45 Of this fair] Edd. 1, 2: & charge of this faire T.MS. The rest of the line is torn away.

46 grove] Ed. 1: grove. Ed. 2.

47 With] Edd. 1, 2: in T.MS.
   quaint,] Ed. 1: quaint; Ed. 2.
49 and] Edd. 1, 2: or T.MS.
50 Boughs] Edd. 1, 2: leaves T.MS. *orig. alt. to* bowes.
52 Or] Edd. 1, 2: & T.MS. *orig. alt. to* or.
54 Eev'ning] Ed. 1: Ev'ning Ed. 2.
59 & number all my rancks & every sprout T.MS. *orig.*
62 Hath lockt up mortal sense] hath chain'd mortalitie T.MS. *orig. alt. to* hath lockt up mortall eyes, *alt. to* text.
66 turn] turning T.MS. *orig.*, a slip of the pen in copying: the word *sing* in the line above has caught Milton's eye.
81 ye toward] Edd. 1, 2: you towards T.MS.
84 enameld] Ed. 1: enamel'd Ed. 2.
89 Elm Star-proof] Ed. 1: Elm-Star-proof Ed. 2.
91 you] Edd. 1, 2: yee T.MS.
   sits,] Ed. 1: sits Ed. 2.
97 banks.] Ed. 1: banks, Ed. 2.
101 ye] Edd. 1, 2: you T.MS.

LYCIDAS

First printed with heading *Lycidas*, under the signature J. M. in *Justa Eduardo King*, at Cambridge, 1638, in a slender volume in which a collection of Latin elegies is followed by a set of English poems with the title 'Obsequies to the memorie of Mr. Edward King': Milton's poem stands last in the volume. The text is carelessly printed (*v.* notes to ll. 67, 73, and 177) and shows scant fidelity to Milton's spelling, punctuation, and paragraphing (*v.* notes to ll. 12, 24–25, 85, 103, 114), but here and there records an earlier reading (*v.* notes to ll. 26, 30, 31, 69, 129, 157). Two surviving copies of the book bear marginal corrections in Milton's hand: one in the Cambridge University Library, to which I refer as 1638ᶜ; the other in the British Museum (C. 21. c. 92), to which I refer as 1638ᴮᴹ. *Lycidas* first appeared in Milton's own works in 1645, Ed. 1, where it stands immediately before *A Mask*. His holograph of the poem, a fair copy, in T.MS. follows *A Mask* and is headed *Lycidas* [Novemb. 1637 *del.*] *In this Monodie the author bewails a lerned friend unfortunatly drownd in his passage from Chester on the Irish seas 1637.* This sub-title or argument has been written in at a later date in Milton's later hand:[1] it first appears in print in Ed. 1 with the added words: *And by occasion foretels the ruine of our corrupted Clergy then in their height.*

In T.MS. Milton starts a fair copy of this poem on the verso of the last page of 'A Mask' (*Comus*), f. 29 *verso*, but soon discards it and starts again on f. 31.

[1] For the distinction between Milton's earlier and later hand *v.* note to ll. 58–63 *infra*.

The cancelled passage runs thus:

> yet once more O ye laurells and once more
> ye myrt'ls browne wth Ivie never sere
> I come to pluck yor berries harsh and crude
> before the mellowing yeare
> and crop yor young

He stops short here, deletes the last two lines, and substitutes

> and wth forc't fingers rude
> shatter yor leaves before ye mellowing yeare

continuing as text (except for an alteration in l. 8, *v. infra*) down to l. 14.

After this false start he begins once more on f. 31, but he keeps the discarded page for drafting and redrafting passages later: *v.* notes to ll. 58–63, 142–50. Throughout he has used T.MS. as a working copy, and has revised passages and altered words after the poem was complete, making a point of writing in the corrections which he made for the printed editions of 1638 and 1645. *v.* notes to ll. 26, 30, 31, 69, 129.

1 Laurels] Edd. 1, 2: laurels 1638. In 1638 initial capitals are throughout infrequent.

2 never-sear] Ed. 1: never sear Ed. 2: never-sere 1638.

8 For] young *alt. to* for T.MS. first draft.

10 *app. crit.* he well knew] I have adopted, as did Wright, the reading which Milton seems to have intended. He has written *well* in his later hand in the margin both of the Cambridge University copy and of the British Museum copy of 1638, to come in between *he* and *knew* in the printed text.

11 rhyme] Edd. 1, 2, 1638: rime T.MS. cf. note to *P.L.* i. 16, Vol. i.

12 bear] Edd. 1, 2: beare T.MS: biere 1638: bier Ed. 3. The printer of 1638 has no special care for eye-rhymes.

19–21 Muse . . . as he passes] Jortin quoted by Newton on *S.A.* 973 writes: ' "Muse" in the masculine for "poet" is very bold.' But there are contemporary examples of this usage. Cf. *O.E.D.* under *Muse* 2 c. 'That memorable sea-battle (Lepanto) sung by a crowned Muse' (i.e. James I) G. Sandys, *Trav.*

21 passes turn,] Edd. 1, 2: passes, turn 1638: passes turn T.MS. Characteristically the MS. has no punctuation.

22 And bid] Edd. 1, 2, 1638: to bid T.MS. *orig.*

24 rill.] rill; 1638.

25 New paragraph Edd. 1, 2, and T.MS.: no new paragraph 1638. Ed. 1 follows T.MS. in giving new paragraphs at ll. 15, 25, 37, 50, 64, 85, 103, 132, 165, and 186. In 1638 no new paragraphs are given at ll. 25, 50, 64, 85, 103.

26 opening eye-lids] Edd. 1, 2: glimmering eyelids 1638, and T.MS. *orig.*: but *opening* in the margin in Milton's later hand. The image 'glimmering eyelids of the morn' was perhaps suggested by the 'twinckling eyelids' of Spenser's Pastorella in the haunting stanza, full of the imagery of light, *F.Q.* VI. xi. 21.

30 *app. crit.*] The first version of this line recorded in T.MS. and in 1638, is, in the Italian manner, a three-foot line intervening between five-foot lines (cf. ll. 4, 19, 21, 33). In the first half of the poem they are noticeably more frequent than in the latter half. In the present instance the line did not satisfy Milton's ear, perhaps because of the clogging consonants in the last three syllables, 'ev'n starre bright'. It is altered in T.MS. in his later hand to 'oft till the starre that rose in Evning bright'.

31 westering] Edd. 1, 2: burnisht 1638, T.MS. In T.MS. *burnisht* is deleted and *westring* in Milton's later hand is written in the margin—a descriptive, altered to a functional, epithet. Cf. l. 58 where *the golden-hayrd Calliope* becomes *the Muse herselfe*. *v.* note to ll. 58–63 *infra*.

   wheel] weele T.MS. Cf. *Com.* note to l. 190 *infra*.

34 clov'n] Edd. 1, 2: cloven 1638: clov'en T.MS. Milton has not begun to distinguish orthographically for metrical purposes *clov'n* from *cloven*, as he does in *P.L. v.* Vol. I, Introd., p. xiii.

36 *Damætas*] Edd. 1, 2, T.MS.: *Dametas* 1638.

39 Thee Shepherd,] Edd. 1, 2. Thee shepherds, 1638. The omission of comma with vocative is consonant with Milton's practice. *v.* Vol. I, Introd., p. xxi.

41 their echoes] Edd. 1, 2, 1638: thire Eccho T.MS. *orig. corr. to* thire Echo's.

42 Hazle Copses] Edd. 1, 2: haze'l copses T.MS.: hasil-copses 1638.

47 *app. crit.* wardrop wear] In T.MS. Milton first wrote *buttons weare*, altered *weare* to *beare*, finally cancelled these words, writing in the margin *wardrope weare*, all in his early hand. He uses the same spelling *wardrope* in *At a Vacation Exercise*, 18.

48 White-thorn] white-thorn 1638: White thorn Ed. 1: White Thorn Ed. 2: white thorne T.MS.

50 No new paragraph 1638.

51 o're] Edd. 1, 2: ore 1638, T.MS.

   lov'd] Edd. 1, 2: lord 1638, corrected in Milton's hand to *lov'd* 1638ᶜ and 1638ᴮᴹ. In T.MS. he began to write *young*, struck it out, and substituted *lov'd*.

53 your] Edd. 1, 2: the 1638, *corr. to* your 1638ᶜ.

   Druids] Ed. 1, 1638; Druids, Ed. 2: Drüids T.MS.

56 Ay] Edd. 1, 2: ay T.MS.: Ah 1638.

58–63 This passage, perhaps the greatest in the poem for sheer poetic power, can be seen in the making in T.MS. Three stages can be traced:

   1. He first wrote in his fair copy:

> what could the golden hayrd Calliope
> for her inchaunting son
> when shee beheld (the gods farre sighted bee)
> his goarie scalpe rowle downe the Thracian lee

   2. Coming back to the passage after completing the poem, he crossed out

the last two lines and wrote in the margin (with a mark to show that the new lines are to follow 'for her inchaunting son'):

> whome universal nature might lament
> and heaven and hel deplore
> when his divine head downe the streame was sent
> downe the swift Hebrus to the Lesbian shore

3. Then he took his spare sheet (f. 29 verso[1]) and began rewriting the lines

> for her inchanting son
> whome universal nature might [*alt. to* did] lament
> when by the rout that made the hideous roare
> his divine [*alt. to* goarie] visage downe the streame was sent
> downe the swift Hebrus to ye Lesbian shoare

4. Finally on the same sheet he rewrote the opening lines of the passage:

> what could the muse her selfe that Orpheus bore
> the muse her selfe for her inchanting son

The text of 1638 follows this last version: Ed. 1 has no substantial variants.

The rewriting of this passage reveals a transitional phase in Milton's handwriting. In the main text of the poem he uses the Greek form of ε which is characteristic of his early hand: in the drafts which I have recorded above he is beginning to introduce an *e* of bold Italian type which he adopted consistently in his later hand: in passage (2) there are two Italian *e*'s, in passage (4) again two among the preponderating Greek ε's. This means that between November 1637 when he wrote his first complete draft of *Lycidas* and the printing of the poem early in 1638 he began the change from Greek ε to Italian *e*. A confirmation is happily supplied by the revised versions in *Comus* of the Epilogue and of a passage in the middle of the poem, ll. 672–705 (*v.* note *infra*, p. 355), where in both cases a sprinkling of Italian *e*'s is to be found. The two revised versions must have been written when Milton was preparing his *Mask* for the press in 1637 (we should bear in mind that 1637, the date of the title-page, could mean any time up to 25 March 1638 according to our modern calendar, but 25 March 1637 according to the calendar of Milton's day). We can be sure then that Milton was beginning to use Italian *e* before he went abroad in April 1638, and we can narrow down the initiation of the change to the period between November 1637—he dates his fair copy of *Lycidas* in T.MS. 'Novemb. 1637' using the ε of Greek form—and April 1638. In his later hand he uses a bold Italian *e* consistently.[2]

63 *Lesbian*] Ed. 2: *Letbian* Ed. 1.
64 No new paragraph 1638.
65 tend] Ed. 1, 1638: end Ed. 2.
66 strictly] Edd. 1, 2: stridly 1638.

[1] *v.* frontispiece *supra*.
[2] *v.* 'The Chronology of Milton's handwriting' (with photographic facsimiles), by H. Darbishire, in *The Library*, Sept. 1933.

thankles] Ed. 1: thankless Ed. 2: thanklesse 1638, T.MS.

Muse,] Edd. 1, 2: muse T.MS.: Muse? 1638.

67 use] Edd. 1, 2, T.MS.: do 1638, *but* use 1638ᶜ and 1638ᴮᴹ.

69 Or with] Edd. 1, 2: Hid in 1638: hid in *corr. to* or with T.MS.

Neæra's] Edd. 1, 2, T.MS.: *Neera's* 1638.

73 when] Edd. 1, 2, T.MS.: where 1638.

76 thin-spun] Ed. 1, 1638, T.MS.: thin spun Ed. 2. In Ed. 1 the hyphen shows faintly.

81 lives] Edd. 1, 2: lives, 1638.

spreds] Edd. 1, 2, T.MS.: spreads 1638.

82 perfet] Edd. 1, 2: perfect 1638, T.MS. Cf. note to *Hymn*, l. 116.

85 No new paragraph 1638.

O] Edd. 1, 2: Oh 1638, T.M.S.

honour'd] Edd. 1, 2, 1638: smooth *alt. to* fam'd, *and finally to* honour'd T.MS.

86 Smooth-sliding] Edd. 1, 2, 1638: soft-sliding. *alt. to* smooth-sliding T.MS.

91 Fellon] Edd. 1, 2: fellon T.MS.: felon 1638.

94 Promontory;] Ed. 2: Promontory, Ed. 1: Promontorie: 1638.

103 No new paragraph 1638.

Camus, reverend Sire,] Edd. 1, 2: Chamus (reverend sire) 1638.

107 Ah!] Ed. 1, 1638: Ah; Ed. 2 *but* Ah! *catchword.*

112 Miter'd] Edd. 1, 2: mitred 1638: mitre'd T.MS.

113 thee] Ed. 1, T.MS.: thee, Ed. 2, 1638. No comma with phrase in apposition is consistent with Milton's practice.

114 Anow] Edd. 1, 2: anough T.MS.: Enough 1638. Milton's characteristic spellings are *anow, anough. v.* Word-List, Vol. I.

116 reck'ning] Edd. 1, 2: reckning T.MS.: reckoning 1638.

118 guest;] Ed. 2: guest. Ed. 1, 1638.

121 Herdmans] Edd. 1, 2: herdmans 1638: heardsmans T.MS.

129 nothing sed] Edd. 1, 2: little said, 1638. In T.MS. Milton first wrote *nothing sed*, deleted *nothing* and substituted *little* in the margin; but later he put an asterisk over *nothing*, meaning that he wished to restore that reading.

131 smite no more] Edd. 1, 2, T.MS.: smites no more 1638.

135 Flourets] Edd. 1, 2: flowerets 1638: flowrets T.MS.

138 Starr] Edd. 1, 2: starre, 1638, T.MS.

sparely] T.MS. *orig.* Milton substituted *faintly* in the margin, but returned to *sparely.*

139 Throw] bring T.MS. *orig.* then *del.* and *throw* written in the margin.

enameld] Edd. 1, 2: enamell'd 1638: enamel'd T.MS.

142 dies,] 1638, Ed. 3: dies. Edd. 1, 2.

142–50] This famous 'flower-passage' was an afterthought. In T.MS. the original fair copy omits lines 142–50 and runs straight on from l. 141 to l. 151. In the margin Milton has written *Bring the rathe &c* with a mark to indicate that the passage is to be inserted between the two lines: he then returns to his first page, f. 29 verso,[1] where he was to work out his final version of ll. 58–63 (*v. supra*), and proceeds to compose the new lines: there are two successive versions:

(1) Bring the rathe primrose that unwedded dies
colouring the pale cheeke of uninjoyd love
and that sad floure that strove
to write his owne woes on the vermeil graine
next adde Narcissus y[t] still weeps in vaine
the woodbine and y[e] pancie freak't wth jet
the glowing violet
the cowslip wan that hangs his pensive head
and every bud that sorrows liverie weares
let Daffadillies fill thire cups with teares
bid Amaranthus all his beautie shed
to strew the laureat herse &c.

(2) Bring the rathe primrose that forsaken dies
the tufted crowtoe and pale Gessamin
the white pinke, and y[e] pansie freakt wth jet
the glowing violet the well-attir'd woodbine
the muske rose and the garish columbine
wth cowslips wan that hang the pensive head
and every flower that sad escutcheon beares [altered finally to *imbroidrie weares*]
   2 let [*altered to* &] daffadillies fill thire cups wth teares
   1 bid Amaranthus all his beauties shed
   to strew &c.

His reversal of the order of the two last lines, letting the English daffodils take the last place instead of the Greek amaranthus, follows a true artistic instinct.

145 Violet,] violet, 1638: Violet. Edd. 1, 2.

146 well-attir'd] 1638, T.MS.: well attir'd Edd. 1, 2.

147 hed] Ed. 1: head 1638, Ed. 2, T.MS. *hed* is an eye-rhyme.

149 *Amaranthus*] Ed. 1, 1638, T.MS.: *Amarantus* Ed. 2.

151 *Lycid*] Lycid' T.MS.

153 frail] sad *alt. to* fraile T.MS.

154 shores] floods *alt. to* shoars T.MS.

155 hurld] Ed. 1: hurl'd Ed. 2, 1638.

157 *app. crit.* whelming] The *humming* of 1638 was corrected to *whelming* in 1638[c] and 1638[BM]. Milton must have had echoing in his mind the line in Shakespeare's *Pericles*, III. i. 64: 'And *humming* water must o'er*whelm* thy corpse.'

160 *Bellerus*] Corineus T.MS. *orig. alt. to* Bellerus.

163 ruth,] 1638: ruth. Edd. 1, 2.

173 waves;] 1638: waves: T.MS.: waves Edd. 1, 2. In some copies of Ed. 1 the mark of a semicolon is discernible, uninked.

175 oozy] Edd. 1, 2: oazie 1638, *corr. to* oosie 1638[c] and 1638[BM]: oozie T.MS. Locks] Ed. 3: locks 1638. Lock's Edd. 1, 2.

[1] *v.* frontispiece *supra*.

176 And hears] listening *alt. to* & hears T.MS.

177. This line is omitted in 1638, but Milton has written it in to 1638^c and 1638^{BM}.

183 Henceforth] Ed. 2, 1638: Hence forth Ed. 1.

191 the Western] Edd. 1, 2: the western 1638: [westren *del.*] the wester'n T.MS.

A MASK PRESENTED AT LUDLOW-CASTLE 1634, &c.

The title *Comus* was first given to the Mask by Dr. Dalton in his *Comus, a Mask, Now adapted to the Stage.* 1738. Thomas Warton was the first of Milton's editors to adopt *Comus* as title (a title which Milton would never have chosen), in his edition of *Poems upon Several Occasions* by John Milton, 1785.

The Mask was first published in 1637 with the title: A Maske | presented| At Ludlow Castle, | 1634: | On Michaelmasse night, before the | Right Honorable, | John Earle of Bridgewater Vicount Brackley, | Lord Praesident of Wales, And one of | His Maiesties most honorable | Privie Counsell. Under the title the name of the author does not appear, but in its stead the motto: *Eheu quid volui misero mihi! floribus austrum | Perditus*—suggesting the same fear of a premature exposure of his poetic gifts that he was to express in the opening lines of *Lycidas*. The letter of Henry Lawes is prefixed to the text.

In *Poems* 1645 (Ed. 1) the Mask stands last of the English poems with a separate title-page: A | Mask | Of the same | Author | Presented | at Ludlow-Castle | 1634 | Before | The Earl of Bridgewater | Then President of Wales | Anno Dom. 1645. The motto is omitted. The letter of Henry Lawes is prefixed, followed by the letter of Sir Henry Wotton.

In 1673 the poem appeared in *Poems &c. upon Several Occasions* by John Milton (Ed. 2) without separate title-page and without the introductory letters, under the shortened title *A Mask presented at Ludlow-Castle, 1634 &c.*

MSS. Two important manuscript copies of the Mask survive: (1) in the Trinity MS. in the library of Trinity College, Cambridge (T.MS.), with the heading *A maske*, 1634; and (2) in the Bridgwater MS. headed *A Maske*, an independent manuscript made in connexion with the production at Ludlow in 1634, now in the library of Bridgwater House (B.MS.). T.MS. has clearly been kept by Milton as a working copy, a copy made by himself and written, except for a very few words (generally in the margin) in his own hand; the deletions and revisions can be seen to have been made at different times: (*a*) in the very act of copying his first draft (*v.* notes to ll. 4/5, 350–66, 659–755); (*b*) on reconsideration at some time before, or whilst, the acting copy recorded in B.MS. was made (*v.* notes to ll. 659–755 and ll. 672–705); (*c*) at some date before or in 1637, when he was preparing a copy for publication at the instance of Henry Lawes (*v.* notes to ll. 243 and 976–1023); (*d*) at some date between 1637 and 1645, when he was preparing his text for Ed. 1 (*v.* notes to l. 214, l. 956).

B.MS. is written in the formal hand of a professional scribe (who makes ignorant mistakes here and there, as in writing *Millobeus* for *Meliboeus*, l. 822).

It would seem to be a fair copy, made for the Earl of Bridgwater, from the acting copy. D. H. Stevens in 'Milton Papers' (*Modern Philology*, 1927) thinks that Lawes himself wrote the names of the actors on the title-page, and some of the stage-directions. I cannot confirm this. We know from Henry Lawes's letter that he played and sang the part of the Attendant Spirit, and it is clear from the manuscript that for the purposes of his production at Ludlow he here and there omitted, and in three places readjusted, parts of the poem as originally written in T.MS. by Milton. How far Milton was his collaborator in this we do not know. The adjustments do no damage to the verbal perfection of the text. First, a portion of the Attendant Spirit's epilogue, twenty lines in all, is borrowed for his prologue (*v.* notes to l. 1 and to ll. 976–1023). (Lawes felt the need to open with a song.) Second, the latter part of the Spirit's song invoking Sabrina is divided between the brothers thus: 871–2 Elder brother; 873–4 Second brother; 875–6 Elder brother; 877–8 Second brother; 879–82 Elder brother: *v.* note to 871–82. Again, the Spirit's appeal to the Lady after her rescue:

> Com Lady while Heaven lends us grace,
> Let us fly this cursed place, . . .

is divided between the Spirit and the Elder brother: ll. 938–43 are given to the Elder brother, ll. 944–55 to Daemon, and ll. 956–7 again to Elder brother. Apart from these adjustments, made for the production at Ludlow, the differences between B.MS. and T.MS. resolve themselves into (1) a few textual variations, generally where B.MS. retains an earlier reading of T.MS. (*v.* notes on ll. 243, 356, 384–5, 429/30, 956), and (2) a number of 'cuts', clearly made in adapting the piece for performance (*v.* notes on ll. 188–90, 195–225, 357–8, 360–5 (*v.* p. 348), 632–7, 679–87 (*v.* p. 353), 697–700, 737–55). A glance at the omitted passages will reveal at once that what is cut is poetical lines or passages of moral reflection fitter for reading than reciting. It is perhaps significant that the speeches cut most drastically (by 59 lines in all) are those of the Lady, played by Alice Egerton, aged 15. The printed text has 1,023 lines, B.MS. 908.

The relation of the manuscripts and the printed text may be figured as follows, taking T.MS. to represent the manuscript as it stood first before various passages were deleted and rewritten, T.MS.¹ to represent the Trinity MS. in its state at the time when a copy, represented by the Bridgwater MS. (B.MS.), was made for Lawes's purpose, and T.MS.² to represent the Trinity MS. as revised for the copy of the first printed edition in 1637.

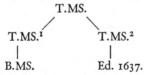

The text of 1637 is undoubtedly derived from T.MS.² in its form as revised

for purposes of publication, and not from B.MS. This is clear from its version
of the first and last lines of the poem (*v.* notes to l. 1, and ll. 979–99) and
from its fidelity to some of Milton's spellings (*v.* notes to l. 11, l. 169, and
l. 265). In two places it introduces passages which are not found in either
manuscript: (1) ll. 357–65, but Todd reports that when he examined T.MS.
these lines were written on a separate sheet (*v.* note to these lines *infra*,
p. 348): (2) ll. 779–806, in which the Lady expounds the sage and serious
doctrine of virginity—where again the lines may have been recorded on a
separate sheet (since lost). The copy of the edition of 1637 from the Bridg-
water Library, now in the Pforzheimer Collection, has pen-and-ink correc-
tions written in, certainly at Milton's instigation, though they do not appear
to be by his hand (I have not seen this copy but only the photographic
facsimile of one page, B.M. N. L. 4^d). The corrections are at lines 20, 49, 73,
131, 223, 417, 443, 474, 781 (*v.* notes *infra*). All these corrections are carried
out in Ed. 1 (1645). It is probable that this corrected copy of the edition of
1637 was presented by Milton to the Earl of Bridgwater.

The text of Ed. 1 (1645) is based on 1637 with some new readings (*v.*
ll. 214, 472, 605, 956), and with considerable modernizing of spelling; in
particular Ed. 1 drops unnecessary final *e* and eschews doubling of final
consonants where the syllable is unaccented (*v.* l. 4 calme and serene aire
1637: calm and serene Ayr Ed. 1; l. 3 aëreall 1637: aëreal Ed. 1).

Ed. 2 (1673) follows the text of Ed. 1 closely: where it deviates, it is gener-
ally in error: e.g. l. 474 sensuality Ed. 2 *for* sensualty Ed. 1, T.MS.; l. 580
further Ed. 2 *for* furder Ed. 1, T.MS.

A clinching proof that each edition follows the last may be found in the
printing of the single word *quest*, l. 321. In 1637, 1645, and 1673 the word is
printed *quest'*. There seems no justification for the aspostrophe: its presence
is, I think, explained by the position of a comma in T.MS. after the word
'cottage' in the line above; this must have been taken by an amanuensis,
making a fair copy, for an apostrophe at the end of *quest*.

In the dramatic structure of the poem and in its stylistic texture Milton
made alterations as he adapted his text first to the exigencies of the produc-
tion at Ludlow, secondly for the printing of it in 1637 as a separate poem to
satisfy those who knew of it as a Mask, and finally for its important place (it
stands last) in his first volume of collected poetry, 1645. The alterations are
few, but they are all significant: Milton reshaped his text with an artist's
insight and with a craftsman's hand. The alterations made for the perform-
ance were made, we must assume, at the instance of Lawes (*v. supra*) in the
interest of the dramatic production. They are almost all in the nature of
rearrangements and 'cuts'. Those to be found in the first printed edition,
1637, are made by a poet scrupulous in his art: the most famous is that in the
Lady's song 'And hould a counterpoint to all Heav'ns Harmonies' changed
to 'And give resounding grace to all Heav'ns harmonies', the technical

musical phrase altered to one of a familiar and general character (cf. a similar alteration in 'Blest pair of Sirens', where 'harsh *chromatic* jarres' are cast out). In two places he allowed a touch of romantic melodrama to pass muster in the acted play: l. 409

> Elder brother: *I could be willing though now i'th darke to trie*
> *a tough passado with the shaggiest ruffian*
> *that lurks by hedge or lane of this dead circuit* . . .

and l. 428, where he pictures his lost sister in a spot

> where very desolation dwells,
> By grots and caverns shag'd with horrid shades
> *and yawninge denns where glaring monsters house:*

but in the printed versions his severe taste rejected the lines italicized above, lines which appear in both manuscripts. To compensate for these omissions he found a place for the same idea, crystallized into abstract terms, at l. 356:

> What if in wild amazement, and affright,
> Or while we speak within the direful grasp
> *Of Savage hunger, or of Savage heat?*

This ruthless compression involved the cutting out of a poetical passage standing here in both manuscripts:

> or else in wild amazement and affright
> so fares as did forsaken Proserpine.
> when the big rowling flakes of pitchie clouds
> and darknesse wound her in.

Characteristically in the printed version Milton expands passages that drive home the moral meaning of his poem: thus he inserts at l. 679 the lines carrying Comus's sophistical appeal to Nature's law, and at the same time ejects the useful dramatic line

> poor ladie thou hast need of some refreshinge (B.MS.);

and he supplies a long eloquent defence of Chastity as *finale* of the Lady's last speech (ll. 779–99), with its immediate effect on Comus (ll. 800–6). The whole of this passage is absent from both manuscripts. Finally he expands and enriches the epílogue, rewriting the whole for publication in 1637.

The text of 1645 shows little rehandling by Milton, but there is one passage of crude melodramatic effect which he had overlooked in 1637:

> Eld bro. But for that damn'd magician . . .
>   . . . Ile find him out,
> And force him to restore his purchase back,
> Or drag him by the curls, *and cleave his scalpe*
> *Downe to the hipps.*

So 1637, following the manuscripts. In 1645 he modified this to the more decorous

> Or drag him by the curls to a foul death
> Curs'd as his life (608–9).

A small stylistic change revealing Milton's sensitive care in the choice of words is in line 214:

Thou flittering Angel girt with golden wings (1637)

—where he altered 'flittering' (perhaps too bat-like?) to 'hovering' (1645); and as a consequence changed 'hovering' to 'lingering' in l. 472.

The first scene . . . *or enters*] 1637, Edd. 1, 2: The first scene discovers a wild wood. A Guardian spirit, or Daemon T.MS.: The first scene . . . wood, then a guardian spiritt or demon descendes or enters. B.MS.

1 In B.MS. before l. 1 there follows a song sung by the guardian spirit.

> From the heavens nowe I flye
> and those happy Clymes that lye
> Where daye never shutts his eye
> up in the broad field of the Skye
> There I suck the liquid ayre
> all amidst the gardens fayre
> of Hesperus and his daughters three
> that singe about the goulden tree.
> there eternall Summer dwells
> and west wyndes with muskye winge
> about the Cederne allyes flinge
> Nard and Casias balmie smells
> Iris there with humid bowe
> waters the odorous bankes that blowe
> Flowers of more mingled hew
> then her purfled scarfe can shew
> yellow, watchett, greene & blew
> and drenches oft with Manna dew
> Beds of Hyacinth and Roses
> where many a Cherub soft reposes

These lines are borrowed, with variants, and in abbreviated form, from what appears in T.MS. as the Epilogue in its first state (T.MS.¹). *v.* notes to ll. 976–99. Milton would have fallen in the more readily with Lawes's adoption of them for the opening lines of the acting version in that they echo the idea and mood of his original opening speech, afterwards cancelled (*v.* note to l. 4/5 *infra*), in which the attendant spirit describes his heavenly abode 'amidst the Hesperian gardens'.

2 immortal] Edd. 1, 2: immortall T.MS., 1637. The doubling of final consonant, characteristic of Milton's early spelling and usual in T.MS. and 1637, is generally, though not always, eschewed in 1645 (Ed. 1); cf. notes to ll. 3, 166, &c. In these minutiae of spelling I have not given collations throughout.

3 aëreal] Ed. 1: aereal Ed. 2: aereall T.MS.: aëreall 1637.

4 milde of calm and serene Ayr] Ed. 1. [Air Ed. 2]: mild of calme and serene aire T.MS., 1637. The idle -*e* at the end of a word is generally dropped in 1645 (Ed. 1).

4/5 After line 4 the following passage stands in T.MS. [I have put deleted words in square brackets]:

  1 amidst the [gardens] Hesperian gardens [on whose bancks] [where the banks]
  2 [aeternall roses grow & hyacinth]
  3 bedew'd with nectar, & celestiall songs
  4 aeternall roses [grow] [yield] [blow] [blosme] grow & hyacinth
  5 & fruits of golden rind, on whose faire tree
  6 the scalie-harnest [watchfull] dragon ever keeps
  7 his [never charmed] uninchanted eye, & round the verge
  8 & sacred limits of this [happie] blisfull Isle
  9 the jealous ocean that old river winds
  10 his farre-extended armes till wth steepe fall
  11 halfe his wast flood ye wide Atlantique fills
  12 & halfe the slow unfadom'd [poole of Styx] Stygian poole
  13 [I doubt me gentle mortalls these may seeme
  14 strange distances to heare & unknowne climes]
  15 but soft I was not sent to court yor wonder
  16 wth distant worlds & strange removed climes
  17 Yet thence I come and oft from thence behold
  18 the smoake & stirre of this dim, narrow spot

No close reader of the Trinity MS. can fail to recognize that Milton set out to make a fair copy, yet also that he soon found himself revising and composing afresh. Cf. note to ll. 659–755 *infra*. In lines 1–4 of the above passage he begins with one construction:

    amidst the Hesperian gardens on whose bancks
    aeternall roses grow

but changes to another:

    amidst the Hesperian gardens *where the banks*
    aeternall roses yield

yet in the end returns to his first thought. More significantly, he becomes aware that this long richly poetical passage is, in relation with his whole design in the Mask, overweighted and out of scale, and he strikes it out, with the exception of the last line. But he saved some of the images and phrases. With ll. 5–7 above cf. ll. 393–5 of the poem:

    But beauty like the fair Hesperian tree
    Laden with blooming gold, had need the guard
    Of dragon watch with uninchanted eye,

and for the Hesperian gardens and the golden tree cf. also ll. 981–3 *infra*.
5 In T.MS. the line first stands as l. 18 of the passage quoted above in note to 4/5. Milton alters it so as to follow line 4 by inserting *above* at the beginning of the line, and deleting *narrow*.

    spot,] Edd. 1, 2: spot 1637. T.MS. has no punctuation here, and throughout Milton punctuates very little in this MS., except for a fairly regular introduction of comma before *and*. *v*. note to l. 7 *infra*.

7 Confin'd,] The comma before the conjunction *and*, as in the next line, *frail, and Feaverish*, is in accordance with contemporary practice, which holds also before the conjunction *or*. Cf. l. 45.

7, 8 Between these lines, originally written in reverse order, T.MS. has 'beyond the written date of mortall change', deleted. At l. 10 *mortal change* is introduced in the final version.

11 the enthron'd] Edd. 1, 2, 1637, T.MS.: the enthroned B.MS. Milton is particular in the spelling of past participles ending in *ed*: if he intends the last syllable to be metrically valid he spells it *ed*, as in *th' unarmed* l. 582; otherwise *'d*. In this place it is perfectly clear that he means *enthron'd* to be read as a disyllable with metrical stress on the first syllable, and *the* as a full metrical syllable. The common modern reading *th' enthroned* is wrong.

12 by] Edd. 1, 2, T.MS.: with B.MS.

13 their] Edd. 1, 2: thire T.MS. Throughout this MS. written, we suppose, in 1634 he spells *thire*. Cf. note to *The Passion*, l. 53 (p. 308 *supra*).

14 ope's] shews T.MS. *orig*.

18] but to my buisnesse now. Neptune whose sway T.MS. *orig*.

20 by] MSS. and Edd. 1, 2: my 1637, *corr. to* by Pforz.

21] the rule & title of each sea-girt Isle T.MS. *orig*.

25 goverment] Ed. 1, MSS.: government 1637, Ed. 2. *goverment* is Milton's spelling. *v*. Word-list, Vol. I.

28 the main] Edd.: his empire T.MS. *orig*.

41 Sovran] Soveran Edd. 1, 2: sovereigne 1637, MSS. Milton's spelling by 1645 was *Sovran* as at l. 639, *v*. Word-list, Vol. I, and I have adopted this spelling.

43 ye] Ed. 1: yee 1637: you Ed. 2, MSS. For the accusative case of this pronoun Milton later used *you* for the emphatic form, *ye* for the unemphatic. *v*. Word-list, Vol. I, and cf. notes *infra* to ll. 438, 513, 967, 1020.

45 From] by T.MS. *orig*.

46 Grape] grapes B.MS.

48 Mariners] manners B.MS.

49 Coasting] Edd. 1, 2: Coasting, 1637, *but comma deleted Pforz*.

53 groveling] Edd. 1, 2, T.MS.: grovling 1637; grovelinge B.MS.

58] In T.MS. Milton first wrote

  wch therfore she brought up and nam'd him Comus

but afterwards corrected *w^ch* to *whome*, and strengthened the line by an un-English inversion, *and Comus nam'd*, thus getting rid of the extra final syllable, an ending which he permits in dramatic blank verse, but never favours.

62 shelter] covert T.MS. *orig*.

63 mighty] potent T.MS. *orig*. 'potent art' is Shakespeare's phrase: *Tempest*, v. i.

64 Travailer,] Ed. 1: travailer T.MS., 1637: Traveller, Ed. 2: traveller B.MS. Milton's spelling is *travailer* in T.MS. also at ll. 200 and 332.

67 fond] weake T.MS. *orig.*

68 Potion works] potions work T.MS. *orig.*

human count'nance] Edd. 1, 2: humane count'nance 1637: humaine countnance T.MS.: humane Countenance B.MS. Milton distinguished between *húman* and *humáne*. *v.* Word-List, Vol. I, and cf. note to l. 297 *infra*, and to *P.R.* i. 298.

69 of] Edd. 1, 2, 1637: of *altered to* o' T.MS.

72 they were] Edd. 1, 2, 1637: before T.MS. *orig.*

73 perfet] perfect Edd. and MSS. But Milton's spelling is *perfet* as in l. 203 *infra. v.* note, and in *Lyc.,* 82.

is] Edd. 1, 2, T.MS.: in 1637, corr. *to* is *Pforz.*

75 before,] B.MS.: Edd. and T.MS. have no stop.

83 robes] Edd., T.MS.: webs B.MS.

84 likenes] Edd. 1, 2: likenesse 1637.

90 nearest & likeliest to give praesent aide T.MS. *orig.*; *give* is then altered to *the*; *aide* to *chance* and finally to *aide.*

91–92 I hear the tread Of hatefull steps] In T.MS. Milton first wrote *virgin steps.* Did he originally plan the entry of the Lady here, or is he anticipating unthinkingly the close of Comus's long lyric, ll. 145–7, where he feels 'the different pace Of som chast footing neer about this ground . . . Som Virgin sure'?

92 At the end of the line in both MSS. *Exit* is written: in T.MS. *Exit* is struck out and *goes out* substituted.

92/93 stage direction] B.MS. is close to the printed text but has 'a glass of liquor' for 'his glass' and 'like men & women but headed like wilde beasts' for 'headed . . . women'. T.MS. reads 'Comus enters wᵗʰ a charming rod & glasse of liquor with his rout all headed like some wilde beasts thire garments some like mens & some like womens they [begin] come on in a wild & [humorous] antick fashion. intrant κωμάζοντες'.

93 fold,] Ed. 1, 1637: fold. Ed. 2.

97 *Atlantick*] Edd. 1, 2: *Atlantik* 1637: Tartessian T.MS. *orig. alt. to* Atlantick: Birch reads *Tartarian.*

99 dusky] Edd. 1, 2: duskie 1637: northren *del*: dusky *in margin* T.MS.: Northerne B.MS. This is a correction made between 1634 and 1637.

108 In T.MS. this line is in part illegible through deletions and through tearing of the paper. Wright reads

        & nice [ ]tom wᵗʰ [her *del.*] scrupulous head.

I can only be sure of

        & [ ]i[ ]e [ ] wᵗʰ scrupulous head.

We both read *Advice* in the margin.

114 in swift] wᵗʰ swift T.MS. *orig.*

117 Tawny] Edd. 1, 2: yellow T.MS. *orig. Yellow sands* is perhaps rejected as too reminiscent of Shakespeare (*Tempest*, IV. i). Cf. note to l. 63 *supra.*

123 hath] has MSS.

125 rights] Edd., MSS.: rites Fenton, 1725. *Right* is a spelling used by Shake-
speare and common in the seventeenth century for *Rite*.

131 art] Edd., MSS.: at 1637 *corr. Pforz.*

132 spets] Edd., spitts T.MS.: spetts B.MS.

134–7] Milton first wrote

> stay thy polisht ebon chaire
> till all thy dues be don & nought left out

Then he writes an insertion between these two lines:

> wherin thou ridst wth Hecate
> & favour our close revelrie *alt. to* jocondrie.

Finally he strikes out this last line, alters *Hecate* to *Hecat*, and finishes the
line *& befriend*, adding as the second line of the couplet 'us thy vow'd
preists till utmost end'. This change of construction necessitates the
alteration of *till* to *of* in l. 137.

137 none] nought T.MS. *orig.* Three final *t*'s in consecutive words at the
end of the line were too much.

139 on th' *Indian*] Edd., T.MS.: on the Indian B.MS.

144 In] wth T.MS. *orig.*

  fantastick] & frolick T.MS. *orig.*

144/5 The Measure] Both MSS. add *in a wild rude & wanton antick*. In T.MS.
the phrase is bracketed.

145 feel] heare T.MS. *orig.*

  pace] 1637: pace, Edd. 1, 2.

146] After this line T.MS. *orig.* continues

> some virgin sure benighted in these woods
> for so I can distinguish by myne art.

Milton then strikes this out and continues as text, l. 147.

147 After this both MSS. have the stage direction 'they all scatter'.

150 charms] traines T.MS. *orig.*

151 wily trains] mothers charmes T.MS. *orig.*

  ere] e're Edd.

154 dazling] powder'd T.MS. *orig.*

155 blear] sleight T.MS. *orig.*: *altered to* blind, *then to* bleare.

156 lest] else T.MS. *orig.*

160 pretence] Edd. 1, 2: praetents 1637: praetence T.MS.

161 glozing] gloweinge B.MS.

164 snares] nets T.MS. *orig.*

166 harmles] Edd. 1, 2: harmlesse 1637: harmelesse T.MS.

167 thrift] T.MS. has in the margin *thirst* in a hand not Milton's.

166–9 So Ed. 1, following substantially 1637 and MSS. Ed. 2 omits l. 167 and
reverses the order of ll. 168 and 169 thus:

> I shall appear some harmles Villager
> And hearken, if I may, her busines here.
> But here she comes, I fairly step aside

But in the Errata of 1673 l. 169 is corrected to

> And hearken, if I may her busines hear,

presumably to avoid the repetition of the word *here* in the next line. But *hearken* and *hear* are tautological and the first version is preferable. In T.MS., followed by 1637, the line is punctuated with unusual care:

> & hearken, if I may, her buisnesse heere.

169 buisnes] buisnesse 1637, T.MS.: businesse B.MS.: busines Edd. 1, 2. *buisnes* is Milton's characteristic spelling. *v.* Word-List, Vol. I. cf. note to l. 18 *supra*.

170 mine] my MSS.

174 unletter'd] Ed. 2, T.MS.: unleter'd Ed. 1, 1637.

175 granges] garners T.MS. *orig.* Warburton comments: 'Altered with judgment to *granges*. Two rural scenes of festivity are alluded to, the Spring [*teeming flocks*] and the Autumn [*granges full*], sheepshearing and harvest home. But the time when the *garners* are full is in Winter, when the corn is threshed.'

175–6 T.MS. has an intermediate reading, cancelled:

> that for thire teeming flocks, and garners full
> in wanton dance adore the bounteous Pan

181 mazes of this tangl'd] Edd. 1, 2: alleys of [these] this arched T.MS. *orig.*

185 se'd] Edd. 1, 2, 1637: sed T.MS.: s'ed B.MS.

188–90] *om.* B.MS.

189 weed] Edd. 1, 2: weeds 1637, MSS. 'In Palmers weed' is a Spenserian phrase. Cf. *F.Q.* II. i. 52.

190 wheels] weeles T.MS. Cf. *Lyc.* 31. Milton's spelling is clearly phonetic: he was a Southerner.

    wain] chaire T.MS. *orig.*

191 came] come B.MS.

193 wandring] youthly T.MS. *orig.*

194] Milton began this line 'to the soone parting light' T.MS., struck this out, & wrote the line as in text.

195 stole] Edd. 1, 2: stolne 1637, MSS. After 'Had stolne them from me' B.MS. omits the rest of the passage down to l. 225 (inclusive).

199 due] thire T.MS. *orig.*

200 Travailer?] Ed..1: Travailer. 1637: Traveller? Ed. 2.

202 eev'n] Edd. 1, 2: even 1637, T.MS.

203 perfet] Edd. 1, 2: perfect 1637, T.MS. *v.* note to *Lyc.* 82 *supra*.

207 shapes] Edd.: shaps T.MS. Cf. *nams*, l. 208.

208 that syllable mens names] Edd. In T.MS. Milton originally wrote 'that lure nightwandring . . .' perhaps meaning to continue 'men', but he altered 'nightwandring' to 'nightwanderers'. Then he deleted the phrase, and substituted 'syllable mens nams' in the margin.

214 hovering] Edd. 1, 2: flittering 1637, T.MS. In the margin of T.MS.
hov'ring is written in a hand not Milton's: the change, made in preparing
his text for Ed. 1, represents a second thought on Milton's part, which led
to his altering *Hovering* to *Lingering* in l. 472 *q.v.*
215 unblemish't] unspotted T.MS. *orig.*

216]   I see yee visibly, & while I see yee
               this duskye hollow is a paradise
               & heaven gates ore my head now I beleeve T.MS. *orig.*

217 Supreme] The word is here accented on the first syllable. *v.* note to *On
Time*, 17 (p. 309 *supra*).
    t'whom] Edd.: to' whome T.MS. The apostrophe indicating a syllable
elided seems to have been inserted when he altered the line from its first
form: 'that the supréme good to whome' &c., where *he* is omitted and
supréme is accented on the second syllable. *v.* Word-List, Vol. I.
219 Guardian] cherub T.MS. *orig.*
223 sable] Edd. 1, 2, T.MS.: sables 1637, *corr. to* sable *Pforz.*
227 fardest] MSS., 1637: farthest Edd. 1, 2. Cf. notes to ll. 321 and 580 *infra*.
furder and *fardest* are Milton's spellings, which I adopt. *v.* Word-List,
Vol. I.
228 venter] Edd., T.MS.: venture B.MS.
229 off] Edd.: hence MSS.
231 *shell*] Edd., MSS.: T.MS. has *cell* in the margin. Dalton has *cell*.
241 *of the Sphear*] Edd. 1, 2: of the spheare T.MS.: of the sphære 1637: to
the spheare B.MS.
243 *give resounding grace*] Edd. 1, 2; 1637, T.MS.²: hold a counterpoint
T.MS.¹ *del*.: hould a counterpointe B.MS. Warton notes: 'Lawes, in setting
this Song, has thought fit to make a pleasant professional alteration: And
hold a counterpoint.' But T.MS. shows, as Todd pointed out, that Milton
himself first used the technical phrase, and altered it to the more general, in
time for the printing of 1637. Cf. note to 'At a Solemn Musick', l. 18, *supra*.
243/4 T.MS. has stage direction 'Comus enters', altered to 'looks in and
speaks'. B.MS. follows the latter.
245 inchanting] enchanting *alt. to* enchaunting T.MS.: enchauntinge B.MS.
252 it] Edd. 1, 2: she 1637, MSS.
254–5] These lines are not in the first draft, T.MS., but are added in the
margin. It looks as if he first wrote 'amidst the flowrie-kirtled Naiades',
then altered to 'sitting amidst the flowrie-kirtl'd Naiads', and finally
reverted to his first thought. B.MS. reads *Niades*.
255] culling thire potent hearbs, & balefull druggs. T.MS. *orig.* but *potent* is
altered to *powerfull*, then to *myghty*, and finally *potent* is written in again.
    potent] Ed. 2, MSS.: Potent 1637, Ed. 1. This is one of the indications
that 1637 is the copy for Ed. 1. There is no significance in the capital P.
256 as] when B.MS.

257–8 *Scylla* wept,/And chid] Scylla would weep/and chide T.MS. *orig.* It looks as if Milton next altered *and chide* to *chiding*, then went back to the preceding line and altered *would weep* to *wept*, and consequently *chiding* to *and chid.*

265 Hail forren wonder] No comma before or after the vocative phrase. This is usual with Milton.

    forren] Edd. 1, 2: forreine 1637, T.MS.: forreigne B.MS. *v.* Word-List, Vol. I.

268 Dwell'st] liv'st T.MS. *orig.*

270 prosperous] prospering T.MS. *orig.*: prosperinge B.MS.

276] After 'answere' in T.MS. 'to give me' is repeated and crossed out.

279 neer-ushering guides] thire ushering hands T.MS *orig.*

280 weary] wearied T.MS. *orig.*

282 i'th] Edd., T.MS.: in the B.MS.

288 loose] Edd. 1, 2, T.MS.: lose 1637.

291 Two such] Edd., B.MS.: such tow T.MS.

294 saw them] Edd.: saw 'em T.MS.: sawe em B.MS.

297 human] Edd. 1, 2: humaine T.MS., 1637: humane B.MS. Cf. note to l. 68 *supra.*

    human, as they stood;] Edd. 1, 2: humaine; as they stood, 1637.

300 colours] cooleness B.MS.

304 find them] find them out T.MS. *orig.*

310 the sure guess] sure steerage T.MS. *orig.*

312 wilde] Edd. 1, 2: wild 1637: wide T.MS. *orig.* but *wild* in margin in a hand not Milton's: wide B.MS.

313 bosky] In T.MS. Milton writes *bosky*, strikes it out, writes it again, strikes it out again, and finally writes *bosky* and keeps it. Shakespeare's 'bosky acres' in *Tempest*, IV. i, must have haunted him.

316] In T.MS. Milton first wrote 'w^{th}in these limits', then 'w^{th}in these shroudie limits', then 'or shrouded in these limits', finally as text.

317 Ere morrow wake] ere the lark rouse T.MS. *orig.*

    low roosted] lowe rooster B.MS.

318 thatcht pallat] Edd. 1, 2: thach't palate 1637: thetch't palate T.MS., but a hand not Milton's, the same that wrote *wild* l. 312 *supra*, writes *pallat* in the margin: thatcht palat B.MS.

321 furder] MSS.: further Edd. 1, 2, 1637. *v.* note to l. 227 *supra.*

    quest'] cf. Introd., p. 338 *supra.*

324 With] & T.MS. *orig.*

325 where] were T.MS. *orig.* Cf. note to l. 190 *supra.*

326 And yet is most pretended] & is praetended yet T.MS. *orig.*

328 it.] Edd. 1, 2, 1637. T.MS. has no stop, nor has B.MS., but the next line begins with capital letter which suggests the beginning of a new sentence.

329 my] this T.MS. *orig.*

331 Stars] Ed. 2: stars Ed. 1, 1637.
332 wontst] wondst T.MS. *orig.*: wonst B.MS.
   travailers] Ed. 1, MSS., 1637: travellers Ed. 2.
340 With thy] with a T.MS. *orig.*
346 whistle] wistle *corr. to* whistle T.MS. *v.* note to l. 190 *supra.*
348 'Twould] Ed. 2: T'would Ed. 1, 1637: t'would MSS.
349 close] lone B.MS. T.MS. has first *lone*, then *sad*, finally *close*.
350–66] What corresponds to this passage in T.MS. is much shorter and
   very much worked over. Lines 357–65 do not appear in either MS., with
   the exception of the half-line 'Eld. Bro. Peace brother peace'. In T.MS. the
   process of composition seems to be as follows:

[351] Where may she wander now, whether betake her
          from the chill dew [in this dead solitude] [in this surrounding wilde]
             amongst rude burrs & thistles
          perhapps some cold bancke is her boulster now
          or gainst the rugged barke of some broad elme
[355] she leans her [thoughtfull] head musing at our unkindnesse
   alt. to
          leans her unpillow'd head fraught wth sad feares
[356] [or else] what if in wild amazment and affright
          so fares as did forsaken Proserpine
          when the big [wallowing] rowling flakes of pitchie clowds
          & darknesse wound her in. 1 Bro. peace brother peace
[366] I doe not thinke my sister so to seeke

In l. [356] *supra* Birch, followed by Newton, Warton, and Todd, misread 'or
else' as 'or lost' (look at the MS. and the mistake is understandable). B.MS.
reads 'or els'. After this line the three lines about Proserpine (*v.* app. crit.
supra, ll. 357–9) are struck out in T.MS.: they remain in B.MS. Newton notes
that the whole passage was altered and 'other lines added afterwards on a
separate scrap of paper'. Warton, followed by Todd, writes: 'some of the
additional lines are on a separate slip of paper.' This slip has been torn away
from the MS., but a strip of its inner margin appears pasted down on to f. 19
(p. 16 of Wright's facsimile). On this stub can be distinctly seen the first
letters of ll. 350–8 of the printed version, and, below these, marks indicating
the first letters of five succeeding lines. It must be assumed from this and
from the following record of variants which Newton, Warton, and Todd—in
one case, l. 361, Todd only—found on the separate slip, that it contained a
fair draft of ll. 350–65 of the printed text.
361 For] which T.MS., noted by Todd.
362 his] the T.MS., noted by Newton, Warton, and Todd.
365 such] this T.MS., noted by Newton, Warton, and Todd.
      self-delusion!] self-delusion? Edd. 1, 2, 1637. This is one of the cases
   where the printer uses *?* for *!*
370 trust] hope B.MS. only.

371 constant] steadie T.MS. *orig.*: misread *stable* by Birch.

376] oft seeks to solitarie sweet retire T.MS. *orig.*

379 bussle] Edd. 1, 2: bustle 1637, MSS.

384–5 Benighted . . . dungeon] Edd. 1, 2, 1637. walks in black vapours, though the noontyde brand/blaze in the summer solstice T.MS. *orig. So* B.MS. T.MS. has the reading of the printed text in the margin.

385 'Tis] 1637: Tis Edd. 1, 2.

388 and] or T.MS. *orig.*, B.MS.

390 a Hermit] Edd. 1, 2: T.MS.: an Hermit 1637: an Hermitt B.MS.

390–1] for who would rob a Hermit of his beads
his books, his hairie gowne, or maple dish T.MS. *orig.*

Milton alters *beads* to *gowne*, then to *beads*, finally to *weeds*, and consequently revises the second line to read as the printed text.

393–5] These lines take up the image launched in the rejected lines of T.MS. in the magnificent opening passage. *v.* note to ll. 4/5 *supra*, ll. 5–7 of the passage quoted. Cf. also ll. 981–3 of the poem.

398 unsun'd] unsum'd B.MS.

399 treasure] treasures B.MS.

400 hope] thinke T.MS. *orig.*

401 on] at B.MS.

402 let] she B.MS.

403 wilde surrounding wast] Edd. 1, 2: *so* 1637 (*but* wild): vast, & hideous wild T.MS. *orig. alt. to* wide surrounding wast: wide surroundinge wast B.MS.

404 me not] not me T.MS. *orig.* but numbered for transposition.

409 controversie] question, no MSS.

409/10 Five lines not in the printed text appear here in both MSS. T.MS. starts with a phrase afterwards cancelled: 'Beshrew me but I would' and continues

I could be willing though now i'th darke to trie
a tough [passado] encounter wth the shaggiest ruffian
that lurks by hedge or lane of this dead circuit
to have 'her by my side, though I were sure
she might be free from perill where she is
but where *etc.*

B.MS. reads as above but with variations of spelling.

410 Yet] but *both* MSS.

hope and fear] hopes & feares T.MS. *orig.*

411 th'event] the event T.MS. *only.*

413 gladly banish] these words are marked for transposition in T.MS.

415 imagine] imagine brother MSS., clearly a dramatic hypermetrical line.

417 you] *om.* 1637, *but inserted Pforz.*

422] For this line T.MS. had originally two lines (struck out):

& may (on any needfull accident
be it not don in pride or [wilfull tempting] in praesumption)

Cf. l. 431.

423 May trace] walke through T.MS. *orig.*

425 rayes] aw T.MS. *orig.* Cf. note to l. 452 *infra.*

426 savage fierce] [savage] salvage feirce T.MS.: salvage, feirce B.MS.
salvage is the familiar form in Spenser.

427 Will] shall T.MS. *orig.*

428 there] even MSS.

429/30 and yawninge denns where glaringe monsters house B.MS. T.MS.
has the same line heavily struck out. *v.* Introd., p. 339, *supra.*

432 Som say] Some say *alt. to* Nay more—*finally* Some say T.MS.: naye more
B.MS.

433 moorish Edd. 1, 2, 1637, B.MS.: moorie T.MS.

434 meager] Edd. 1, 2, 1637, T.MS.: meagar B.MS.: wrinckled, wrincl'd *in
margin.* T.MS. *orig.*; *both del.*

436 goblin] goblinge B.MS.

437 Hath] Has 1637, MSS. In T.MS. *orig.* the line ran 'has power over true
virginity' with *powér* a disyllable.

438 ye] Edd. 1, 2: yee 1637, T.MS.: you B.MS.

439 *Greece*] Ed. 2: Greece Ed. 1, 1637.

442 This line is inserted in the margin T.MS.
silver-shafted] silver-shafter B.MS.

443 she] we 1637, *corr. to* she *Pforz.*

448 That] the B.MS.
unconquer'd] In T.MS. Milton first wrote *aeternall,* then *unvanquish't,*
finally *unconquer'd.*

452 and blank aw] of her purenesse *alt. to* of bright rays, *alt. to text* T.MS.
Milton's hesitation between *rays* (cf. l. 782 'the Sun-clad power of Chastity')
and *aw,* in describing the effect of Chastity (cf. l. 425 and note *supra*), is
perhaps connected with his memory of Britomart, who represents Chastity
in the *Faerie Queene.* Cf. F.Q. III. i. 43, 'Such was the beautie and the shining
ray / With which faire Britomart gave light unto the day', and IV. vi. 33,
where Artegal finds Britomart's countenance 'goodly grave and full of
princely *aw*'. *Awe* could be used in the seventeenth century in a subjective
sense (= reverent fear) or in an objective sense (power to inspire reverent
fear).

454 a soul is found] it finds a soule T.MS. *orig.*

456 This line is added in the margin T.MS.

460 Begin] begins T.MS. *orig. and* B.MS.

465 But] Edd.: & T.MS. *and* B.MS.
leud and lavish] the lascivious T.MS. *orig. alt. to* lewd lascivious *finally to*
lewd & lavish: lewde lascivious B.MS.

468 quite loose] loose quite T.MS. but marked for transposition.

471 Sepulchers] In T.MS. Milton began to write *monuments*.

472 Lingering] Edd. 1, 2: Hovering 1637: hovering T.MS., hoveringe B.MS. Cf. note to l. 214 *supra*. At l. 472 there is no correction in T.MS. indicating the reading for Ed. 1, as there is at l. 214.

474 sensualty] Ed. 1: sensualtie T.MS.: sensuality Ed. 2: sensualitie B.MS., 1637, *corr. to* sensualtie *Pforz.*: *sensualty* is the form which Milton requires metrically.

476 Against this line in T.MS. *Hallow within* has been deleted.

480 In T.MS. Milton appears to have written first 'list [bro.] list methought I heard'.

481 far off] Ed. 1: far of Ed. 2: farre off 1637: farre-of T.MS.
    hallow] Edd., T.MS.: hollowe B.MS. In T.MS. against this line Milton writes in the margin 'hallow farre of'.

485 Som roaving Robber] In T.MS. Milton first wrote 'some curl'd man of the swoord' *del.*: above is written 'hedge' as if he started a new phrase, but in the margin he writes 'some roaving robber'.

486 sister, agen agen and neer,] Ed. 1: sister: agen agen and neere 1637: sister, agen, agen, and neer, Ed. 2: sister. [yet] agen agen & neere T.MS.: sister: agen, agen & neere B.MS. The lack of punctuation in *agen agen and neer* expressing the brother's breathless excitement is clearly intended.

487 Best draw . . . guard] Milton first gave this line to the first brother: 1 *bro.* T.MS.

488] After this line Milton first wrote 'had best looke to his forehead, heere be brambles' *alt. to* 'he may chaunce scratch his forehead'.

489/90 *The attendant Spirit . . . Shepherd*] he hallows [hallo] the guardian Daemon hallows agen & enters in the habit of shepheard T.MS.: he hallowes and is answered, the guardian daemon comes in habited like a shepheard. B.MS.

490 what are you?] Edd. 1, 2: what are you, 1637: no punctuation in MSS.

491 iron stakes else] pointed stakes T.MS. *orig.*

492 that?] MSS.: that, Edd.

493 my father Shepherd] Edd. 1, 2: *so* 1637 *but* Shepheard: fathers shepheard MSS.

496 sweeten'd] Ed. 1, 1637: sweetn'd Ed. 2: sweetned MSS.
    dale] valley T.MS. *orig. alt. to* dale. Cf. notes to l. 58 and l. 28 *supra*.

497 thou] *om.* B.MS.
    Swain?] Edd. 1, 2: Swaine, 1637: shepheard, MSS.

498 Slip't from the fold] Ed. 1, 1637: *so* Ed. 2, *but* Slipt: leapt ore the penne T.MS. *orig. alt. to* slip't from his fold: slipt from the fould B.MS.

499 the pen't] hath the pen't T.MS. *orig.*

512 *Thyrsis*] shep. T.MS. *orig.*

513 *Spir.*] Shep. *corr. to* Dæ. T.MS.

ye] Edd. 1, 2: you 1637; MSS.

518 Hell] Ed. 2: hell Ed. 1, 1637.

519] In T.MS. this line is inserted in the margin.

523 Deep skill'd] enur'd T.MS. *orig.*: *alt. to* deepe learnt *finally to* deepe skill'd.

528 And the] In T.MS. Milton inserted after *and* the word *makes* but afterwards struck it out.

531 hilly crofts] pastur'd lawns T.MS. *orig.*

545 With flaunting Hony-suckle] Milton had trouble with the epithet. In T.MS. he first writes s——g [word illegible, *del.*] (Birch and Newton read *spreading*, Wright suggests *suckling*); then in the margin tries *flaunting*, alters to *blowing*, and finally returns to *flaunting*.

546–7 These two lines were written in reverse order but marked for transposition in T.MS.

547 meditate] meditate upon Ed. 2 only. *Meditate* in this sense (cf. meditate the thankles Muse, *Lyc.* 66) is not, and never was, an English usage, but is simply a Miltonic borrowing from Vergil. Cf. *Ecl.* i. 2, *musam meditaris avena*, meaning 'practise poetry'.

548 a close] the close T.MS. *orig.*

551 ceas't, and listen'd] cease, & listen T.MS. *orig.*

553 drowsie frighted] Edd. 1, 2, B.MS., 1637. In T.MS. the *r* of *frighted* has been altered to *l*—no one can tell by what hand—and many editors have adopted the reading *drowsie-flighted*, notably Newton, Dalton, and, of modern editors, Masson, Grierson, and Elton. The present editor accepts *drowsie frighted* as Milton's intention. *v.* the excellent note by Lascelles Abercrombie on *drowsie frighted steeds* in *Proceedings of the Leeds Philosophical Society*, vol. ii, Literary and Historical Section, Part I, pp. 1–5.

554 sleep.] sleepe. 1637: sleep, Ed. 1: sleep; Ed. 2. T.MS. has no stop, but the next line begins with a capital letter, *At last*, indicating a new paragraph: in general the lines begin with minuscules.

555–6] T.MS. shows an interesting process of reshaping in these two lines, in particular a shuffling of epithets. Milton first wrote

> At last a soft and solemne breathing sound,

then altered *soft* to *still*, afterwards to *sweet*, and proceeded

> rose like the soft steame of distill'd perfumes.

B.MS. records this stage of composition:

> at last a sweete, and solemne breathinge sound
> rose like the soft steame of distill'd perfumes.

T.MS. records the later stages of reshaping:

> At last a soft and solemne breathing sound
> rose like a steame of slow distill'd perfumes

finally altered to

> rose like a steame of rich distill'd perfumes.

'Possibly Gray had noticed this very curious passage in Milton's manu-script; for in his *Progress of Poesy* he calls the Æolian lyre, "Parent of sweet and solemn-breathing airs."' Todd.

556 steam] Ed. 1: steame 1637, T.MS.: stream Ed. 2.

558 ere] B.MS.: e're T.MS. Edd. Milton came to distinguish rightly *ere* (= before) from *e're* (= ever).

563 did] might MSS.

573 prævent] Ed. 1: prevent Ed. 2.

574 aidless] In T.MS. Milton first wrote *helplesse*, struck it out and wrote *who tooke him* at the end of the line, struck this out and returned to *helplesse*, but in the end substituted *aidlesse*.

578 with that] & with that T.MS. *orig.*

580 The line begins 'and this' T.MS. *orig. del.*
    furder] Ed. 1, MSS.: farther 1637: further Ed. 2. *furder* is Milton's spelling. *v.* Word-List, Vol. I.

581 ye] Edd. 1, 2: yee T.MS., 1637: you B.MS.

594 In T.MS. this line began originally 'till all to place' *del.*

597 self-consum'd;] self-consum'd, Edd. 1, 2: selfe consum'd, 1637, B.MS. T.MS. has no stop but a space between *selfe consum'd* and *if this fail*, as if a cheek or stop were indicated. Hence I refrain from the easy emendation *self-consumed*, supplying the missing syllable.

598 rott'nness] Edd. 1, 2: rottennesse, 1637, MSS.

605 Harpyes] Ed. 2, T.MS. Harpyies Ed. 1, 1637.
    or all] or T.MS. *orig. all* is inserted above the line.
    forms] *v. app. crit.*

607 restore his purchase back] release his new got prey T.MS. *orig.*

608-9 *app. crit.*] For the significance of this reading *v.* Introd. note, p. 339 *supra.* In T.MS. Milton struck out *hipps* and began to write *lowest* but deleted this and returned to *hips.*

610 thy] the B.MS.

611 sword] [swo] [steele] swoord T.MS.

614 unthred] unquilt T.MS. *orig.*

615 all thy sinews] every sinew T.MS. *orig.*

616 thy self] *om.* B.MS.

626 ope] open B.MS.

627 names] hews T.MS. *orig.*

632-7 *om.* B.MS.

636-7 The following lines are added in the margin in T.MS.:

> & yet more med'cinall then that ancient Moly
> that Mercury to wise Ulysses gave *orig. alt. to text.*

For Milton's pronunciation of *med'cinal v. S.A.* 627 and note.

639 sovran] Ed. 1: sov'ran Ed. 2: soveraine 1637, T.MS.: soveraigne B.MS.
v. note to l. 41 *supra*.

648 when we go] Edd. 1, 2: as we goe T.MS. *orig. alt. to* when on the way,
finally to when we goe.

649 the necromancers] his necromantik T.MS. *orig.*: the Negromancers
B.MS. For this spelling cf. the Italian form given by Florio in his *Worlde of
Wordes*, 1598: '*Negromante*, a nigromant, an enchanter'.

650 dauntless hardihood] suddaine violence T.MS. *orig.*

652 shed] powre T.MS. *orig.*
liquor] potion T.MS. *orig.*

653 But] and T.MS. *orig.*
sease] cease B.MS.

656 will they] they will T.MS., but marked for transposition.

657 Ile] I MSS.

658] & good heaven cast his best regard upon us T.MS. *orig.*

658/9 The stage direction is the same in B.MS. (*but* 'soft Musick' *om.*), 1637,
and Edd. 1, 2. In T.MS. 'soft Musick' *om.* and the second sentence is as
follows: 'Comus is discover'd with his rabble & the Ladie set in an in-
chanted chaire. She offers to rise.'

659-755] The opening scene in Comus's palace between the Lady and Comus
was planned differently in the first version in T.MS. It opened thus:

[659] nay Ladie sit, if I but wave this wand
yor nerves are all chain'd up in alablaster
and you a statue [fixt] or as Daphne was
4 root-bound, that fled Apollo. why doe ye frowne
[667] heere dwell no frowns nor anger, from these gates
sorrow flies farre. see here be all the pleasures
7 that [youth & fancie] fancie can beget [invent in] on youthfull thoughts
when the [briske] fresh blood [return] grows lively & returnes
[671] brisk as the Aprill budds in primrose season
[706] Oh foolishnesse of men! that that lend thire eares

In the later version adopted in B.MS., 1637, and Edd. 1, 2, Comus, speaking
first: 'Nay Ladie sit . . .' is interrupted after four lines [659-62] by the
Lady: 'fool, do not boast, Thou canst not touch the freedome of my mind
. . . while heavn sees good' [662-5]. Milton has written these lines in the
margin, marked for insertion midway in the fourth line above, after *Apollo*.
In the earlier version Comus goes straight on with no interruption from
the Lady (for the second interruption *v.* note to ll. 672-705 *infra*), not
making his offer of the cordial julep until he reaches the end of his speech:
'There was another meaning in these guifts' [754], which he follows by
'Think what, & look upon this cordiall julep' . . . 'this will restore all
soone'; on which the Ladie replies: 'stand back, false traitor/thou canst not
touch the freedome of my mynd'. The revised version is dramatically more
effective, the speeches of Comus and the Lady skilfully broken up, and the

climax better placed. B.MS. follows the revised version in its first form.
v. note to ll. 672–705 *infra*.

660 nervs] Ed. 1, 1637: nerves Ed. 2, MSS.
    Alablaster] MSS., Edd. *v.* Word-List, Vol. I.

662 do not boast] thou art over-proud T.MS. *orig.*

665 hast] MSS., 1637: haste Edd. 1, 2.

666 you] Edd. 1, 2, 1637, B.MS.: ye T.MS.

669 fancy] Milton began to write *youth & fancie*, then deleted the words and
wrote *fancie* T.MS.
    beget on] restored in T.MS. after *invent in* has been tried.

672–705 In T.MS. this is the passage on 'the pasted leaf', which constitutes
the second interruption in Comus's long unbroken speech as originally
conceived. It is indicated by the instruction written into the margin
opposite l. 7 [671] of the passage quoted in my note to ll. 659–755 *supra*:
'that which follows here is in the pasted leaf begins ["poor ladie" *del.*]
"and first behold" &c.', and the lines themselves have survived on a
separate small sheet pasted on to the inner margin of f. 21 verso. The
passage as first written corresponds substantially with ll. 672–8, 688–705,
the two groups joined by the line afterwards deleted, 'poor ladie thou hast
need of some refreshing'. Later, when this line was struck out, a passage
corresponding to ll. 679–87 has been written in to the margin. It is to be
noted that in this passage on 'the pasted leaf' there are signs of the changing
phase of Milton's handwriting belonging to the period Nov. 1637—April
1638: *v.* note to *Lyc.* 58–63, pp. 332–3 *supra*. This means that the passage
must have been written at the same period as the revised version of the epi-
logue, ll. 976–1023 (*v.* notes *infra*), when Milton was preparing his copy for
the press in 1636–7. An earlier copy of the passage on 'the pasted leaf' must
have supplied the text for B.MS., which retains the line, 'poor ladie thou
hast need of some refreshing', and lacks the lines afterwards inserted in the
margin, ll. 679–87 as well as ll. 697–700. The passage stands thus in B.MS.:

> [672] and first behould this cordiall Julep, heere
>   that flames, and dances in his christall bounds,
>   with spiritts of baulme, and fragraunt sirrops mixt;
> [675] Not that Nepenthes wch the wife of *Thone*
>   in Egipt gave to Jove-borne *Hellena*
>   is of such power to stirre up Joye as this
> [678] to life soe freindly, or soe coole too thirst,
>   poore ladie thou hast neede of some refreshinge
> [688] that hast been tired aldaye without repast,
>   a kindly rest hast wanted. heere fayre Virgin
> [690] this will restore all soone; *La:* twill not false traytor
>   twill not restore the trueth and honestie
>   that thou hast banisht from thy [thoughts *del.*] tongue wth lies,
>   was this the Cottage, and the safe aboade
>   thou touldst me of? what grim aspects are these?
> [695] these ougley headed Monsters? Mercie guard me

[696] hence with thy brewd enchauntments, fowle deceaver
[701] were it a drafte for Juno, when she banquetts
I would not taste thy treasonous offer, none
but such as are good men can give good things
and that wch is not good, is not delitious
to a well govern'd and wise appetite;

688] Before this line B.MS. has the line (deleted in T.MS.) 'poore ladie thou hast need of some refreshinge', which, however banal poetically, has clearly dramatic value. Milton got rid of it by interposing a sophistical appeal, on Comus's part, to Nature's laws: ll. 679–87.

have] hast T.MS. *orig.*, B.MS.

689 have] hast T.MS. *orig.*, B.MS.
but] heere T.MS. *orig.* and B.MS.

690 'Twill] Edd. 1, 2: t' will MSS.: T'will 1637.

691 'Twill] Edd. 1, 2: t' will T.MS.: twill B.MS.: T'will 1637.

695 ougly] T.MS., 1637: ougley B.MS.: oughley Edd. 1, 2.

696 brew'd inchantments] hel brewd liquor [opiate *on pasted leaf*] T.MS. *orig.*

697–700] *om.* B.MS.

698 forgery] forgeries T.MS.

707 Furr] gowne T.MS. *orig.*

709 sallow] shallow B.MS.

712 fruits, and flocks] & wth fruits T.MS. *orig.*

713 Thronging] cramming T.MS. *orig.*

714 Milton first wrote 'the feilds wth cattell & the aire wth fowle'. T.MS. *orig.*

717 To deck] to adorne T.MS. *del. deck* was the first reading and the last.

721 Pulse] pulse T.MS. *orig. alt. to* fetches, *finally to* pulse.

722 Freize] freise T.MS.: freeze B.MS.

723] th' all giver would bé unthankt would be unprais'd T.MS. The apostrophe over the first *be* indicating elision suggests Milton's metrical reading of the line.

725 master] maister T.MS. Milton was later to adopt this as his chosen spelling.

727 And live like] living as T.MS. *orig.*

730 th'earth cumber'd & the wing'd aire dark't wth plumes T.MS. This magnificent line looks like an afterthought: it is written in the margin.

732–5   the sea orefraugh would heave her waters up
above the shoare, and th' unsought diamonds
would so bestudde the center wth thire starre light
were they not taken thence that they below
would grow enur'd to [day. *del.*] light & come at last T.MS. *orig.*

733–4 would so emblaze with starrs, that they below B.MS., *making one line of two.*

737 and] nor *alt. to* and, *finally to* nor T.MS.

737–55] *om.* B.MS.

740 currant] current *corr. to* currant T.MS. Milton distinguished, by spelling, current (stream) from currant ('that will pass as good money').

742 it self;] Newton. There is no stop in the printed editions.

743 a neglected] an neglected T.MS. *orig.*

744 with languish't head] & fades away T.MS. *orig.*

749] they had thire name from thence coarse beetle brows T.MS. *orig.*
course] Edd. 1, 2: coarse T.MS. This is an earlier example of the spelling *coarse* than any noted in *O.E.D.*, which states: 'Our earliest contemporary example of the spelling *coarse* is in Walton, 1653.'

755 and be adviz'd, you are but young yet.] & looke upon this cordiall Julep. T.MS.[1] The next passage, firmly struck out (*v.* note to ll. 659–755 *supra*), introduces Comus's offer of the cordial julep, and corresponds roughly with the later version, ll. 672–703 *supra*. The whole passage representing this first version runs thus:

> & looke upon this cordiall julep
> that flames & dances in his crystall bounds
> wᵗʰ spirits of balme & fragrant syrops mixt
> not that nepenthes wᶜʰ the wife of Thôn
> in Ægypt gave to Jove borne Helena
> is of such power to stirre up joye as this
> to life so freindly or so coole to thirst
> poore Ladie thou hast need of some refreshing
> that hast bin tir'd all day wᵗʰ out repast
> & timely rest hast wanted heere [sweet Ladie] faire virgin
> this will restore all soone. La. stand back false traitor
> thou canst not touch the freedome of my mynd
> wᵗʰ all thy charmes although this corporall rind
> thou hast immanacl'd while heaven sees good
> was this the cottage & the safe abode
> [amoungst these ougly musl'd monsters mercie guard me]
> thou toldst me of? what grim aspects are these?
> these ougly headed monsters mercie guard me

The remaining lines are much worked over, but the main sequence may be traced as follows:

O my simplicitie what sights are these
how have I bin betrai'd with dark disguises
[and soothing lies] & soothing flatteries, hence with thy treacherous kindnesse
hence wᵗʰ thy hel bru'd liquor lest I throw it   [bru'd sorcerie]
against the ground, were it a draft for Juno
[I hate it from thy hands]
I should reject thy treasonous offer, none
but such as are good men can give good things

758 mine eyes,] mȳe eyes T.MS.: my eyes B.MS. Neither printed editions nor MSS. have any stop after *eyes*.

763 would] ment T.MS. *orig.*

764 cateress] Ed. 1: cateres Ed. 2: cateresse 1637, T.MS.: Chateresse B.MS.

765 Means] intends T.MS. *orig.*

772 blessings] blessinge B.MS.

777 feast] feasts B.MS.

779–806] *om.* both MSS. *v.* Introd. note, p. 339 *supra.*

780 anough] Ed. 1: anow Ed. 2: enough 1637. *anough,* or *anow,* is Milton's later spelling. *v. Lyc.* 114 and note.

781 contemptuous] Edd. 1. 2: reproachfull 1637. *corr. to* contemptuous *Pforz.*

794 rapt] rap't Edd. 1, 2, 1637. Milton's spelling was *rapt.* Cf. *Il Pens.* 40, *P.L.* vi. 23.

806–10   come [y' are too morall *del.*] no more
      this is [your] meere morall stuffe the tilted lees
      & setlings of a melancholy blood. T.MS. *orig.*

813/14 The stage direction in T.MS. is: the brothers rush in strike his glasse downe the [monsters] shapes make as though they would resist but are all driven in. Dæmon enter wth them. B.MS. has 'glasse of liquor' and 'the Demon is to come in with the brothers'.

814 you let] yee left B.MS.

 scape] passe T.MS. *orig.*

816 rod] art T.MS. *orig.*

821 Some other means I have] there is another way T.MS. *orig.*

 that] both MSS.: which Edd. 1, 2, 1637. I have restored *that* to the text from the MSS., since the repetition of *which* in the next line is difficult to reconcile with Milton's sensitive ear.

822 *Melibœus*] Millobeus B.MS.

825 smooth] smoote B.MS.

826 Virgin pure] Milton first wrote *virgin* then *goddesse chast,* deleted these words, returned to *virgin,* and added *pure.*

828 That] whoe B.MS.

829 She] Ed. 1, 1637, both MSS.: The Ed. 2.

831 flood] floud *alt. to* streame, *finally restored* T.MS.

834–5   held up thire white wrists to receave her iŋ
      and bore her straite to aged Nereus hall T.MS. *orig.*

white is then altered to *pearled; to receave* to *and* [carie] *take,* finally to *and took;* finally *and bore* to *bearing.*

834 pearled] pearkled B.MS.

846 make] leave T.MS. *orig.*

846/7 and often takes our cattell wth strange pinches T.MS.

847 *om.* B.MS.

849 rustick] lovely T.MS. *orig.* Birch reads *lively.* 'lovely lays' is a haunting Spenserian phrase.

851 pancies, pinks, and gaudy] pancies & of bonnie T.MS. *orig.*

853] each clasping charme & secret holding spell T.MS. *orig. alt. to* the clasping charm & [melt each] thaw the numming spell.

857 In hard besetting need] in honourd vertues cause *alt. to* in hard distressed need. T.MS.

858] and adde the power [call] of some strong verse T.MS. *orig.*

860] Listen virgin where thou sit'st T.MS. *orig.*

867 Listen and appear to us] Before this line B.MS. has 'The verse to singe or not'. T.MS. has in the margin 'to be said'.

869 By th'earth shaking] T.MS.: by th'earth shakinge B.MS.: By th earth-shaking 1637 (there is just room for the missing apostrophe): By the earth-shaking Edd. 1, 2.

869–74] Added in the margin T.MS.

871–82 In B.MS. these lines are divided up and apportioned alternately to the Elder and the Second brother; ll. 883–9 to the Dæmon. *v.* Introd. note, p. 337, *supra.*

879–82] Crossed out in T.MS.

883 that] of B.MS.

883–4] Added in margin T.MS.

883–9] *v.* note to 871–82 *supra.*

889/90 stage direction] by water-Nymphes Edd. 1, 2: wth the water nymphs T.MS.
    and sings Edd. 1, 2: Sings T.MS.

893 *azurn*] azur'd B.MS.

894 *Turkis*] Turquis T.MS. *orig.*: Turkiss B.MS.
    Emrauld] emrald T.MS. *orig.*

895 that my rich wheeles inlayes T.MS. *orig.*

897 *set*] rest B.MS.

898 *velvet*] *om.* B.MS.

900 *request*] In T.MS. Milton began to write *behest.*

904 charmed] Milton began to write *magic.*

907 inchanter] enchanter T.MS.: inchaunters B.MS.

910 Brightest] vertuous T.MS. *orig.*

911 thy] this B.MS.

918] In the margin Milton writes 'Sabrina descends' T.MS.

919] Against this line Milton writes 'the ladie rises out of her seate' T.MS.

921] To waite on Amphitrite in her bowre T.MS. orig.

924 brimmed] crystall T.MS. *orig.*

927 tumble] Ed. 1, 1637, T.MS.: tumbled Ed. 2.
    the] from T.MS. *orig.*

937 After this line T.MS. has *song ends: so* B.MS.

938 Lady] In B.MS. the scribe first writes *Lady*, then alters it to *sister* : these lines, 938–43, are given to Elder brother.

938–57. In B.MS. these lines are divided between the Elder brother and the Daemon. *v.* Introd. note, p. 337, *supra.*

948 met] come T.MS. *orig.*

951 there] neere MSS.

953 their] thire T.MS. (as everywhere in this MS. for *their*): this B.MS.

956 grow] Edd. 1, 2: are 1637, T.MS. *orig.*, B.MS.: grow T.MS. in margin.

957 sits] raignes T.MS. *orig.*

957/8 stage direction] T.MS. reads 'the scene changes, and then is præsented [then is presented B.MS.] Ludlow towne & the præsidents castle then enter [come in B.MS.] countrie dances & such like gambols &c. [and the like &c. B.MS.] at [After *orig.*] those sports the Dæmon wth ye 2 bro. & the Ladie enter [come in B.MS.]'.

958 Song. Spir.] the Dæmon sings T.MS.: the spiritt singes B.MS.
    anough] Edd. 1, 2: enough 1637, MSS., cf. note to l. 780 *supra*.

962 Milton wrote first: 'of speedier [toeing] toes & courtly guise'; then altered *speedier* to *nimbler*, finally to *lighter*, and for *courtly guise* tried *such neat guise*, and finally *such court guise*.

963 such as Hermes did devise T.MS. *orig.*

965/6 stage direction: This second Song presents . . . mother] 2 Songe presents . . . mother B.MS.: 2 Song T.MS.

967 *ye*] Edd. 1, 2: yee 1637, T.MS., B.MS.

971 *patience*] T.MS. *alt. to* temperance, *then* patience *restored*.
    truth,] 1637: truth. Edd. 1, 2.

973 to a crowne of deathlesse bays T.MS. *orig.*

975/6 *The dances ended, the Spirit Epiloguizes*] Edd.: they dance. the dances all ended the Dæmon sings. or sayes T.MS.¹, *so* B.MS. In the second version, T.MS.², The Dæmon sings or says.

976–1023] These lines, of which ll. 976–99 are adapted for the acting version of *The Mask* as Prologue in B.MS. (*v.* note to l. 1 *supra*), appear in two versions in T.MS.: (1) on f. 27 *verso*, struck out (T.MS.¹), (2) on f. 29, revised and augmented by fourteen lines (T.MS.²). B.MS. follows T.MS.¹ with some lines omitted.

    T.MS.², of which the handwriting belongs to the period between November 1637 and April 1638 when Milton was beginning to use Italian *e*'s along with Greek *ε*'s (*v.* note to *Lyc.* 58–63, pp. 332–3, *supra*), provides the copy for 1637 and Milton's final text. The same phase of his handwriting is to be noted in the passage on the pasted sheet which has survived. *v.* note to ll. 672–705 *supra*.

976 To the Ocean] From the Heavens B.MS. *v.* note to l. 1 *supra*.

979 broad] plaine T.MS.¹ *orig.*
    fields] field B.MS.

979/80   farre beyond ye earths end
                 where the welkin [cleere] low doth bend   T.MS.¹

981–3] Cf. note to 4/5 *supra*.

982] Of Atlas and his daughters three T.MS.¹ *orig. Atlas* was altered to *Hesperus*; then *daughters* to *neeces*, but *daughters* finally restored.

983 where grows the right-borne gold upon his native tree T.MS.² *orig.*
984–7 *om.* T.MS.¹, B.MS.
988 There] T.MS.¹, B.MS.: That there T.MS.², 1637: *so* Edd. 1, 2. In Errata Ed. 2 *That there* is corrected to *There*, which would seem to have Milton's authority: it was his first thought and his last.

 eternal] Edd. 1, 2: eternall T.MS.²: æternall 1637, T.MS.¹

990 cedar'n] myrtle T.MS.¹ *orig. alt. to* cedar'ne.
991 balme, & casia's fragrant smells T.MS.¹ *orig.*
992 humid] garnish't *alt. to* garish, *finally to text* T.MS.¹
995 purfl'd] watchet *alt. to* purfl'd T.MS.¹

 After this line T.MS.¹ has 'yellow, watchet, greene, & blew'. So also B.MS. In T.MS.² the line is struck out. For Milton's delight in colour, characteristically kept in check, cf. notes to 'Blest Pair of Sirens' *supra*, and note that 'the golden-hair'd Calliope', *Lyc.* 58, gives place to 'The Muse herself'.

996 with *Elysian*] oft with manna T.MS.¹: so B.MS.: wᵗʰ Sabæan T.MS.² *orig. alt. to text.*
997 (List mortals, if your ears be true)] This line does not appear in T.MS.¹, nor in B.MS. In T.MS.² Milton writes it in the margin when he has struck out the line, *yellow, watchet, greene, & blew.*
999 young *Adonis* oft] Edd., T.MS.²: many a cherub soft T.MS.¹, B.MS.
1000–11] *om.* T.MS.¹, B.MS.
1012 But now] Edd., T.MS.²: now T.MS.¹: Now B.MS.

 my task is smoothly don] my message well is don T.MS.¹ *orig.*; *message* was then altered to *buisnesse*, and finally the phrase changed to text.

1014 green earths] Edd. 1, 2: greene earths T.MS.², 1637: earths greene T.MS.¹ *orig.*, B.MS.
1020 ye] Edd. 1, 2: yee 1637, T.MS.¹,²: you B.MS. Milton seems to adopt at this time no settled form for the accusative case of this pronoun, cf. note to l. 43 *supra*. His care is for the sound that is appropriate in the given line.
1022–3 In the album of Cerdogni, a Neapolitan nobleman residing in Geneva, Milton wrote, on his return journey from Italy:

—if Vertue feeble were
Heaven it selfe would stoope to her
Johannes Miltonius
Anglus
Junii 10° 1639.

1023 stoop] Edd. 1, 2: stoope T.MS.², 1637: bow T.MS.¹ *orig.*

 The End] Ed. 1, 1637: *om.* Ed. 2: Exit the end. Finis T.MS.¹: The end. T.MS.²: Finis B.MS.

PSALMS I–VIII. *Done into Verse, 1653*

First printed in 1673, Ed. 2. These renderings of the Psalms into English,

I 'Done into Verse', 1653. II–VIII 'Done' between 8 and 14 August 1653, and the following group, Psalms LXXX–LXXXVIII, 'done' in April 1648, differ from the early renderings published in 1645 (*v.* pp. 121–3 and 305–6 *supra*) in that they are close translations from the Hebrew. In the present group done in 1653 he experiments with a number of different metres; in the following set written in 1648 he uses consistently the simplest possible metre, the so-called common metre (favourite with hymn-writers), and, to demonstrate the closeness of his translation, prints in italics 'all words that are not the very words of the Text'. I have inserted commas where necessary: other places where I have remedied defective punctuation are noted below.

Psalm I

5 *Jehovahs*] Ed. 2. Milton's practice is to put proper nouns in italics, as *Jehovah* here and in *Paradise Lost*. I have followed his practice in this group of Psalms. For the spelling of the possessive case without apostrophe *v.* note to *P.R.* i. 115 *supra*.

13 judgment]: jugdment Ed. 2.

Psalm II

5 dear.] Ed. 2 has no stop. I have remedied defective punctuation in these two groups of Psalms. *v.* notes *infra*.

22 averse,] averse Ed. 2.

Psalm III

3 rise;] rise Ed. 2.
9 count;] count Ed. 2.
23 Lord;] Lord Ed. 2.

Psalm IV

2 righteousness;] righteousness Ed. 2.
13 chose,] chose Ed. 2.
36 abounds.] abounds Ed. 2.
41 Cell,] Cell Ed. 2.

Psalm V

10 delight;] delight Ed. 2.
11 makes,] makes Ed. 2.
15 ly;] ly Ed. 2.
20 low.] low Ed. 2.
23 if] If Ed. 2.
26 sooth;] sooth Ed. 2.

Psalm VI

6 sore;] sore Ed. 2.
8 sake,] sake Ed. 2.
18 prai'r,] prai'r Ed. 2.

Psalm VII

1 flie,] flie Ed. 2.
3 crie;] crie, Ed. 2.
12 free'd] fre'd Ed. 2. I have adopted the spelling *free'd* of Psalm lxxxvi. 46, *infra* as printed in the text of Ed. 2. *vide supra.*
56 made;] made, Ed. 2.
61 *Jehovahs*] Jehovah's Ed. 2. *v.* note to *Psalm* i. 5 *supra.*

Psalm VIII

2 earth!] earth? Ed. 2. For the printers' confusion between ? and ! *v.* Vol. I, Introd., p. xxii.
4 bearth] Ed. 2. For the spelling *v.* note to *P.L.* ix. 624.
8 oppose.] oppose Ed. 2.
20 meet,] meet. Ed. 2.
22 slide, and] slide. And Ed. 2.

PSALMS LXXX–LXXXVIII

April. 1648. J. M. Nine of the Psalms done into Metre, . . .] Milton's attempt here (*v.* introductory note to Psalms i–viii *supra*) to distinguish the words which are an exact translation of the Hebrew text has not been a complete success. Dr. Rabin judges that the not altogether satisfactory distribution of italics is partly due to Milton, partly to the printer. I have made some slight corrections, according to Dr. Rabin's advice, in the marginal translations of the Hebrew words: he notes that the transliteration corresponds to the Spanish-Jewish pronunciation then current among scholars.

Psalm LXXX

1 Israel] I have not italicized proper names in this group, since Milton is deliberately using italics for his own purpose of differentiation, *v.* subheading.
6 out-spread,] out-spread Ed. 2.
8 dread.] dread Ed. 2.
10 Manasse's] Ed. 2. Milton's form of the word is rather that of the Latin Vulgate than the Hebrew.
14 voutsafe] vouchsafe Ed. 2. But Milton's spelling *voutsafe* at l. 78 should be adopted here, and at l. 30. *v.* Word-List, Vol. I.
15 shine,] shine Ed. 2.
28 throw.] throw Ed. 2.
30 voutsafe] vouchsafe Ed. 2. *v.* note to l. 14 *supra.*
38 fast,] fast Ed. 2.
42 over-spread,] over-spread Ed. 2.

Psalm LXXXI

6 bring,] bring Ed. 2.
29 (margin) Besether] Be Sether Ed. 2.

Psalm LXXXII

5 (margin) Tish-phetu] Tishphetu Ed. 2.
7 might,] might. Ed. 2.
8 strong?] strong Ed. 2.
18 on,] on Ed. 2.
22 high,] high Ed. 2.

Psalm LXXXIII

14 be,] be Ed. 2.
27 Phitistims] Ed. 2. *Phitistim* is the Hebrew form with final *m*. In *S.A.* Milton uses throughout the Latin form *Philistine* (in the Argument *Philistins*).
34 Coast,] Coast Ed. 2.
42 speed,] speed Ed. 2.
66 Jehovah] Jehova Ed. 2.

Psalm LXXXV

26 shew,] shew Ed. 2.
42 met,] met Ed. 2.

Psalm LXXXVI

25 and 27] *gods* is spelt here deliberately with initial minuscule, as in l. 36 *God* is spelt with initial capital. *v.* notes to *Hymn* 224 and *S.A.* 1176.

Psalm LXXXVIII

14 pit,] pit Ed. 2.
20 deep,] deep. Ed. 2.
22 regard;] regard, Ed. 2.
54 Ere] E're Ed. 2.
68 persue] Ed. 2. *persue* is Milton's spelling in his later years.

POEMATA

Epigramma Salsilli ('Cede Meles, . . .')

3 undas, Ed. 2: undas Ed. 1
4 te, Milto, per Ed. 3: te Milto per Edd. 1, 2.

ODE

1 *Etra,*] *Etra* Ed. 1.   *ò*] *o* Ed. 2.   *Clio,*] *Clio* Edd. 1, 2.

2 *intreccierò*] *intrecciero* Ed. 2.   *corona,*] *corona* Edd. 1, 2.

3 *più*] *piu* Ed. 2.

4 *Elicona;*] *Elicona,* Edd. 1, 2.

6 *A*] *A'* Edd. 1, 2, the apostrophe here representing accented *A* (cf. Intro-duction, *supra*, p. xv).   *virtù*] *virtu* Ed. 2. So too in ll. 12, 19, 24, 44, 69.

7 *può*] *puo* Ed. 2.

8 *preda*] *preda,* Edd. 1, 2.   *valore,*] *valore* Edd. 1, 2.

9 *può*] *puo* Edd. 1, 2.   10 *onore;*] *onore,* Edd. 1, 2.

12 *ferirò*] *feriro* Ed. 2.   *Morte,*] *morte.* Edd. 1, 2. The question of the capitalization of abstract nouns is often uncertain in Italian poetry, but this seems a clear case of personification.

16 *Però*] *Pero* Ed. 2.

17 *sà*] *sa* Ed. 2.

20 *nei*] *ne i* Edd. 1, 2.

21 *è sol*] *e sol* Ed. 2.

23 *Ridillo tu, Giovanni,*] *Ridillo tu Giovanni,* Ed. 1.

26 *brama,*] *brama;* Ed. 1, 2.

27 *udío*] *udio* Edd. 1, 2.

30 *più raro.*] *priù raro.* Ed. 1: *priu raro.* Ed. 2.   *Così*] *Cosi* Edd. 1, 2.   *l'Ape Ingegnosa*] Cf. Tasso, *susurrando predava Ape ingegnosa, Rime* (1583), p. 47.

37 *amante,*] *amante* Edd. 1, 2.

38 *Milton,*] *Milton* Edd. 1, 2.   *natío*] *natio* Edd. 1, 2.

42 *più*] *piu* Edd. 1, 2.

43 *divino,*] *divino* Edd. 1, 2.   *rintracciando,*] *rintracciando* Edd. 1, 2.

48 *virtù*] *virtu* Edd. 1, 2.   49 *Flora*] i.e. Florence.

59 *ode*] *Ode* Edd. 1, 2.   *all'Anglia*] *all Anglia* Edd. 1, 2.   *più*] *piu* Edd. 1, 2.

61 *più*] *piu* Edd. 1, 2.

62 *Natura*] *natura* Edd. 1, 2.   *terra,*] *terra* Edd. 1, 2.   63 *a*] *á,* Ed. 1.

66 *mor[t]al*] *moral* Edd. 1, 2 (*v.* Introduction, p. xvii, *supra*).

68 *ferminsi*] *fermin si* Ed. 2.   70 *ai*] *a i,* Edd. 1, 2.

71 *Chè*] *Che* Edd. 1, 2.   *Poema o storia*] *Poema e storia* Ed. 2.

72 *già*] *gia* Edd. 1, 2.   76 *vanto;*] *vanto,* Edd. 1, 2.

77 *dirà*] *dira* Ed. 2.   *è concesso*] *e concesso* Ed. 2.

80 *preclaro,*] *preclaro* Edd. 1, 2.

Joanni Miltoni

4 cuncta orbis Ed. 1: cuncta, orbis Ed. 2.

16–17 *I have corrected the lineation and punctuation.* Edd. 1, 2 have:

eruditionis ambages comite assidua autorum Lectione.
Exquirenti, restauranti, percurrenti.
At cur nitor in arduum?
Illi in cujus virtutibus &c.

The full stop after Lectione *in the printed texts leaves the sentence ungrammatical; and the line-division is meaningless. That the words* At cur nitor in arduum? *form a glyconic verse seems to be mere accident.*

20 Florentinus, Newton: Florentinus Edd. 1, 2.

Elegia i

24 prima, Warton: prima Edd. 1, 2.
31 *Perhaps* facundus (cf. Eleg. vi. 31).
60 Amor; Newton: Amor. Edd. 1, 2.

Elegia ii

12 tuo, Ed. 2: tuo Ed. 1.
21 *I have added commas before and after* Academia
24 *Perhaps* totas . . . scholas

Elegia iii

13 luxi, dignissime Warton: luxi dignissime Edd. 1, 2.
36 meos; Newton: meos. Edd. 1, 2.

Elegia iv

 1 *I have added commas before and after* mea littera
10 viri; Newton: viri, Edd. 1, 2.
23 *I have added commas.*
24 erat; Newton: erat. Edd. 1, 2.
35 *commas added by Warton.*
44 Dei, Newton: Dei. Edd. 1, 2.
47 multam sit: Newton: multam, sit Edd. 1, 2.
51 Musis, Newton: Musis Edd. 1, 2.

Elegia v

25 Jam, Philomela, Warton: Jam Philomela Edd. 1, 2.
27 utrinque *conj.* Chr. Wordsworth.
33 opacæ, Newton: opacæ Edd. 1, 2.
43 puellâ, Warton: puellâ Edd. 1, 2.
44 Phoebe, Warton: Phoebe Edd. 1, 2.
49 thalamos, Aurora, seniles, Warton: thalamos Aurora seniles, Edd. 1, 2.
56 amplexus, Phœbe, subire Warton: amplexus Phœbe subire Edd. 1, 2.
62 *Perhaps* Opem;

67 Aspice, Phoebe, tibi Warton: Aspice Phoebe tibi Edd. 1, 2.

72 toros; Warton: toros, Edd. 1, 2.

81 languentem, Phœbe, diurno Warton: languentum Phœbe diurno Edd. 1, 2.

85 Frigora, Phœbe, mea Warton: Frigora Phœbe mea Edd. 1, 2.

93 tu, Phœbe, tuo Warton: tu Phœbe tuo Edd. 1, 2.

134 *I have added commas.*

135, 137 *commas added by Warton.*

136 *Perhaps* ad nimbis aspera cela

Elegia vi

12 *Perhaps* iocos

24 merum; Newton: merum. Edd. 1, 2.

31 *Perhaps* facundam (cf. Eleg. i. 31).

75 tuas, rex ime, domos Warton: tuas rex ime domos Edd. 1, 2.

84 colit; Newton: colit. Edd. 1, 2.

Elegia vii

1 *I have added commas before and after* Amathusia

5 imbelles, dixi, transfige Warton: imbelles dixi transfife Edd. 1, 2.

14 *commas added by Warton.*

21 æterno Ed. 2: ærerno Ed. 1. In the copy of 1645 given by Milton to the Bodleian (MS. Lat. Misc. f. 15) the first *r* of *ærerno* has been corrected in ink to a *t*. But an asterisk (such as is found elsewhere in Milton's manuscripts) directs the reader to a marginal correction; of which there survive only the last two letters, *io*. These point, I think, to *ætherio*, as Milton's own correction. He has *ætherio . . . Olympo* in *Mansus* 100; and it is found in Martial 9.3.3.

26 *Perhaps* melle

31 *commas added by Warton.*

35–36 *Perhaps* nequit, adductum . . . arcum, Qui . . . solet, vincere

45 *I have added commas before and after* stulte

In proditionem Bombardicam

2 infandum, perfide Fauxe, nefas Warton: infandum perfide Fauxe nefas Edd. 1, 2.

6 rotis: Warton: rotis Edd. 1, 2.

In eandem ('*Purgatorem animae . . .*')

5 ait, Warton: ait Edd. 1, 2.

   sacra, Warton: sacra Edd. 1, 2.

Ad Leonoram

3 mirum, Leonora, tibi . . . major Warton: mirum? Leonora tibi . . . major, Edd. 1, 2.

Ad eandem ('*Altera Torquatum* . . .')

4 te, Leonora, foret! Warton: te Leonora foret! Edd. 1, 2.
6 lyrae! Todd: lyrae, Edd. 1, 2.

Ad eandem ('*Credula quid* . . .')

1 *I have added commas before and after* Neapoli

Apologus de Rustico & Hero

1 malo Newton: Malo Edd. 1, 2.
3 captus 1695: Captus Ed. 1.

In obitum Procancellarii

25 *commas added by Newton.*
29 Apollinis *conj.* Warton.
46 *I have written* Ennæa *for* Aetnæa *The legend of Proseropine connects her with Enna, not with Aetna.*

In quintum Novembris

44 inulta. Newton: inulta, Edd. 1, 2.
49 fines; Warton: fines, Edd. 1, 2.
52 *commas added by* Warton.
74 haeres, Todd; haeres Edd. 1, 2.
76 noctes); Warton: noctes) Edd. 1, 2.
84 salaces. Ed. 2.
92 Dormis, *scripsi*: Dormis Edd. 1, 2.
   artus? Ed. 2; artus Ed. 1.
94 cathedram, venerande, tuam Warton: cathedram venerande tuam Edd. 1, 2.
108 pontum Ed. 2.
123 mone: *scripsi*: mone Edd. 1, 2.
137–8. *I have added a comma after* aulae *deleting the comma placed after* visus *in* Edd. 1, 2.
138 resolvens *conj.* Newton.
152 antrum, Newton: antrum Edd. 1, 2.
153 umbris, Warton: umbris Edd. 1, 2.
154 vortunt; Newton: vortunt, Edd. 1, 2.
162 propago: Warton: propago Edd. 1, 2.

169 *Perhaps* volt
174 Ossæ. Newton: Ossæ Edd. 1, 2.
180 culmen. Newton: culmen Edd. 1, 2.
185 tot, Newton: tot Edd. 1, 2.
198 officiis, vaga divâ, tuis Warton: officiis vaga diva tuis Edd. 1, 2.
208 Nec mora, Warton: Nec mora Edd. 1, 2.
219 omnem. Ed. 3: omnem Edd. 1, 2.

In obitum Præsulis

6 præsulis; *scripsi*: præsulis. Edd. 1, 2.
44 subterraneas. Newton: subterraneas Edd. 1, 2.

Naturam non pati senium

22 Pallas; Newton: Pallas Edd. 1, 2.
38 Raptat Ed. 2: Raptat, Ed. 1.
44 rotarum. Newton: rotarum, Edd. 1, 2.
58 vastâ] *Perhaps* iustâ
60 *commas added by Warton.*
63 Phoebe, tuusque, et, Cypri, tuus, nec Warton: Phoebe tuusque et Cypri tuus nec Edd. 1, 2.

De Idea Platonica

1 Dicite, sacrorum Warton: Dicite sacrorum Edd. 1, 2.

Ad Patrem

6 *commas added by Warton.*
13 istâ, Ed. 2: istâ Ed. 1.
14 Clio, 1695: Clio Edd. 1, 2.
26 aras, Newton: aras Ed. 1, 2.
35 orbes, Ed. 2: orbes Ed. 1.

Psalm 114

In this and the two pieces following punctuation, accents and breathings wrongly given in Ed. 1 and Ed. 2 are here tacitly corrected, and iotas subscript have been added where they are missing.
The verses *In Effigiei Eius Sculptorem* were added in Ed. 2 after the lines *Ad Salsillum*. In Ed. 1 they are printed beneath the portrait given as frontispiece.

Ad Salsillum

5 lectum, Ed. 2: lectum. Ed. 1.
17, 24 *commas added by Warton.*

Mansus

1–2 *commas before and after* Manse *added by Warton.*

24 Phœbi, Newton: Phœbi Edd. 1, 2.

96 virtus, Newton: virtus Edd. 1, 2.

Epitaphium Damonis

Of the *Epitaphium Damonis* the British Museum preserves (C. 57. d. 48) a printed text earlier than that of 1645 (pretty certainly belonging to 1639–40). It is distinguished by two notable misprints (*onundus* for *oriundus* in line 6 of the *Argumentum*, and *umbtacula* for *umbracula* in line 216 of the poem. At line 53 of the poem it anticipates Warton in correcting *nymphæ.* to *nymphæ,* It has numerous other variants of punctuation and spelling, none of them worth recording—the punctuation is, in general, plainly inferior to that of Ed. 1.

20 funere, Warton: funere Edd. 1, 2.

36 præmia, Warton: præmia Edd. 1, 2.

53 nymphæ, B.M. MS., Warton: nymphæ. Edd. 1, 2.

82 te, Thyrsi, futurum Warton: te Thyrsi futurum Edd. 1, 2. I corrected *te* to *de te* in the Oxford type-facsimile of 1924. The correction was adopted by Grierson in his edition of 1925. In vol. xviii of the Columbia Milton it is assigned to C. S. Jerram.

115, 117, 120 *I have changed the punctuation* (sepultam? reliquit; sonantes. Edd. 1, 2).

125 pigebit, Newton: pigebit Edd. 1, 2.

152 medentûm. Newton: medentûm Edd. 1, 2.

153 medentûm, Newton: medentûm Edd. 1, 2.

154 *After* Gramina *Edd. 1, 2 have a comma, which I have removed.*

166 Jögernen, Newton: Jögernen Edd. 1, 2: Jogernen B.M. MS.

185 ver, Newton: ver Edd. 1, 2.

195 *Perhaps* orbem

198 lubrica, *scripsi:* lubrica Edd. 1, 2.

Page 86 in Ed. 1 concludes the volume with the word FINIS. In Ed. 2 the verses *Ad Joannem Rousium* follow the *Epitaphium Damonis,* and the FINIS, accordingly, disappears.

Ad Joannem Rousium

Of this poem, first printed in 1673, the Bodleian Library possesses a transcript sent by Milton to Rous, dated 23 Jan. 1646/7. The transcript was preserved in a copy of the 1645 Poems, MS. Lat. Misc. f. 15, where it was placed between the English and Latin Poems.[1] 'Generally supposed to be in Milton's hand', says Masson (ii. 379), 'but probably, I think, a transcript

---

[1] The MS. sheet is now separated from the volume and is catalogued as MS. Lat. Misc. d. 77.

by some calligraphist.' A facsimile of a portion of this MS. forms the frontis-piece of Beeching's larger edition of Milton. But today no responsible editor, perhaps, would claim it as Milton's autograph.

6 *Correcting* Sedula . . . nimii *to* Seduli . . . nimis *we get a perfectly good Phalaecian for a verse which yields no kind of metre. Moreover,* Sedula *contradicts* non operosa *in line 3.*

22 per] *Perhaps* super (*giving an anapaestic dimeter*).

39 *Both grammar and metre seem to demand* erraveris ex (*another anapaestic dimeter*).

51 virûm] *Perhaps* vatûm. Milton seems to have intended a choriambic trimeter; and it is difficult to believe that he thought the first syllable of *virum* long.

From Milton's Common-place book

Carmina Elegiaca

In the first poem the first line in the MS. is punctuated thus:

Surge, age surge, leves, iam convenit, excute somnos

So too (but with the omission of the first comma) the penultimate line. In the rest of the poem no punctuation is discernible.

In the second poem there is no discernible punctuation, except a comma in line 5 after *Eurialus*.

i. 1 *For* excute *the MS. had a cancelled* arcere. *So too in line* 19.

3 praenuncius ales] *The photograph shows only* p   le. The text printed is that recorded from the lost MS. by A. J. Horwood.

11 zephyritis MS.: ? Zephyri vis.

13 Segnes] ? Segnis es: *Or did Milton mean* Segnes *to be voc. sing.?*

15 somnos *corrected in the MS. from* somnum.

ii. 4 *The photograph shows no more than* Str.tus purp. . eo. But Horwood was able to read *procubuit*. For the missing last word I have printed, conjecturally, *thoro* (*toro*): the Columbia edition gives *strato*, reluctante metro. The metre is the familiar lesser *Asclepiad*, and not, as the Columbia editors say absurdly, choriambic trimeter. [Since this was written the Columbia Milton in a supplement to vol. xviii (1938) withdraws *strato* and proposes, independently, *thoro*.]

H. W. G.

APPENDIX

The Printing of 'Paradise Regain'd', 'Samson Agonistes', and 'Poems &c.' published in 1645 and 1673

THE first edition of *Paradise Regain'd* and *Samson Agonistes* is a slim octavo volume with the date 1671 (see the title-page facsimile, p. 1 *supra*). A careful list of Errata in both poems is given at the back of the volume:

Errata in the former Poem (*Paradise Regain'd*)

I, verse 62. after *being* no stop.
I, v. 226. for destroy r. *subdue*
I, v. 373. for demuring r. *demurring*
I, v. 400. for never r. *nearer,*
I, v. 417. for Imports r. *Imparts*
II, v. 128. after threatens insert *then*
II, v. 313. for Thebes r. *Thebez*
II, v. 341. for pill'd r. *piled*
II, v. 371. no comma after *knowledge,* but after *works,*
III, v. 324. for shower r. *showers*
IV, v. 102. no stop after *victor*

Errata in the latter Poem (*Samson Agonistes*)

verse 126. for Irresistable r. *Irresistible*
v. 157. for complain'd r. *complain*
v. 222. for mention'd r. *motion'd*
v. 354. before such r. *And*
v. 656. no stop at the end
v. 660. for to r. *with*
v. 1248 for divulg'd r. *divulge*
v. 1313 for race r. *rate*
v. 1325 for Mimirs r. *Mimics*
v. 1552. for heard r. *here*

The first edition is dated 1671. Starkey the bookseller states in his Catalogue of Books offered for Sale that *Paradise Regain'd* with *Samson Agonistes* was printed 29 May 1670. The Licence leaf in the book itself is dated July 2. 1670, and in the Term Catalogues the book appears under the general date Nov. 22 1670. *Price bound* 4/*s.* Apparently publishers at this time used the next year's date from as early as the month of October.

A second edition in similar form with a similar title-page (differing only in the date and in the omission of the printer's initials) appeared with the date 1680. The printer has ignored the list of errata in Ed. 1.

There is little evidence of Milton's detailed supervision of the printing of the volume of 1671, nothing like the many significant corrections of the sheets of the first edition of *Paradise Lost*, as they went through the press.[1] I have noted such as are of interest in *Paradise Regain'd* and *Samson Agonistes* in my textual commentary, *q.v.* The page of Errata betrays Milton's hand, *v.* p. 373 and commentary *supra*.

In 1688 a Folio edition of the two Poems (Ed. 3) was published with the following title-page:

> Paradise Regain'd. | A | Poem. | In IV Books. | To which is added | Samson Agonistes. | The Author | John Milton. | London, | Printed by R. E. and are to be sold by | Randal Taylor near Stationers-Hall. | MDCLXXXVIII. *Samson Agonistes* has a separate title-page.

The volume of *Poems* containing *Lycidas*, *A Mask etc.*, and *Poemata* was first published in 1645, and a second edition, enlarged, in 1673. *v.* title-pages, pp. 110, 111 *supra*.

In 1695 appeared the first collective edition of Milton's poetical works under the aegis of Jacob Tonson. This folio edition had a covering title-page as follows:

> The | Poetical | Works | of | Mr John Milton. | containing, | Paradise Lost, Paradise Regain'd, | *Sampson Agonistes*, and his Poems | on several Occasions. | Together with | Explanatory Notes on each Book of the | *Paradise Lost*, and a Table | never before Printed. | London: | Printed for *Jacob Tonson* at the *Judges-Head* near the *Inner-Temple-* | *Gate* in *Fleet-street*, MDCXCV.

The separate title-page for *Paradise Regain'd* and *Samson Agonistes* (Ed. 4) is similar to that of 1688 (Ed. 3), but with John Whitelock's name substituted for Randal Taylor.

The separate title-page for *Poems upon Several Occasions* (Ed. 3) is as follows:

> Poems | upon | Several Occasions. | Compos'd at several times. | By Mr John Milton. | The Third Edition | London: | Printed for *Jacob Tonson* at the *Judge's* Head, near the *Inner-* | *Temple-Gate* in *Fleet-street*. 1695. |

The publisher has changed the order of the Poems, perhaps with the intent of placing first those that were best liked: *Lycidas*, *L'Allegro*, *Il Penseroso*, *A Mask*, *Arcades*, *On the morning of Christ's Nativity*: thereafter the sequence follows that of 1673 (Ed. 2), except that *At a Vacation Exercise* and *On the New Forcers of Conscience* are placed immediately before instead of after the Sonnets.

By 1705 Tonson must have acquired the copyright of all Milton's poetical works.

[1] *v.* Vol. I, Introd., p. x, and Appendix, p. 315.

The most important editions issued in the eighteenth century are as follows:

1705. *The Poetical Works* in 2 vols. 8vo, for Jacob Tonson.
1713. *Paradise Regain'd, Samson Agonistes,* and *Poems.* 12mo, for J. Tonson.
1720. *The Poetical Works* in 2 vols. 4to, for J. Tonson: Tickell's edition.
1725. *Paradise Regain'd, Samson Agonistes,* and *Poems.* for J. Tonson. 8vo. The Sixth Edition, Corrected: Fenton's edition.
1730. The same, 2 vols. 8vo; also Fenton's edition.
1747. *Paradise Regain'd, Samson Agonistes,* and *Poems.* for J. R. Tonson and S. Draper, R. Ware, J. Hodges, R. Wellington, C. Corbett, J. Brindley, R. Caldwell, and J. New. 2 vols. 12mo.
1752. *Paradise Regain'd, Samson Agonistes, and Poems upon Several Occasions,* A New Edition, with Notes of Various Authors by Thomas Newton. For J. and R. Tonson and S. Draper. 1 vol. 4to.
1758. *The Poetical Works.* Printed at Birmingham by Baskerville. 2 vols. large 8vo.
1785. *Poems upon Several Occasions* with Notes Critical and Explanatory by Thomas Warton. 8vo.
1791. The same with alterations and additions, by Thomas Warton. 8vo.
1795. *Paradise Regain'd* with Notes of Various Authors by Charles Dunster.
1798. *Comus,* A Mask, with Notes Critical and Explanatory, and a Copy of the MS. belonging to . . . the Duke of Bridgwater, by Henry John Todd.

Of the many editions issued in the nineteenth and twentieth centuries the following deserve notice:

1801–1826. *The Poetical Works* with Notes of Various Authors, edited by H. J. Todd. First edition 1801; third edition, with important additions, 1826.
1851. *The Poetical Works,* edited by J. Mitford.
1859. *The Poems,* edited by T. Keightley.
1874. *The Poetical Works,* edited by D. Masson.
1892. *Samson Agonistes,* edited by A. W. Verity.
1903. *The Poetical Works,* edited with Critical Notes by William Aldis Wright.
1924. *The Complete Poetical Works,* edited by W. V. Moody.
1925. *The Poems,* edited by H. J. C. Grierson.
1932. *Paradise Regained,* edited by E. H. Blakeney.
1931–8. *The Works of John Milton:* the Columbia University edition.
1943–8. *John Milton's Complete Poetical Works reproduced in Photographic Facsimile,* edited by H. F. Fletcher: the University of Illinois edition.